DATE DUE

05 19 97			
MAY 21 02			

DEMCO 38-296

LEADING MANUFACTURING EXCELLENCE

LEADING MANUFACTURING EXCELLENCE

A Guide to State-of-the-Art Manufacturing

Patricia E. Moody

John Wiley & Sons, Inc.

New York • Chichester • Weinheim • Brisbane • Singapore • Toronto

This text is printed on acid-free paper.

HD 9725 .M57 1997   :turing.

                                     'anada.

Leading manufacturing   rk beyond that
   excellence   ed States Copyright
                                     r is unlawful.
Requests for permission or further information should be addressed
to the Permissions Department, John Wiley & Sons, Inc.

This publication is designed to provide accurate and authoritative
information in regard to the subject matter covered. It is sold with
the understanding that the publisher is not engaged in rendering legal,
accounting, or other professional services. If legal advice or other expert
assistance is required, the services of a competent professional person
should be sought.

Library of Congress Cataloging-in-Publication Data:

Moody, Patricia E.
    Leading manufacturing excellence : a guide to state-of-the-art
manufacturing / Patricia E. Moody.
        p.   cm.
    Includes index.
    ISBN 0-471-16341-4 (cloth : alk. paper)
    1. United States—Manufactures—Management.   2. Total quality
management—United States.   3. Production management—United States.
4. Manufacturing processes—United States.   I. Title.
HD9725.M57   1997
670'.68'5—dc21   96-49899
                                                               CIP

Chapter 17 excerpted and adapted from the book *Visual Systems: Harnessing the
Power of a Visual Workplace* (Amacom, New York, 1997). Copyright © 1996,
Gwendolyn D. Galsworth, all rights reserved.

Printed in the United States of America

10   9   8   7   6   5   4   3   2   1

for Delia Richard Moody
1917–1972

Contents

Acknowledgments

This project came together with the help and active support of many professional colleagues and friends whose involvement is deeply appreciated. Thanks to

Steven Wheelwright, who pointed me in the right direction;

Jon Wettstein (plant manager), Elsa Berenberg, Prudence Sullivan, Carolyn Edwards, Roy Leonardi, Ed Bourdeau, Paul Mantos, Bill Mulcahy, Donna McIntyre, Karl Hummel, and Russ Snyder, all of Digital Equipment Corporation;

Daniel Holbrook of the Charles River Museum of Industry in Waltham, Massachusetts.

Patricia E. Moody

"Spinning Silk." Boston Manufacturing Company, circa 1890. Reprinted with permission of the Waltham Historical Society.

Introduction

Twenty years ago I learned a choral piece based on William Blake's "Jerusalem." A few lines from his poem stuck with me all these years, a sad vision of industry gone wrong—England's "dark satanic mills." Here is the original poem.

> And did those feet in ancient time
> Walk upon England's mountains green?
> And was the holy Lamb of God
> On England's pleasant pastures seen?
> And did the countenance divine
> Shine forth upon our clouded hills?
> And was Jerusalem builded here
> Among those dark satanic mills?
>
> Bring me my bow of burning gold!
> Bring me my arrow of desire!
> Bring me my spear! O clouds, unfold!
> Bring me my chariot of fire!
> I will not cease from mental fight,
> Nor shall my sword sleep in my hand,
> Till we have built Jerusalem
> In England's green and pleasant land.

The poem does not simply suggest a yearning to return to the pastoral world we want to believe existed before the mills. I believe it suggests the *potential* for utopia dreamed of by many early innovators (Francis Cabot Lowell and his associates included).

We have come so far since the early days of Lowell's Industrial Revolution. We have managed to leave behind most of the dehumanizing horrors of other industrializing nations—child labor, unsafe conditions, and 12-hour, 6-day work schedules.

In two generations we created a middle class. We have successfully supplied two world wars and postwar prosperity.

We in the United States have incredibly rich natural resources and a gloriously diverse heritage of liberated, energized immigrant workers and their descendants.

Our system of government is geared toward generation of wealth. The structure for educating our citizens is in place. And we still subscribe to a humanistic view of humanity's potential.

In this book the reader will find many approaches to the basic question of how we can compete more successfully. Each section is preceded by an overview; the book is organized so that each chapter stands alone. When read in its entirety, the presentation of manufacturing strategy proceeds from theory and analysis of company and industry through formulation of appropriate competitive strategy and the tactics required to execute that strategy.

We have included a number of current topics that represent real opportunities for improvement—the empowerment of production workers, time-based competition, and the role of flexibility in manufacturing. The last section addresses the challenging area of change management.

Patricia E. Moody

PART ONE

HISTORICAL PERSPECTIVE

The first chapter of *Leading Manufacturing Excellence* looks at vital statistics describing the comparative strengths of U.S. manufacturing and concludes with an existing approach to filling industry's needs for a better prepared workforce. The section on industry/academic strategic collaboration looks at the need for educational reform to support U.S. strategic requirements in manufacturing and engineering and one university program started by Lester Thurow to answer that need.

Romeyn Everdell traces the evolution of U.S. manufacturing from its beginnings in textiles on the banks of the Charles River ("that Muddy Water") in Waltham, Massachusetts, to Sunnyvale. Two repeating patterns emerge:

- U.S. leadership in innovation began in the early 1800s.
- Each time labor costs became uncompetitive, the industry moved, but the innovators stayed.

1 VITAL STATISTICS

Patricia E. Moody

Where will the United States be in the next millenium as fierce economic competition becomes the world's focus? Is the United States in its era of final decline or, as more optimistic theorists claim, will it consolidate its strengths—its industry, its tradition of wanting and taking responsibility for global leadership, its diverse and creative cultural energies, its love of money and manufactured things, its size and natural resources?

The economic future is filled with question marks and surprises. The answers will not come simply internally and, as the United States begins to feel the pressures of being a global player and of having less control over its plans and future, anxiety drives us to want the answers now.

We do have some key pieces of information, vital statistics on leading indicators, that we need to watch and think about over the next three to five years. The data describe and raise questions about the United State's global market share, productivity, competitors' strengths, and U.S. manufacturers' strategic focus. Before *Leading Manufacturing Excellence* appeared, a group of M.I.T. scientists, engineers, and economists released the results of its examination of the condition of U.S. industry in its book entitled *Made in America.*[1] From data gathered on eight major industries—computers, commercial aircraft, consumer electronics, steel, chemicals, textiles, autos, and machine tools—the group reached conclusions about the problems, including preoccupation with short-term returns, lack of cooperation, difficulty translating technology breakthroughs into products, and neglect or misuse of human resources. Among its recommendations are educational reform and restructuring government's role in building stronger industries.

SHARE OF WORLD MARKETS

As Table 1–1 shows, the U.S. share of global markets is challenged by strong competition from Japan, Germany, and Korea. We concede that the United States now holds less of the world auto market; other industry positions are also threatened.

- The U.S. market share of the world car (excluding trucks) market stands at 6.1 percent, Japan at 30.0 percent, Germany at 25.0 percent, and Korea at 1.0 percent and growing.
- In consumer electronics Japan has virtually won the game with total world share of TV and VCR sales of 29.0 percent and radios/small electronics of 38.0 percent.

TABLE 1-1   World market share (1986)[a]

	USA Rank			Japan Rank			Germany Rank			Korea Rank		
	%	Exp	Imp	%	Exp	Imp	%	Exp	Imp	%	Exp	Imp
Auto												
Cars	6.1	6	1	30.6	1	12	24.9	2	3	1.3	11	NA[b]
Trucks	8.8	4	1	36.3	1	NA	13.2	3	6	0.1	22	NA
Chemicals												
Drugs	16.1	2	1	2.5	11	3	16.2	1	2	NA	NA	NA
Plastics	25.4	1	17	4.0	7	6	12.3	3	1	NA	NA	NA
Computers	23.7	1	1	22.0	2	8	10.7	3	2	2.2	11	15
Electronics												
TV, VCR	4.2	6	1	29.4	1	NA	14.9	2	2	NA	NA	NA
Radio, etc.	3.0	10	1	38.3	1	15	4.7	6	2	9.9	2	NA
Household												
Appliances	4.9	7	1	15.9	2	NA	19.7	1	4	5.2	6	NA
Paper	7.5	5	1	3.5	8	8	11.5	4	2	0.5	17	NA
Primary Steel	NA	NA	4	11.4	4	7	19.6	1	2	4.8	8	5
Textiles	5.9	5	1	NA	NA	9	9.1	1	2	4.9	9	NA

[a] World = Noncentrally controlled economies

[b] NA = Country rank is lower than 22 as exporter and/or 20 as importer

Source: UN International Trade Statistics Yearbook.

- The United States's 16.0 percent share in drugs equals Germany's.
- In computers, the United States holds 23.7 percent against Japan's 22.0 percent and Germany's 10.7 percent. While we may generally assume that American innovative skills will continue to hold the lead, it is alarming to think that the U.S. high-tech industry may go the way of consumer electronics.
- In household appliances, an industry where Black and Decker is making a strong showing worldwide, the United States holds only 4.9 percent, against Germany's 19.7 percent and Japan's 15.9 percent.

Domestic Auto Market

The fight for market share has intensified as each major competitor refuses to cut back production rates; consequently, inventories are building. It has been estimated that there will be five cars for every four buyers in the nineties—a good buyer's market, but the overinventoried position sounds a death knell for less-competitive car manufacturers and dealers.

In 1986, approximately 70 percent of U.S. cars were built here by U.S. companies. In 1987 it had slipped to 67 percent. According to a recent M.I.T. study, in 20 years the United States has gone from an auto export surplus to an import deficit of $60 billion.[2]

FOREIGN COMPANIES IN THE UNITED STATES

As in the auto industry, other foreign competitors have established manufacturing facilities within the United States. The presence of foreign manufacturers, not simply through arm's-length ownership from acquisition and buyout deals, is growing. According to the Bureau of Economic Analysis, in 1985 there were more than 1,500 foreign-owned manufacturing facilities operating on U.S. soil, representing sales of $185,377,000,000. Surprisingly, the largest number of foreign-owned companies manufacture chemicals (34 percent of total manufacturing), followed by autos (Table 1–2).

COMPARATIVE HOURLY WAGES
FOR PRODUCTION WORKERS

We know that one of the causes of high U.S. manufacturing costs (and therefore loss of U.S. competitiveness) is labor rates. The numbers are discouraging.

TABLE 1–2 Affiliates of foreign companies in the United States (1985)

	Number	Sales[a]	Inventories[a]
Total	9,824	630,113	64,764
Mfg. Total	1,549	185,377	29,322
Auto	25	9,647	1,807
Chemicals	176	62,464	8,916
Computers	37	2,902	NA
Electronics	27	5,028	
Household Appliances	5	1,824	3,483
Paper	37	6,724	780
Steel	51	8,839	3,245
Textiles	78	2,955	621

NA = Not available

[a] in millions of dollars

Source: Bureau of Economic Analysis.

Clearly, U.S. labor costs have contributed to pricing the nation out of certain markets, specifically the very low (i.e., Hyundai) and very high (i.e., Mercedes and BMW) ends. For example, hourly wages for auto workers in the United States averaged $12.81 in 1986, compared with $8.72 in Germany, $4.00 in Japan, and $2.02 in Korea. Unfortunately U.S. wages, which represent a major portion of total manufacturing costs, have not been changing significantly. In Germany, which holds the second biggest chunk of global auto markets, wages have increased from $6.08 in 1984. The shockingly low figure in Korea can only point to a continued challenge as its auto industry catches up.

TRENDS

Research and Development Expenditures

To stay competitive as technological innovators, the United States needs to dedicate more earnings to research and development (R&D). Table 1–3 shows that while the percentage of R&D spending as a portion of the U.S. GNP has stayed relatively flat, the two biggest competitors, Japan and Germany, have increased theirs.

As shown in Table 1–4, only 14 percent of total U.S. R&D spending goes to computer development, compared with 12 percent for Japan and 14 percent for Germany, even though the United States is being strongly chal-

TABLE 1–3 R&D funding as percentage of GNP

	USA		Japan		Germany	
	Total	Nondefense	Total	Nondefense	Total	Nondefense
1970	2.6	1.6	1.9	1.8	2.1	2.0
1980	2.3	1.8	2.2	2.2	2.4	2.3
1981	2.4	1.8	2.4	2.4	2.4	2.3
1982	2.5	1.9	2.5	2.5	2.5	2.4
1983	2.6	1.9	2.6	2.6	2.5	2.4
1984	2.6	1.8	2.6	2.6	2.5	2.4
1985	2.7	1.9	2.8	2.8	2.7	2.5
1986	2.7	1.8	NA	NA	2.7	2.6

NA = Not available

Source: National Science Foundation.

lenged in this area. Also note the heavy Japanese focus on R&D in consumer electronics, an industry it already dominates.

Areas of Competitive Focus

A research report published by Boston University's Manufacturing Roundtable identifies from the responses of 217 industry participants the key areas of competitive focus.[3] In order of importance, these companies rate their need to be competitive as follows:

1. Conformance quality.
2. On-time delivery performance.
3. Quality.
4. Delivery.

TABLE 1–4 Percentage of R&D funding by industry

	USA	Japan	Germany
Auto	9	15	14
Chemicals	11	20	16
Computers	14	12	14
Electronics (consumer)	22	27	24

Source: National Science Foundation.

5. Speed.
6. Product flexibility.
7. After-sale service.
8. Price.
9. Broad line (features).
10. Broad distribution.
11. Volume flexibility.
12. Promotion.

From this ranking it is clear that quality and cost will continue to be addressed but that the new areas of opportunity are speed, customer service, and flexibility.

Following the rating of priorities, companies developed action lists. In order of importance, quality and statistical process control (SPC) are at the top of the action programs list. It is interesting to note that in 1984 the top three priorities were production control systems, workforce reductions, and supervisor training. Evidently U.S. manufacturers are getting closer to their customers by looking beyond the mechanics of production to issues of quality and responsiveness.

Planned changes in labor costs or in the makeup of the workforce emerge from the survey. Indirect labor will be reduced in the categories of material handling, quality control, supervising, manufacturing management, accounting, finance, and administration. Increases are planned for the design and R&D engineering sections, along with direct labor, management information systems (MIS), and purchasing.

Our comfortable standard of living, supported by high wages, has weakened our competitive position in several industries; the automobile sector illustrates this situation. Rather than attempting to compete on labor costs, we need to address the issues of improved customer service (from order administration through delivery of quality product), speed, and flexibility. Specific recommendations for improvement in these three key areas are addressed in more detail in subsequent chapters.

INDUSTRY/ACADEMIC COLLABORATION
TO IMPROVE MANUFACTURING

The U.S. educational system, from kindergarten through graduate school, is not functioning to produce the numbers and types of skilled workers and managers needed to compete globally. The very fact that foreign languages are not now a general public education requirement is one example. Declining math and science national test scores is another. Although the need for industry/education collaboration is now in the discussion and organization stages, educational reform works slowly and requires strong outside threats to respond. A few innovative programs including the M.I.T. Leaders in Manufacturing Program have pioneered reform.

Engineer Shortage

The December 5, 1988, issue of *Aviation Week and Space Technology* addressed the problem of supply and demand of engineers in emerging technology areas of the U.S. aerospace/defense industry. This industry, which represents a significant amount of the GNP, is being impacted by a shortage of both entry-level and experienced engineers. It is also one of the two strong U.S. industries (out of eight) according to the M.I.T. Commission on Industrial Productivity. Robotics, artificial intelligence, electronics, and systems and software engineering positions are some of the difficult slots to fill.

There are several factors contributing to this problem:

- Demographics—the college population is low.
- East Coast companies have difficulty recruiting because of that region's high cost of housing.
- Courses in emerging technologies may not be generally available at the undergraduate level.
- Some experts feel that the current U.S. educational approach limits development in the sense that engineering students may be trained to solve specific problems, but they are not absorbing what is called a total systems approach. The need for manufacturing engineering to relate problem solving to all the stages of the product delivery cycle, from engineering through distribution, is just now being accepted and built into curricula.
- The average age of aerospace engineers is increasing. A National Science Foundation Study showed the number of engineers in its over-50 age group increased 23 percent from 1976 to 1986.

Performance Evaluation for the U.S. Educational System

Former U.S. Senator Paul Tsongas, former head of the Massachusetts Board of Regents, proposed a partnership between the public colleges and the high-tech industry. As head of the body governing 29 public colleges and universities, he wanted to change current policies to improve the quality of public education. He proposed the formation of an academic review panel to evaluate candidates for college boards of trustees, the inclusion of business executives on college trustee boards, and the seating of more college professors, presidents, and administrators on corporate boards.

These collaborative ideas grew from Tsongas's feeling that the dominant need is to ensure the survival of the American standard of living and quality of life by achieving true competitiveness in international trade. To meet this challenge the United States needs a superbly trained, educated, and motivated workforce. The United States is competing with the Pacific Rim nations and Europe, both of which trade entities have stronger, more effective educational systems.

One of Tsongas's specific recommendations to improve the quality of the U.S. educational processes is the introduction of performance-based funding allocations—in his words, "Excel and you'll get more funding; botch it and we'll cut your funds."[4] The issues of accountability and quantitative performance evaluation are quite clear in the private sector; he wants to see them revisited in the academic world. Politics tends to interfere with public higher education. The former senator believes the powers-that-be should agree to a merit-based philosophy of decision making within the institutions, as well as come to an understanding on the larger issues of the missions of individual institutions and their structures. This means that both the business and academic communities need to agree on the educational requirements that will best satisfy our need to compete in international business.

Educational reform is driven from enlightened self-interest, in which each sector sees its own success and/or survival linked to the success and/or survival of each other sector. The following experimental education program is geared specifically toward satisfying these needs.

Senator Edward Kennedy says that, "Unless we act now, America will soon be without enough hands on deck to get the work of America done."[5] A Labor Department study has predicted a problem caused by a surge in new jobs and a decline in the birth rate, compounded by what Kennedy calls a potential skills gap between available workers and job openings. Collaboration between industry and education can provide the initial energy to start reforming U.S. education and training to overcome these problems.

The M.I.T. Leaders in Manufacturing Program— Developing a New Type of Manager

The Leaders for Manufacturing Program is a new joint educational and research program established to help the United States recapture world leadership in manufacturing. It represents an exciting collaboration between the M.I.T. Schools of Engineering and Management and 11 of the nation's leading manufacturing corporations. The program is funded by a $30-million collaboration between the university and 11 companies—Alcoa, Boeing, Digital, Eastman Kodak, Hewlett-Packard, Johnson & Johnson, Motorola, Polaroid, General Motors, Chrysler, and United Technologies.

The goals of the program are to develop a model curriculum for educating a new generation of leaders in manufacturing and to draw some of the nation's best students into careers in manufacturing industries. (See recommendations of Romeyn Everdell in Chapter 2).

Lester Thurow, the Dean of the Sloan School of Management at Massachusetts Institute of Technology, feels that its new combination management/engineering graduate degree program is exciting and necessary. A common criticism of M.B.A. programs is that they do not adequately address the type of training managers will need to lead U.S. industry. According to Thurow: "Today, most top managers in Europe and Japan have a technical education, while most U.S. managers don't. As a result, foreign companies have been more willing to take risks on new technologies."[6]

Professor David Hardt of the M.I.T. School of Engineering agrees with Cohen and Zysman (authors of *Manufacturing Matters: The Myth of the Postindustrial Economy*) that it is manufacturing, not the service sector only, that creates wealth. It is misleading and dangerous to think that the United States can safely abandon basic production and become fast-food purveyors to the world.

Curriculum

The two-year program includes academic course work and six months of on-site research experience with a sponsoring organization under close faculty and industrial supervision. The program's purpose is to define the combination of educational experiences that will yield graduates who can be measurably more effective in the definition, design, manufacturing, and delivery of high-quality products and systems.

The fellows, as the degree candidates are called, all take a management core curriculum, as well as selected electives. Within the School of Engineering, they design individual programs in an engineering department. In addition, all students take a required weekly professional seminar, the program's major mechanism for bringing together its disparate constituencies of management and engineering faculty and students and company sponsors. During the seminar, students and faculty also look closely at each of the sponsoring companies, with student teams developing presentations and companies bringing in their best in-house instructors.

The program represents a commitment to integrating engineering and management concerns. Engineers and managers are encouraged to learn more about each other and to begin to speak the same language.

An example of the intensive, but typical, two-year curriculum for a dual degree includes 13 management and 6 engineering courses, 4 seminars, 3 projects, and 4 theses. Graduates are expected to leave the program with many of the following:

- A broad understanding of manufacturing, from the product design concept to its production, use, and field maintenance.
- An understanding of production planning, scheduling, inventory control, manufacturing policy, and management accounting.
- An understanding of the role that human factors (e.g., labor relations, psychology, and ethics), logistics, marketing, vendor support, and economics play in all aspects of manufacturing systems.
- Self-confidence in approaching the design and management of innovative manufacturing and processing systems and a tolerance for ambiguity during times of change.
- An in-depth understanding of at least one technology and its integration into an overall system (e.g., mechanical assembly or integrated factory information systems).
- An understanding of materials processing technologies and methods of modeling, simulating, and controlling processes.
- Working understanding of computer-based design, manufacturing system automation and control, and communications systems.
- An understanding of emerging technologies and materials that will impact manufacturing beyond the next decade.
- Increased leadership strengths and improved management, communication, and interpersonal skills.

The Students

The first 20 fellows were 12 of the top applicants to the Engineering Graduate School and 8 of the top applicants to the School of Management. This program represents a new educational model in the area of university/manufacturing alliances, as well as interdepartmental collaboration. Professor Bitran of the Management Science Department declares, "We want to be copied. And we want companies to count on the program's graduates."[7]

GLOBAL COMPETITION

In the late eighties, the President's Commission on Industrial Competitiveness completed a two-volume study with specific recommendations on how to meet U.S. global competitive challenges. The commission included leaders from industry, academia, banking, government, and various professional organizations. In *Volume I, The New Reality*,[8] the recommendations included:

In research and development and manufacturing
- Create a federal department of science and technology.
- Increase tax incentives for research and development.
- Commercialize new technologies through improved manufacturing.

In human resources
- Increase effective dialogue among government, industry, and labor.
- Build labor/management cooperation.
- Strengthen employee incentives.
- Deal with displaced workers.
- Improve workforce skills.
- Improve engineering education.
- Improve business school education.
- Create partnerships in education.
- Develop education technology.

In international trade
- Minimize impact of controls on competitiveness.
- Export expansion.
- Export financing.

How many recommendations have been acted upon four years later? Although we are working on strengthening our trade position, most activity is happening in the human resources category; the first group of recommendations on R&D and manufacturing remain relatively untouched.

Joint Research and Development

According to a report of the Conference Board entitled *1992: Leading Issues for European Companies*,[9] there is an EC-administered $180-million fund dedicated to promote cooperation among research labs of member states. This combination of R&D resources, particularly in the electronics field, may enable the Europeans to beat Americans and Japanese to market (see Table 1–5). The first phase of the joint research and technology programs, Esprit, was launched in 1984, scheduled to run 10 years. Part 1 of Esprit involved 450 participating organizations. Part 2 will deal with advanced microelectronics, software development, advanced information processing, office automation, and robotics. Later phases will explore new industry technologies such as CAD/CAM.

TABLE 1–5 Three global trading blocks

	U.S.	Japan	EC
Population	243.8M	122.0M	323.6
Share of world GNP	25.9%	9.4%	22.1%
Total labor force	121.6M	60.3	143.0
Agricultural	3.4	4.6	11.9
Nonagricultural	118.2	55.7	131.1
GNP Growth Rate 1987	2.9%	4.2%	2.9%
Exports (US$ millions)	250.4	231.2	953.5[a]
Imports (US$ millions)	424.1	150.8	955.1[a]

[a] Includes trade between EC members.

Source: The Wall Street Journal, 2/13/89 and 1/23/89.

Regulations Impacting U.S. Manufacturers

The accords will affect how U.S. manufacturers do business in Europe. Technical standards vary from one European country to another; French and Italian electric plugs, for example, have three prongs, while West German plugs have two. Hopefully, the rules will be standardized, along with manufacturing safety standards and other product specifications. Other areas included for standardization are

- Motor vehicle emission standards.
- Measuring instruments.
- Machine safety.
- Food additives.
- Noise levels in lawn mowers, household appliances, and hydraulic equipment.
- Pharmaceuticals, high-tech medicines, and certain devices.
- Labor issues (which may increase worker mobility within Europe): engineering training standards, comparability of vocational training qualifications, and mutual recognition of higher educational diplomas.

Transport time, and therefore customer delivery times, should be reduced as border checks of paperwork are simplified.

SUMMARY

We have reviewed briefly the factors impacting U.S. manufacturers' ability to compete globally, including

- The loss or threatened loss of market share.
- The invasion by foreign manufacturers.
- Research and development expenditures.
- Internal focus on quality, flexibility, and customer service.
- The need for education/industry collaboration.
- European Community reforms.

Of all the issues faced, U.S. manufacturers can really address only four directly: labor costs, R&D spending, internal manufacturing strategic focus, and educational reform. But effective focus on even one will realize some of the potential for productivity gains.

ACKNOWLEDGMENTS

Thanks to Paula Cronin, of *M.I.T. MANAGEMENT,* who contributed her piece on the Leaders in Manufacturing Program, to Dean Lester Thurow and Professor Don Rosenfield of the M.I.T. Sloan School, and to Paul Tsongas for their very generous and timely contributions to this chapter.

Research describing market share and other key data was performed by Monique Richardson of the Simmons College Graduate School of Management Library.

NOTES

1. Michael L. Dertouzos, Richard K. Lester, Robert M. Solow, and the M.I.T. Commission on Industrial Productivity, *Made in America* (Cambridge, Mass.: The M.I.T. Press, 1989), 79.
2. Ibid., p. 18.
3. Jeffrey G. Miller and Aleda Roth, *Manufacturing Strategies, Executive Summary of the 1988 North American Manufacturing Futures Survey,* Boston University School of Management Manufacturing Roundtable, 1988.
4. Quoted from Senator Tsongas's speech before the Massachusetts High Tech Council, February 1989.
5. Boston *Globe,* January 30, 1989, p. 31.
6. Boston *Globe,* June 19, 1988, p. 97.
7. Alfred P. Sloan School of Management, *M.I.T. MANAGEMENT* (Winter 1988): 2–8.
8. United States Presidential Commission on Industrial Competitiveness, *Global Competition: The New Reality* (Washington, D.C.: Government Printing Office, 1985): 45–46.
9. Catherine Morrison, *1992; Leading Issues for European Companies* (New York: The Conference Board, 1989).

STATISTICAL REFERENCES

Arpan, Jeffrey S., and David A. Ricks. *Directory of Foreign Manufacturers in the United States*, 3d ed. Atlanta: Georgia State University, 1985.

Duns Analytical Services. *Industry Norms and Key Business Ratios*. Murray Hill, N.J.: Dun & Bradstreet Inc., 1983–84 through 1987–88 (annual).

Industry Surveys. New York: Standard & Poor's, 1988.

International Labor Office. *Yearbook of Labor Statistics*. Geneva: International Labor Office, 1987.

International Monetary Fund. *International Financial Statistics Yearbook*. Washington, D.C.: International Monetary Fund, 1987.

National Science Foundation. *International Science and Technology Update*. Springfield, Va.: NTIS, 1987.

――――. *Research and Development in Industry, 1984*. Springfield, Va.: NTIS, 1986.

"100 Leading National Advertisers." *Advertising Age* 59 (Sept. 28, 1988): 41.

Pennar, Karen. "The Factory Rebound May Be More Fantasy Than Fact." *Business Week* 3083:98 (Dec. 12, 1988): 101.

"Projections 2000." *Monthly Labor Review* 110 (Sept. 1987): 3–62.

RMA Annual Statement Studies, FY 1988. Philadelphia: Robert Morris Associates, 1988.

Rosenbaum, Andrew. "Europe: Fortress―or Facade?" *Industry Week* 238 (Feb. 6, 1989): 54–55.

"Special Report: Reshaping Europe: 1992 and Beyond," *Business Week* 3083 (Dec. 12, 1988): 48–73.

Survey of Current Business 68 (July 1987).

U.N. Department of International Economic and Social Affairs. Statistical Office. *Industrial Statistics Yearbook 1985*. New York: United Nations, 1987.

――――. *International Trade Statistics Yearbook 1986*. New York: United Nations, 1988.

UNESCO. *Statistical Yearbook*. Paris: UNESCO, 1987.

U.S. Bureau of Labor Statistics. *Handbook of Labor Statistics 1983*. Washington, D.C.: GPO, 1985.

U.S. Bureau of the Census. *Annual Survey of Manufacturers*. Washington, D.C.: GPO, 1983–1986 (annual).

――――. *Statistical Abstracts of the United States*. Washington, D.C.: GPO, 1988.

U.S. Dept of Commerce, Bureau of Economic Analysis. *Direct Investment Abroad: Operations of U.S. Parent Companies and Their Foreign Affiliates, Preliminary 1986 Estimates*. Washington, D.C.: GPO, 1988.

――――. *Foreign Direct Investment in the United States: Operations of U.S. Affiliates, Preliminary 1985 Estimates*. Washington, D.C.: GPO, 1987.

U.S. Dept of Commerce, International Trade Administration. *U.S. Industrial Outlook*. Washington, D.C.: GPO, 1988.

U.S. National Center for Education Statistics. *Digest of Education Statistics*. Washington, D.C.: GPO (Dept. of Education. Office of Education Research and Improvement CS88–600), 1988.

———. *Projections of Education Statistics to 1997–98*. Washington, D.C.: GPO (Dept. of Education. Office of Education Research and Improvement CS88–607), 1988.

GPO: Government Printing Office
NTIS: National Technical Information Service

2 FROM LOWELL TO SUNNYVALE

MANUFACTURING IN THE UNITED STATES

Romeyn Everdell

Editor's note

As the United States approaches the next millenium, large segments of U.S. industry ("smokestack America") are facing crises. The question remains: Can U.S. manufacturers compete in basic manufacturing on a worldwide basis or is U.S. industry over the hill? Is the U.S. competitive position like that of a professional athlete weakened by age, unable, like the United Kingdom, to stay in the game? Or can industry be revitalized in a competitive response to the challenges from Japan, West Germany, and now South Korea? This book takes the position that industry is a team sport. With fresh players, updated strategy and training, and new management, it is not only possible to regain the competitive edge, we actually know how to do it.

There is an old but compelling cliche that those who fail to study history are condemned to repeat the mistakes of the past. We have neither the time nor resources to repeat mistakes. It is important, therefore, to review the evolution of manufacturing before addressing the current challenge and response.

MANUFACTURING BEGINNINGS

Manufacturing had a noble beginning, and in spite of traumatic events in its uneven progress, we recognize that it was our tool-making ability that distinguished humans from their animal ancestors and built civilization as we know it. From man the *faber* (Latin for "maker") gradually evolved the artisans and craftsmen of the middle ages. The medieval guilds and shops were our first manufacturing facilities. However, *modern* manufacturing received its initial impetus from the Renaissance. The Age of Reason focused on the mind rather than the spirit and fueled the explosion of science and engineering. Leonardo da Vinci was the first in a long line of technical innovators: Edison, Bell, Ford, and the current giants such as Shockley, Packard, and Jobs.

Modern manufacturing as we know it began in England between 1765 and 1815 with the Industrial Revolution—a child of the marriage of emerging technology and the handcrafts. Manufacturing became a major influence for good—availability of low-cost products—and evil—"the dark satanic mills" that led to social stress, labor/management conflict, and the still-to-be-resolved communist/capitalist schism. Modern manufacturing, with its origins in human labor (the worker) and human mental skills (the engineer), remains a major factor in defining the quality of life of society and is therefore worthy of our interest, understanding, and involvement.

U.S. MANUFACTURING MILESTONES

Wickham Skinner suggests in a chapter he wrote entitled "The Taming of Lions: How Manufacturing Leadership Evolved 1780–1984," from the book *The Uneasy Alliance,* that there are five stages to the evolution of manufacturing in the United States:

1800–1850 The age of the technical capitalists

1850–1890 The introduction of mass production

1890–1920 Scientific management in manufacturing

1920–1960 The golden years of U.S. manufacturing

1960–1980 The decline of the American factory

Basically these milestones identify responses to evolving technologies, changing markets, proliferation of products in an increasingly wealthy nation, and intense competition (see Figure 2–1).

FIGURE 2–1 Evolution of manufacturing in the United States

TIME PERIOD		1800	1850	1890	1920	1960	1980
STAGES	Renaissance to Industrial Revolution	Technical Capitalists	Mass Production	Scientific Management	Golden Years	Decline	Challenge from Overseas
KEY PLAYERS	Leonardo DaVinci to Cartwright	Francis Cabot Lowell Watt	Bell Edison	Taylor Ford	Knudsen Charlie Wilson Shockley		
FACTORIES	• Crafts • Guilds • Cottage industries	• Water power • Large labor force • Technical innovation	• Conversion to steam and electrical power • High volume • Increasing automation	• Product proliferation • Job shops appear • Replacement of labor with machinery	• Rapid product obsolescence • Further reduction of labor through automation • Heavy investment in equipment	• Inflexible factories • Equipment obsolescence	
MANU-FACTURING MANAGEMENT	Craftsmen to Apprentice	• Factory agent	• Agent plus foreman	• Increasing production staff • Production manager	• Complex production staff, high overhead	• Attempt to increase control and use computers	

20

TIME PERIOD	1800	1850	1890	1920	1960	1980
ORGANIZATION	• President intimately involved • Small staff of supervisors • Agent runs mill	• Plant manager with foremen • Top management in technical innovation and equipment investment	• Foremen lose power to production manager • Top management less involved	• Large specialized staff • Factory run by numbers	• Bureaucracy • Manufacturing isolated, run by numbers	
COMPETITION	• Competition because of success	• Competition from low wage regions	• Competition increasingly result of economy of scale	• Competition based on customer satisfaction • Largely within U.S.	• Cost competition from overseas	

Summary of U.S. Manufacturing Trends

As the nation grew and prospered, more U.S. assets were used to develop a manufacturing base. While the jobs created by this investment and continuing wage increases improved the living standard, over time there was also a gradual but dramatic reduction in direct labor per unit of product. The reduction in direct labor content was achieved by a growing production staff of industrial engineers, planners, and controllers until a bureaucracy of manufacturing middle management developed that increased overhead costs and partially offset the reduction in direct labor. Paralleling this trend came the need for top management to give greater attention to selling and marketing, accounting and financing, and legal skills to meet competition in an increasingly regulated environment and to keep the investment in production fully utilized.

Manufacturing in the 1800s was the only game in town. By 1980, largely because of early successes, it had fallen low on the totem pole on the stack of management concerns. To put flesh on these broad trends and to better understand the implications and impact of the current dilemma, let us look at each of Skinner's five periods in more detail.

1800–1850, THE AGE OF THE TECHNICAL CAPITALISTS

The Boston Manufacturing Company

Before 1800, the United States was a nation largely of farmers and maritime merchants. Much of the demand for manufactured goods was met by imports shipped from Europe, India, and the Orient. As a result, significant amounts of capital started to accumulate in the hands of New England's merchants and shipowners. One critical import was machine-woven cotton textiles from England, a major product of the British Industrial Revolution.

In 1811 a successful Boston merchant, Francis Cabot Lowell, went to England, visited Manchester, the center of that revolution, and in an astonishing act of memory became the first U.S. industrial spy. He returned to Boston with mental blueprints of the power loom, a proprietary British invention. On his return, using his own and additional capital from his association with fellow maritime merchants, Lowell formed the Boston Manufacturing Company and built the first American power loom textile mill in Waltham, Massachusetts, in 1813. With the help of a brilliant mechanic, Paul Moody, Lowell adapted and expanded the technology taken from England to produce a completely integrated manufacturing process at a single site, starting with raw cotton and ending with finished cloth.

In one extraordinary leap, Lowell created a stock corporation, formed an integrated manufacturing facility with a significant competitive edge, and hired the first manufacturing engineer. Lowell's enterprise brought the stockholders just over 19 percent average annual return on investment between 1817 and 1821. In 1822, as the company grew, the return was a tax-free 27.5 percent. The original Boston Manufacturing Company of Waltham expanded to the banks of the Merrimack River in Lowell, Massachusetts. Competitors were quick to develop, and many more mills followed throughout New England wherever water power, the required energy source, was available. A fascinating history of these beginnings and their impact on American society can be found in *The Enterprising Elite—The Boston Associates and the World They Made.* °

Key Developments of the Period

It is important to recognize that the initial development was technology. The acquisition of capital to realize the potential was vital, but it was the second step. The implication of the word *capitalism* tends to obscure this fundamental principle.

In Lowell's original organization, three items stand out: (1) management structure, (2) sales, and (3) the labor force. The early mills were run by a mill agent who managed the day-to-day business. The agent reported to the treasurer, who was, or reported to, the president. The treasurer handled purchasing and managed all financial affairs. Sales were achieved by a separate commercial firm paid commissions. This activity also fell under the control of the treasurer. As a result, there was very little overhead to spread over a large manufacturing labor base.

Despite all the technological innovations in carding, combing, spinning, and weaving, a textile mill of this period had a huge labor force. In the mid-1800s labor represented in excess of 40 percent of cost of sales (at Amoskeag, the largest textile mill in the world, wages were still 35 percent of gross income by 1900). The labor force was of great concern to Charles Dickens because of his reaction to the dreary factories of the British Industrial Revolution. His novels vividly portray the social consequences of the Industrial Revolution in England: Factory profits made the rich richer, while subsistence wages created appalling living conditions for labor in the factory cities.

Lowell copied only the English loom design and evolved an ingenious solution to the labor problem. He devised the concept of hiring young, unmarried women off the farm, training them, and acting *in loco parentis.* They lived in mill-owned, supervised housing. As a social engineer, Lowell viewed his effort as improving the limited opportunities available to women

---

°For this and other references, see bibliography at end of chapter.

off the farms. The "singing loom girls," whose ethics and behavior became the concern of the benevolent mill owner, were his answer to the wretches laboring in the Manchester mills. This interesting experiment did not last, but at least the beginnings of the U.S. factory system were both innovative and progressive.

Between 1820 and 1850, the success of the Boston Manufacturing Company stimulated growth in other textile mills, and Lowell started the capital goods industry through sale of textile machinery. Arms manufacturing, another seminal manufacturing activity, developed the concept of interchangeable parts and opened the door to mass production. Canals, followed by railroads around 1830, reduced the cost of transporting raw materials and finished products to and from manufacturing facilities and expanded the impact of as well as the market for, these factories.

At the end of the 18th to the middle of the 19th centuries, manufacturing began to rival farming and maritime shipping. The new game in town attracted a nucleus of wealthy, technically oriented entrepreneurs. They were interested in and involved with manufacturing equipment and process and wanted to deal intelligently with the new industrial workforce. The early managers gave manufacturing their full attention.

1850–1890, INTRODUCTION OF MASS PRODUCTION

Evolution of the Factory and the Workforce

The Civil War and migration of farming to the West changed the isolated Eastern factory towns to an urban industrial region. Technological restraints were removed by the invention of energy and communications devices—the steam engine, telegraph, electricity, and electric motor. Manufacturing broke free of location restraints; plants could be located close to raw material, markets, or labor. Factory wages attracted the subsistence farmers and stimulated demand for manufactured products. Technology was applied to both new products and the manufacturing process. The era of mass production arrived.

Labor became available as agriculture receded and emigration from depressed regions in Europe increased. The early stage of automation reduced costs dramatically by trading investment in manufacturing equipment for reduction in direct labor. Production output increased. Although new products came into being, variety within a product was limited. Each plant produced relatively few products. Top management focused on economies of scale. Managers were involved directly with production technologies and concerned with gaining a satisfactory return on the escalating investment in manufacturing equipment.

Lowell's noble experiment, founded on an enlightened labor policy, deteriorated. It was too costly to train the transient flow of inexperienced farm girls. A permanent workforce was the cost-effective answer. As high profits created competition and pressure on prices, the need to reduce labor costs, coupled with the freedom of plant location, started the search for low-cost labor regions—initially the post–Civil War South. As the permanent workforce settled in, the social mores of the male breadwinner and the physical demands of many of the new jobs created an increasingly male-dominated factory.

The financial requirement to keep expensive production machinery fully utilized under growing competition put pressure on labor, the major variable cost, particularly in periods of depression. Top management delegated all responsibility for the labor force to the agent and he in turn to the foreman. The foreman was king, responsible for hiring, firing, directing, and controlling labor. The reaction of the foremen to pressure for increased output inevitably led to labor problems and helped develop and expand unionism. However, business prospered, labor requirements grew, and industrial urbanization continued.

The Amoskeag Manufacturing Company— A Case in Point

The textile industry was a leading indicator in the manufacturing community. Hareven and Langenbach's *Amoskeag, Life and Work in an American Factory City* details the fascinating history of a textile factory located in Manchester, New Hampshire, across three periods of manufacturing history. Amoskeag was a direct descendent of the Waltham–Lowell system. In the mass production era it became the largest cotton textile mill of its time. It declined as textiles moved south.

Although the mill was started along the banks of the Merrimack River, the automatic loom gradually replaced Lowell's water-powered loom. The process was technologically driven and became very successful because of the application of mass production techniques. The labor force, which reached a high of 17,000 workers, consisted of New England mill girls, later replaced by French Canadians and Europeans. The earliest agent was a model of corporate paternalism, but the benevolence of his regime deteriorated as size, makeup, and competitive pressures impacted the labor/management relationship. Finally, the seeds of decline grew as new mills opened in the South with cheaper labor and equipment better suited to the changing product. But until the end of the 19th century Amoskeag was a profitable model of manufacturing in its era.

General Characteristics of the Period

The period of mass production was a logical extension of the 1800–1850 origins. Sales were still conducted largely through independent companies. Management was financially and technologically oriented; top management, a small group generally located away from the plant, consisted of a president (who sometimes doubled as treasurer) and a slowly growing staff of clerks. Manufacturing overhead grew as size and complexity required greater numbers and layers of foremen, superintendents, and department heads, with the agent at the top of this expanding pyramid. Technology also required expansion of the indirect labor force involved with maintenance, material handling, inspection, and payroll-related duties. During this period of large, direct labor forces, however, indirect labor costs were insignificant.

1890–1920, SCIENTIFIC MANAGEMENT IN MANUFACTURING

Enter the Consultants

At the turn of the century, outsiders (the first consultants) began to impact all industry. The innovators included Frederic Taylor, Frank Gilbreth, Henry Gantt, Charles Bedeaux, and Lyndall Urwick, who founded a more systematic approach to manufacturing. Their new techniques came to be known as *scientific management*, a somewhat misleading term for the origin of industrial engineering.

The age of mass production had generated a group of operational concerns:

- Personnel problems—hiring, training, and integrating labor into an increasingly complex manufacturing process.
- Manufacturing or process engineering—the design of production equipment to suit product and volume.
- Rate setting—the determination of the expected number of pieces to be produced per worker and piecework pay rates.
- Material control—the management of logistics from raw material through work-in-process, storage, and finally shipment.

The Birth of Industrial Engineering

The initial efforts of people such as Taylor and Gilbreth focused primarily on reduction of direct labor costs through methods and time study. The systematic approach of these pioneers required the addition of a staff of industrial engineers. The valid assumption was that a dollar spent on trained staff would realize two dollars of direct labor savings. They formally analyzed methods used to run production equipment or perform manual tasks, improved each method, compared before and after with a stop watch to determine the degree of improvement, and computed the savings. The contribution of Bedeaux was to take this time data and establish a standard hour for each direct labor operation based on the number of pieces that normally could be produced in 60 minutes. He used this time standard as a basis for standard hour incentive pay plans to replace the piecework plans set rather arbitrarily by foremen.

The industrial engineers reduced labor; increased output; and, by distributing the savings to the worker as well as the company, increased workers' wages. A by-product of these productivity programs was a dramatic reduction in the foreman's power by taking away his ability to determine workers' pay. Even setting the base rate (paid for standard performance or below) became the responsibility of the personnel department, which was influenced by area wages.

Growth of Production Staff

Another important by-product of industrial engineering was the use of the standard hour as the basis for developing the standard cost of labor and estimating product costs and prices. The labor standard also became a control tool, used to compare actual to standard and to generate variances. The opportunity to monitor labor performance led to the addition of whole departments of cost controllers. The manufacturing arm soon grew trained staffs of salaried specialists gathered into production departments:

- Methods and time study.
- Cost accounting.
- Personnel.
- Material control.
- Manufacturing engineering.

Most of these functions originally had been part of the foremen's responsibilities. Cost accounting expanded the skill level and workload of the corporate clerk, a one- or two-person crew in the 1800s. Manufacturing engineering evolved from the relatively few master mechanics and inventors who had designed the automated equipment on which the Industrial Revolution was built. The number of manufacturing engineers grew as new technologies became available to accelerate the replacement of manual labor with machines. Industrial engineers (efficiency experts, often accused of speed-up) tried to apply labor more efficiently by reducing the time required by the remaining workers to produce goods. Management began to use the new standards to look for unfavorable variance from direct labor standards. A significant change emerged as top management moved away from direct involvement with manufacturing toward a delegation of responsibility to a growing production management staff, while monitoring quantitative performance measures (management by objectives or MBO).

As important as was the impact on all industry of the systems engineers, the activities of specific manufacturers were equally important. Under the stimulation of technological giants such as Edison and Bell, new products and new industries vastly expanded the manufacturing base. Among these facilities were a few model factories (e.g., the Hawthorne Works of Western Electric in Chicago) that applied all the new scientific management techniques to operating high-speed machinery. This period saw the introduction of Henry Ford's moving assembly line and the culmination of his manufacturing masterpiece: the River Rouge complex in Dearborn.

Managing Labor

There was a growing concern that mass production had been achieved at the expense of the worker. The emerging dominance of an engineering view of the world, fueled by the popular belief that progress equaled improved technology, was changing the production labor force from man the *faber* to man the machine. The most biting commentary on this change was the Charlie Chaplin film *Modern Times*.

Unions had been hard at work to ensure the worker a financial share in the industrial revolution, but unrest in the labor force went deeper. Experiments at the Hawthorne Works were the first efforts to apply industrial psychology to the monotonous and dehumanizing effect of tasks broken down into small, repetitive elements. The Hawthorne experiments seemed to suggest that monotonous, unskilled, repetitive jobs could be accommodated if the foremen showed more concern for the human or spiritual side of the worker, suggesting that the Age of Reason's rationality had gone too far.

Benevolent experiments built on paternalism were tried at Draper, Hershey, Kohler, and others. They all foundered on the owners-know-best restraint on the freedom of the individual, complicated by the diversity of an increasingly pluralistic and educated workforce. Labor unrest continued while well-intentioned efforts to deal with it generally deteriorated into an adversarial relationship between union and management.

Impact of Customer Demands

Important manufacturing strategy changes in this period were influenced by the proliferation of not only new products but product variety. The Ford manufacturing ideal of any color as long as it's black did not last. Marketing became a vital concern driving product design and manufacturing. The use of separate sales companies proved uneconomical and too remote. As a result, top management gave more attention to the creation and management of specialized internal departments for sales and marketing. Concern with marketing accelerated the drift of top management away from exclusive interest in manufacturing and finance. At the same time, manufacturing faced increasing problems dealing with product change and proliferation in plants originally designed for simpler and often dramatically different items.

The Decline of Amoskeag—A Harbinger of the Future

Through the advantage of hindsight, the history of Amoskeag in this period is a remarkable forerunner of what occurred 50 years later throughout U.S. industry. The principal difference is that competition came from the low-cost-labor American southland rather than offshore. New and more advanced textile factories with lower labor rates created cost competition. Amoskeag reacted by going from one shift to a three-shift, seven-day schedule. Tripling production capacity did not help the saturated textile market. Prices fell and profits dropped.

With lower margins, management was reluctant to invest to upgrade the manufacturing process. It chose instead to run fully depreciated and rapidly deteriorating machinery at higher rates for longer hours. Management reduced labor rates with arbitrary piece-rate changes. Labor/management relations worsened. By 1920 the surge of demand to supply the U.S. troops in World War I with uniforms, blankets, and the like masked the symptoms of decay. As a result, the problems that would bring about the tragic ending of this once noble enterprise by the mid-1930s were not addressed.

1920–1960, THE GOLDEN YEARS OF U.S. MANUFACTURING

World War I Aftermath

U.S. manufacturing entered a period of world domination at the end of World War I. The Versailles Treaty levied heavy reparation payments on the defeated nations, which had a depressing effect on world markets. When the pent-up domestic demand of the war years was satisfied, the U.S. economy went into a tailspin in 1929, triggering a prolonged worldwide depression throughout the 1930s. This period forged the crucible that carried the United States into the golden era of manufacturing after World War II. In the 1930s, management had to cut back to survive. With labor still a major cost factor, the brunt of this effort fell on the newly organized manufacturing arm, now headed by a manufacturing manager, whose power and influence grew. The strategies used to stabilize operations were to have serious effects later.

Labor unrest continued during the Depression. With layoffs and speedups the order of the day, unions grew in size and power. Although some industries were enlightened and tried to handle labor with wisdom and fairness, economic disaster tended to breed desperate measures. The Amoskeag story ended tragically. Management, deciding it could not justify an investment in the Manchester facility, used the cash flow from operations to fund a trust for the benefit of the owners. Strikes occurred in 1922, 1933, and 1934. The last two were bitter and violent, and in September of 1935 the mill shut down. Liquid assets had been siphoned off to the trust fund, leaving a shattered economy in Manchester, a city of 75,000.

Labor/Management Power Struggles

Union influence varied. On one extreme was Sam Gompers, head of the garment workers union, who actually introduced industrial engineering to the garment trades, lowered costs, and saved the needle workers' jobs. At the opposite extreme was the longshoremen's union, which allied itself with gangsters to take over the docks. Abuses and conflict on both sides hardened labor/management relations into adversarial positions.

Automation Extended—The Product Volume Dilemma

Observing the success of mass production and frustrated with the intractable demands of labor, management emphasized increased automation as a solution. Not only was the process automated, but conveyor lines, transfer equipment, and assembly lines were developed to automate material handling. Unfortunately, automation efforts had the negative effect of reducing manufacturing's ability to be flexible and accommodate product change. As a result, growing distinctions among types of manufacturing began to be recognized (see Table 2–1).

New products and product styles proliferated, forcing production in the direction of the job shop. But manufacturing management, recognizing the increased costs involved, pushed in the direction of high-volume, minimum flexibility facilities. Striving to meet market needs or stimulate demand, sales and marketing became adversaries of manufacturing, which was looking for a few high-volume products. The conflict sometimes reached the point at which sales and marketing were not allowed in the factory. Complaining about product proliferation, manufacturing tried to freeze

TABLE 2–1 Three types of manufacturing

Type	Product	Characteristics
1. Pure process	Chemicals, steel, wire and cables, liquids (beer, soda), canned goods	Full automation, low labor content in product costs, high-volume output, facilities dedicated to one product
2. High-volume manufacturing	Automobiles, telephones, fasteners, textiles, motors, household fixtures	Automated equipment, partial automated handling, moving assembly lines, most equipment in line, factories dedicated to various models of product
3. Job shops (low volume)	Capital goods, hand tools, hardware, instruments	Machining centers organized by manufacturing function, not in line, high labor content in product costs, general-purpose machinery with significant changeover time, little automation of material handling, large variety of product

schedules. The words "give us long lead times" became the rallying cry of the factory.

Growing Manufacturing Bureaucracy

Overhead continued to increase as material handlers, equipment maintenance and changeover personnel, inspectors, and planning and inventory controllers were added to industrial and manufacturing engineering staffs.

Two unanticipated problems resulted:

1. *Growing overhead costs.* Costs of indirect labor (burden) were measured as a percentage of direct labor. As direct labor costs were reduced, an increasingly financially oriented management became alarmed at the rise in the percentage of burden. Some programs for direct labor reduction were even rejected because overhead percentages increased. In other cases indirect labor was cut arbitrarily. The confusion over burden absorption clouded the issue of cost control throughout this period, even leading to occasional decisions to *add* direct labor to improve burden rates.

2. *Bureaucracy sets in.* The sheer size and makeup of factory overhead personnel created a conservative, risk-averse bureaucracy. Middle management specialists looked at the production process with tunnel vision and parochial interest. By 1960 the plant staff could best be described as a

group of blind people feeling an elephant, each describing it in the limited context of his or her experience. Not only did the bureaucracy make change difficult, it failed to see the whole process (elephant) and often duplicated, canceled, or offset the efforts of the individual. Bright, ambitious activists left for more challenging fields.

World War II Aftermath

With these growing cracks in the manufacturing foundation, why were these the golden years? The reasons lie in the impact of World War II. The prewar depression ensured that the fittest survived. The country entered the 1940s equipped with a lean, mean, and hungry manufacturing community. The conversion of U.S. industry to war production is an incredible story of quick response. Aided by statesmen such as Bob Lovett from the War Department, one of the great manufacturing men of his age, Bill Knudsen from Ford planned, guided, spurred, expedited, and coordinated the conversion. U.S. manufacturers made it work. After the war, the U.S. government recognized that post–World War I reparations had contributed to the 1930s depression and the rise of Hitler. Jack McCloy went to Germany with the Marshall Plan to finance the rebuilding of that devastated economy, and the American Caesar, General Douglas MacArthur, went to Japan to direct its reconstruction. The result was that the United States primed the pump—a growing export market—that sustained the domestic surge of postwar demand. The combined effects of pent-up demand, the export market financed by U.S. loans, and little worldwide competition generated a huge market for U.S. products. Until 1960 no one could match U.S. costs, but the arrogance of success meant that no one was keeping an eye on Japan and West Germany.

Introduction of Quantitative Methods

Another impact of World War II on manufacturing was the growth of a specialized quantitative problem-solving approach called *operations research* (OR). Operations research had been used to solve a wide variety of war-related problems by teams of multidisciplinary scientists. After their wartime success, some OR scientists turned to manufacturing, attracted by an area full of unresolved problems. This stimulated the development of powerful mathematical techniques and the beginnings of truly *scientific* management applications for manufacturing. From creative chaos emerged an alphabet soup of techniques:

> SQC—statistical quality control. Statistics applied first to inspection, then to control processes, and subsequently to problem solving; used to eliminate defects and their attendant cost.

EOQ—economic order quantity. Mathematical solution of the lot size problem, which trades off setup costs against excess inventory costs.

LP—linear programming. Complex mathematics that solve for optimum decisions among conflicting costs and restraints.

PERT—planning, evaluation, and review technique. Project planning to determine the project cost, the critical path, and the shortest time to completion.

MRP—material-requirements planning. The explosion of product quantities through a bill of material to determine quantity and dates of required components to meet finished-goods assembly schedules.

LOB—line of balance. Line balancing to determine the optimum assignment of tasks to assembly-line workers at varying line speeds.

These complex quantitative approaches were sponsored by a growing number of manufacturing consultants and technical societies mirroring the specialization and departmentalization in the manufacturing organization (see Table 2–2).

The specialists pushed their solutions on an industrial population lacking the academic background or training to evaluate and understand them. Top management had neither the experience in manufacturing nor the time to evaluate, select, and sponsor these new techniques. Furthermore, they were preoccupied with marketing, product planning, investment strategies, and a growing need to meet regulatory and legal issues.

Impact of the Computer

When the computer arrived on the scene, the young technicians and sales representatives of that industry were very much at home with quantitative

TABLE 2–2 Some specialized technical societies and their functions

Technical Societies	Manufacturing Specialty
ASQC	Inspection and quality control
AIIE	Industrial engineering
SME	Manufacturing engineering
MHI	Material handling
APICS	Product planning, scheduling, and inventory control
NACA	Accounting and cost control
PMA	Purchasing
TIMS	Operations research
AIDS	Mathematicians dedicated to applying quantitative methods to aid decision making

approaches and immediately saw manufacturing applications and dramatic marketing implications. Most of the new techniques were difficult to handle manually. A hasty marriage of the quantitative specialist with the computer and software industry took place. The technical societies jumped aboard to sell solutions to all of manufacturing's problems.

Top management, mystified by the problems and the bewildering array of acronyms presented as solutions, viewed the computer as an automation device. They rushed toward computerization, partly to keep up with the Joneses and partly in the hope that computer automation could replace indirect labor as earlier factory automation had reduced direct labor. The race was on. An unprepared manufacturing bureaucracy tried frantically to upgrade quantitative skills and computer knowledge in the scramble to get smart. There were enough successes to fuel the effort because the problems were real and the techniques were sound when properly applied. However, the consultants and data-processing industry generally made more money than the users.

The Final Surge of Demand

Meanwhile, down in the factory, foremen and factory managers focused on the two narrow objectives by which they were measured: Beat the standards and ship the maximum amount of dollars. They made the numbers and profits improved. Although labor was still an adversary, its size had dropped to between 10 and 20 percent of cost of sales for job shops and to under 10 percent in high-volume manufacturing. Flexibility was a problem and factory overhead was climbing, but GNP grew and productivity increased almost every year. Who said there were cracks in the foundation?

1960–1980, THE DECLINE OF THE AMERICAN FACTORY

The Turning of the Tide

What then finally went wrong? Perhaps the best example is the automotive industry. A remarkable full-scale account of this period as it affected Detroit and the automotive industry can be found in David Halberstam's *The Reckoning*. In 1960, General Motors held a substantial cost advantage over its rivals. Economies of scale, good engineering, and styling to meet customers' whims had given it the lead. Ford, the early leader based on its strength in manufacturing innovation, had slipped into a poor second. GM did not dare drop prices to reflect its cost advantage. Fear of government action under the Sherman Antitrust Laws required a concerted effort to keep at least two other viable competitors in business. The law had the unintended effect of actually reducing competition.

In 1973 a general slowdown in U.S. industrial growth began. Supply had finally caught up with demand. The investment in reconstruction of Japan and Western Europe, particularly West Germany, had brought new factories. These countries began to import less as revived industries prospered in domestic markets, supported by the hidden import duty of a high U.S. dollar. "Stagflation" appeared in the United States (aggravated by the OPEC crises and increased oil prices). Productivity leveled off. Because U.S. management had been measured on earnings per share and return on investment, management did not want to look worse by investing in the plant and equipment. As volume and profits sagged, the desire to look good in the short term was achieved by running depreciated and increasingly obsolescent equipment—shades of Amoskeag.

The Japanese Challenge

The 1970s were bad enough, but things began to look worse. Japan started to ship attractive cars in increasing quantity to the United States at $1,000 lower cost than the best U.S. producers. Toyota is generally given credit for the low-cost manufacturing edge. Japan had accepted MacArthur's admonition that its future lay in economic competition as opposed to disastrous military adventure. First it rebuilt its industrial base, which it then matched with an educational program particularly strong in mathematics and engineering. Japan accepted the old criticism of its prewar consumer products as poor-quality imitations and set out to do better. Large teams of industrial managers visited the States in the 1960s. They learned all they could about American manufacturing. Moreover, they learned with a critical eye and with two extremely wise philosophies: Keep it simple and deal with the whole, not just the parts.

Like Francis Cabot Lowell 100 years earlier, they put together what they had seen in an innovative and brilliant adaptation. Nearly all the elements of the Toyota concept were gleaned from the United States. The breakthrough came from the way the pieces were combined in a holistic approach. Toyota's cars were cheaper, were better designed, were less costly to maintain, had fewer defects, and (especially valuable in the OPEC crisis) had lower gas consumption. Table 2–3 shows the cost advantages as seen through the eyes of a U.S. car-rental agency. Table 2–4 shows a productivity comparison between a U.S. and a Japanese engine plant.

Detroit's answer was a typical response to any catastrophe: first denial, then rage, followed by recognition of the problem, and finally a belated response. Admittedly Japan had lower labor costs and a much newer manufacturing infrastructure. But its impact was far more profound because its

TABLE 2–3   1977 Hertz incidence of repairs study[a]

Model	Repairs/100 Vehicles
Ford	326
Chevrolet	425
Pinto	306
Toyota	55

[a]First 12,000 miles.

strategy and system of manufacturing produced a quantum jump in product-cost reduction. Because of some of its more obvious aspects, the Toyota system was called just-in-time (JIT).

The Just-In-Time Principles

JIT principles in hindsight seem obvious, but they had not been part of the U.S. philosophy (for the following discussion of JIT, the writer is indebted to Ed Hay of Rath & Strong Inc., Lexington, Massachusetts):

1. Eliminate waste: Waste is anything that does not add value to the product.
2. Henry Ford was correct: The most efficient way to manufacture is to be able to make and move one unit at a time—not just in assembly but throughout the whole process.
3. If you don't need it now, don't make it now: Produce each day only what is sold each day.
4. Repeal Murphy's law: Instead of living with problems, initiate a process of continuous problem solving.

JIT Approach to Labor

JIT looked at labor with fresh eyes. If direct labor represented less than 20 percent of the cost, obviously cost improvement and productivity gains must lie elsewhere. Toyota backed off the philosophy of deskilling and

TABLE 2–4   Focused factory

	Toyota	Ford
Engines/Day/Employee	9	2
Square Feet	300,000	900,000

Toyota's productivity level is 4.5 times Ford's, with two-thirds to one-half lower capital investment.

speeding up labor. In contrast, it involved the direct labor workforce in some of the work usually done by indirect labor or the manufacturing staff. These activities included quality control, maintenance, cleanup, and problem solving. Time and training required to update labor skills was provided during the work week in sessions called *quality circles*.

JIT Approach and Inventory

Inventory was looked upon as waste, not as an asset. For years U.S. foremen had used inventory (making more than required at the moment) to increase output (long runs), bridge long changeover times, level out demand variation, and cover breakdowns or quality losses. JIT recognized that inventory covered other problems. The Japanese reduced inventory until production was interrupted (called *stressing the system*); then they solved, for example, the quality-control problem before continuing production and reducing inventory further to uncover the next problem. In the United States, stopping production was a mortal sin. Any inventory reduction that jeopardized output only proved that inventory was necessary—not just in time, but just in case. JIT looked at the size of inventory as a measure of how much progress was being made in problem solving. For that reason JIT has often been called *zero inventory*, a definition that is far too narrow.

JIT Approach to Quality

The concept of eliminating waste attacked another Achilles' heel of U.S. industry. Quality and reliability problems had been reduced in America by applying the methods of giants in the domestic quality-control field: Juran, Shainin, Seder, Fiegenbaum, and others. They were frustrated at being able to stimulate only a portion of the potential progress using their methodology for making it right the first time. U.S. management assumed quality improvement was costly and went only as far as competition required. The quality-control advocates successfully turned to military and space hardware manufacturing, where there was no room for defects. In frustration, one of them, Deming, went to Japan; he became almost a deity. The Japanese recognized all the costs of poor quality (inspection, lost labor and material, inventory, salvage, and so on) and vigorously attacked the causes. Production costs dropped and customer satisfaction increased.

JIT Approach to Product Flow and Flexibility

U.S. factories had developed serious layout and run-size problems. JIT rearranged the factory, improved the flow, and shortened supply lines.

U.S. factories were divided into job shops (equipment clustered in functional groups—all milling machines together, all grinders together) or high-volume manufacturing (equipment in line according to product operation sequence), depending on volume and product variety. The auto industry's assumption was that demand would permit high-volume manufacturing. However, model changeover, variety, and options had demonstrated that massive, fully automated production lines were too rigid and therefore too expensive to meet market changes. Some factories became a mixture of job shop and high volume with less than optimum flow.

The JIT approach became one of flexible machining centers (job-shop concept) that could be moved as product changes warranted (product-line concept), with flexible labor capable of running any and all of the machines required. Labor was balanced and machine speeds adjusted to run at the rate the schedule required, not maximum machine speed. In the United States, a foreman would generate an "unfavorable variance" if a machine was slowed down (underutilized). The accounting and performance measurement systems guaranteed poor flow because each machine had to run at maximum speed. The result was considerable interruption and inventory buildup as operations were started and stopped.

To achieve smooth flow and still accommodate product variety under the JIT concept, machine changeovers were analyzed just as the early industrial engineers had studied direct labor operations. Changeover time was reduced until there was no penalty for running a single piece. The flow was no longer interrupted when the same machines were used to make different items. The result was a *flexible factory* that could run at any speed and tolerate product changes paced to customer demand.

The difference between job-shop and high-volume manufacturing became less distinct as factories sought the benefits of both: product variety with assembly-line flow, that is, flexibility and low cost. Such a factory produced only what was needed rather than building up inventory at high speed and then shutting down to use it up.

JIT Production Objectives

JIT made the schedule the goal. Labor stopped only when the schedule was complete, regardless of the time of day. If schedule completion took place before the end of shift, workers stopped producing product and went into training, problem solving, cleanup, or other nonproduction job activities.

As the flow improved and products moved quickly, dramatic results occurred. Work-in-process inventory dried up, causing lead time to shrink, making manufacturing far more responsive to customer changes. Simpler systems were possible because there was less semifinished material on the floor at any one time.

JIT manufacturing strategy is best summarized by an old industrial engineering principle: Improve the method before setting the rate. Only after the factory was focused properly on the optimum arrangement and product flow would automation be applied, whether in terms of equipment (robotics, transfer equipment) or computerization (computer-aided manufacturing—CAM). The United States occasionally would automate a mess by developing expensive equipment and systems to deal with an environment that had not been optimized.

The JIT measure of performance was final product output versus schedule—more being as bad as less. Total manufacturing cost per unit produced, rather than direct labor variance from standard, became the key number in evaluating manufacturing productivity.

Managing the JIT System

In well-managed Japanese industries, top management served an apprenticeship in all departments, including manufacturing. At the corporate planning level, they coupled product planning with manufacturing planning. Significant changes in product design would generate revisions to the factory. The rebuilt Japanese manufacturing base would be revamped and upgraded constantly with substantial investment. Japan avoided the cancer of obsolescence leading to decline demonstrated by the Amoskeag story and, more recently, the U.S. steel industry. Japanese managers took a longer-range view.

In the manufacturing organization, there was one technical arm—production engineering. These staff-support technicians were taught manufacturing not as a group of differing disciplines and techniques but as an application of a common body of knowledge integrating industrial engineering, manufacturing engineering, quality engineering, planning, scheduling, and factory accounting principles. The manufacturing organization was flat: factory manager to foremen supported by a relatively small but well-trained production engineering staff.

Japanese labor management requires a high level of worker loyalty, discipline, and dedication, which may well change with time and affluence. Several JIT principles did break down the adversarial and dehumanizing elements of the U.S. approach:

1. Labor was cross trained to be flexible enough to run a large variety of equipment.
2. Labor was not tied to individual output goals (the standard incentive plan) but to meeting schedule.
3. Direct labor could stop the process to force problem solving rather than running defects for subsequent repair and rework.
4. Downtime was utilized to perform maintenance, housekeeping, problem solving (in quality circles), and cross training.

In short, direct labor approached a salaried-employee concept, although the levels of labor were adjusted periodically to match the rate of customer demand. Finally, burden rates were divorced from labor (labor-based accounting) and applied to the process (process accounting). This eliminated variance control and burden absorption as a misleading and unreliable basis for decision making.

JIT Cost Performance

The average cost improvement from JIT, primarily resulting from a continual problem-solving effort, has been about a 40 percent reduction in manufacturing costs. The bulk of the savings came in overhead costs: inspection, changeover time, material handling, scrap, rework, storage, and accounting and staff support. A significant savings comes from smaller factories per unit of output. As in the United States, direct labor reduction is a function of automation, but only when the factory is ready for it. The lowest cost to achieve growth through increased market share is the prime goal, with earnings per share and return on investment as measures of success rather than ends in themselves.

Domestic Organizational Developments

During the 1960 to 1980 period of decline, there were some significant developments in U.S. management. An output of the sixties was the human potential movement. Industrial psychologists had been around a long time, as the Hawthorne experiments in the 1930s illustrated, but behaviorists such as B. F. Skinner at Harvard began to look toward a broader application of their theories in industry. A growing number of behavioral scientists suggested that companies needed to use potential in the workforce and lower-level management. Large and complex organizations, full of technical specialists, had evolved into a collection of separate departmental functions. Each knew more and more about less and less and were managed by a small top-management group that seemed to know less and less about more and more, at least as viewed from the manufacturing perspective.

Coalescing around the acronym OD (organization dynamics), behaviorists challenged the traditional hierarchical structure with a bottom-up approach, a concept requiring extensive behavior modification. The OD advocates also emphasized the importance of the *process* of organizational interplay rather than the pure *content* of the specialities (engineering, scheduling, accounting, and so forth). While the Japanese had adopted a consensus style of bottom-up management, the OD fraternity went further. Its members addressed not only low-level input and consensus but suggested revamping the authoritarian approach to one that would be more effective in managing change and avoiding higher-level management isolation. David Halberstam's *The Reckoning* indicates dramatically the severe problems arising from that isolation.

As of 1980, a conflict between OD and the old military–high-command approach had developed. OD became known as the soft science, the implication by the traditionalists being that tough decisions and strategies would suffer. The soft scientists and the combat-weary generals with their engineering-trained hard scientists mixed like oil and water.

Business schools also appeared to be deeply divided on this score: Harvard and Stanford advocated the traditional top-down, aggressive, financially oriented decision making; Yale was the home of the behavioral, consensus concept, more sensitive to human potential. M.I.T.'s Sloan School was the prime advocate of system, content, and technology, as well as the need for technically trained management. However, all of these graduate programs are now in various stages of transition, and perhaps the ultimate revision will contain the best elements from each school. At the very least, it appears that the labor/management problem is finally moving out of an adversarial standoff, and the military school of industrial command will be modified significantly to meet and manage change.

THE END OF THE 20TH CENTURY— CHALLENGES AND RESPONSE

U.S. manufacturers have made significant strides, assisted by the falling dollar and low oil prices. Manufacturing is still a mystery to a large segment of the financial, political, and academic communities. The prestigious graduate schools of business are just beginning to look at manufacturing as something more than a low-level effort that happens between order booking and shipment. But Japan and West Germany have wielded the two-by-four that got U.S. management's attention. At the end of the Reagan administration, significant cost reduction (often called *restructuring*) using some of the JIT concepts had improved dramatically manufacturing costs. Much to the surprise of economists and Wall Street, profits and productivity of well-managed U.S. companies improved. There is more to be done, however, and some industries may never recover.

The Challenge

This country has used adversity (the 1929 depression and the war years) to strengthen the survivors and reach extraordinary new levels of competence. Overseas competition may well be another trial by fire. It may force key revisions to manufacturing strategy and reestablish a low-cost base, balancing the skills at which U.S. manufacturing still excels: innovative and entrepreneurial attitudes, engineering ability, marketing acumen, financial sophistication, and legal or regulatorial ability. This review of manufacturing history has tried to suggest strategic considerations and revisions to restore our competitive edge in the world and to provide a framework for subsequent chapters in this book. Six recommendations to U.S. management are offered:

1. Develop a coherent body of knowledge for both academic and in-house educational programs as a means to train more competent manufacturing personnel. Financial and engineering staffs learn their trade with the aid and support of excellent academic programs, but manufacturing staffs do not. An increasingly complex world requires more than warm bodies to fill manufacturing management ranks.

The successful model of airline pilots' and computer programmers' training suggests that a degreed graduate program is not the only solution, and the body of knowledge from which to teach still needs drastic .revisions and general agreement on content.°

2. At all levels of academia and industrial management, recognize the importance of attracting (and maintaining) the brightest and best minds in manufacturing. Today, manufacturing is not a career path to the top. We have a vicious cycle to break: Good students are not attracted to manufacturing courses, and good teachers are not attracted to teach them. What M.B.A. is going to go to Peoria, Illinois, for $35,000 a year to work in a factory, when a $100,000 consulting, arbitrage, or merger and acquisition job is available in New York, Boston, or San Francisco?

3. Revamp traditional cost accounting to reflect how costs really act. Methodology exists in the realms of *direct costing* as an improved method of dealing with fixed and variable costs and *process costing* to move away from labor-based overhead accounting. Managing to the wrong objectives is hardly the intent of management by objectives. The NACA, CPA firms, and accounting courses must be involved. Productivity must be redefined, and manufacturing goals and measurements should be redirected to a variety of goals (quality, delivery, share of the market, return on investment, earnings per share). Goals and performance measurements must support and reward revised manufacturing strategy.

4. At the highest levels of management, reconsider the financial bias toward short-term returns that has inhibited investment in technology at critical times in industry. Francis Cabot Lowell in 1810 and Japanese industrialists in 1970 recognized that industry is *technology driven,* U.S. industry

---

°Editor's note: The M.I.T. Leaders in Manufacturing program, a new, innovative dual degree at the Sloan School, combines M.B.A. and masters engineering work to produce a new kind of manufacturing leader. See Chapter 1.

has been increasingly *financially* driven since World War II. Success is impossible without sound marketing and financial skills, but the best marketing organization with the largest financial resources can only delay death from technological obsolescence of product or plant. Can we resist the feeding frenzy of the 1980s financial markets and fund a continual investment program to regain and maintain technological leadership in our manufacturing base?

5. With the exception of pure process industries (chemicals and oils, for example), every company should thoroughly understand what is behind the acronym JIT and develop a tactical plan to move toward or improve on that strategy. Toyota took 10 years to pioneer the concept, making many mistakes along the way. With large bureaucracies to challenge, to convince, and to restructure, the task for American manufacturers will take time and committed top management. Fortunately, savings accrue from the first years, but the effort must continue over time. Zero inventory, zero direct labor, and zero defects may never be attainable but are important targets. U.S. management must replace fad management (jumping from SQC to CAD, CAM, MRP, OR, OD, and so on) with a program of continual problem solving under a sound production strategy.

6. Develop an organization and set of informing mission statements that

- Manage change. The exponential growth of technology suggests that changes will continue to accelerate. Flexible factories, people, and systems are required.
- Upgrade skills at all levels. We need to be smarter as automation and computers perform manual clerical work. We need prepared workers to plan, make decisions, and solve problems.
- Manage specialization. The tools and systems of manufacturing incorporate machine design, applied statistics, computer systems, materials science, behavioral science, and so on. Manufacturing managers need to understand the application and effects of using resources that necessarily evolve from specialists. The broader liberal arts curriculum answers the need for people who can deal with specialists within the context of understanding the total manufacturing environment. Manufacturing is a human/machine interface better managed by generalists than specialists—a lesson the Japanese have demonstrated.

Is all this possible? Table 2–5 shows the performance of a TV assembly facility located in Franklin Park, Chicago, before and after it was acquired by a Japanese company using the JIT system. The facility is run by the same workforce and is still located in a high-labor-cost Northern urban environ-

TABLE 2–5 Quasar: U.S. operations

	Prior Management	JIT Management (2 years later)
Direct Labor Employees	1,000	1,000[a]
Indirect Labor Employees	600	300
	1,600	1,300
Daily Production	1,000 Units	2,000 Units
Assembly Repairs	130%	6%
Annual Warranty Costs	$16M	$2M[b]

[a] Same employees.
[b] 2 × units or 16:1 improvement.

ment. The only change is a management team with a different strategy and philosophy.

The opportunity exists. The need is critical. Quasar is not an isolated example. The next period for U.S. manufacturing has begun. Our world leadership in manufacturing can be regained, but it will take a change in management's perception, interest, and understanding of manufacturing as a profession. It will also take a manufacturing staff of fewer, brighter, and better professionals with the talent and broader educational background to pull it off. This text suggests that we already have the tools and the know-how.

BIBLIOGRAPHY

Clark, Kim, Robert Hayes, and Christopher Lorenz. *The Uneasy Alliance.* Cambridge, Mass.: Harvard Business School Press, 1985. See chapter by Wickham Skinner, "The Taming of Lions: How Manufacturing Leadership Evolved 1780–1984," pp. 63–110.

Dalzell, Robert F. Jr. *The Enterprising Elite—The Boston Associates and the World They Made.* Cambridge, Mass.: Harvard University Press, 1987.

Halberstam, David. *The Reckoning.* New York: William Morrow and Company Inc., 1986.

Hareven, Tamara, and Randolph Langenbach. *Amoskeag, Life and Work in an American Factory City.* New York: Pantheon Books, 1987.

Hay, Edward J. Jr. *Just-in-Time Breakthrough: Implementing the New Manufacturing Basics,* New York: John Wiley & Sons, 1988.

Skinner, Wickham. "The Productivity Paradox." *Harvard Business Review* (July–Aug. 1986): 55–59.

PART TWO

THE STRATEGIC MANUFACTURING PLANNING PROCESS

Strategies and tactics. Strategy refers to competitive approaches toward winning a market niche: being best in quality or lower in price, for example, or offering the most features or the newest idea. Tactics are the methods of supporting and executing the chosen strategy. In seeking to be the market innovator, for example, appropriate tactics would include large expenditures for research and development and a flexible and fast new-product introduction capability.

In Chapter 3, four managers from Hewlett-Packard fully describe the manufacturing strategy process, including industry and company analysis. A third component of the planning process currently receiving more press in the United States is the element of global competitive requirements, covered by Linda Sprague in Chapter 4. The question of how much planning is enough is answered in Chapter 5 by Jeanne Leidtka. In the area of worker empowerment, Chapter 6's three authors, Steve Cabana, Ron Purser, and Janet Fiero, detail a proven process for empowered decision making. Tom Wallace's years of experience in executive consulting are reflected in Chapter 7, "Sales and Operations Planning."

USING MANUFACTURING AS A COMPETITIVE WEAPON

3

THE DEVELOPMENT OF A MANUFACTURING STRATEGY

Sara L. Beckman

William A. Boller

Stephen A. Hamilton

John W. Monroe

Editor's note

In this chapter, four authors explain the methodology that Hewlett-Packard has developed—a five-step strategic manufacturing planning process that can help a company reestablish manufacturing's position as a critical contributor to the success of the company's business strategy. They show how this planning process is particularly effective in helping companies compete when measured by critical success factors, including quality, features, price, and availability. The process, which combines academic theory and real-world applications, works for HP's customers as well.

47

INTRODUCTION

In 1958, John Kenneth Galbraith wrote that the United States had solved the production problem. Nothing has proved to be further from the truth. As management attention was diverted from improving manufacturing capability to problems of mass distribution, advertising, and marketing, U.S. manufacturing capabilities began their decline. Meanwhile, some of the more successful international competitors identified a new secret weapon: manufacturing. As numerous recent studies report, U.S. manufacturing productivity has declined severely, and much of the product we now consume is manufactured in other countries.

Many reasons are cited for the U.S. manufacturing crisis. Some claim that lower labor rates in other countries are to blame, and they chase cheap labor around the world in an attempt to manage costs. Others believe that foreign competition is not as burdened by government regulation as are U.S. manufacturers; they seek changes in U.S. policy and tax structures. Still others attribute the loss of a competitive edge to a general deterioration of the American work ethic. They try to understand the cultural contribution of the competitors' environments and argue the feasibility of transferring cultural characteristics to the U.S. worker.

While all of these problems, and others, are likely contributors to the U.S. competitiveness dilemma, no single one is the sole cause. The beginnings of the U.S. decline appear to be rooted in much more distant history. Wickham Skinner traces the origin of the problem to the turn of the century, when top management in America stopped making manufacturing issues (process technology development, equipment innovation, production architecture) principal concerns in their strategic agendas. The President's Commission report on global competition corroborates Skinner's observation. It claims that there has been a general failure by American industry to devote enough attention to process technology and to manufacturing as a whole. Clearly, there is a significant need for U.S. manufacturers to recognize the critical role that manufacturing plays in the accomplishment of business objectives and to integrate the manufacturing function as a partner in strategy development and execution.

AN APPROACH TO INTEGRATING MANUFACTURING

At Hewlett-Packard (HP), we have developed a strategic manufacturing planning process that we believe can help your company reestablish manufacturing's position as a critical contributor to the success of the company's business strategy. It combines many of the techniques proposed by the academic community, tools from real-world manufacturing, and the collective

U.S. manufacturing experience to create an understandable process that works. It not only benefits us, but has been proved successful by some of our major customers from aerospace, food processing, telecommunications, and other industries.

Our five-step approach to manufacturing strategy development is as follows:

1. Start with the business strategy. More specifically, understand why customers will prefer your product or service to the competitors'.

2. Create a manufacturing strategy that is *linked* to the business strategy. In other words, specify manufacturing's contribution to making customers choose your product or service instead of your competitors'.

3. Identify manufacturing tactics to execute the strategy. This requires understanding how to manage and control the people, processes, materials, and information needed to deliver products or services in a way that meets the objectives of the strategy.

4. Organize for manufacturing success. Organization design, including structure and performance measurement, must match strategic needs, or success will be limited.

5. Measure the results and initiate further change. Strategies must be altered continually to meet the needs of a constantly changing environment. Feedback loops are critical to the continuous-improvement process.

This process must begin at the top. The highest levels of management must commit the corporation to a strategic direction that is clearly defined and well communicated throughout and conduct periodic reviews to ensure that its direction is being followed. Here, in more detail, is a description of the strategic manufacturing planning process.

START WITH THE BUSINESS STRATEGY

What is a business strategy? Unfortunately, *strategy* is both an underdefined and overused word. In the most basic sense, a definition of strategy is the *science* and *art* of military *command* exercised to meet the enemy in combat under *advantageous conditions*. Current management literature tailors this definition to the business environment. Hayes and Wheelwright suggest that business strategy "specifies the scope of that business in a way that links the strategy of the business to that of the corporation as a whole, and (describes) the basis on which that business unit will achieve and maintain a competitive advantage."[1]

Most authors agree that a business strategy must do the following:

1. Describe the methods of competition (e.g., occupy a specific niche of the marketplace that is not currently occupied by other major competitors—Niche A).
2. Define the contributions of each product and function to the goals of the business (e.g., low-end product offerings will keep low-end competitors from moving into Niche A).
3. Allocate resources among products and functions (e.g., manufacturing will receive X dollars to develop flexible manufacturing capabilities for building custom products for customers in Niche A). Competition is the focus of the business strategy. The strategic statement must describe both the customer-driven goals of the business and the allocation of resources to achieve those goals, and it must be based on facts about the competition.

Development of a business strategy, a necessary prerequisite to generation of a manufacturing strategy, is a difficult and iterative process. It depends on input from many different sources. External sources (customers, competitors, and the economic environment) should drive some objectives, while an assessment of internal strengths and weaknesses should drive others. General Foods, for example, has been able to gain a significant competitive advantage in the dessert foods marketplace by employing its proprietary process for making gelatin products. In fact, antitrust suits have been brought against General Foods because it has such a large proportion of the market. By understanding the desires of the customer and by using its process capabilities wisely, General Foods has resoundingly beaten its competitors in this marketplace.

Critical Success Factors

Ultimately, a business strategy must begin with the customer. Why will customers buy your products or services rather than those of your competitors? We offer a short list of possible answers. Customers buy products or services based on their perception of one or more of the following characteristics:

- Low product or service cost.
- High product or service quality.
- Prompt product or service availability.
- Distinguishing product or service features.

Definition of your desired position in each of these characteristics, as compared to your primary competitors virtually defines your business strategy.

Business Segmentation

Difficulties may arise during the process of identifying critical success factors, however, if your company is actually in more than one business. In this case, you must include a business segmentation exercise as a part of your strategic planning process.

A business segment is a set of products or services and customers that shares a distinct set of economics. The opportunities to obtain competitive advantage through manufacturing may differ significantly by segment. Therefore, it is critical that a proper segmentation be made early in the planning process. While there are many ways to segment a business, the only meaningful one is based on the real needs of the customer and the cost structure required to meet those needs.

An example might make this a little more clear. At HP, we are in many different businesses. Customers for our test and measurement instruments (e.g., oscilloscopes) require a wide variety of product technology with lasting value—which implies broad product mix, inclusion of current technology, and support for the old technology. A critical success factor in this market is providing features. The minicomputer (e.g., HP 3000) marketplace, on the other hand, requires much less hardware product variety. (In fact, product standardization is becoming an issue for these customers.) Market growth is relatively quick, and new computing technologies are being developed rapidly. Two critical success factors in this business are quality and features. Finally, customers for the personal computers (e.g., Vectra) and terminals virtually dictate high volume and a high degree of product standardization. In this marketplace, price and availability are the most critical success factors. Figure 3–1 summarizes the three different businesses.

Note that while each business emphasizes different critical success factors, it does not ignore the others. All businesses will pay some attention to cost, quality, availability, and features. Focus on the primary success factors is critical, however.

Business segments do not remain static. They will change over time as customer requirements, internal capabilities, competitors' strategies, available technology, and economic environment change. Further, they are likely to change as products or services move through the various stages of their life cycles. Thus, constant monitoring and reevaluation of the true business segmentation and the associated manufacturing missions are essential to long-term success.

A coherent, well-focused business strategy allows all of the functions in a manufacturing business to work together with a shared vision of the orga-

FIGURE 3-1 **Important product/market characteristics**

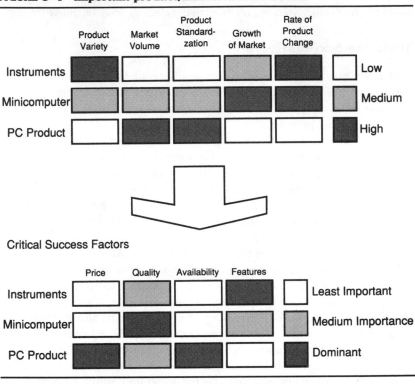

Critical Success Factors

nization's purpose and direction. It provides the guidance for all decision making, resource allocation, and performance measurement activities in the organization, as well as a common basis for communication throughout. It is the critical first step in the strategic manufacturing process.

CREATE A *LINKED* MANUFACTURING STRATEGY

Manufacturing, marketing, R&D, finance, and human resources must all create strategies that collectively and synergistically comprise the overall strategy for the business. These strategies are referred to as functional strategies. Each may have a slightly different emphasis on achievement of one or more of the objectives of the business strategy.

For example, in its management of the customer interface, marketing may be responsible primarily for the availability objective. R&D may be more accountable for the features of the product in the product-development process. R&D should also take responsibility for a large portion of the quality and cost objectives, since they are both greatly affected during product design. However, manufacturing may retain significant liability for cost, quality, and the management of both new-product introduction and ongoing production. We are chiefly concerned here with manufacturing's role.

Just as there are numerous definitions of business strategy, there are several of manufacturing strategy. Hayes and Wheelwright define a manufacturing strategy as "a pattern of decisions actually made, and the degree to which that pattern supports the business strategy. . . . It is the collective pattern of these decisions that determines the strategic capabilities of a manufacturing operation."[2] Roger Schmenner puts it more simply when he defines a manufacturing strategy as "a plan that describes the way to produce and distribute the product."[3]

Most authors agree on a few common characteristics of a manufacturing strategy:

- First, the manufacturing strategy must support the business strategy by focusing the manufacturing activity on a small set of objectives dictated by customer need.
- Second, it should describe allocation of resources within the manufacturing function in a way that allows achievement of the manufacturing objectives.
- Third, it will be reflected in the patterns of actual decisions (e.g., capacity expansion, automation) made by the manufacturing function. If the decisions made over time by the organization are not consistent with the stated strategy (and many times they aren't), then the stated strategy is displayed by the enacted strategy.

A key aspect of *linking* the manufacturing strategy to the business strategy is to have manufacturing team members determine the contribution that manufacturing can make in each of the areas of customer need: cost, quality, availability, and features. Providing an advantage in the *cost* category implies being able to produce goods or services for the lowest total cost, where total cost includes cost of ownership throughout the product or service life. Advantages in *quality* must be obtained from some conformance to or betterment of customer requirements for products or services. *Availability* measures the capability of delivering the product when and where desired, as well as the ability to respond to changes in market demand and opportunities. Manufacturing makes a contribution to an availability objective by being flexible and/or responsive. Finally, manufacturing can contribute product or service *features* whenever its process allows inclusion of unique attributes in the product design or service. This requires that manufacturing be innovative in its development of new process tech-

FIGURE 3–2   Critical success factors

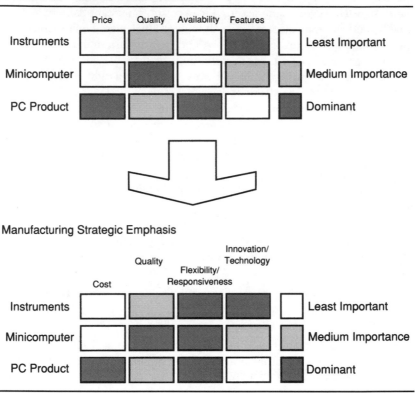

Manufacturing Strategic Emphasis

nologies. Integrated circuit fabrication facilities, for example, often allow inclusion of more capability in an integrated circuit, thus encouraging use of new attributes in a product design.

Following through with our HP example (see Figure 3–2), we see that manufacturing's strategic emphasis in the instrument business is on flexibility/responsiveness and innovation/technology, which allows it to respond with the features required by its customers. Minicomputer manufacturing's emphasis is on quality and flexibility/responsiveness, which allows it to meet requirements for both quality and product features. Finally, personal computer manufacturing must focus on cost and responsiveness to answer its customer needs for low-cost and off-the-shelf availability. Again, note that while each manufacturing strategy differs in its primary emphasis, all elements have some role to play in the strategy.

It is interesting that American manufacturing has focused traditionally on cost in its effort to maximize machine and human utilization in the manufacturing process. The Japanese, on the other hand, have had a nearly unilateral obsession with quality. Both may be right—it depends on what the customer wants. Manufacturing can be supportive of the business strategy only when the strategic objectives are made clear and the contribution of the manufacturing function is well understood and described.

Strategic Decision-Making Categories

Once a manufacturing organization understands its points of strategic emphasis (cost, quality, flexibility/responsiveness, or innovation/technology), it has the basis for making further strategic decisions. These decisions fall into a number of categories, which may include the following:

1. Capacity/facilities

    How many sites?

    How large?

    Where located?

    How focused (e.g., on products, markets, processes)?

2. Workforce/organization

    Skill sets required?

    How measured and compensated?

    What composition?

3. Information management/systems

    How structured?

    Who owns?

    Degree of automation?

4. Vertical integration/sourcing

    How vertically integrated (forward or backward)?

    How many suppliers?

    What types of supplier relationships?

5. Process technology

    What types?

    How automated?

    Make or buy?

6. Quality

    What is it?

    How measured?

    Who's responsible?

FIGURE 3-3 Manufacturer's strategic decision-making matrix

	Cost	Quality	Availability	Features
Capacity/ Facilities	+	+	++	
Workforce/ Organization	+++	+++	++	+
Information Management	++	++	+++	
Vertical Integration/ Sourcing	+++	+++	++	+++
Process Technology	++	++		
Quality	+++	+++	+++	+++

+   Least important
++   Medium importance
+++ Most important

This list is but one of many. Each company will want to select its own list of characteristics most relevant to the execution of its business and manufacturing strategies. The result of this exercise may be a matrix like the one shown in Figure 3–3.

Consultants and other outside observers of manufacturing companies often examine the patterns of decisions made by the companies in categories such as those shown in Figure 3–3 to determine the de facto manufacturing strategy of the firm. For example, a company that continues to invest in hard automation dedicated to the manufacture of a single product is unlikely to be pursuing a strategy of flexibility to accommodate rapid product change. If it claims to be, it needs to be told that its pattern of decision making is not supportive of its stated strategic direction.

Some Tools for Manufacturing Strategy Development

Most business strategies focus primarily on product- and market-related characteristics rather than on manufacturing- or process-related items. A couple of tools that help translate product-focused business strategy to process-focused manufacturing strategy are useful.

FIGURE 3–4   Product/process life-cycle matrix

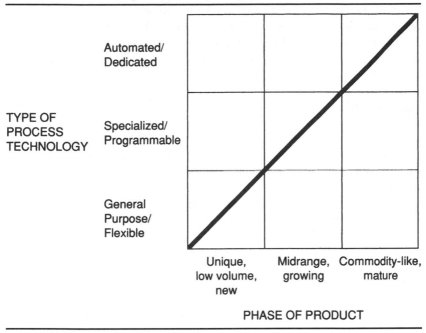

Hayes and Wheelwright[4] formalized the concept of the product/process life-cycle matrix displayed in simplified form in Figure 3–4. In this matrix, products are characterized as falling into one of three categories, often because of their position along the product life cycle. Products that are unique, customized, or sold in very low volumes comprise the first category. Products often fall into this category when they are first introduced. On the other end of the spectrum are highly standardized, commodity-like products that are likely sold in large volumes. These are typically considered to be mature products that are at the peak of their product cycles. In the middle are products that are relatively stable and standardized and sold in medium volumes, usually into a growing marketplace.

Intuitively, one can define the characteristics of the process technology required for each product category. Unique products require manufacturing flexibility. A job-shop or general-purpose process environment best meets this requirement. For midrange products requiring superior quality and room for innovation, a specialized or programmable technology is appropriate. The mature, standardized product must be consistent and produced at the lowest possible cost. This is achieved with highly automated and dedicated process technology. Thus, we define the types of process technology along the other dimension of our matrix.

In general, if a production process is mapped properly to the requirements of the product it is to build, the facility should be found on the diagonal of this matrix. Dedicated automation rarely will be found in a factory intended to build many different, unique products. Similarly, programmable automation is likely to be too costly for a facility building commodity-like, standardized products.

Understanding the position of your company's products on this matrix should provide some useful insights. For example, do all products require the same type of technology? If not, should some products be redefined? Or should the process technologies currently employed be changed? If more than one technology is employed, should separate plants be established, or can they share one facility? Where are your competitors positioned? What position should be assumed to obtain an advantage over them? Do planned new-product introductions fit with existing process technology? What types of capital equipment should be purchased to meet future needs? Overall, the matrix provides a useful thinking tool and framework for the development of a manufacturing strategy.

A recent article on the development of the Korean microwave manufacturing capability exemplifies movement on this matrix.[5] When the Koreans first began to develop their version of the microwave oven, their production process was almost entirely manual. As they developed ovens that they were able to sell in volume to a world market, however, they were able to purchase automated equipment for their manufacture. Further, they moved from doing primarily assembly activities to actually fabricating some of the critical components of the ovens themselves in dedicated, automated facilities. Over time they moved from the lower-left-hand to the upper-right-hand quadrant of the matrix.

Another concept useful to the creation of manufacturing strategies is *factory focus,* popularized by Wickham Skinner in 1974.[6] A simplified version of the concept is depicted in Figure 3–5. An operation with a small number of process technologies is called *process focused.* Steel producers generally are thought of as being process focused because they use a common set of processes to produce a small number of fairly homogeneous end products. An operation manufacturing similar products, possibly using several different process technologies, is called *product focused.* Most electronic-equipment manufacturers have product-focused facilities. They produce televisions, computers, or video recorders using whatever collection of processes is required to do so (e.g., printed circuit board fabrication and assembly, mechanical assembly, final product assembly, and test). When a facility produces a large number of products and uses many different technologies it is said to be an all-purpose facility.

A company with a few homogeneous product lines can have a simple infrastructure for managing its processes, whereas a company with a large

FIGURE 3–5 Simplified version of types of factory focus

Complex, Large Numbers of Products with Divergent Requirements	**PROCESS FOCUSED** Specialized, technology-based, needs centralized planning	**ALL-PURPOSE** Lacks mission, complex, difficult to manage
Simple, Few Homogeneous Product Lines	**PRODUCT/PROCESS FOCUSED** Unique mission specialized area, responsive, needs centralized planning	**PRODUCT FOCUSED** Responsive, suitable for decentralized planning

PRODUCT COMPLEXITY (vertical axis)

Simple, Few Similar Process Technologies — Complex, Several Divergent Process Technologies

◄——— **OPERATING COMPLEXITY** ———►

number of products with divergent requirements usually has a more complex production process. Product-focused facilities are often believed to be most desirable; however, process-focused facilities can be equally effective in some circumstances.

All-purpose facilities generally should be avoided. One can imagine the difficulty in achieving any particular competitive advantage from a facility that is attempting to be all things to all customers. Often, after years of rapid growth and many new-product introductions, a facility will lose focus and become all-purpose. Companies that find themselves with such facilities should seriously consider change. Can the facility be separated into a number of smaller product- or process-focused facilities? Should the facilities be separated physically or organizationally? Can the problem be solved by creating a plant within the plant? Having a focused factory is considered critical to long-term success.

Both of these concepts—product/process mapping and factory focus—allow the user to identify alternate manufacturing strategies and to map these alternatives against the requirements of the business strategy and, ultimately, of the customer. The manufacturing strategy must describe the contribution that manufacturing makes to the cost, quality, availability, and features objectives of the business and must provide direction for achieving that contribution.

IDENTIFYING MANUFACTURING TACTICS

Webster's defines a *tactic* as "the technique or science of securing the objectives designated by the strategy." The business strategy, derived from a clear understanding of customer needs and the company's position relative to the competition, has driven identification of the strategic emphasis of the manufacturing function. Manufacturing will emphasize some combination of cost, quality, flexibility/responsiveness, or innovation/technology. Achievement of these objectives in turn requires selection of appropriate management actions or manufacturing tactics.

There are two levels, then, at which a manufacturing function needs to be managed. At a macro, or strategic, level, there are structural issues, such as number of facilities and their locations focuses, and capacities. Degree of vertical integration and choice of process technology and overall organization structure are other structural issues at the strategic level (see the earlier section, "Strategic Decision-Making Categories").

Other issues are managed at a more micro, or tactical, level within the manufacturing organization itself. These tasks can be categorized into three interrelated activities:

1. Control of the manufacturing process.
2. Control of the manufacturing resources including people, materials, and tools.
3. Control of manufacturing information.

Successful manufacturing requires that (1) the right resources (people, materials, tools) be in the right place at the right time, (2) the right processes be executed properly at the right time, and (3) the information to enable and improve execution be available just as needed to enable appropriate, localized decision making. The emphasis in executing any one of these activities, however, must be on the areas of concentration dictated by the manufacturing strategy—cost, quality, flexibility/responsiveness, or innovation/technology.

Manufacturing tactics, then, specify the methods by which process, resource, and information control are executed to optimize their contributions to cost, quality, availability, and features of the end product. This linking of manufacturing tactics, manufacturing strategy, business strategy, and ultimately customer requirements is critical to a company's long-term competitive success.

Over the last decade, a number of concepts have been added to the manufacturing manager's arsenal, including total quality commitment (TQC), just-in-time (JIT), and computer-integrated manufacturing (CIM). Although these methodologies have received considerable attention in both academic and trade media, they do not represent radical change in manufacturing requirements. Rather, they are modern tools or methods for responding to the old problems of controlling the process, the resources, and the information, respectively. They are evolved from older concepts of quality control, materials management, and line management.

Whether a company chooses to employ TQC, JIT, or CIM philosophies is a choice to be made according to customer need. If any of these programs are implemented, they should be used with a focus on the cost, quality, availability, and features objectives suggested by the business plan.

Let's return to our HP example once again (Figure 3–6). In the instrument business, the R&D/manufacturing link is the most critical to managing the introduction of features required by the customer. In the minicomputer business, TQC programs (as well as the R&D/manufacturing link) are important to meet quality and features needs. In the personal computer business, hard automation is required to minimize cycle time at the lowest possible cost, thus allowing customer requirements of low cost and instant availability to be met. Bottom line? Your choice of manufacturing tactics must be linked directly to customer needs for cost, quality, availability, and features.

ORGANIZE FOR MANUFACTURING SUCCESS

At all levels, the manufacturing organization must be structured and managed to support execution of the business and manufacturing strategies. Volumes have been written[7] on the importance of matching organizational structure with strategy, yet most organizations are poor at explicitly recognizing the linkages.

To begin, the overall structure of the manufacturing organization must match the selected manufacturing strategic emphases. Organizations that must be predictable in certain types of environments can be organized in a hierarchical fashion. They can run themselves largely through application of clear, well-understood rules and procedures. When exceptions occur to these rules or procedures, a decision request can be passed up through the management hierarchy and direction received. U.S. military operations are the most extreme example of this type of organization. Using strict rules and

FIGURE 3-6 Manufacturing strategic emphasis

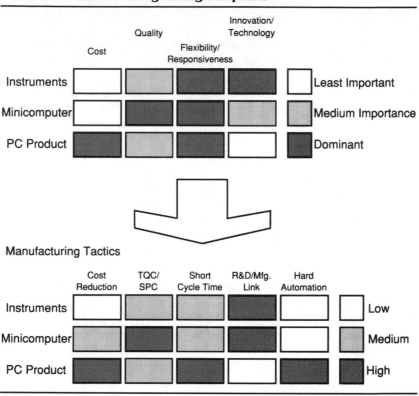

procedures to guide day-to-day decision making and a structured hierarchy for giving direction during times of stress, military operations operate in reasonably well-structured environments.

Companies concerned about gaining competitive advantage in an environment of constant change will seek a more fluid organizational structure. Such structures typically will be flatter and leaner. They will rely less on the use of rules and procedures and more on decisions made at the lowest levels of the organizational structure. The currently popular development of high-performance work teams fits this type of thinking. Work teams are developed at the level of the factory floor to get workers directly involved in decision making about the processes they run. Such teams are trained to handle variability and change on their own without referring rule exceptions to the hierarchy for resolution.

Organizations that are more rigidly, or hierarchically, constructed will often handle a specific change by creating a suborganization with a more fluid structure. IBM was able to rapidly introduce its new personal computer product by creating a small, independent development organization in Florida. By doing so, it facilitated the communication required to rapidly and successfully launch the new product. The Japanese have used similar spinoff structures to introduce new products ranging from cameras to cars. A fitting match of the organizational structure to the current strategic needs has proved crucial in all of these cases. Once the organizational structure has been put in place, the performance measurement and capital justification systems must be designed to both match the organizational structure and encourage the behavior desired by the manufacturing strategic objectives.

Performance measurement systems play a particularly important role in the execution of a strategy. Will you measure your managers on achievement of cost objectives (the bottom line) even when time-to-market is your critical success parameter? Many companies do. Current popular literature on developments in cost accounting[8] recommends significant changes in our traditional approaches to cost roll-up, product pricing, and thus performance measurement. It has been said: "Tell me how you'll measure me and I'll tell you how I'll act." Performance measurement systems *must* be designed with your strategic direction in mind, or it is unlikely that your strategic objectives will be met. The design of such systems is not well understood today. The systems you design will require constant feedback and fine-tuning until new and more effective measurement systems become widely accepted.

Similarly, the process used for project justification must also match strategic requirements.[9] The commonly used return-on-investment approaches are fundamentally cost focused. They don't directly accommodate inclusion of quality, availability, and feature improvements, either short or long term.

Quality projects should be measured on contributions to quality, availability projects on improvements in availability, and production process innovation projects by their impact on feature enhancement. The application of short-term economic measures to all manufacturing projects is insufficient. New methods of project justification must be found and used by companies wishing to optimize variables other than cost in their business strategies. The manufacturing organization must be structured to meet the strategic needs of the business, taught the strategic objectives involved in the investment decisions that express the functional strategy, and then measured on its ability to meet those objectives.

MEASURE THE RESULTS

How can a manufacturing business ensure that its strategy becomes more to the organization than just a document that collects dust on the bookshelf? It must provide a system of checks and balances and feedback loops that allow constant monitoring of progress against the strategic objectives.

First, if a strategy is really made up of the patterns of decisions that an organization makes, one ought to be able to check its execution by simply monitoring decision patterns over time. A major food-processing corporation we worked with stated that its strategy is to be responsive and flexible in its manufacturing function. Examination of its capital spending plans, however, revealed that more than 80 percent of the budget was being approved for cost-containment projects. This pattern of decisions suggested that a different strategy—cost reduction—was actually being executed. Watch the decisions that your manufacturing management makes over time and determine whether your strategy is being executed as defined.

We discussed performance measurement at length in the section entitled "Organize for Manufacturing Success" as an element of organizational design. It bears repeating here that the performance measurement system must be restructured to support execution of the strategic objectives. To be most effective, the system must also provide competitive norms to reinforce the strategic objectives. The system must reflect contributions to quality, availability, and features, as well as to cost, or the organization will focus on cost to the exclusion of the other factors. Recently, the CEOs of both Hewlett-Packard and Motorola have made quality a primary objective for their organizations and achieved significant improvements.

In 1979, John Young, HP's CEO, challenged his management teams to improve the quality of the company's hardware products 10-fold in the upcoming 10 years. This stretch objective for the eighties fundamentally altered HP's management style. HP had always been known for high product quality, but it was experiencing an initial in-process failure rate of roughly 3 percent on a number of products. By 1985, HP engineers had achieved three orders of magnitude improvement in their printed circuit board manufacturing quality, providing first-pass failure rates in the 30 parts per million range, and the quest continues.

Former Motorola chair Robert Galvin established a similar objective, the result of which was the award of the Malcolm Baldrige Award for Quality to the *entire* Motorola Corporation. In both of these examples, the companies have succeeded in meeting their CEOs' objectives only by establishing quality as a performance measure at least equal in importance to any cost objectives that already existed. In short, strategies can be made to live only in organizations in which the performance measurement systems appropriately reflect primary customer needs, and the competitive response and investment management decisions are made with the strategic direction in mind.

FIGURE 3-7 Five-step strategic planning process

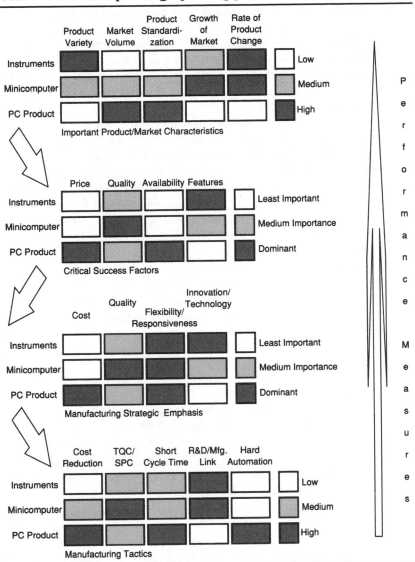

SUMMARY

We have proposed a five-step strategic planning process that is summarized in Figure 3–7. The strategic planning process must begin at the top of the company with commitment from corporate leaders to a focused set of customer needs. These customer needs will likely be contained in the categories of product or service cost, quality, availability, and product or service features.

The manufacturing strategy must, in turn, be derived by the manufacturing team from the business strategy. It will describe in more detailed terms the directions that the manufacturing function will take in playing its role, along with marketing, R&D, finance, and human resources, in achieving the objectives of the business.

Strategies can only be executed through close management of tactics. In manufacturing, tactical activities will involve managing and controlling processes, resources, and information. Perhaps the current concepts of TQC, JIT, and CIM will be useful in identifying supportive tactics.

The manufacturing organization's structure itself must match the requirements placed on it. Use of team-based management techniques, creative compensation systems, and innovative applications of communications technology may be techniques worth considering as required by your strategic direction.

Finally, no strategy can be deemed successful unless there are tangible assessments made of progress against the objectives dictated by the strategy. These assessments must consider explicitly the performance of the competition. Performance measurement and project justification systems must support the strategy and provide feedback for changing the strategy as needed.

NOTES

1. Robert H. Hayes and Steven C. Wheelwright, *Restoring Our Competitive Edge: Competing Through Manufacturing* (New York: John Wiley & Sons, 1984), 29.

2. Ibid.

3. Roger W. Schmenner, "Look Beyond the Obvious in Plant Location," *Harvard Business Review* (Jan.–Feb. 1979): 126–132.

4. Robert H. Hayes and Steven C. Wheelwright, "Link Manufacturing Process and Product Life Cycles," *Harvard Business Review* (Jan.–Feb. 1979): 133–140.

5. Ira C. Magaziner and Mark Patinkin, "Fast Heat: How Korea Won the Microwave War," *Harvard Business Review* (Jan.–Feb. 1989): 83–92.

6. Wickham Skinner, "The Focused Factory," *Harvard Business Review* (May–June 1974): 113–121.

7. See, for example, J. D. Thompson, *Organizations in Action* (New York: McGraw-Hill Book Company, 1967); P. R. Lawrence and J. W. Lorsch, "Differentiation and Integration in Complex Organizations," *Administrative Science Quarterly* 12 (June 1967).

8. See, for example, Robin Cooper, "You Need a New Cost System When. . . ," *Harvard Business Review* (Jan.–Feb. 1989): 77–82.

9. Jack R. Meredith and Marianne M. Hill, "Justifying New Manufacturing Systems: A Managerial Approach," *Sloan Management Review* (summer 1987): 49–61.

STRATEGIC ANALYSIS FOR GLOBAL MANUFACTURING

4

Linda G. Sprague

Editor's note

This chapter shows how a global manufacturing strategy can be developed fully to complement overall business objectives. Dr. Sprague's process of manufacturing strategy development requires completing a series of planning grids, followed by capacity and technology analysis. As more information about manufacturing capabilities is plugged into the planning grids, the production function's role becomes that of a driver, rather than a follower, of strategic decisions.

MANUFACTURING STRATEGY—THE MISSING PIECE

Most strategic plans contain a barn-door-size hole. This alarming fact is disguised by the hefty weight of documents that feature comprehensive analyses of markets, segments and niches, products old and new, competitors' likely market postures, and elaborate financial projections. Occasionally, one finds a brief section toward the end devoted to implementation, which speaks of investment in high-technology approaches to meet compelling market challenges and opportunities. When the strategic plan encompasses worldwide markets, the implementation section may refer obliquely to exploitation of existing capacity close to existing markets.

What's missing is the manufacturing strategy necessary to execute the marketing strategy. Strategic planning for manufacturing capacity remains the missing link in corporate strategy nearly two decades after the first clear alerts were sounded by Wickham Skinner in 1969. It is serious enough when business strategies for domestic activities are concerned; it can be life threatening when global plans are being developed.

Strategic analysis for long-range business planning typically revolves around markets and products. A widely used structure is based on three dimensions for business strategy formulation:

- Customer groups served.
- Customer functions served.
- Technologies used.[1]

Figure 4–1 is an example of the classic use of this framework for the photo-typesetting industry.[2] The vertical axis identifies customer groups or market segments—in this instance newspapers, commercial printers, typesetting houses, and businesses doing typesetting in-house. The horizontal axis iden-

FIGURE 4–1   Three-dimensional structure for business strategy development

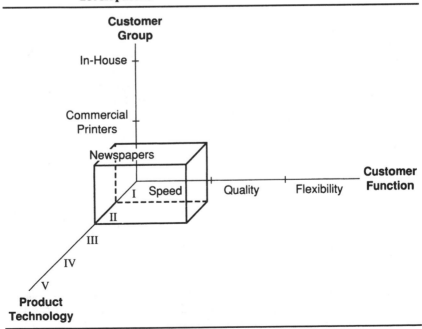

tifies functions or benefits desired by the customer—here, speed, quality, and flexibility. Technologies are shown as the third dimension—for the photo-typesetting industry these are generations through which the product technology has evolved and continues to evolve. The photo-typesetting technology generations are

I. Letter matrix through fixed lens, to film, and to plate.

II. Letter disc through interchangeable lens, to film, to plate.

III. Computer library through CRT, through lens, to film, to plate.

IV. Computer library through CRT to plate.

V. Computer library to laser printer.

This product technology is evolving from mechanical/photographic, through mechanical/optical/electronic/photographic, to pure computer-based electronics. The implications for required process technologies in manufacturing are profound. A decade ago, being in this business meant having mechanical production capabilities. Today it means having to work successfully with computer and laser technologies: The older technologies are diminishing in importance.

Strategic planning using Abel's three-dimensional structure can lead to understanding the approaches to market segments with subsequent development of specific market strategies. As the product technology develops and evolves, market strategies can be refocused, and in some instances product technology developments can be anticipated.

For example, the small cube in Figure 4–1 describes the approach that was successful in selling second-generation photo-typesetting equipment to the newspaper industry on the basis of speed. Third-generation equipment added the potential for higher quality and greater flexibility, making it attractive to commercial printers; this segment is also represented in Figure 4–1. Thoughtful use of this framework can play an important role in the development of business strategies in industries facing substantial product technological development.

However, from the perspective of the manufacturing and logistics arms of the organization, a view of business planning based on only three dimensions (customer groups, function, and technologies) is woefully incomplete. The process technologies required to create the product technologies are left in the shadows. As the example in Figure 4–1 shows, product technology development can, and too often does, force dramatic change in process technology requirements.

The evolution of photo-typesetting product technologies has meant a shift from the manufacture of electromechanical devices toward the production of software-driven, computer-based systems. The impact on manufacturing capacity planning—for both physical technology and workforce expertise—has been wrenching. The frameworks used for analysis of such change are incomplete; they do not go the next step and add the dimension of process technology. And, when global marketing and distribution is involved, this framework must be augmented by geography.

Without a fully conceived and developed strategic program supporting manufacturing and logistics, effective implementation of a business strategy is impossible. The track record for implementation of corporate strategy has been spotty. One reason may be that most strategic planning is truncated. The hole in the plan is the lack of manufacturing and logistics strategy development as part of the corporate strategy.

HOW TO DEVELOP STRATEGIC PLANNING GRIDS

The first step in plugging the major hole in strategic planning is to integrate manufacturing and logistics into the process. We can begin by laying out a simple grid. Then we will add dimensions to the basic grid, building a set of grids that fully describes the problem.

Let's start with Figure 4–2, in which one side represents the marketplace and another the product. We use the example of three types of lawn mowers (nonpowered, powered, and riding mowers) used to teach the fun-

FIGURE 4–2   Market/product grid

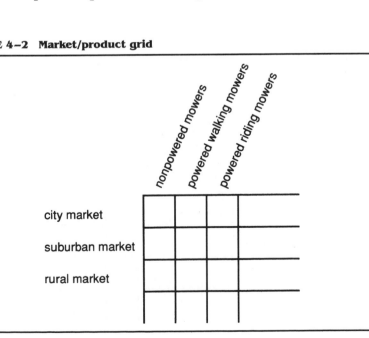

damental marketing concepts. The marketplace is broken down into three segments—city, suburban, and rural. Forecast volumes are entered into the cells in this grid, which is the basic framework commonly used by marketers to identify and explore specific product opportunities or market niches.[3]

Describing the three types of lawn mowers does not fully tell the technology story: The powered mowers are based on two types of power, gasoline and electricity. Figure 4–3 adds the product technology dimension that will move us closer to the critical issues facing manufacturing—the process technology requirements and options.

Global marketers will expand the market axis to show geographic location. The addition of this international dimension is shown in Figure 4–4. Finally, in Figure 4–5, the key manufacturing axis is shown—process technology requirements (e.g., injection molding, painting). Bringing this final dimension into focus provides the basic information necessary for the development of a complete strategic plan.

Step 1: The Market/Product Grid

The market/product grid sets the foundation for the development of the marketing strategy. For an international organization, the market segments are further specified by country. Present and projected sales volumes typically are shown in each cell to provide some sense of time, essentially adding a third dimension to the basic grid.

FIGURE 4–3 Market/product technology grid

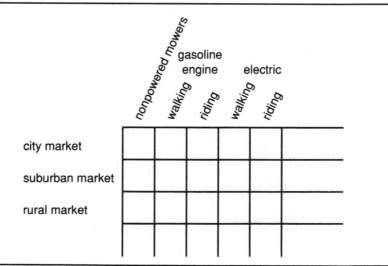

FIGURE 4–4   Geographic market/product technology grid

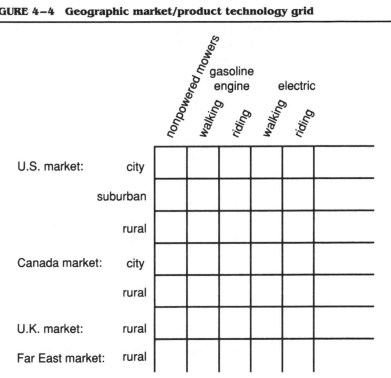

FIGURE 4–5   Product technology/process technology grid

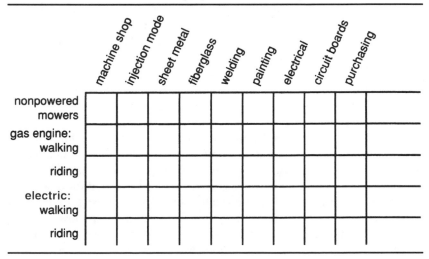

The information provided by such market analyses is of fundamental value for the business-strategy planning process. This basic framework can be enriched considerably with segment and niche details and by delineation of complete product lines. However, completion of Step 1, the market/product grid, is not sufficient without the next part of the process—the development of complementary manufacturing and physical distribution segments of the strategy. Without these vital next steps, the strategic plan, for all its bulk, will be incomplete.

Manufacturing and logistics organizations within the firm need information provided by a systematic conversion of baseline market forecast data into projections of specific product technologies and their relative importance over time. From this information, manufacturing sees the resulting implications for required production technologies. From a market forecast for engines we can develop capacity requirements for forging crankshafts or assembling carburetors. To complete the strategic analysis for an international organization, the geographic locations of capacity availability, present and projected, must be added.

Step 2: The Market/Product Technology Grid

The product delineation shown in a traditional market/product grid is based on customer-focused product differentiation: The objective is market niche analysis. Differentiation of products by their technology may result, but it is not the point of the exercise. The lawn mower analysis grid is a good example of this. As it happens, these three products (nonpowered, powered walking, and powered riding) differ substantially with respect to their technologies, although market segmentation was the basis for the distinction.

The first step in the development of the market/product grid into a tool for operations analysis and planning is to add product technology factors to it. To continue with the lawn mower analysis, the grid must be broken down further into gas- or electric-powered engines.

Not surprisingly, rural markets show the biggest demand for riding mowers. If that demand should shift to suburbia, capacity requirements, location of demand, and logistics (warehousing and transportation costs) would also change. This becomes clearer when each cell contains both present and projected volumes. There are also clear implications for research and development priorities for products. Anticipated further population movement back into cities, for example, would probably dictate lower gas riding mower forecasts, although there would also be a need for new products in the urban market. This information can also be of use for additional market analyses, particularly if markets are segmented geographically.

Working through the completion of the grid in Figure 4–4, with its geographic and technology volume forecasts, may allow us to spot a profitable opportunity, for example, in the demand for older product technologies in lesser developed parts of the world. This framework provides a mechanism for identifying such opportunities.

The projected volumes by product technology also have implications for future after-sale service and accessory requirements. This business has received new attention from U.S. suppliers because its profit margins are usually multiples of the original equipment margins. The extra revenue does not come easily, however. The service business is difficult to translate into capacity requirements. The product line needs to be taken apart first, separating purchased from in-house parts.

Step 3: The Product Technology/Process Technology Grid with a Strategic Capacity Requirements Explosion

U.S. manufacturers need to understand shifting capacity requirements. With export demand pumped up by the low value of the dollar, it is dangerous not to understand the capacity issue thoroughly in all its forms. Specifically, analysis of true capacity requirements allows us to consider various strategic responses:

1. We can consider gearing up or down quickly and define relevant costs/paybacks in advance.

2. We can compare the costs of increasing different capacities: Are we just adding a shift of hourly workers, for example, or would we be looking at renting and equipping a new facility?

3. We can compare the effect on lead times of each strategic response in capacity planning.

Long-range changes in capacity needs implied by shifts in products and their technologies can be identified on the product technology/process technology grid. This is the critical link between market strategy development and strategic operations planning. For lawn mowers, the grid looks like that of Figure 4–5.

It is common for manufacturing organizations using their material-requirements planning systems to carry out demand explosions for parts and for elements of capacity. This typically is accomplished as part of a relatively short-range program of execution, not as part of a strategic planning process. The short-range focus, although highly valuable for day-to-day operations and control, cannot provide visibility for long-range needs for new production technologies.

For example, material-requirements planning/driven capacity planning may generate good demand data short term on total circuit board requirements, but it will not tell us if and when a technologically different board type will shift process/capacity plans (e.g., moving from single- to multilayer boards). Nor can it illuminate the potential for older technologies whose future competitive importance may be underestimated.

The product technology/process technology grid is essentially a strategic capacity-requirements explosion with each cell containing present and projected levels. It is based on information too often ignored in the strategic planning process—the forms of process technology currently in use and estimates of those required in the future. The estimates are not easy to develop, in part because alternatives are often possible, particularly with respect to the purchase or subcontract of some processes.

Unfortunately the information within these cells, both present and projected, is not easy to gather. At the least, a bill of material explosion capability is required, along with specific process data (routings) and utilization data (run times by machine or work center, setup and changeover data). Labor use data can also be factored in. Where a fully developed capacity-requirements planning system is available, organization of base data for the present situation is fairly straightforward. A firm that does not have this material-requirements planning (MRP) capability will find conversion of product demand into meaningful capacity load numbers to be a daunting, although worthwhile, task. Even when the information about present process capacities and utilizations is at hand, developing estimates of future technology requirements is bound to be difficult. We usually see an overabundance of short-range data coupled with a lack of longer-range information about technological processes.

Alternate technologies, or approaches to technologies, pose a particular problem in forecasting process requirements. Purchased parts provide a good example of the kind of issues that become apparent during the development of process capacity-requirements projections. For example, if a firm purchases all of its circuit boards today because analysis has shown that insufficient volume exists to produce them economically in-house, simply extending current values of purchased parts into the future will mask opportunities for economic production as volumes increase.

Incorporating forecasts of future process economics is important as well. To continue the circuit board example, as break-even volumes for economic production of boards drop, the parameters for make/buy decisions are changed.

The product technology/process technology grid makes clear aggregate volume needs by process, yielding baseline data for consolidation. When each cell in the grid contains present and projected volumes, the information can be reorganized to show changes in overall capacity requirements as well as shifts in process mix requirements.

FIGURE 4-6   Present and projected process technology requirements

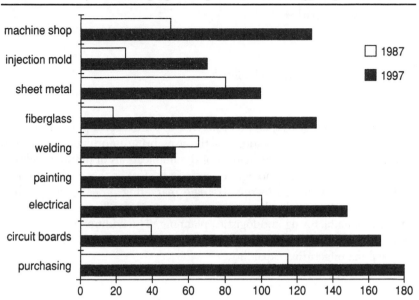

The capacity-requirements projection (Figure 4–6), for example, shows that in 10 years the product will require work in welding but significantly more (proportionally) in new technologies, fiberglass, and circuit boards.

Analysis of this information results in estimates of aggregate capacity needs (the size of the building) and the relative needs of process technology (the relative sizes of the process centers within the building). It can also highlight research and development needs for process technologies, as well as long-range requirements for technical expertise.

To bring these grid analyses full circle, process technologies can be mapped against geographic location, present and proposed. When studied along with a geographic market/product technology grid (Figure 4–4), the maps will highlight manufacturing location options that offer the best support for the competitive situation. The geographic grids also provide baseline information for the development of long-range logistics and after-sale support programs to complement the marketing strategy.

Strategic planning for global markets and the manufacturing and logistics to support effective presence in those markets require planning information along these dimensions:

- Market by segment.

- Product by product line.
- Geographic market.
- Product technology.
- Process technology.
- Geographic process availability.
- Time.

We have used grids that are basically two-dimensional plots of multidimensional information. Rotations of the axes bring information pairs into focus, permitting systematic analysis of the implications of product technology shifts on process technology requirements. Just as the market/product grid identified trade-offs in the strategic marketing process, the product technology/process technology grid (Figure 4–5) facilitates trade-offs in strategic manufacturing and logistics planning. The addition of geographic location information makes this a particularly valuable tool for the planning of global manufacturing capability.

STRATEGY: PRODUCT DRIVEN OR PROCESS DRIVEN?

Most organizations assume that product technology requirements will drive manufacturing process demands. This is often the case, but process technology advantages can be exploited for competitive market position, particularly when a low-cost market opportunity opens up. Although the sequence we have used is the one textbooks traditionally show, with the market-product grid as the pacesetter, there are situations when the driving force can be the process technology advantage. Process technologies that provide the ability to deliver a customized product in a matter of days, for instance, can offer a major competitive advantage.

The personal computer clone business is an example of competitive advantage through fast delivery of customized units. A mail-order system, for example, can be delivered from Wisconsin in five working days (the actual final assembly takes about half a day). The basic system is made up of one hard disk, one motherboard, one controller, one floppy disk drive, one power supply, and one case—all pieces currently available on the market. The product competes with other IBM–AT clones that are twice as expensive. It fills a niche created by a rare IBM marketing strategy error. When IBM decided to move the market away from its five-year-old AT design, it failed to note the numbers of users who were satisfied with the IBM design but not the price and who were not eager to move up to their next product offering, the System 2.

WHERE TO GET THE DATA

The real problem in the development of these grids is data availability. Present market and product line detail are the most likely data to be available. Projections—particularly of new product and product technologies—will of course be forecasts with the usual accuracy problems.

The data-conversion process is deceptively simple. It requires a file inversion. Data are collected by product and exploded through the material-requirements planning system to component parts. The data must be manipulated into meaningful capacity categories. Conversion of demand to load tends to be the least well done, so the result is that we often load facilities by dollars. It doesn't work.

The first grid shown (Figure 4–2), the market/product grid, generally can be drawn quickly with readily available data from current reports and regular marketing planning documents. Beyond that, data availability in the form required for these frameworks becomes a serious problem, particularly when international sales and production are involved.

An added complexity is the difficulty of multicurrency conversion. We can expect that worldwide currencies will continue to fluctuate. Strategic planning in the face of these paper fluctuations will be difficult.

Further, currency complications are compounded by the peculiarities of cost accounting systems, those used in the United States included. The important caveat for this or any other exercise intended to shed light on aspects of global manufacturing and logistics is to avoid making long-term decisions based on short-term oddities.

Data-availability problems notwithstanding, these grids, which focus attention on process technology requirements, provide a window on future needs, conventional and innovative. Complementing market-based strategic planning frameworks with others based on manufacturing and logistics requirements results in business strategy planning with a higher probability of successful implementation. It can also highlight competitive options focused on manufacturing and logistics strengths. The barn-door-size hole can be closed.

NOTES

1. D. A. Abell, *Defining the Business: The Starting Point of Strategic Planning* (Englewood Cliffs, N.J.: Prentice Hall, 1980).

2. From data in "Bobstgraphic Division (A)," case prepared by Nancy Newcomer, Research Associate, under the supervision of Professor John A. Murray, IMEDE, Lausanne, Switzerland, 1980.

3. E. N. Berkowitz and R. A. Kerin, *Marketing* (St. Louis: Times Mirror/College Publishing Company, 1986).

BIBLIOGRAPHY

Abell, D. A. *Defining the Business: The Starting Point of Strategic Planning.* Englewood Cliffs, N.J.: Prentice Hall, 1980.

Berkowitz, E. N., R. A. Kerin, and W. Rudeluis. *Marketing.* St. Louis: Times Mirror/College Publishing Company, 1986.

Heckman, C. R. "Don't Blame Currency Values for Strategic Errors." *Midland Corporate Finance Journal.* New York: Stern Stewart Management Services Inc. (fall 1986): 45–55.

Porter, M. E. "From Competitive Advantage to Corporate Strategy." *Harvard Business Review* (May–June, 1987): 43–59.

Skinner, W. "Manufacturing—Missing Link in Corporate Strategy." *Harvard Business Review* (May–June 1969): 136–145.

CHARACTERIZING YOUR ENVIRONMENT— STRATEGIC PLANNING SYSTEMS

5

IS MORE NECESSARILY BETTER?

Jeanne Liedtka

Editor's note

Most U.S. manufacturing companies operate in a climate of uncertainty and change. This chapter outlines a strategic planning approach that categorizes industry and company factors in four groups of varying degrees of complexity and uncertainty—the Dinosaur Bowl, Mission Control at Miami, Nintendo Warriors, and Dogfight-Aerial Combat—and suggests appropriate planning methods for each.

What are the implications for manufacturing managers trying to match a firm's strategic planning process with its environment? A key issue is that, after all the elaborate analyses have been completed, it is often manufacturing that determines whether a strategy will succeed. A manufacturing organization can be structured by appropriate use of technology and simple, efficient planning methods to deal effectively with environmental pressures such as uncertainty and complexity. Methods that facilitate dealing with change (shorter cycle times, setups, order processing, and flexibility) are explored more fully in Joe Blackburn's piece on time-based competition and Sara Beckman's chapter on flexibility.

In the 20 years since the concept of strategic planning appeared in the business literature and subsequently took hold in the minds of corporate America, the assumption has been that if *some* planning was good, *more* planning must be even better. That assumption has begun to be questioned seriously of late, with the growth of interest in entrepreneurship and intrapreneurship, for example. What price do we pay for our carefully integrated strategic plans with their long time horizons? Is it more than just the cost of the bureaucracy of staff planners who maintain them? Is what is good for General Motors generally good for the rest of American business?

For too long manufacturing managers have been willing to relegate involvement in strategic planning issues to senior management and staff planners while they focused exclusively on issues such as product quality and production efficiency. This is a luxury they can no longer afford in an atmosphere of escalating uncertainty resulting from globalized competition, technological innovation, and demographic changes in the workforce. With the least flexibility to change and the longest lead times for capacity additions, manufacturing would benefit more than any other company division from an accurate crystal ball. Increasingly, the production efficiency of tomorrow rests on today's ability to put in place the proper internal capabilities to respond to new developments, whether they be in customer demand, product or manufacturing technology, or competitors' behavior.

Yet, business firms operate in environments that differ dramatically from each other. Thus, cookie-cutter techniques are unlikely to produce satisfactory solutions across the board. The first step toward putting in place a successful process for making important strategic decisions for your firm is to take a close and careful look at your environment. This has important implications for the *type* of planning process you use, as well as for the ultimate competitive strategy that you select.

CHARACTERIZING A FIRM'S ENVIRONMENT

There are many ways to describe the different types of environments that firms operate in. None can be considered right or wrong, since each focuses on a particular aspect or characteristic. Some, however, have proved to be more useful than others.

Michael E. Porter, a professor at the Harvard Business School, has developed a popular framework that focuses on the characteristics of the industry that a firm operates in.[1] An industrial economist by training, Porter argues that the range of profitability within an industry is determined by five structural characteristics.

The first is the *threat of new entrants.* If it is easy for new firms to enter an industry, Porter argues, profitability will be decreased in the price wars initiated as they attempt to gain market share from already entrenched competitors. Deregulation, for instance, facilitated the entry of numerous new carriers, such as People Express, into the airline industry. In the price wars that followed, profits plummeted.

The level of *rivalry among existing firms* is another important factor in Porter's scheme. Intense rivalry is likely to destabilize the industry, with much the same consequences as the entry of new competitors. Structural factors such as high fixed costs, lack of product differentiation, and slow growth all contribute to increased rivalry as firms scramble to fill excess capacity through the use of price cuts. The paper industry in its maturity offers a case in point with its bitter rivalry and low profitability.

The *threat of substitute products,* a third factor, must be assessed by looking outside a firm's own industry at products that perform a function similar to one's own. The ready availability of alternatives for the customer tends to reduce profits by placing an upper limit on the price that can be charged, even in times of shortage. Firms often make the mistake of defining their competition too narrowly, of ignoring new developments outside of their industry, which may later lead to erosion in the demand for their own products. The use of personal computers to perform word processing, for instance, has annihilated demand for traditional typewriters in a way unforeseen by most of the industry even 10 years ago.

Finally, *the bargaining power of suppliers and buyers,* respectively, constitutes the final two important structural characteristics of industry in Porter's theory. At one extreme, powerful suppliers are likely to demand top dollar for raw materials, while at the other extreme, powerful buyers resist a firm's attempt to pass these cost increases along to them. The result is decreased profitability for the industry caught in between. Strength often comes from concentration. Consider the hypothetical case of a small manufacturer of automobile windshields in Detroit. Forced to accept substantial price increases from a small group of glass manufacturers who control the supply of raw materials, but unable to pass these increases along to the big three car companies (each of which constitutes too substantial a portion of its business to lose), the windshield manufacturer suffers the loss of profits.

These five factors, Porter argues, have important implications for the selection of one of the generic strategies through which firms compete with each other. These strategic alternatives include the following:

- Cost leadership (being the competitor with the lowest cost).
- Focus (targeting a particular segment of the market to serve).
- Differentiation (distinguishing oneself from one's competition via some unique capability, e.g., superior quality, customer service).

The alternative may also be a combination of these three.

Though Porter's view of the environment is intuitively appealing and useful in helping managers think about the *content* of an appropriate strategy, it does not help us address *how* to plan or illuminate the internal *process* of arriving at a strategy within the firm.

COMPLEXITY AND UNCERTAINTY, TWO ADDITIONAL PLANNING FACTORS

Researchers in the field of organizational theory generally have used broad concepts in describing the qualities of the environment to which an organization ought to respond in designing its internal processes. The two aspects usually focused on have been complexity and uncertainty, the most critical determinants of a firm's planning process. The appendix discusses some common measures that have been used as indicators of the degree of environmental complexity and uncertainty.

Complexity

Complexity refers to the number of different factors in a firm's environment to which it must pay attention. These things are often related or interconnected in some way. The term *complexity* frequently is used interchangeably with other terms such as *heterogeneity* or *diversity*.

The complexity of a firm's environment is a function of both internal and external factors. For example, a firm with numerous product lines probably operates in a more complex environment than a single-product firm. It has more customers' needs to be attentive to, more competitors' actions to monitor, more inputs to analyze and integrate. A change in any one factor (customer needs, for example) is likely to have a ripple effect on other factors (e.g., competitors' behavior). Thus, a firm that operates in a more complex environment needs to spend proportionately more time monitoring or scanning its environment for new developments. Firms that operate in more homogeneous, less complicated environments can afford to do less of this. Consider, for example, the situation of a large, multiproduct firm such as General Electric, which has made products as diverse as lightbulbs and nuclear generating equipment. Clearly the complexity of the firm's operations requires that it devote substantial effort to tracking new developments in all of its many areas of participation.

Uncertainty

Uncertainty, our second important quality, relates to the degree of change in a firm's environment and to the frequency, extent, and (most importantly) predictability of that change. The more frequent, significant, and unpredictable a firm's environment, the more uncertain it is. The term *uncertainty* can be used interchangeably with *turbulence, dynamism,* and *instability.* Operating in a field like consumer electronics, characterized by frequent and significant technological change, a firm such as Matsushita would be considered to operate in an environment high in uncertainty. Procter & Gamble, on the other hand, a firm with a more stable technology in the household products area, would experience more certainty.

Though these descriptions of the environment may seem self-evident at first, they have important (and often unnoticed) implications for how firms make important strategic decisions. Rating each of the two qualities low or high for a given company (see Figure 5–1), we find that firms operate in one of four possible environments.[2] After a discussion of planning processes in general, we will return to each of the four quadrants to explore the impact of these very different environmental contexts.

DIMENSIONS OF THE PLANNING PROCESS

Having looked at the characteristics that we will use to describe the firm's environment, we now turn to a discussion of the dimensions of the planning

FIGURE 5–1   Simplified matrix for identifying a firm's strategic planning environment

	Low complexity	High complexity
Low uncertainty	I	II
High uncertainty	III	IV

process itself. Four different aspects of the planning process appear to be related, ultimately, to the context in which the firm finds itself.

Degree of Centralization

The first aspect is the degree of centralization of the planning process—whether it is primarily top-down or bottom-up. This refers to the level in the organization where the alternatives for strategic action are generated and evaluated. In a top-down process, senior management is responsible primarily for strategy formulation. Its decisions are then passed down through the ranks to middle- and first-line levels of management for implementation. Conversely, in a bottom-up process, lower levels of management have an important voice in creating and selecting alternate strategies, as well as for implementing them.

Who Makes the Strategy, Line or Staff?

Another dimension of the planning process, sometimes related to the degree of centralization, is the role of staff in relation to line management in the formulation of strategy. In some organizations, strategy is formulated largely by a staff of planning experts, usually located at corporate headquarters. These may be employees of the firm or outside consultants hired from major consulting firms such as McKinsey, the Boston Consulting Group, or Bain and Company. In other firms, strategy formulation is the responsibility of line management—of the managers who actually run the business on a day-to-day basis.

The first two dimensions, then, relate to *who* in the organization generates the firm's strategy. The final two dimensions deal with the nature of the process itself.

Comprehensiveness of Process

The third dimension examines the comprehensiveness of the process, which is concerned with the exhaustivity and extensivity of the process. It encompasses such specific factors as the time horizon of the process, as well as the linkage of the planning process to other organizational processes such as budgeting, performance appraisal, and management incentives. Increasing comprehensiveness also results in increased formality in the process, implying additional paperwork, deadlines, and levels of review. These are usually necessary in a decentralized organization to process and integrate numerous inputs efficiently. To illustrate the differences in the degree of comprehensiveness, we might contrast the very different processes involved for the entrepreneur who makes decisions spontaneously, based on gut feelings, versus the large, multinational firm whose strategic plan, and the analysis supporting it, result in a 200-page document reflecting years of effort.

Impetus Driving the Process

The final aspect of the planning process that we will concern ourselves with is the firm's analytic orientation. By *analytic orientation,* we mean the focus of and the impetus behind the process. At the extremes, a firm's process can be either internally focused and reactive in nature or externally focused and proactive in nature. The focus of an internal, reactive orientation is usually to *solve problems* that have arisen and to emphasize the gathering, analyzing, and generating of data on the firm itself (such as revenue and earnings-per-share targets) as the basis for strategic decision making. As a result, the firm usually adapts *after the fact* to changes in its environment. In contrast, the external, proactive orientation is focused primarily on the search for new opportunities. In this process, the gathering of outside data dominates (e.g., market growth rates, assessments of competitors' behaviors). The goal here is to manipulate the firm's environment, or strategy, in *anticipation* of a change occurring.

Linking a Firm's Strategic Planning Process to Its Environment

Having defined, thus far, two important characteristics of a firm's environment (complexity and uncertainty) and four dimensions of the strategic planning process (degree of centralization, role of staff versus line management, degree of comprehensiveness, and analytic orientation), we arrive at the critical question: Do these relate to each other in a way that is significant? The answer is yes, and we begin to understand why as we examine the different impacts that complexity and uncertainty have as we try to plan long term.

Coping with Complexity

Essentially, complexity is *knowable;* uncertainty is not. In other words, if complexity refers to having a large number of different factors in the environment, it ought to be analyzable and therefore *controllable* if we as a firm devote sufficient resources to paying attention to it. That implies having a comprehensive bottom-up planning process that has a lot of staff support and an external, proactive orientation.

Complex environments require decentralization for good reasons. The more specialized markets a firm participates in, the less knowledge senior management has about any one of those markets. As a result, the detailed knowledge necessary to make important strategic decisions occurs only at lower levels in the organization. Thus, only the managers in the relevant area of specialization are equipped to formulate strategies for their products. Imagine Jack Welch attempting to become an expert on all relevant aspects of each of General Electric's products. That would be inefficient, unworkable, and maybe even dangerous to the long-term health of the firm.

Simultaneously, however, decentralization requires a whole staff of people somewhere at corporate level and a comprehensive system with lots of paperwork and deadlines to integrate all of those divisional plans into one coherent plan for the organization as a whole. The process must be formal as a means of control. The diversity of products and markets creates the need for a proactive external orientation. It would be impossible to accomplish corporate objectives in a reactive mode. The potential for inconsistent and incompatible responses is too high.

Coping with Uncertainty

Uncertainty, on the other hand, is inherently unknowable. If a change is rather specifically predictable (the change in the number of 25-year-olds between 1990 and 2000, for example), it does not involve much uncertainty. After all, the number of individuals who will be 25 in either 1990 or 2000 have already been born. Consider the greater difficulty in predicting the number of births in 2000. This is substantially less predictable and hence more uncertain. Regardless of the resources devoted to its analysis, it is difficult to plan for uncertainty. As a result, in an uncertain environment, extensive planning processes may accomplish little.

Unlike complexity, uncertainty fosters centralization, elimination of staff planning specialists, decreased comprehensiveness, and an internal, reactive orientation. Centralization offers decreased response time and improved control. Senior management seeks the assistance of technical experts, rather than planning specialists, to selectively monitor certain aspects of the environment (such as technology). The rate of change leaves the firm with little time, substance, or ability to integrate. In this situation, comprehensive or centralized planning systems may be worse than useless: They may have an adverse effect on performance by reducing the organizational flexibility needed to move quickly. Plans with long-time horizons become outdated overnight. Information is obsolete before it reaches headquarters. Formality decreases response time. Worst of all, people become committed to strategies based on assumptions and predictions that turn out to be wrong. A number of researchers have found a negative relationship between comprehensive planning systems and firm performance in an unstable environment.

FIGURE 5–2 Simplified strategic planning matrix with paradigms

	Low complexity	High complexity
Low uncertainty	I: The Dinosaur Bowl	II: Mission Control at Miami
High uncertainty	III: Nintendo Warriors	IV: Dogfight - Aerial Combat

Returning to our four-quadrant model discussed earlier, we can now describe the ideal types of planning systems for each quadrant (see Figure 5–2). Remember that analysis of your industry and company environment is the first step. Although life-cycle stages may change, this will help identify where your company fits on the spectrum of relative uncertainty and the spectrum describing relative complexity. Once the company environment has been identified, the amount and type of strategic planning required can be selected. The objective here is to build flexibility and quick response or to generate more detailed information through a centralized structure. Too much planning in a high-tech environment, for example, will probably defeat the whole purpose of the exercise. Too little planning detail in a more formal situation will undermine the credibility of the plan.

Quadrant I: The Dinosaur Bowl

Complexity: Low

Uncertainty: Low

Planning system: Minimal—centralized, reactive; lacking staff planners and comprehensiveness.

Termed the dinosaurs, few firms remain in this type of halcyon environment. The sweeping changes in both government regulation and technology have rendered extinct the previously stable, monopolistic environment in which they ruled. Once upon a time, lack of complexity here offered little rationale for elaborate planning. The few firms that remain are in previously static environments (utilities and insurance bureaucracies), whose goal usually is to maintain the status quo. They are interested primarily in problem solving; planning is geared toward internal control, with a short time horizon. If we looked to the sports world for an analogy, we would find our dinosaurs bowling—same pins, same alley, your own ball every time. Of course, it takes skill and practice, but once you have it down, the dynamics of the game rarely change.

Quadrant II: Mission Control in Miami

Complexity: High

Uncertainty: Low

Planning system: Proactive, extensively decentralized, comprehensive, including staff planners.

Here, we find the consummate planners—the General Electrics of the world. Generally large, multiproduct firms, the diversity of their operations requires that they decentralize their planning system to facilitate the extensive environmental scanning necessary to formulate an intelligent and coherent overall strategic thrust. Valuing rationality as a dominant goal, the task of coordinating the far-flung planning network requires staff planners who enforce formal standards of reporting to reduce distortions as information flows upward.

We've moved to the Super Bowl, and everyone on the sidelines is wearing headsets to keep up with the action. Life is complex, competition is head to head, and focusing exclusively on your own game is no longer sufficient when you share the field with your competitor. So you get to know the competitor's game as well as your own. The game is played with carefully planned plays; otherwise, you'd have chaos. If you do your homework, however, the strategies of your competitor should ultimately be fairly predictable. The gridiron, unlike the bowling alley, is no place for a team without a carefully conceived, thoroughly researched plan of attack that anticipates the opponents' moves.

Quadrant III: Nintendo Warriors

Complexity: Low

Uncertainty: High

Planning system: As in Quadrant I, decentralized and lacking comprehensiveness, but with technical experts replacing staff planners and a mixed analytic orientation.

Frequently seen in the start-up phases of a new industry such as biotech, where the behavior of both government regulators and potential customers is unpredictable and where the technology itself has not yet stabilized, the combination of low complexity and high uncertainty fosters centralized decision making and little comprehensiveness to ensure a rapid response to environmental changes and maximum flexibility. The action is fast paced and new developments are unpredictable; the firm must be free to act quickly, unencumbered by layers of bureaucracy and red tape. To achieve such minimal response time, decision-making responsibility must rest in the hands of those at the top of the organization. Planning here serves a different focus: It provides a forum through which senior management communicates to employees to calm their fears in the face of vulnerability from external threats and to reinforce the firm's centrally determined mission. As a result, it takes an internal, reactive orientation. At the same time, however, this is balanced by the existence of those selected technical gurus, who pay a great deal of attention to a few critical external factors.

This is the type of environment in which the entrepreneurially managed firm thrives. Lean and quick on its feet, the image is of the entrepreneur as Nintendo warrior, with joystick in hand, dodging alien spacecraft on a path guided more by his or her own vision of the future than by the latest statistics on share of market.

Quadrant IV: Dogfight—Aerial Combat

Complexity: High

Uncertainty: High

Planning system: Hybrid—decentralized; low comprehensiveness; external, proactive orientation; and the use of technical experts.

The hybrid planning process in this quadrant is forged out of the need to meet the incompatible demands of highly complex, uncertain environments. The high uncertainty suggests the need to allow for rapid response to change while maintaining control. The entrepreneur, joystick in hand, is the analogy we've used.

High complexity, however, forces decentralization. The number of games being played simultaneously is too much for even the most adroit warrior. Time pressures prevent the integration efforts required to synthesize the information derived during the multiple searches for new opportunities being conducted throughout the firm. As a result, control over policy making at senior management levels is effectively forfeited. Industries such as consumer electronics with numerous competitors both small and large, constant innovations in product and production technologies, and changing consumer tastes offer a case in point.

Imagine a basketball game in which each team has its own ball; think of the coach on the sidelines attempting to call plays—or the team members attempting to execute them. Visualize a dogfight (aerial combat) in progress. The squadron commander may monitor who is winning or losing the pilots' individual battles, but he or she is unable to tell them *how* to fight. In the heat of the moment, that responsibility must fall to the pilots alone.

Structuring Your Strategic Planning System— Be Selective

What are the implications of these observations for management practice? They are straightforward, in a general sense: Good strategic planning requires that you begin with an understanding of the environment in which your firm operates and of the role of manufacturing in that strategy. The types of elaborate and comprehensive planning systems that have routinely come to be associated with good management are undoubtedly appropriate and commendable for some firms but potentially could spell disaster for others. Like most aspects of the art of managing, strategic planning has few universal rules. Instead, it has a series of prescriptions, with the usefulness of any one of these being contingent on a variety of factors. Those we've examined here—the levels of complexity and uncertainty in the firm's environment—are certainly among the most important for managers to consider in structuring the strategic planning process most suited to the special qualities of their own environments. The appendix to this chapter discusses some measures that have been commonly used as indicators of the degree of environmental complexity and uncertainty.

NOTES

1. Porter lays out his theory in his seminal book called *Competitive Strategy, Techniques for Analyzing Industries and Competitors* (New York: The Free Press, 1985). *Competitive Advantage, Creating and Sustaining Superior Performance* (New York: The Free Press, 1980) follows up at a more detailed level.

2. Obviously, these qualities operate on a continuum from low to high. We have reduced the complexity of the real world into the simplicity of four quadrants to illustrate our point more clearly.

APPENDIX TO CHAPTER 5: DIAGNOSING YOUR ENVIRONMENT

Measures of complexity

Environments that are less complex	Environments that are more complex
Single-product firms with few subsidiaries	Diversified firms with many subsidiaries
Regionalized competition	Global competition
Little vertical integration	Significant vertical integration
Few competitors	Numerous competitors
Single-channel distribution system	Multichannel distribution systems
Short lead times on component parts	Long lead times on component parts
Few internally shared facilities	Multiple internally shared facilities
Few manufacturing technologies involved	Multiple manufacturing technologies involved
Single-customer base with standardized needs	Differentiated customers with specialized needs

Measures of uncertainty

Environments that are less uncertain	Environments that are more uncertain
Stable manufacturing or product technology	Changing manufacturing or product technology
Small and stable group of competitors	Numerous competitors with new industry entrants
Modest product modification activity	Frequent innovation and new-product introductions
Good information concerning competitors' strategies and behaviors	Poor information concerning competitors' strategies
Predictable customer demand patterns at the aggregate industry level	Changing customer demand patterns at the aggregate industry level
Secure raw material availability	Questionable raw material availability
Low likelihood of product obsolescence	High likelihood of product obsolescence
Consistent product quality	Erratic product quality
Entrenched, long-standing government regulation	Changing degrees of government interference

FROM MERE POSSIBILITIES TO STRATEGIES THAT WORK

6

THE SEARCH CONFERENCE METHOD FOR PLANNING IN AN ERA OF RAPID CHANGE

Steven Cabana

Ronald Purser

Janet Fiero

Editor's note

Hierarchies work well in some situations, but where groups of employees must be creative, flexible, and attuned to the market and technology, other organizational structures work better. Steve Cabana and his coauthors have worked with the heart of the self-managed teams concept, and in their search conference they take participants into a better approach to true empowerment.

ACCELERATING CHANGE REQUIRES ACCELERATED PLANNING

One thing is clear. The time-honored expert, top-down approach to planning is becoming obsolete. Many manufacturing executives know they are now facing a complex, dynamic, and uncertain environment and articulate that understanding quite well, while still using planning processes suited to the era of Norman Rockwell and the *Saturday Evening Post.*

In the old days top management figured out the strategy and the troops implemented the actions to achieve the plan. Management was able to stay on top of the changing markets. The world was relatively stable and predictable. But today the world is turbulent. Top management needs the knowledge and skills of people who interact every day with customers or hold informal leadership roles that relate to our strategic challenge. No longer can management look at past market and historical data to predict the future on a linear timeline. Yes, the heavily analyzed, aggregated financial and economic data that our experts have prepared is necessary but surely not sufficient to mobilize the workforce to a future desired by all.

In the past, strict financial controls and administrative procedures worked to keep people oriented on a straight, linear path to the one right solution. Today this just doesn't work. Top management needs the people to adapt to changing circumstances without direction from the top. This will take changes in education, recognition, compensation, and most of our organizational structures.

That's how you used to motivate people and build a world-class strategy. So what happened? Just reflect for a moment on the changes we have seen in the world around us in the past several decades:

- The rapid acceptance of imported consumer electronics and automobiles in the U.S. market from the late 1960s to the present.
- The oil-price crisis and power of OPEC from the mid-1970s to the late 1980s.
- The almost overnight emergence of the "little tigers" (Taiwan, South Korea, Hong Kong, and Singapore) in Asia as manufacturing giants.
- Toyota's development and worldwide diffusion of lean production (e.g., an integration of individually developed production and control equipment and procedures, such as short cycle times, JIT, TQM, TQC, continuous improvement, single sourcing/long-term relations with a small number of suppliers, multifunctional machines, compulsory task rotation in teams).
- The explosion of desktop computers and the software industry since the mid-1980s.
- The loss of community and neighborhoods and the breakdown of families in the West.
- The collapse and breakup of the Soviet Union, end of communist dictatorships in Eastern Europe, and emergence of China as an economic power.

- The GATT agreements since the 1960s, the 1985 liberalization of Japanese financial markets (which allowed capital to leave the country for the first time), and now NAFTA.

- Deployment of advanced global telecommunications.

- The compression of space and time, first by the fax and then by the Internet.

- The recent shift in value from the point of production to the point of sale with more of the consumer's dollar ending up with the company that controls the distribution channel and less with the factory.

- Accelerated environmental degradation worldwide.

Today we must recognize that people need to learn and plan together in real time if we want to survive. That means inventing new ways of involving people to develop and implement strategies that keep us on our feet when we feel most vulnerable. Is there any help out there for us?

In 1959, social scientists Fred Emery and Eric Trist were called to help the senior executives of two aircraft-engine companies in England, Bristol and Siddeley Aero-Engine, create a single operating company, Bristol-Siddeley Aero Engines. The merger was forced on them by their major customer, the British Royal Airforce. Emery and Trist gathered the key people together for a process they called a search conference (SC), so named because the primary function of the conference was to allow all possibilities to surface.

In searching for meaning in these emerging possibilities or sudden shifts and changes, including those in the bulleted list, conference participants are usually confronted with unexpected new directions and new ways of approaching old issues. In essence, when uncertainty is high, the primary task of strategic planning changes from incremental improvement in market share and position to searching for new strategic goals or initiatives. Emery and Trist had discovered how a systems approach to planning coupled with democratic, task-oriented work groups could be a powerful motivating force for effecting strategic change. A precise body of information and experience has accumulated since 1960, making it possible to design search conferences with a high probability of success.

WHAT IS A SEARCH CONFERENCE AND HOW IS IT USED?

Search conferences are large group meetings designed to engage the collective learning and creativity of people, inspiring them to find common ground around new strategies, future directions, and joint actions. The process combines the best practices associated with strategic planning, systems thinking, and creative group dialogue—empowering people to take part fully, rise above self-interest, and make decisions for the common good. The search conference method is designed to assist the enterprise in creating strategies and action plans that enable it to achieve a flexible and proactively adaptive relationship between itself and its constantly changing environment. The conference involves a group of 20 to 45 employees and managers in collaborative, task-oriented activities—a collective learning process that is more akin to jigsaw puzzle solving than traditional, linear problem solving.

Seeking collectively for a desired future state, the search conference process increases the effectiveness of strategic planning by giving participants—those actually knowledgeable about the system—more control over their long-term purposes and directions. The process produces not only a shared vision but a set of concrete strategic goals and action plans that employees are committed to implementing. This method has been used throughout the world for conducting participative strategic planning sessions for organizations at the corporate, division, plant, and departmental levels. It has also been used in new-product development efforts, customer–supplier partnerships, joint ventures, and mergers.

Microsoft, for example, used the method to facilitate new-product development, conducting four back-to-back search conferences that culminated in a meeting for integrating ideas, strategies, and action plans. This resulted in a comprehensive strategy for each of the product lines within the division. The process has been used at least 13 times in the organization. Exxon Chemical sponsored a search conference on the future of customer–supplier relationships in the tire industry in 2010—inviting its major customer, Goodyear Tire and Rubber, to participate in creating a strategic partnership. At Hewlett-Packard, one plant used the search to organize work so people would be able to see themselves as owners. In another HP facility, in danger of being shut down, the search conference was used to bring people together and to make hard choices for survival that entailed dropping four product lines and the jobs associated with them in order to secure a meaningful future for the business.

A Ford Electronics facility conducted a search in 1982 to determine how to survive in its marketplace. The result was a mindset shift. Rather than making parts for Ford it decided to become a learning lab for new technology and management practices that could be exported to other Ford facilities. That led to redesign of the facility, implementation of total quality management (TQM), presentation of a prestigious quality award, and expansion of the plant from 900 to 1,800 people. Levi Strauss in Canada was featured on CNBC recently for its innovative management practices. Almost a decade ago it outlined the business plan it now has in place in a search conference. The critical shift in mindset was to form a partnership with the union and go forward together to create the future.

SEARCH CONFERENCE COMPONENTS

The search conference is the centerpiece of a three-phase process that also includes planning, designing, and implementation and diffusion phases. The SC itself is normally a two-and-a-half-day event and is usually held off-site in a retreatlike setting. Participants are selected based on criteria such as their knowledge of the system, whether they offer a diverse perspective, their potential for taking responsibility for implementation, and the degree of respect they have in the organization. Participants attend not as representatives of stakeholder groups but because of their importance to the conference task. The idea is to get the right pieces of the puzzle together, those people who are critical to achieving the purpose of the search conference. Therefore, precise specification of the purpose of a search conference is crucial, because it determines how the conference system is defined, which, in turn, shapes the criteria for participant selection.

Participants in a search conference work on planning tasks in a mixture of whole-community sessions and small groups. As a whole community, participants scan their external environment, review their history, and analyze the strengths and weaknesses of their current system. This provides a shared context for their most important task: the development of strategic goals and action plans.

Strategic issues relevant to a system are debated and discussed by the entire conference community, while areas of agreement and common ground are mapped out through a process of generating, analyzing, and synthesizing data into an integrated community product. Learning and planning to achieve shared purposes is an evolving process, which means the outcomes of the search conference are open-ended; they cannot be predicted in advance: "In a search conference you don't know where you will end up; it is an adventure," asserts Chet Terry, manager of employee development, who helped plan a search conference for Xerox whose purpose was organizational renewal.

Because more people are involved directly in the planning process, the search conference is a highly participative event. The plans and strategies developed in a search conference reflect the unique character and culture of an organization, thereby increasing the probability that effective implementation will follow. "The level of observed commitment employees had to the plan they created coming out of the search conference was unprecedented," recalls Dan Dotin, vice president of the Illinois customer business unit at Xerox. Managers and employees are refreshed by participation in a process that is task oriented, open-ended, and practical.

WHY THE SEARCH CONFERENCE WORKS

Since its invention in 1960, the search conference has developed into a highly reliable method for democratic planning. It is simple, straightforward, and theoretically sound. SC has certain core principles that make it effective and, when understood, lead to flexibility in planning an SC (see Box 6–1).

Meeting Conditions for Effective Communications

A search conference seeks to realize the rich potential of face-to-face human interaction. Its intent is to establish the conditions for effective and influential communications and create a shared context for collaborative group work.

Certain conditions for effective communications are necessary to sustain for several days an open dialogue among diverse people responsible for the strategic direction of the enterprise. Sustaining a fully democratic dialogue requires the development of trust. An absolutely essential part of the search conference concerns creating the conditions for trust among participants. This means that the planning environment must contain the following elements:

1. The conference is structured so that all information is shared openly and things are as they appear (i.e., no master plan, hidden agendas, or secret deals going on behind the scenes—all information is available).

BOX 6–1 Core principles of the search conference

- Meeting conditions for effective communications and dialogue.
- Open systems thinking.
- Right system in the room.
- Puzzle learning and direct perception, not expert-driven problem solving.
- Democratic structure.
- Searching for common ground by making conflicts rational.

2. Participants experience through pooling their perceptions of their organization in its environment a mutually shared objective view of the world—a sense that they all live in the same world and can make sense of it as real and knowable.

3. Official status differences are minimized by working within self-managing groups governed by a ground rule that everyone's perceptions carry equal weight. The sharing of perceptions related to the past, present, and future of the enterprise, especially the focus on shared ideals, establishes the sense that participants at the conference are psychologically similar and share like concerns.

Solomon Asch, a prominent social scientist, produced groundbreaking research on the conditions for effective and influential communications in groups that are critical success factors for search conference design. The first condition—openness—is critical to all facets of search conference design and management. In operational terms, this means ensuring the conditions that things are as they appear to be (i.e., that this isn't a trick to get people's commitment to a course of action management has already decided on). Joint action is more likely to emerge when communication among participants reveals that discussions are open and accessible to all parties.

For this reason, all data in a search conference are public and in open view for inspection by all. Individual note taking or filling out worksheets is discouraged in favor of recording perceptions on flip charts, while managers of the process refrain from becoming involved in the content of group discussions. Indeed, all group work is self-managing. If the group or any individual perceives any hint of manipulation, the condition of openness will be violated and the development of trust inhibited.

The search conference is designed to produce what Asch called a "mutually shared field." In the first phase of a search conference participants focus on the environment, thereby establishing the presence of a field with commonly perceived features. With the emergence of this shared context, people can validate their perception of a shared starting point. The third condition, basic psychological similarity, is established primarily through the sharing of human ideals that are elicited when people articulate and decide on a desirable future (using a process to rationalize conflict between groups). As these conditions are established, the fourth condition of trust develops and evolves.

Open Systems Thinking

Based on an open system view of organization, the search conference is designed to facilitate learning how to plan and adapt strategies in an environment of increasing turbulence and uncertainty. The evolution of the environment to a condition of turbulence—where the ground rules of business shift in unpredictable ways—makes a systems approach to planning necessary. Organizations are systems and must be viewed as complete in themselves, composed of parts or subsystems. Yet organizations, as undivided wholes, are not understood simply by looking at interrelationships and dynamics between parts. Every organization also has an overriding system principle that serves to organize and govern different parts and subsystems into a functional whole. In a search conference the system principle is translated into a set of strategic goals.

As living systems, organizations must remain open and responsive to their environments if they are to maintain their coherence and survive. A well-functioning open system has the capacity for active adaptation, that is, a continuous organizational learning and planning capacity. Open systems are constantly engaged in learning from the environment and adapting plans in response to what they learn. As Box 6–1 illustrates, the design of a SC consists of three phases organized into a task sequence that follows the logic of an open systems approach to learning and planning. An open system—whether it is a corporation, a new product, or a new organization to deal with an emerging need—is also defined by a shared purpose, mission, core process, or primary task. Defining this shared purpose is critical to determining the boundaries that demarcate the system from its environment.

Similarly, a search conference creates a temporary organization that brings together a large group of people to plan the future of a system. One of the first steps involved in designing a search conference is defining the purpose or conference task. There must also be some compelling business reason or challenging issue for convening a search conference, the nature of which will determine the people who participate in the conference event.

Puzzle Learning

Because the search conference shifts planning away from a focus on means (tactics, operations, and short-term goals) to searching for ends (ideals, strategies, and long-term purposes), the learning component is different from that of problem solving. Planning in a turbulent environment is more like puzzle solving than problem solving. Puzzle solving is a function of the perceptual synthesis of a group of people: The search for possibilities is more important than a reliance on existing conceptual knowledge.

When a situation is complex and unpredictable, puzzle solving allows a nonlinear learning process to take place. Previously hard-won learning may not only be unhelpful, it may prevent forward movement (hence the need for unlearning). Puzzle learning requires one to piece things together as new patterns emerge. The challenge is to determine what is required for a piece to fit; until that piece is found, it isn't clear how to find the next pieces. Because the path to a puzzle solution is nonlinear, routine procedures or predefined steps will only lead to dead ends.

Organizations have become overly reliant on information junk food. High-level strategic planning efforts often have relied solely on the information produced by experts, basing plans on statistical, financial, and aggregated data and piecemeal views of the environment. This kind of information is still necessary but is insufficient. Actions based on such data will be limited by incomplete perceptions of the environment, which fail to take into account more intuitive knowledge, anecdotal reports, and synthetic forms of knowledge about what is happening in the environment. This implies that expert knowledge is not privileged. In the search conference, each participant attends because of his or her potential for contributing knowledge and expertise about some piece of the overall puzzle. Everyone is considered an expert in the search conference.

Direct Perception and Ecological Planning

The search conference is based on the theory of direct perception, the belief that ordinary people have an innate ability to directly perceive meaning from the environment. Contrary to this view, our corporations are organized around the traditional machine-age beliefs that discrete bits of information must be abstracted, added up by experts, and somehow integrated before meaningful knowledge is available. That gets us into trouble because it limits our ability to see and act when sudden changes occur. The search conference allows people to regain confidence in their innate abilities for direct perception, searching, and puzzle solving their way to seeing and understanding patterns, trends, and complex situations.

Executives have long recognized the importance of direct perception (i.e., a firm grounding in reality versus abstraction) and that a great deal of information needed for strategic planning never becomes hard fact. Bill Gates, for example, is known to meet regularly with the CEOs of all the major hardware and software firms. This enables him to spot trends and anticipate developments. Studies confirm that personal sources of information exceed impersonal sources in perceived importance by 70 percent compared to 29 percent in managers' decision making. Since the environment contains an abundance of richly detailed information, any person with an intact perceptual system and a long, rich experience as part of the industry in question can access this information directly from the contextual environment.

The first phase of every search conference requires putting people directly into a mode of learning from the environment. During this time of the search conference, participants draw on their perceptions of the environment, synthesize these into scenarios, and report their collective interpretations. They produce realistic and sophisticated local theories of their situations. They gain confidence in their abilities to self-manage and see the true value of their perceptions and experience. This search through all the possibilities with a well-chosen group of people helps produce realistic plans.

Democratic Structure and Self-Management

The search conference is a temporary organization that locates responsibility for the coordination, control, and implementation of planning tasks in self-managing work groups. Status differences between managers and employees are put aside as people work together in groups that have total responsibility for controlling and coordinating their own affairs to achieve jointly agreed-upon objectives. There are no areas off-limits and no division of labor between thinkers and doers. Instead, the self-regulating work group constitutes the basic building block of organization. This increases the adaptive behavior of individual members and enhances the conditions for mutual collaboration.

If people are expected to provide input and improve already established plans they are not involved in a search conference but a participative event. The leadership in such a conference has chosen not to share authority and responsibility for the coordination and control of work. They are the thinkers and the people are the doers. This situation prevents the formation of a viable learning and planning community. It may raise energy and create more awareness of the whole, but, in short order, people return to a state of bureaucratic apathy and lack of commitment to plans. Remember that the critical knowledge for active adaptive planning is not in the heads of a few specialists or executives: It is widely distributed among all employees. And if we don't include people who represent every aspect of the puzzle, we risk staying frozen in old assumptions and ways of operating.

Creative Working Mode: Get Outside of Command and Control's Limitations

Through a democratic structure and clearly specified, time-bound tasks, the search conference establishes a creative working mode. This mode is in operation when groups display high levels of energy, learning and cooperation, and sustained concentration toward completing tasks on time. It is a condition that fosters group creativity and innovation.

Wilfred Bion's famous research on groups taught us how to achieve and sustain the creative working mode. Bion found three patterns in groups not performing at optimal levels. A dependency orientation is the most common pattern experienced by people in traditional command-and-control organizations. Here members look to a leader to sustain the functioning of their group. Individuals do not develop creative relationships with each other, instead depending on a supervisor's control. When this dependency is operating, the emotional tone of the group is negative, and low levels of energy and learning are present. In the grip of dependency, the learning process is similar to the process of television viewing—people are largely passive, uncritical, and mentally lazy.

Another pattern in command-and-control systems occurs when the official leader or expert is perceived in such a way that members feel they must either fight or flee. When group members are in a fight mode, their concern is with winning their arguments, not with mutual understanding. In flight, a group may unconsciously ignore directives, appearing impatient, edgy, and distracted. Under these conditions in which groups feel threatened and insecure, emotions become extraordinarily intensified, intellectual abilities become markedly reduced, and only routine work is accomplished.

Additionally, animated discussions (usually between several members) may take precedence in a group, diverting attention toward some new hopeful idea. These discussions can end up going in circles. So there is often a lot of hopeful talk, but no real committed action. None of these unproductive behaviors will create achievable plans. The search conference is designed and managed to minimize the outbreaks of such behaviors and keep people in the creative working mode.

Rationalizing Conflict

The rationalization of conflict is quite different from the consensus decision-making process. The rationalization of conflict procedure puts matters into proper perspective; it allows all parties to perceive the true ratio of agreement to disagreement. This is done in the full community by first asking for questions for clarification only and then asking whether there is anything that particular subgroups report they are not prepared to fully support and make happen. Contentious items are placed on a disagree list. Only the redundancy existing across the various small-group reports is removed. The integrated product possesses the richness of all the small-group reports. Its language is that of participants, in their own words.

In a search conference, we are not assuming that consensus within the community will or should exist at all times. If consensus does occur, it is an added bonus, but it's not the ultimate goal, which would be unrealistic, especially in cases where there are legitimate adversarial positions. Rather than striving for consensus, the search conference focuses on identifying those areas in which people concur, building agreement so that groups can also safely and rationally discuss their differences. Arguments and sorting out differences is essential when everyone's future is at stake.

In a search conference we don't try to put conflict on hold, sweep it under the rug, or facilitate it away. Instead, we deal with it directly by making conflict rational, objective, and discussible. Finding common ground, however, is not an end in itself, because that shifts the purpose away from task-oriented strategic planning. Finding agreement is a means to an end, the end being serious commitments to action plans that are focused on achieving a more desirable future for the system.

Let's look at an example of search conference implementation from Motorola. We will learn how the company was able to use this method to tap the deep well of human energy, commitment, and tenacity to deal with the challenges of innovation and growth of the business.

SEARCHING FOR GROWTH: AN ENTREPRENEURIAL UNIT WITHIN MOTOROLA

The new director of the minichip business unit within Motorola decided to hold a worldwide strategic planning event in January of 1995. Minichip designs and produces the newest, smallest semiconductors that feed the wireless equipment business of Motorola. The foundation for the business had been put in place by the first director in the 1990s (manufacturing capability was built; initial products were designed; and internal champions were chosen in Europe, the United States, Japan, and the Far East). According to the new director: "We are poised to grow but how to do it is the question we want to come together to answer." He wanted this first planning session under his leadership to be different than past experiences with strategic planning, which typically had focused on tactics rather than long-term and global strategies.

Twenty-five key personnel gathered in Tokyo for three days to create a future toward which they could all work. They would leave the planning session with each participant part of a self-managing team responsible for involving others in the goals for the desirable future and keeping implementation on track. The search began at 3 P.M. of the first day. Our first task was to review the nature of a search:

- The search is essentially a translation of open system thinking into a design for strategic planning.
- There are different types of task environments faced by organizations, and the semiconductor task environment is turbulent and uncertain.
- Planning methods based on technical and economic criteria aren't adequate for this type of environment.
- We can change to be adaptive instead of passively adapting to change.

- We will act as equals, be self-managing, and consider all ideas valid.
- We will create space for dialogue and work mostly in small groups for specific tasks.

Our second task was to document the external environment. What has happened in the last three to five years that is novel and significant? As people sit in a large semicircle facing the flip charts, we post their comments: Reduction of U.S. military budget, the GATT treaty, semiconductor focus, NAFTA, European Community has gotten bigger, PCS auctions, merging financial institutions, wireless growth and acceptance by the consumer, computers are everywhere, the Hubble telescope, Asian market now the consumer market, United States is becoming a service economy, wealth redistribution is occurring globally, manufacturing in third-world countries is increasing, Motorola is tripling sales, access to Internet for all, savings and loan crisis, quality is now necessary to compete, computer-aided designs, proliferation of airbags, consumers reject errors in high-tech, power PC introduced, and so on.

Our third task is for subgroups to work on desirable and probable futures for the world. The desirable future taps into their ideals but must be achievable by 1999. The probable future reflects the world if current trends continue. The next appropriate task is charting the desirable and probable futures of minichip's industry context or task environment. The likely future reflecting its industry context included the following:

- Wireless technology and markets will expand and diversify.
- Third-world economic growth will result in improved living standards and further democratization.
- Regional economic alliances will result in a shift in market shares/manufacturing bases globally.
- Wireless technology will evolve, allowing a phone number and communication tool to move with an individual.
- Higher levels of system integration will develop in the personal communication arena.

The next morning we are ready to move from a focus on scanning the environment to learning about the minichip unit itself as a system. Our new task is to remember the unit's history. A circle is formed with the whole group present. The people who were there at the beginning speak first to share their experience. After they begin, others add their voices. For the next hour we listen quietly as the stories people tell bring the group's history to life. Events seem to be linked with the different leaders over the last decade. The newest people listen in rapt attention. It is obvious the founders faced significant turning points 10 years ago on the journey to creating this unit:

- There were many false starts; their own organizer wouldn't support their independence, so an internal customer funded their birth.
- The group found office space and the business became a reality.
- With pride, one of the elders recalled for the group the day that George Fisher, then CEO of Motorola, called their little division "the king's jewels" upon which the future of the whole company rested.
- There were territorial issues with other units and arguments over the merits of different technologies.

The purpose of the history session is to ensure people share a common knowledge base of the minichip operation's origins and all the major milestones and changes it has gone through to get where it is today. At this point there is sufficient trust in the room to move into a thorough assessment of the operation's current strengths and weaknesses. The best way to do this is to ask three questions simultaneously: What do we want to keep? What do we want to throw away? What do we want to create or invent?

Motorola's minichip unit is already a well-run operation, so there are many strengths, including the small-group team environment in product development, tenacity, benchmarking, worldwide job rotation, an empowered environment and the close communication that makes it work, strong credibility with customers, excellent training and a good U.S. staff, a clear and appropriate mission, an ability to influence others (e.g., offshore suppliers, contract houses), current capacity ahead of demand, project planning abilities, and good support for the regions. Like any organization, minichip wants to jettison a number of items. These include the strategic business unit boundaries, tariffs, the current situation in the characterization lab, wafer costs that are too high, internal conflicts around products and people, inadequate back-end reliability, dependence on one internal customer, and the R&D approach for a product group.

The flip chart fills quickly with items people want to create or invent: Creating worldwide centers of excellence, generating systems solutions, defining wafer technology platforms, entering a new market, gaining more regional autonomy and funding, expanding benchmarking, adding external customers, creating a concise packaging roadmap with the present modeling tools, finding new ways to listen to customers and markets, reducing cycle time for new-product introductions, partnering with customers, and shifting leadership to the regions in product development to eliminate redundancies across regions.

In an uncertain, turbulent environment an organization requires a well-defined, desirable future expressed in six to eight strategic goals. Active adaptation to the global and task environments means the organization has the ability to align its actions to these goals and can modify, drop, or add a particular goal in real time as the environment changes. At this point we break people into small groups to work on designing a plan for the minichip operation through 1999. The scenarios they create may include a definition of market, applications, new technologies, new products, new platforms, organizational structure, and business size. The groups work for several hours and then report their scenarios.

The similarities and differences among the groups are then integrated using the rationalization of conflict method described earlier. The list of differences contains two items that were not reconcilable after extensive discussion. These were put aside so people could focus on the more workable points.

The combined goals for the desirable future of the minichip operation for 1999 may be overly optimistic:

1. We will have the largest portion of the worldwide market, which means we must grow faster than the market. Specific market and product figures are identified to get us there. We will participate in at least one emerging market/application.

2. Worldwide centers of excellence will exist for marketing applications, design and development, manufacturing, and global teamwork.

3. We will drive the semiconductor, packaging, and assembly/test technology platforms and have guaranteed access to them.

4. A systems solution approach and key customer partnerships will be in place.

5. Development and manufacturing cycle time will be reduced and give us a key competitive edge (seven days from order to customer's dock).

6. Quality and reliability will be greater than Six Sigma, and qualification cycles will disappear.

We have completed the first two phases of the open systems approach to planning in turbulent environments and understand the shifts and changes in and effect on minichip's environment. After evaluating the current situation at minichip and identifying its most desirable future, we are ready to deal with constraints. Constraints can feel overwhelming and paralyze people who don't have a learning and planning community ready to work together to create the future they want to achieve. The people in the room have gelled into such a community. That means they are capable of taking their vision for the future and subjecting it to the cold, hard face of reality that constraints represent, a task made more manageable in the community environment.

Since minichip is a small unit within Motorola, it is natural to expect that a significant portion of its constraints will be within Motorola, which proves true. The final integrated list has two clusters of constraints. External constraints include defense-spending cuts, strategy limited by competitors' strategies and Motorola's equipment market share, the degree of customer acceptance of both its products and the wireless system, political situations, trade barriers, tariffs, and the situation in China and Asia. Internal constraints include organizational structure issues that limit minichip's ability to provide system solutions, technology availability from R&D, and capital funding and human resource issues. Because it will take some time to develop the centers for excellence, group members say they will need considerable time to improve the development cycle time and internal customers are reluctant to allow them to support external customers with advanced technologies.

As predicted this becomes the low point of the search conference. At first participants are overwhelmed by the magnitude of the constraints and a sense of powerlessness sets in, but they soon develop creative strategies to deal with their difficulties. For example, some of the potential strategies for overcoming the limits arising from a competitor's strategy include hiring some of their key people, duplicating their technology, and buying the competitor or forming a joint venture or alliance with them. The group could work to understand its competitor's internal structure and create a history map of its evolution, understand its customer focus, benchmark its products for strategic missteps and limitations, and determine its research and development expenditures and their effectiveness. Minichip could also ignore its competitor's strategy, go its own way, pull out of that market, or invest elsewhere.

A crucial outcome is making constraints seem positive; in the process, groups often find their work in the search conference has provided major strategies for moving toward their goals. We now check to see whether the plan is still desirable and achievable in light of the present constraints. A vigorous dialogue continues for 45 minutes, and one change is made to the business goals.

The morning of the third day is a time for extensive work on action planning. At least one-third of the time in a search conference is allocated to action planning to ensure it works in the long term. The minichip group decides to take the six richly detailed strategic goals and form them into three clusters. They chose technology, marketing, and organizational structure, which is against our advice to stay away from abstract categories and stick with the original six goals.

Participants then join one of three self-managing task forces—each of which then develops action plans (strategies and tactics) to achieve those clustered goals. They agree that no one leaves until they determine the following:

- Time parameters for each group.
- Criteria for monitoring progress.
- Future meeting times.
- Guidelines for self-managing.
- Recruitment of other organizational members into the implementation phase.

Participants know that they are now on their own, fully responsible, and will not appreciate a manager telling them what to do. Collaboration has by now become an expected behavior.

We review the principles that will keep the work on track for the next six months to a year: self-management, temporary democratic structure, and continuation of the creative working mode. We caution them that reverting to a committee structure will bring about predictable consequences: territorial bickering, refusal to address primary issues, a rapid decline in attendance, energy, and enthusiasm, and a waste of the gains you have made in the search conference. We remind them to work to keep responsibility for control and coordination of work within their group rather than with a manager.

Six months later, the minichip director summarized his assessment of the results from the search conference: "The three task forces are all doing well: The technology task force has built upon our strengths and is beginning key programs to fill our technology voids. The marketing task force has made significant progress expanding our markets and beginning a systems solution approach to our customers. The task force on centers of excellence has initiated a critical shift. No longer will the design of new products be centered in the U.S. but instead are dispersed into the regions. This allows us to respond adaptively to customer needs and avoid redundancy by having the expertise in one center available to other regions. Critical resources have been added in the regions in support of the goals developed during the planning session. For example: a design engineer in Japan, an applications engineer in Europe, and a new product development champion in the United States."

The search conference at Motorola was a positive and motivating experience for managers. The emphasis on developing shared agreements around a desirable set of strategic goals has brought discipline and focus to the managers in this extended global business. The minichip director remarked: "I am delighted with the leadership emerging from our Japanese operations. We shared the essence of the future we want to create with the entire organization through staff meetings and communication meetings. We are maintaining the focus on the goals rather than just the action plans. Organizational members are clear about our desirable future and can align their activities accordingly (even if they are not directly involved in a task force). Commitment to the goals of our desirable future is high, and we have gained a greater sense of a family environment worldwide rather than just in the United States. This will pay dividends for us over the long term."

Unique to the search conference is its direct, experiential approach to learning and planning in real time that helps to develop the organizational capacity for active adaptation. A greater number of people in the organization will be exposed to open systems thinking, learning how to adapt plans and strategies, and adjusting and redefining their paths toward moving targets and goals that are constantly shifting in turbulent environments. The future is always an abstraction—it never really arrives. An active, adaptive capacity depends on strategic actions undertaken in the present.

Organizations succeed in today's environment when their people are involved in implementing and revising their plans to stay actively adaptive. A map of the immediate terrain is often all that is available. Successful managers will be those who involve their people in a planning approach that helps them adapt to rapid change.

7 SALES AND OPERATIONS PLANNING

TOP MANAGEMENT'S HANDLE ON THE BUSINESS

Thomas F. Wallace

Editor's note

Balancing supply and demand doesn't have to happen by accident. Tom Wallace recommends a deliberate approach that looks at a company's big objectives and drives mix and detail issues accordingly. By using a simple spreadsheet, the numbers make the options clear, and internal organizations will find themselves more in control and less driven by unexpected, but constant, changes.

Let's eavesdrop on a tense executive staff meeting at the Acme Widget Company.

President: "This shortage situation is terrible. When will we get our act together? Whenever business gets good, we run out of product and our customer service is lousy."

VP operations: "I'll tell you when. It's when we start to get some decent forecasts from marketing . . ."

VP marketing (interrupting): "Wait a minute. We forecasted this upturn."

VP operations:	". . . in time to do something about it. Yeah, we got the revised forecast—four days after the start of the month. By then it was too late."
VP marketing:	"I could have told you months ago. All you had to do was ask."
VP finance:	"I'd like to be in on those conversations. We've been burned more than once by building inventories for a business upturn that doesn't happen. Then we get stuck with tons of inventory and run out of cash."

And the beat goes on. Poor customer service, dissatisfied customers, high inventories, finger pointing, cash flow problems, demand and supply out of balance, and missing the business plan are the norm in many companies, but it doesn't have to be that way. Today many companies are using a tool called sales and operations planning to help prevent these problems.

Sales and operations planning (S&OP) is a *business process* that helps companies keep demand and supply in balance. It does this by focusing on aggregate volumes—the big picture—so that mix problems—the details— can be handled more successfully. The S&OP process is rigorous; it occurs on a monthly basis and includes, among others, the kinds of people cited earlier: top management. It's a new process that's been around for only a dozen years or so.

Dick Ling, an independent consultant based in Wilmington, N.C., more than any other person is the inventor and prime mover of sales and operations planning. Ling states, "It's a real thrill for me to see S&OP having such a positive impact in so many companies . . . including Compaq Computer, 3M, Motorola, Gillette, Kodak, and Caterpillar as well as the ones featured later in this chapter."

THE S&OP SPREADSHEET

One of the most important elements in this business process is the S&OP spreadsheet (see Fig. 7–1). Using this tool, key people review each major product family. The information—displayed in aggregate rather than in detail—shows sales performance to forecast, production performance to plan, and the resultant inventory levels and/or customer order backlogs. See Figure 7–1 for an example of how the information is displayed. In this example, for a make-to-stock product family called medium widgets, the demand/supply strategy specifies a target customer-service level (shipments on time and complete) or 99 percent. The target finished inventory necessary to support this shipping performance has been set at a 30-day (or one-month) supply. See the area in Figure 7–1 identified by *A*.

FIGURE 7–1 Sales and operations plan for June 1998

Family: Medium widgets (Make-to-stock)	Unit of Measure: 000 Units
Target customer service Level: 99%	Target INV Level: 10 Days on Hand

	March	April	May	June	July	August	September	October	November	3rd 3 months	4th 3 months	Next 12 months	Fiscal year	Business plan
Sales														
Forecast	100	100	100	105	105	110	110	110	110	345	345	1,335	$12,770	$12,700
Actual	110	98	114											
Difference +/–: Month	+10	–2	+14											
Cumulative		+8	+22											
Production														
Plan	100	100	100	105	110	115	115	115	115	345	350	1,365	1,272	1,300
Actual	100	102	99											
Difference +/–: Month	0	+2	–1											
Cumulative		+2	+1											
Inventory														
Plan	50	50	50	30	35	45	50	55	45	45	50			
Actual	40	44	30											
Days-on-hand	8	9	6	6	7	9	10	11	9	9	10			
Customer service %	97%	98%	89%											

Demand Issues and Assumptions:
1. Forecast assumes no competitor price changes
2. Accelerated export demand will continue through middle of next year

Supply Issues:
1. June and July production plan represents maximum effort due to vacations

114

Let's examine the 30-day-supply inventory target for a bit. Why does this company feel it needs 30 days of finished goods inventory? The answer is that its experience over the recent past has shown that 30 days is the minimum level necessary to provide 99 percent customer service. Should this 30-day-supply target be considered as a constant, fixed far into the future? Definitely not. The principle of continuous improvement should drive this company to improve its sales, production, and logistics processes so that 99 percent customer service is attainable with only, say, a 25-day supply. And then a 20-day supply. And then 15. But for now, the realities of life are that it takes a month's worth of inventory to provide the 99 percent service level. In Figure 7–1 part *B*, actual sales are compared to those estimated. For the past three months, sales have been running ahead of the forecast by 22,000 units. Actual production performance to the plan is evaluated in part *C*. It's close to perfect.

Area *D* shows inventory performance to plan and the actual customer-service performance. We can see a serious problem developing here: Because the forecast was oversold, the actual inventory dropped below plan. The result is that customer service has dropped to 89 percent for May, far below its 99 percent target. Showing the customer-service numbers next to the inventory numbers is strongly recommended, because it helps people avoid suboptimal decisions. Many companies lurch from "the inventories are too high; cut the inventories" to "build inventory; we have too many back orders." Understanding the interplay between finished inventories and customer service is aided by viewing this situation organically, which can help greatly in maintaining the demand/supply balance.

The new sales forecast is shown in *E*. Toward the right of the page are shown a total for the next 12 months and totals in units and dollars for the fiscal year, ending in December in this example. As a result, these totals are made up of both sales history (January through May) and sales forecast (June through December). Area *E* also shows the forecasted dollars in the business plan, allowing for an easy comparison between the business plan and the S&OP forecast for the fiscal year's volume. Based on these data, the top-management team will probably elect to change the business plan accordingly. The assumptions underlying the forecast are listed in area *H*. The future production plan, based on the new forecast and other considerations, is shown in *F*, and the relevant supply (production/procurement) issues are listed in *J*. Area *G* contains the future inventory projection for finished goods. It shows that the target inventory of 10 days on hand will not be reached until September.

In summary, Figure 7–1 is an example of a proven, effective format for sales and operations planning information. The intent is to have all of the relevant information for a given product family on one piece of paper. This enables each family's situation, both in recent past and future outlook, to be viewed completely. For decision-making purposes, this has proved to be far superior to displays of information that focus only on sales, inventory levels, or production.

THE S&OP PROCESS

The essence of the S&OP process (Figure 7–2) is decision making. For each product family reviewed, a decision is made based on recent history, recommendations from middle management, and the executive team's knowledge of business conditions. The decision can be any of the following:

a. Change the sales plan.
b. Change the production plan.
c. Change the inventory/backlog plan.
d. None of the above; the current plans are okay.

These decisions represent the agreed-upon plans by the president and all involved vice presidents and are documented and disseminated throughout the organization. They form the overall orders for the marketing, sales, manufacturing, materials, finance, and product development departments. (New product plans are reviewed within S&OP in terms of their impact on the demand/supply picture.) These groups break down the aggregate plans

FIGURE 7-2 The monthly sales and operations planning process

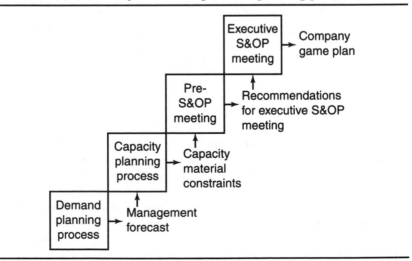

from S&OP into the necessary level of detail: individual products, customers, regions, plants, and materials.

Sales and operations planning, however, is not a point event that occurs in a two-hour executive meeting each month. Rather, preliminary work begins shortly after month end and continues for several days. This phase, called pre-SOP, involves middle management and others throughout the company (see Figure 7–2). It includes the following:

- Updating the sales forecast.
- Reviewing the impact of these changes on the production plan and determining whether adequate capacity and material will be available to support them.
- Identifying alternatives where problems exist.
- Formulating agreed-upon recommendations for top management regarding overall changes to the plans and identifying areas of disagreement where consensus is not possible.
- Communicating this information to top management with sufficient time for its review before the executive S&OP meeting.

Therefore the information contained in Figure 7–1 represents the recommendation coming from the pre-SOP team to top management regarding medium widgets. It's then top management's job to make a decision: accept the plan as submitted or change it. In the example in Figure 7–1, the below-target inventory levels between June and August may be viewed by top management as unacceptable, because the company will not be providing good customer service. The company may decide to incur the additional, and perhaps substantial, costs of paying for extreme overtime, subcontracting, or bringing in temporary help, so that the inventories—hence customer service—can get back on target sooner than September.

Thanks to pre-SOP, the executive S&OP meeting should not take long; two hours or less is the norm with companies that understand the process. The net result of S&OP for the top-management group should be fewer meetings, less time spent in meetings, more productivity in its decision-making processes, and a higher quality of work life. And most of the middle-management people involved in the pre-SOP process will experience the same benefits.

SUCCESSFUL USERS

Now let's look at some companies making effective use of this powerful new tool. We'll focus on a major player in consumer package goods, a manufacturer of aerospace and industrial components, a chemical company making, highly seasonal products, and a foundry.

Procter & Gamble—Cincinnati, Ohio

Annual sales: $33 billion

Products: Consumer package goods

Customers: Grocery chains, drug chains, mass merchandisers, distributors (make-to-stock/make-to-demand)

Procter & Gamble is a leader and an innovator. More than any other company in its field, P&G has been out in front in areas including supply chain management, quick response/efficient consumer response, and value pricing. So it comes as no surprise to see the company making effective use of a leading-edge business process such as sales and operations planning. Within this global company, S&OP is used in many different areas, ranging from foreign countries with broad product lines to individual product categories in the United States. These categories are large business units and contain a number of individual brands such as Tide, Pampers, Head and Shoulders, Crest, Pringles, and Max Factor.

Mike Kremzar, vice president of product supply, customer services worldwide, is the process owner for manufacturing resource planning (MRP II) including implementation of S&OP. Kremzar says: "MRP II is changing the way we operate the total supply chain. The general managers of the business units now can operate their profit centers with the knowledge of the impact of their decisions on the total system. The S&OP process provides the data, the forum, and the measurement tools that let these leaders continue to make good decisions for their brands but now with full team understanding including cost, inventory, and service impacts."

One of these general managers, who has been using the S&OP process for two years, states: "For the first time, sales and operations planning lets me feel like a true general manager. I now know the cost implications of the decisions that we make every month. Our entire business team—marketing, sales, product supply, finance, R&D—is working more effectively since we have stopped defending different volume estimates all month. We can pull together with a single number forecast that has everyone's full support."

Here's Kremzar again: "The benefits from sales and operations planning have been significant and continue to grow. Some of our business units have experienced a 20 percent improvement in inventory with a 25 percent improvement in customer service levels while costs have decreased!

"Generally, our implementation time for complete, Class A MRP II takes about 18 months, and of course S&OP comes up early in that time frame. We've found that, as Tom Wallace says, good things start to happen early, often in the first month or two of implementation."

Moog Inc.—East Aurora, New York

Annual sales: $500 million

Products: Aerospace and industrial valves and controls
(primarily make-to-order; some make-to-stock)

Moog prides itself on doing things well. Great technical competence, superior management processes, and a high regard for its employees characterize this company, which is featured in the book *The 100 Best Companies to Work For in America*.

Bill Talboys is the senior manufacturing executive for Moog's systems group, which includes divisions producing space products, missile components, industrial valves, and electronic controls. "Running a variety of complex businesses, most make-to-order and some make-to-stock, is a real challenge," Talboys states, "but now that we've implemented S&OP, it's a good deal easier to keep track of these different units and to make the right decision on demand and supply. S&OP gives us far better control of our businesses. For example, our space products division—space station and satellite components—has had a dramatic upturn in demand over the last 12 months, and thanks to S&OP, we've increased capacity much earlier than we otherwise would have. This enormous demand is still a challenge, but it's much more manageable thanks to the better forward visibility that S&OP provides. Further, in some of our businesses, as a direct result of S&OP we've reduced lead times to customers by up to 50 percent."

A question heard frequently is whether S&OP will work in areas other than traditional sales and manufacturing. Well, the people at Moog have proved that it does—they're using sales and operations planning in product development. Here's Mike Baczkowski, who's in charge of the systems group's new-product development activities: "Our development folks live in an unpredictable world; uncertainty abounds. This is particularly true with our ultra high-tech products like space and missile components. We do our best to schedule each job realistically, but almost invariably we get surprises. Engineering is late, or the customer changes his mind, or the prototype we just built fails the qualification test, or dozens of other things.

"That's the bad news. The good news is that we're beginning to adapt sales and operations planning to our part of the business: new product development. It's uncanny. Even though individual projects move around, the aggregate numbers for resource requirements—drafting, model shop, the development lab—tend to be more stable. S&OP gives us *a window into the future;* we can see what our upcoming workloads will be far better than before. We're able to prioritize better, and hence react better. I think even Tom Wallace is surprised that it's working so well in an atypical environment like product development."

Richard C. "Bing" Sherrill, group vice president and general manager, adds: "We're now running six sales and operations planning processes. In the beginning, some of the S&OP meetings took over two hours but as each business unit comes under control, the meeting time has dropped dramatically.

"There are three reasons why I attend every S&OP meeting every month. First, I get the pulse of the operation: what are current sales, where are the forecasts going, how are shipments doing. Second, I always learn something important about our people, our processes, our products, and—last but certainly not least—our customers. The S&OP sessions are consistently among the most productive and most informative meetings I attend. Thirdly, my attendance encourages the attendance of the functional managers, which in turn assures that we have all the decision-makers in the room and that we have a common picture of our business. Consensus and buy-in become much easier to get."

Vigoro Consumer and Professional Group— Winter Haven, Florida

Annual sales: $100+ million

Products: Fertilizer and ice-melter products (primarily make-to-stock; some make-to-order)

Is your business seasonal? If so, you'll appreciate the situation facing Vigoro, a manufacturer of fertilizers and ice-melter products. In much of the business, more than 80 percent of annual sales occur in three or four months. Thus it's necessary to start production long before the selling season starts. The timing of when to begin the prebuild, at what rates, the resultant inventory buildup, and cash flow requirements are important issues that must be planned thoroughly—and then authorized or modified by senior management.

"Sales and operations planning really helps with the kind of seasonal planning that we have to do," claims Ken Holbrook, president of Vigoro Consumer and Professional Group. "This is particularly true in dealing with mass merchandisers. Recently we were able to virtually double our consumer business by capturing a major new customer—and, thanks to S&OP, we did it with our eyes open. We've been able to superimpose that volume on top of our existing plans—and make early, informed decisions on needed capacity increases. Further, we'll be tracking the entire situation in our monthly S&OP cycle and be able to make adjustments proactively—and thus provide superior customer service."

Jay Ferguson, chief financial officer, puts it succinctly: "I'm the guy that corporate calls to ask questions about our inventory levels and cash flow. S&OP can be a big help in providing the answers to questions like why did we start the prebuild on Ice Melter products in June rather than August, how much cash will we need to fund the prebuild, is prebuilding a better economic decision than capacity expansion, and so on. And, from a broader company-wide point of view, anything that helps our business planning process and provides better customer service has to be a big plus—and S&OP certainly qualifies."

Joe Rocco, Vigoro's VP of operations, likes what sales and operations planning has done for his manufacturing team: "We have nine fertilizer plants in the United States and one in Canada, and we view this network as a real asset in terms of being geographically close to the customer. The hard part is allocating production and coordinating plans so that the total supply chain does what we want it to do. We've brought a high level of ownership to our plant managers, and they're able to plan proactively versus reacting to last minute volume swings. Each plant sets its own production plan; when the totals don't come out right, it's their job to work together to reallocate production so that the total system is producing the right amount to meet our customer's needs. It's been a real help in building teamwork in this highly seasonal, multiplant environment; we now have a common language and a shared view that gets updated every month."

Cast-Fab Technologies—Cincinnati, Ohio

Annual sales: $50 million

Products: Iron castings and sheet and heavy-plate fabrications
                  (make-to-order)

"Our business is highly cyclical," says Jim Bushman, Cast-Fab's CEO and president, "we're the extreme first link in the supply chain. Our products represent the foundation of large machines. Our customers supply these machines to the companies who produce products—both consumer and industrial—that are everyday household words. The cycles of the capital goods industry can be very volatile for our type of business."

Cast-Fab is purely a make-to-order shop, completely dependent on incoming customer orders to replenish its sales backlog. Remember years ago when foundry lead times ranged from 12 to 40 weeks? Well, those days are gone forever; Cast-Fab's customer lead times don't exceed six weeks and in most cases are shorter. And Cast-Fab works hard at not allowing those lead times to stretch out as order volume picks up.

Bob Meier, VP of sales, puts it in perspective: "sales and operations planning provides a company-wide view of changing markets and individual customer needs (the demand side), while enhancing the company's overall flexibility and response time (the supply side). S&OP addresses the very same issues that are vital to our customers—what they're going to need and how we're going to get it to them."

Steve Timmons, VP of operations, chimes in: "Our sales and operations planning meeting provides a monthly, structured forum for us to review future capacity changes. Do we still get surprises? Sure, but the surprises are less of a shock and we are developing proactive thinking. Because we're looking ahead every month, we're able to make production rate changes sooner, and at times spread the impact. This means these changes are easier for us and our workforce to respond to. And they cost less."

Bushman adds: "Our executive S&OP meeting takes about two hours, once per month. In that meeting, we approve or modify recommendations made by the cross-functional sales, manufacturing, and finance pre-SOP team. We set the company game plan. We dollarize the sales and operations plan, compare it to the business plan to see how we're tracking on the fiscal year, and make changes where appropriate. It's a very effective investment of our time."

RECAP

To sum up, here's what these and other executives are saying about sales and operations planning:

1. S&OP gives executives and managers better control of the business. It provides a window into the future and thus helps top management make better decisions.

2. S&OP enhances the company's flexibility to respond to customer needs and to ship complete orders on time.

3. Top management's role is crucial. For the process to work, the president or general manager must be engaged directly via his or her leadership at the executive S&OP meeting.

4. Changes in production rates can be made less radically and hence with lower costs and less negative impact on the workforce.

5. Inventories and order backlogs can be managed *proactively* to support the company's delivery- and lead-time objectives.

6. The sales and operations plan can be converted to dollars to test the validity of the business plan, which may have been set many months earlier.

7. S&OP provides a more holistic view of the business, because sales demand, production, inventories, and customer lead times are viewed simultaneously for a given product family and set of resources. Thus S&OP enhances teamwork at both the top- and middle-management levels.

8. Bottom line: sales and operations planning has been shown to help companies improve customer service, reduce inventories, shorten customer lead times, and control costs.

FREQUENTLY ASKED QUESTIONS ABOUT SALES AND OPERATIONS PLANNING

Q. Why does top management need to be involved directly?

A. Stewardship and leadership. Many of the decisions made in S&OP affect the financial plan for the current year, and top management owns that business plan. It has a stewardship responsibility for it, and only top management can make decisions to change the plan.

　　When the business plan is not changed to reflect the new sales and operations plan, there's a discrepancy between the financial numbers top management expects and the forecasts and production plans being used to operate the business. Best-in-class performance in this area means that the business is managed—at all levels—using only one set of numbers. Through their direct involvement, the leaders of the business make a strong statement that S&OP is the process that they use to manage this highly important part of the business: bringing demand and supply into balance . . . and keeping them there.

Q. How much time is required of top management?

A. One meeting per month, lasting less than two hours. This event, called the sales and operations planning meeting, can often replace several other meetings and thus result in a net reduction in meeting time. For the president (CEO, general manager, managing director), preparation time is zero.

Q. How is this possible? How can something so productive require so little time?

A. Most of the heavy work is done in what's called the pre-SOP process: forecasting, capacity planning, and the pre-SOP meeting itself. Refer to Figure 7–2.

Q. What about software?

A. Virtually all companies generate their S&OP spreadsheets via spreadsheet software. This means that it's inexpensive, easy to change, and tailored specifically to the needs of the business. The main software task in implementing S&OP is to automate the transfer from the main business systems into the spreadsheet.

Q. How long does it take to implement S&OP?

A. It's taken most companies between six months and a year to become proficient with sales and operations planning. As with any new process, there's a learning curve involved. Further, that curve is lengthened because the S&OP cycle occurs monthly; incremental expertise is gained only once per month.

The good news is that benefits are apparent within several months. Early on, people are able to identify and correct problems that wouldn't have been visible until much later. Further, sales and operations planning is relatively inexpensive to implement. It doesn't cost a lot and relatively few people are involved. The important issue is whether top management is prepared to adopt a new business process. Is it willing to run the business using a more effective tool?

THE FUTURE

What's in store for sales and operations planning down the road? Well, we see several trends emerging, one being the obvious: wider acceptance overall. The word's getting around that this process is powerful and neither difficult nor costly to implement. One general manager said that S&OP is so good it almost seems like cheating.

Second, we'll see more extensive use of S&OP in a global context. Dick Ling, who's had more experience in this arena than anyone else, claims: "You really can't run a global manufacturing business effectively without S&OP. If you have global customers, do global marketing, produce global products or do global sourcing, you need a global S&OP process."

Third, sales and operations planning will become recognized as an essential core of executive information systems (EIS) in manufacturing companies. If you're putting together an EIS without making provisions for S&OP, you're probably heading down the wrong path.

Last, the onset of MRP simulation software—making full master scheduling and material-requirements planning runs in a minute or two—will make possible what I call the "top-management war room." Imagine that your company has successfully implemented sales and operations planning. Your top-management team is meeting once per month to authorize sales, production, and inventory plans that will harmonize demand and supply. One of the executives—the president or perhaps the CFO—raises a question: If we can pull up the new product launch by six weeks, we're sure we can beat the competition to the market. Can we do it? If so, what other products might be impacted?

The S&OP display for this product family is projected onto a large screen from a PC, which contains the entire resource-planning database for the company. During a brief time-out, the simulation software runs the master schedule and MRP. Within several minutes, you have answers: Plan A is feasible but will impact product X; Plan B is feasible but will impact products Y and Z; and Plan C will have the least total cost but will cause serious backlogs across much of the product line.

The phrase "top-management war room" certainly comes to mind. I predict that within five years this type of capability will be widespread: sales and operations planning linked with simulation software running at the speed of light—supporting major demand/supply decisions with facts rather than guesses—in a top-management setting. This is not blue sky. It's coming.

BIBLIOGRAPHY

Ling, Richard C., and Walter E. Goddard. *Orchestrating Success—Improve Control of the Business with Sales and Operations Planning.* Essex Junction, Vt.: Oliver Wight Publications, 1988.

Rucinski, David. "Game Planning." *Journal of the American Production and Inventory Control Society,* first quarter, 1982. (This is an interview with the president of the U.S. pharmaceutical division of Abbott Laboratories, discussing its experiences with sales and operations planning.)

PART THREE

NEW STRATEGIES

Part 3, "New Strategies," covers all business functions that must be included in the development of manufacturing strategy from the beginning of the order cycle in white collar areas to manufacturing quality control and logistics. The issue of manufacturing flexibility as the key to building more competitive facilities is fully developed in Sara Beckman's chapter. Burgess Oliver offers his own very successful down-home approach to team building in Chapter 9. Bob McInturff looks at three success stories from the perspective of human resource management. Chapter 11, from Jackie Hammonds of Honda of America, shows how the number-one U.S. expert on quality circles pioneered this system. Joe Blackburn covers the big challenge of time-based competition. Another powerful improvement tool, kaizen, has taken hold—Tony Laraia's Chapter 13 takes you into the process. Another simple, powerful tool, Wayne Smith's pull systems, is covered in Chapter 14. Chapter 15's "Production Planning Simplicity," takes the mystery out of a frequently overcomplicated process. In Chapter 16 Michael Harding, veteran purchasing practitioner and consultant, cuts through antiquated practices to a more multifunctional approach. Finally, visual systems, a powerful, immediate approach to improving the environment, is presented by Gwen Galsworth.

8 MANUFACTURING FLEXIBILITY

THE NEXT SOURCE OF COMPETITIVE ADVANTAGE

Sara L. Beckman

Editor's note

What is flexibility? Why should U.S. manufacturers become more competitive in this area? In this chapter Sara Beckman answers these questions, discusses in detail the types of variability to which flexibility responds, and cites examples of appropriate use of production flexibility.

INTRODUCTION

A new philosophy about manufacturing is sweeping industry: Manufacturers are learning to be flexible and to use flexibility, along *with* quality and productivity, as a competitive weapon in a rapidly changing and fiercely competitive marketplace. A number of factors are contributing to the heightened interest in flexibility:

- The rate of new-product introduction has increased as product life cycles have shortened, particularly in the so-called high-tech industries.

129

- Increasing competition from foreign producers is challenging U.S. manufacturers to provide their traditionally broad product mix at lower cost. The Japanese set the stage for low-cost, high-quality manufacturing primarily with standardized products. U.S. consumers prefer multiple-option products but want them at cost and quality levels similar to those provided by the Japanese on comparable products.
- Customization has become critical to the penetration of both foreign and domestic marketplaces. More sophisticated consumers throughout the world expect products to be tailored to their specific needs. A few years ago, computer users in China had to live with English keyboards; they can now procure computers that use their native language.
- Technology is evolving at an increasingly rapid rate, requiring manufacturers to quickly assimilate new materials, as well as new process and product technologies, into their organizations.

In short, change is the name of the game. And flexibility is the response that successful companies are employing to cope with it.

At the same time that the need for flexibility is growing, new technology in the form of flexible manufacturing systems (FMS), computer-controlled equipment, and robotics is being developed that allows for more actual flexibility on the production floor at lower cost. Simultaneously, information technology developments are facilitating information transfer, thus improving the overall responsiveness of the organization. While there are many mechanisms for achieving flexibility that are not technology based, technological developments have been critical drivers in the creation of flexible organizations.

Although the coexistence of the need for flexibility and the technology to provide it is unprecedented in recent manufacturing history, the concept of flexibility as a primary dimension of manufacturing performance is not new. Wickham Skinner proposed in 1978 that flexibility, cost, quality, and dependability were the critical aspects of manufacturing performance. Of these, cost, quality, and dependability have all received considerable attention and are fairly well understood. Recent advances in cost accounting and capital investment justification techniques continue ongoing efforts to understand manufacturing costs. Concepts of quality control have been well established for many years and have received additional notoriety in the form of total quality control programs. In addition, although the definition of dependability has changed some over the years from achieving monthly shipping targets to meeting customer due date requirements, it, too, is well understood. *Flexibility* remains the most poorly defined and understood dimension of manufacturing performance.

Although a number of authors, primarily academic, have recently begun to address the topic of flexibility, the conflicting definitions purporting to explain why flexibility is needed and what the means are for achieving it are still confusing. This chapter attempts to reduce that confusion. We will describe the reasons an organization would want to be flexible and the importance of linking those reasons to the firm's overall strategic direction. Second, we will describe how organizations can achieve flexibility. Finally, we will discuss the trade-offs to be made in developing a flexible organization.

WHAT IS FLEXIBILITY?

In the most basic sense, *flexible* means "responsive to change; adaptable; capable of variation or modification." Alternatively, *flexibility* is defined as "the ability to respond effectively to changing circumstances." Manufacturing flexibility might then be defined as the ability of a manufacturing organization to deploy and redeploy its resources effectively in response to changing conditions. Several authors have attempted to describe flexibility. A summary of their work is provided in Table 8–1. The definitions provided range from narrow to broad, from describing types of variability to describing mechanisms for achieving flexibility, and from applications to the field of economics to illustrations from management science. Collectively, they present a very confusing picture.

Because flexibility is a response to changing conditions, to variability, it seems most reasonable to begin defining it by categorizing and describing the types of variability to which a manufacturing organization must respond.

Requirements for Flexibility

There are five primary sources of variability that may require a manufacturing organization to be flexible: demand variability, supply variability, new-product introduction or product variability, new process introduction or process variability, and workforce and equipment variability. As we describe them, think about your organization and the extent to which it must cope with each of the types of variability.

Demand Variability

Demand variability is well recognized as a source of disruption in manufacturing. A plethora of demand-forecasting models attests to the fact that demand variability is an important factor in manufacturing businesses. These models attempt to assess trends and seasonality in demand and to identify levels of aggregation at which forecasts can be made most accurately. Inventory planning models, of which the economic order quantity (EOQ) models are the most popularly used, were also developed in response to a need to cope with variable demands on manufacturing. The advent of just-in-time

TABLE 8–1 Definitions of flexibility

Author	Type of Flexibility	Definition
Gerwin[a]	Mix flexibility	The processing at any one time of a mix of different parts loosely related to each other
	Parts flexibility	The addition of parts to the mix and removal of parts from the mix over time
	Routing flexibility	The dynamic assignment of parts to machines—that is, the rerouting of a given part if a machine used in its manufacture is incapacitated
	Design-change flexibility	The fast implementation of engineering design changes for a particular part
	Volume flexibility	The accommodation of shifts in volume for a given part
Buzacott[b]	State flexibility	The ability of the system to process a wide variety of parts of assemblies without intervention from outside to change the system
	Job flexibility	The ability of the system to cope with changes in the jobs to be processed in the system
	Machine flexibility	The ability of the system to cope with changes and disturbances at the machines and workstations
Browne[c]	Machine flexibility	Ease of making changes to a given set of parts
	Process flexibility	Ability to produce a given set of part types, each possible using different materials, in several ways
	Product flexibility	Ability to change over to produce a new (set of) product(s)
	Routing flexibility	Ability to handle breakdowns and to continue producing a given set of parts
	Volume flexibility	Ability to operate profitably at different production volumes
	Expansion flexibility	Capacity of building a system, and expanding it as needed, easily and modularly
	Operation flexibility	Ability to interchange the ordering of several operations for each part type
	Production flexibility	Ability to produce a large universe of part types
Jaikumar[d]	Process flexibility	Ability to reroute a part when a machine is down
	Program flexibility	Ability to run the system unattended during a shift
	Product flexibility	The total incremental value of new products that can be fabricated within the system for a defined cost of new fixtures, tools, and parts programming

[a] D. Gerwin, "The Do's and Don'ts of Computerized Manufacturing," *Harvard Business Review* 60, vol. 2 (March–April 1982), pp. 107–116.
[b] J. A. Buzacott, "The Fundamental Principles of Flexibility in Manufacturing Systems," *Proceedings of the First International Conference on Flexible Manufacturing Systems* (Brighton, UK, 1982).
[c] J. Browne, "Classification of Flexible Manufacturing Systems," *The FMS Magazine*, April 1984, pp. 114–117.
[d] R. Jaikumar, "Flexible Manufacturing Systems: A Managerial Perspective," unpublished working paper, Harvard Business School, 1984.

manufacturing has renewed focus on demand variability and its impact on the design of the manufacturing process.

Demand variability arises in two forms. It may be caused by the existence of a broad product mix, which may also vary over time. Automobile manufacturers typically provide a wide variety of options, thus practically ensuring that they never produce two cars in a row that are exactly alike. They must learn to cope with demand variability in the form of a broad and variable product mix.

Demand variability may also arise in the form of volume variability. Suppliers to retail sales channels often experience considerable variability in sales on a seasonal basis as their customers make holiday, beginning-of-school, and other seasonal purchases. Volume variability may be experienced by a manufacturer of a single product line or may compound the already complex management problem of broad product mix.

Thus, breadth of product line and variation in demand volume are both sources of demand variability with which manufacturing organizations must cope. How many different products does your organization sell? Do sales vary much from month to month? If your answers are "many" and "a lot," then your organization is clearly dealing with *demand variability*.

Supply Variability

Supply variability has also been widely recognized as a source of disruption for a manufacturing operation. Models to set safety stock levels and reorder points all recognize uncertain delivery lead times and variable incoming material quality as factors. Scrap and rework rates are accounted for in setting yield factors in materials-requirements planning systems. Minimizing supply variability is recognized as a basic tenet of just-in-time manufacturing.

As with demand variability, there are different dimensions of supply variability. First, the number of different parts to be procured is certainly a source of complexity similar to that introduced by the number of different products along the demand dimension. It likely implies that the organization must deal with a number of different suppliers as well.

In addition, timeliness of parts delivery and quality of parts received contribute to supply variability. Despite improved relationships with suppliers, uncertainty as to delivery and quality still remains. As the new Apple Macintosh facility was ramping up production in early 1984, it suffered two highly publicized experiences with supply uncertainty. A defective shipment of CRTs arrived from Japan that shut down the assembly facility briefly. About the same time, a shortage of memory chips also closed the facility. Despite just-in-time ties with vendors, supply was not 100 percent guaranteed. Furniture manufacturers, too, must cope with different qualities of raw materials as lumber is drawn from different locations. A sugar beet refiner deals with variability in sugar content of the raw beets fed into the refinery. Although these companies are in different industries, they must all deal with uncertainty about quality and timeliness of material delivery.

The introduction of new materials is yet another source of supply variability. Airframe manufacturers are still learning to fabricate composite (rather than aluminum) parts. Semiconductor manufacturers are accommodating gallium arsenide and ceramic substrates.

Number of different parts sourced, uncertainty as to timing and quality of delivery, and new materials all contribute to supply uncertainty in a manufacturing business. Does your company purchase many different component parts? Are those parts ever delivered late? Are they of variable quality? Have you introduced any new materials to your manufacturing process lately? If you answered yes to any or all of these questions, then your organization must be dealing with *supply variability*.

Product Variability

Product variability can range from the introduction of completely new products to the daily changes implemented on existing products. The rapid pace of technological evolution is causing industries to experience shorter product life cycles and higher product turnover. From 1964 to 1976, for example, IBM introduced only two families of mainframe computers. Between 1976 and 1980 new computer families were introduced at the rate of one per year. New-product introduction is therefore imposing a major requirement for flexibility on manufacturing businesses.

Closely related to new-product introduction is product change. Your company would be highly unusual if it didn't experience numerous engineering change orders on its products throughout their lives. Whether these changes are initiated by the customer, by engineering, or by production itself, they are clearly sources of variability with which the organization must cope.

Thus, new-product introductions and changes to existing products constitute what we call *product variability* for a manufacturing business. Does your organization experience product variability?

Process Variability

Process variability comes in two forms: introduction of new process technology and introduction of new process management techniques. Installation of new process technology is often closely related to the development and introduction of new products. Semiconductors, for example, have become smaller as the technology used to produce them has become capable of accurately embedding more functionality in smaller spaces on these devices. In this case, by necessity, introduction of product and process technologies go hand in hand.

In the machining industry, on the other hand, computer-controlled equipment and flexible manufacturing systems have significantly changed processes for manufacturing complex machined parts by reducing setup times and improving accuracy. While use of the new equipment is not necessarily required to build new products, the performance of the process is greatly improved.

In all, new process technologies such as these—whether developed internally, procured from equipment vendors, or copied from competitors—create complexity for manufacturers. In addition to the changes effected by the introduction of new process *technologies,* there is change associated with new process *management* techniques. In the recent past, materials-requirements planning (MRP) caused hundreds of companies to make fundamental changes in the management of their production processes. More recently, just-in-time (JIT), total quality commitment (TQC), design for manufacturability (DFM), and computer-integrated manufacturing (CIM) have all had an impact on the way that manufacturing organizations do business. These changes in process management can be accompanied (though not necessarily) by the introduction of new process technology as well.

Introduction of process change, whether in technology or in process management, imposes a degree of variability on the manufacturing organization. Do process technologies evolve rapidly in your industry? Do you have to develop new processes for the new products you introduce? Are you keeping up with the latest trends in new process management? If so, then your organization is dealing with what we call *process variability.*

Workforce and Equipment Variability

Finally, both labor and equipment employed in the production process are sources of variability. Labor turnover, absenteeism, and efficiency are causes of uncertainty in planning production. Economic conditions, the location of the manufacturing facility, the personnel policies of the company, and the treatment of the workforce influence the degree to which labor uncertainties are experienced.

In terms of consistent production of quality product and machine uptime, variations in equipment reliability can also create a source of uncertainty that has been well recognized in management models for doing job shop and preventive maintenance scheduling. Machines that wander out of tolerance as they operate, or that require frequent repair, cause an increased requirement for flexibility in a production operation. Thus, both *workforce and equipment variability* constitute the fifth type of variability to which manufacturing organizations must be responsive.

Summary—Five Types of Variability

We have argued that flexibility in manufacturing must be developed in response to some well-defined strategic need. In this section, strategic needs

TABLE 8–2 Uncertainty and complexity dimensions of variability

Type of Variability	Uncertainty Forms	Complexity Forms
Demand variability	Fluctuation in: Product mix Volume	Product mix
Supply variability	Changing delivery: Quality Timeliness	Number of parts New materials
Product variability		New products Changes to existing products
Process variability		Changes in process: Technology Management
Workforce and equipment variability	Labor: Absenteeism Turnover Equipment downtime	

have been described in terms of variability in the variety of forms shown in Table 8–2. A clear understanding of the types of variability your organization chooses to contend with to provide a competitive advantage is critical. Note that the source of variability need not necessarily always be external to the business itself. Once the workers and equipment sets are chosen and either hired or installed, workforce and equipment variability are largely internally generated. Demand variability, on the other hand, is more likely to originate outside the organization with the customer. Product variability lies somewhere in between. Hopefully, product changes are driven largely by customer demand, but they may also be due to internal reasons. Manufacturing may wish to have a product redesigned to make it more manufacturable, or marketing may ask that an additional feature be added. The organization must decide with how much and what type of variability it wants to contend, whether internally or externally derived. Let's examine a few examples of organizations that have developed flexibility in response to a perceived strategic need.

IBM's quick-turnaround-time–integrated circuit fabrication facility in East Fishkill, New York, is capable of building prototype ICs routinely in 18 days and, on an expedite basis, within 3 days. Most competitors require at least a six-week turnaround time on new designs. Strategically, this allows IBM to develop and introduce new products rapidly, as well as to economically produce custom ICs for pilot runs and small-volume sales. IBM is choosing to deal competitively with what we have called product variability.

Allen-Bradley spent $15 million over a period of two years to construct a fully automated motor-starter assembly plant in Milwaukee, Wisconsin, that today builds more than 700 different versions of motor starters in lot sizes as small as one. Orders received at the plant on one day are manufactured, tested, packaged, and shipped the next. At a time when most of its competitors were moving to the Far East to obtain low-cost labor for manual product assembly, Allen-Bradley has been able to obtain a considerable edge. In this case, Allen-Bradley is seeking competitive advantage in its ability to effectively and efficiently manage demand variability.

Even in the automobile industry, where long production runs on fixed-setup assembly lines have been a longstanding tradition, flexibility is being strongly considered in plant design and redesign decisions. General Motors plans to invest $52 million in an automated, highly flexible manufacturing plant in Saginaw, Michigan, to machine and assemble a family of axles for several different models of cars. The plant is a direct response to the shortening of product life cycles in the auto industry. It provides manufacturing capabilities that accommodate themselves to rapid design changes and product customization requirements.

For lower-volume automobile manufacturers (e.g., Saab, BMW, and Alfa-Romeo) manufacturing flexibility provides an opportunity to compete with the high-volume, low-cost producers. BMW pioneered sophisticated techniques for varying product mix randomly down common production lines, allowing increased resource use despite low unit-volume production. Austin Rover made extensive use of computer-aided engineering to reduce the new-product introduction cycle from five years to three and a half years, permitting it to bring new designs to market more quickly. Alfa-Romeo is piloting a flexible final assembly process using the Volvo group-assembly production model to achieve benefits similar to those sought by BMW.

All of these companies recognize manufacturing flexibility as a critical aspect of being competitive in their marketplaces and are organizing their manufacturing resources to achieve it. The possibility that your organization may have to cope with all five types of variability at one time is a daunting prospect. Yet, most of our organizations deal with them all. Whether we can handle all of them well is a good question, and one worth considering in the development of the strategic direction of the business. Let's look at the types of mechanisms companies use to make themselves more flexible along each of the dimensions we've described. Where conflicts among these mechanisms arise, potential for not achieving the strategic objectives of the firm exists.

CREATING PRODUCTION FLEXIBILITY

Traditionally, manufacturing organizations appeared flexible to the outside world by carrying inventory. To protect the production organization from the vagaries of customer demand, they carried finished-goods inventory. To obviate the disastrous impact of supply variability, they carried raw-materials inventories. And in case of variability in the process itself, in either equipment or labor, they carried work-in-process inventory. Thus, as shown in Figure 8–1, the production organization was well protected from the variability of the outside world, as well as from internally generated variability, and the organization as a whole appeared capable of responding to variability in demand, supply, and workforce and equipment.

Total quality commitment and just-in-time philosophies have forced a rethinking of the use of inventory as protection for the production organization. Many manufacturing organizations have steadily reduced their inventory levels to the bare minimum and expect the production organization to be able to respond directly to the variabilities it faces. Other organizations are struggling to eliminate that last layer of inventory, perhaps because they have not yet provided production with the capabilities it needs to respond to change in the absence of inventory.

FIGURE 8–1 Inventory buffers protecting production from supply, demand, and workforce and equipment variability

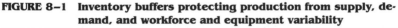

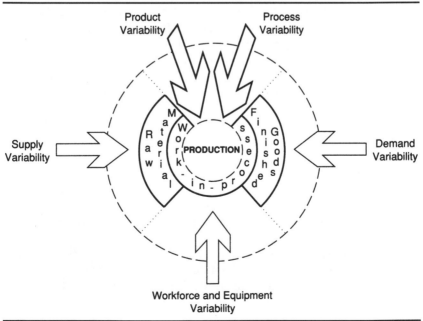

In addition to the philosophical changes encouraged by TQC and JIT, new product and process introductions are becoming more and more important. Inventory not only rarely protects production from changes in product or processes, it often becomes a deterrent to accommodating the required changes. Does your organization ever wait to implement an engineering change to a product because it wants to use up existing inventory first? The production organization is being forced to invent and implement a new set of coping mechanisms for dealing with all of the different types of variability.

The New Flexible Production Organization

Much has been done in production organizations to improve their flexibility. New, more flexible automation is at the heart of much of this change. Workforce flexibility is absolutely critical. And some cases require carrying some form of excess capacity—in operations research terms, *slack resources.*

Automation

Allen-Bradley's motor-starter plant is one of the best publicized examples of the use of automation to achieve flexibility, but there are others. Motorola's Bandit facility in Boca Raton, Florida, uses automation to produce a wide variety of pagers on demand. Benetton, the Italian sportswear company, has not only automated the knitting process for producing clothing but has integrated the entire supply chain—from raw materials through the retail outlets that sell its wares. By doing so, it is able to respond rapidly to changing demands all over the world.

There are several different aspects to automating for flexibility. Numerical control and other equipment programmed for rapid setup allow for quick modification in response to product mix variability, new-product introduction, and product change. Automatic tool-changing ability or the ability to keep different tools online similarly accommodate changing product mix and often new products as well. Automated material-handling equipment and sophisticated part-loading devices can expedite delivery of materials to the production system. Finally, investment in multipurpose equipment provides flexibility as well. Thus, there are a number of aspects of automation to keep in mind if flexibility is an objective of your organization.

Another important aspect of most automated environments is automated information management, often referred to as CIM. Provision of just-in-time information to the people or equipment performing the production process can play a critical role in providing ultimate flexibility. Computer-aided design/computer-aided manufacturing (CAD/CAM) links allow for rapid translation of new product designs or design changes from the drawing board to the production floor. Real-time scheduling systems allow products to be rerouted around bottleneck activities. Data collection for feedback and control purposes is equally important. Having sensors and computer controls for detection and handling of unanticipated problems (e.g., poor material quality, equipment breakdowns) allows for rapid response to these forms of variability.

Automation, then, whether of the physical process or of the associated material flows, can be an important means of achieving flexibility in the production organization. In the quest to implement the latest process technologies, however, the human aspects of the production system must not be neglected.

Workforce Flexibility

Development of a flexible workforce must go hand in hand with implementation of flexible automation if automation is a chosen solution. In other cases, a flexible workforce alone may provide the needed degree of flexibility. There are a number of ways in which production organizations are improving the flexibility of their workforces.

Many companies are attempting to integrate shop floor workers more fully into the production process. In doing so, companies typically provide extensive training to the workers in statistical process control techniques so that they can attempt to stabilize the process, even in the face of constantly changing inputs or required outputs. Further, the company may cross train workers in multiple tasks. Cross training increases production flexibility in several ways: It familiarizes employees with all activities throughout the production process, thus giving them a better picture of the whole and how their job affects overall output. It allows for efficient redeployment of the workforce as demand changes. Absent employees' jobs can be more easily covered and workstations can be quickly restructured without considerable disruption or need for extensive retraining.

Cross training to achieve flexibility is not, however, restricted to manufacturing industries. Lechmere Inc., a 27-store retail chain owned by Dayton Hudson, had used the traditional approach to covering variability in customer traffic through their stores by hiring a large number of part-time workers who could be scheduled to cover peak demand requirements. Around Sarasota, Florida, where unemployment rates run as low as 4 percent, this approach was not feasible. Instead, the Sarasota store offers its employees raises based upon the number of jobs they learn to perform. Having motivated a highly cross-trained workforce, it can accommodate changes in customer demand by rapidly redeploying the workforce as needed. Cross training was an important element of Lechmere's ability to compete in the Sarasota environment.

Another tool used by many companies is the concept of flex force. Employing a flex force entails qualifying a list of people from the local community who are interested in periodic, part-time work—people the company can call during periods of need. These people do not become permanent parts of the company payroll, so they do not cost the company anything when they are not working, but they are an available, trained resource that can be tapped when necessary. They can be used either to respond to variability in demand volume or to fill in capability gaps caused by other types of variability. For example, demand for printed circuit board assemblies may be such that an unusually high amount of hand load work is required in a given month. Availability of a ready, trained workforce may be useful in responding to such a demand. A flexible workforce, achieved through increased employee involvement, workforce cross training, or development of a well-trained flex force, is likely to be a critical aspect of achieving production flexibility.

Other Mechanisms

There are a number of other ways for production to become more flexible that do not necessarily require investment in equipment or a flexible workforce. In the quest for just-in-time manufacturing, many organizations have reduced setup times significantly. They have done so through parts kitting, equipment dedication, production sequencing, and other such techniques. Decreased setup times improve production's responsiveness to various types of variability.

The production organization may also choose to carry excess capacity (slack) so that it can be made available during periods of peak demand or so that there are extra resources to be deployed as product mix varies. The company may maintain excess capacity internally in the form of employees or equipment. Or it may choose to develop strong relationships with subcontractors to provide services in time of high demand. In particular, the company may contract capacity to supplement its bottleneck operations. For example, a sheet metal production facility that chronically runs short of capacity at its punch presses may occasionally choose to subcontract some of its punching requirements.

Summary

There are a number of techniques that production can employ to become more flexible in response to any of the five types of variability, including the following:

- Employ flexible automation.
- Integrate manufacturing information management.
- Cross train the workforce.

- Employ a flex force.
- Reduce setup times.
- Maintain excess capacity, internal or external.

Most organizations use a combination of these techniques to improve production's overall flexibility.

FLEXIBILITY IS NOT PRODUCTION'S JOB ALONE

Thus far we have focused our discussion on the activities that production can undertake to improve the flexibility of a manufacturing business. It is critical, however, that all functions in a manufacturing business be involved in the achievement of flexibility. In particular, marketing and R&D have important roles to play. Production cannot and should not be asked to shoulder the entire burden of providing flexibility by itself.

Marketing's Role in Creating a Flexible Organization

The marketing organization plays an important role in managing the interface between the customer and the manufacturing organization. In assuming this role, it can have a significant effect on the amount of demand variability that eventually hits the production operation. There are a couple of ways that marketing can effectively smooth demand before it reaches production, neither of which should significantly affect customer perception of responsiveness from the organization.

First, marketing is responsible for planning and executing promotional activities that have direct impact on demand. By planning these activities to coincide with periods of low demand, marketing can effectively smooth production's build schedule. Postholiday sales are a good example of attempts to smooth demand (and thereby revenue). While it is unusual to actually find a marketing organization that thinks about manufacturing in its planning of promotional events, it doesn't seem unreasonable to expect that they could. They are accustomed, after all, to hosting sales to rid the organization of excess inventory *after* production has built it. Why not plan ahead?

Marketing also plays a critical role in the definition and positioning of the product. If it performs this exercise creatively, it can reduce significantly the impact of a broad product mix on production. Hewlett-Packard's signal analysis division, for example, recently introduced a line of new instrumentation products that consist of multiple modules integrated in a single rack. Each module has different functionality. Together, a collection of modules creates an instrument that meets a certain set of customer specifications. By mixing and matching the modules, the specific requirements of any given customer can be met; production has only to build the small number of modules that make up the total instrument.

The customers perceive that they are receiving customized products, while production is dealing with a minimal product mix. By defining product features in small packages that can be combined as required to meet customer requirements, marketing was able to minimize the impact on production of multiple customer demands.

Thus, marketing can have a significant impact on the variability and on the perceived flexibility of the company. It can either reduce the absolute variability experienced by the organization through promotional events, or it can support definition of a broad product mix through modularity in product design. In the latter exercise, it must work closely with the R&D organization as well as with manufacturing.

R&D's Role in Achieving Flexibility

As rapid new-product introduction becomes increasingly important to successful competitive positioning, R&D's role in providing flexibility will grow. Most often, the way in which R&D can make a contribution to the overall flexibility of the organization is through application of a set of standard design rules and standard components in their designs. Both are critically important to the ability of the entire organization to produce and deliver new products to the marketplace in a timely fashion.

It is becoming popular to embed a set of design rules in the computer-aided design packages used by product engineers. These rules direct the designer to use product characteristics that best match the production process currently in place. They may, for example, describe part-spacing requirements on a printed circuit board assembly or optimal fold angles on a sheet metal box. In any case, they are intended to reflect the cost trade-offs inherent in the production process in which the product will be made.

Some systems even go so far as to present the designer with explicit cost information. At Hewlett-Packard's Roseville networks division, an expert system called the manufacturing knowledge expert (MAKE) provides cost estimates to printed circuit board assembly designers that allow them to make trade-offs during the design process. They can immediately see, for example, the impact of including a part in their design that will have to be hand loaded rather than automatically inserted. Selecting the low-cost solution will probably result in the fastest throughput time as well, because it likely employs the most available processes.

Just as critical to flexible operations is the use of a common set of parts in a product design. Many manufacturing organizations have undertaken programs to significantly reduce the number of parts used in their products.

IBM, for example, reports a 25 to 30 percent reduction in the number of parts used to produce its goods. Others report similar reductions. Using parts from a common and existing set of preferred parts provides an obvious advantage for achieving flexibility. Production doesn't need to qualify a new set of vendors on a new set of parts; it can use parts it already procures to build the new product. New products can be built and tested much more quickly. In addition, fewer parts implies the possibility of fewer setups, thus reducing cycle time and improving the ability to respond to broad product mix. In sum, R&D has an important role to play in the achievement of manufacturing flexibility through adherence to a strict set of design rules and selection from a limited set of preferred design parts.

ORGANIZATION STRUCTURE AND FLEXIBILITY

We have described the individual roles that production, marketing, and R&D have to play in the achievement of flexibility, each of which is important and unique. But they must all ultimately play together to provide flexibility, and their ability to do so is a function of the design of the organization.

In his "information processing view of an organization," Jay Galbraith provides a nice description of the effect of variability on an organization and of the design choices that an organization makes to respond to variability.[1] An organization that deals with little variability from any source can be run largely through the application of rules and procedures. Any exceptions can be processed by passing them up the hierarchy. As the organization faces increasing variability, however, the number of exceptions to be handled becomes overwhelming and the efficiency of the hierarchical organization begins to break down. In some cases, replacement of the rules and procedures with more broadly based guidelines helps. Ultimately, however, the organization will likely have to select a new structure that is more suited to the variable environment in which it operates. It has a couple of options.

First, the organization may choose to improve its communications ability both laterally and vertically. The more effectively and efficiently information can be communicated either across the organization or up and down the hierarchy of command, the more rapidly the organization can deal with change. The advent of computer-integrated manufacturing (CIM) clearly addresses communication requirements. By managing common manufacturing information and ensuring that the most current information is available as needed, CIM improves the organization's responsiveness to variability. Tracy O'Rourke, CEO of Allen-Bradley, claims that the most difficult part of the implementation of its automated motor-starter plant was not the automation but the information-management system that overlays the automated factory. Clearly, well-executed information management is what allows the factory to build 700 different versions of the product on demand.

The organization may also choose to restructure into what Galbraith calls "self-contained tasks," by which he means structuring the organization into subunits that are focused on well-defined outputs. Further, each subunit is provided with all of the resources it needs to provide its output. Hewlett-Packard's (HP) product-focused organization is a good example. Rather than complicate a large organization with handling the rapidly expanding product line of instrumentation and computational products, HP spun off individual product divisions that had full capability and responsibility for a limited set of products. Each division contained marketing, manufacturing, R&D, finance, and personnel functions to support its product charter. Only the sales organization remained centralized. Each division had to deal only with the variability imposed by the specific marketplace for its products, a much simplified set of the total HP demand.

Another form of self-contained tasks commonly found in practice is the application of group technology to form-machining centers or cells. In this case, parts with common characteristics or requiring a common set of equipment or tooling are grouped together. All of the production equipment needed for their manufacture is colocated in a cell, many of which may make up the total production floor. These cells then concentrate on the production of a limited number of similar types of parts and do not experience the full variability of the factory.

It is important to understand that these concepts can be applied at various levels in the manufacturing organization. While sweeping organizational changes must be instigated by senior management, there are similar applications of these concepts that can be made at middle- and lower-management levels as well. Application of just-in-time concepts, even in small parts of a factory, effectively tightens communication linkages between individuals. (There is no longer a wall of inventory preventing communication between workstations.) Computerized information management within a work cell is another possibility.

Quality circles, which are today evolving into high-performance work systems, are yet another form of self-contained task. They effectively serve to bring together all individuals involved in the creation of a specific output to work on the problems associated with producing that output in an efficient, effective manner. By limiting their focus to a small number of outputs, they effectively limit the variability with which they must deal.

Organizational structure is critical to the achievement of manufacturing flexibility. Through improved communication linkages, either vertical or horizontal, and the creation of self-contained tasks, an organization's ability to handle variability, to be flexible, can be greatly improved.

THE FLEXIBILITY MODEL

We have defined the five types of variability for which an organization may wish to develop flexibility: demand, supply, product, process, and workforce and equipment variability. Further, we have described the roles not only of the production function, but of the marketing and R&D functions as well in responding flexibly to demand for change. Finally, we have discussed the importance of organizational structure in the organization's ability to be flexible. We have a model of manufacturing flexibility (Figure 8–2).

There are many trade-offs to be made. First, the organization must understand which types of variability are to be dealt with in achieving its competitive advantage. Will it attempt rapid and frequent new-product introduction? Or will it produce a limited product line for which volume variability is an issue? Is it operating in a business (e.g., sugar refining or logging) in which supply variability is a significant factor? Or is process variability the name of the game as it is in the semiconductor industry? Whatever its primary mode, it is important that your company understand what types of variability it is dealing with, because each may require different

FIGURE 8–2 R&D and marketing roles in managing variability

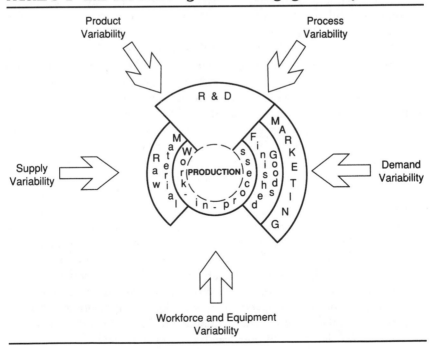

types of flexibility on the part of the organization. Ultimately, most of the trade-offs occur in production, where all variability not managed elsewhere comes to rest. There are many questions to be asked. Will the flexible equipment that is being purchased to build the existing broad product mix also accommodate numerous new-product introductions? Or would it be better to employ a more manual process under the assumption that *people* are easier to set up for new products than equipment is? Will limiting part count in an attempt to minimize the impact of broad product mix on production cause it to be inflexible in new-product introduction efforts? The production function has much to gain from an understanding of how it will achieve flexibility along all of the required dimensions.

The astute manufacturing manager will make clear both the types of variability to which his or her organization must respond and the role that the marketing and R&D organizations are expected to play in creating the ultimate flexible organization. It is only through cooperation among the functions and a full understanding of the trade-offs to be made that a manufacturing business can be truly flexible.

FLEXIBILITY IS A STRATEGIC DIRECTION

Now that we understand what flexibility is and how to achieve it in a manufacturing organization, let's return to the strategic perspective with which we started. For years, U.S. manufacturers have focused on cost reduction as a primary source of competitive advantage. Through increased machine use and direct labor utilization, they sought to deliver goods to the marketplace at the lowest possible cost. Meanwhile, their Japanese competitors, listening to the words of Deming and Juran, selected quality as their primary focus. Through application of total quality control (TQC) and statistical process control (SPC) along with quality circle and employee involvement structures, they pursued productivity improvement *through* quality improvement. U.S. manufacturers persisted in believing that quality could be achieved only at great cost and, as a result, continued to lag behind in both productivity and quality.

What we did not understand during those times of great focus on single dimensions (i.e., cost or quality) of manufacturing performance is that we could successfully pursue more than one dimension simultaneously. Why? The dimensions are not orthogonal but rather may be fully complementary. Quality and cost were eventually seen as complementary: Pursuing quality made cost reduction, or productivity improvement, possible. There is a growing belief that flexibility, too, can be an objective complementary to cost reduction.

FIGURE 8–3 Hayes–Wheelwright product/process matrix

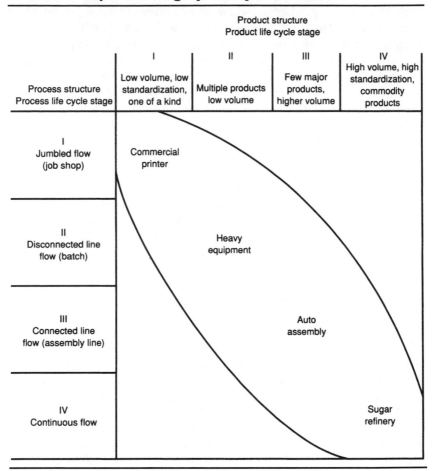

The Changing Product/Process Matrix

Hayes and Wheelwright[2] popularized the concept of the product/process matrix shown in Figure 8–3. The best place to position a manufacturing organization, they argued, was on the diagonal of the matrix where process capabilities are best matched to product requirements. The existence today of flexible equipment changes this picture (see Figure 8–4). By employing flexible automation along with the techniques described in this chapter for achieving flexibility, organizations are able to afford low-cost factories that can serve multiple types of product requirements.

The new term being used to describe this picture is *economies of scope*. In contrast to *economies of scale* where cost advantage was gained

FIGURE 8–4   Product/process matrix historical evolution

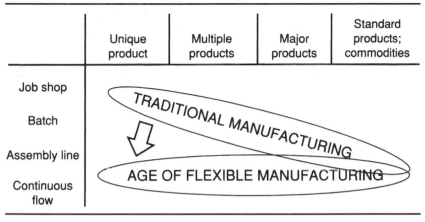

through production of great volumes of few items, economies of scope implies that similar gains can be achieved by producing many different products whose individual volumes add up to large total plant volume. Flexibility is critical to achieving economies of scope.

Flexibility and the Japanese

Although Japanese manufacturers appear to be evolving new capabilities for manufacturing flexibility rapidly, they have traditionally not been as flexible as U.S. manufacturers. A comparison of the two approaches sheds some light on the strategic role of flexibility in market positioning.

The Japanese focus considerable attention on maintaining flexibility on the shop floor to allow rapid response to manufacturing disruptions, such as machine breakdowns and quality problems (the category we have labeled workforce and equipment variability). To do so, they use cross-trained labor, investment in redundant equipment (excess capacity), U-shaped rather than L-shaped layouts, and other such techniques. Historically, U.S. manufacturers have focused more on resource utilization and have therefore tended more often to dedicate labor and equipment to specific tasks. Furthermore, the Japanese choose local suppliers and through JIT materials-management techniques are able to maintain flexibility to respond to engineering design changes, production schedule changes, quality problems, and other related changes without huge inventory write-offs.

There is, however, an apparent limit to the amount of flexibility that is considered acceptable to ask of a Japanese manufacturing organization. Production schedules frequently are frozen at a certain point, and Japanese companies often reduce product-line breadth or increase customer minimum-order sizes rather than allow significant variation in demands placed on the manufacturing organization. U.S. manufacturers have created markets through product differentiation and have been much more responsive to the demands of the marketplace because of their ability to customize products and maintain multiple-product options.

Support of lifetime employment policies in Japan may limit its flexibility in handling demand volume fluctuations through workforce sizing. Unionization of the workforce and existence of lengthy work-rule lists may provide a similar limitation in the United States; however, Japanese attitudes toward flexible use of the workforce are currently being debated by the United Auto Workers. The NUMMI (New United Motors Manufacturing Inc.) concept—an American-flavored Japanese labor-management system—requires assembly-line workers to go from performing individual, narrowly defined tasks to working as part of a team. Application of such a concept gives management greater flexibility in running the plant but requires workers to have a broader skill base.

Finally, there are indications that Japanese organizations are rigid in handling new-product introductions. To develop and introduce new products successfully, they often establish separate new-product development project teams that operate independently of the rest of the organization (a form of self-contained task). IBM used a similar technique for the development and introduction of the PC Jr.

Thus, relative to the United States, the Japanese emphasize shop floor flexibility in response to machine and quality disruption but limit their responsiveness to marketplace demands for customization and broad product mix. They do not view workforce size as a source of adaptability but do extensive cross training so the workforce in place can be used flexibly. They apparently have difficulty innovating and introducing new products efficiently within their existing structures. Such contrasts suggest that there are in fact different strategic approaches to flexibility.

CONCLUSION

Flexibility is an important strategic choice to be understood and made by manufacturing businesses today. An astute manager will first recognize the different reasons for having flexibility—responsiveness to demand, supply, product, process, or workforce and equipment variability—and then put in place the mechanisms appropriate to achieving the desired type and level of flexibility. When used judiciously as a complement to cost and quality objectives, flexibility is potentially the new basis for competition in the next decade.

NOTES

1. Jay Galbraith, "Organizational Design: An Information Processing View," *Interfaces* (May 1974): 28–30.

2. Robert H. Hayes and Steven C. Wheelwright, *Restoring Our Competitive Edge: Competing Through Manufacturing* (New York: John Wiley & Sons, 1984), 208–223.

PEOPLE DEVELOPMENT AND THE TRANSFORMATION TO TEAMS

9

Burgess Oliver

Editor's note

Self-directed work teams and empowerment are best described by someone who has been there. Indeed, Burgess Oliver credits much of the success of his organization to employees working together, harnessing their creativity and energies to tackle innovation.

Reach, teach, empower, and equip have been the critical people-development processes in the five-year journey to creating self-managed work teams at Northern Telecom's Nashville Repair and Distribution Center.[1] Burgess Oliver, director of operations, provided the spark for this team development and employee growth. Throughout this chapter, he will share how NRDC moved through these processes and the requirements for the individual leading the process, the *we* characteristics, actions taken, systems required, results, and restarts. Trusting others, also addressed, is the final necessary ingredient that brought teamwork to NRDC.

A PERSONAL EDUCATION

I started down the path toward believing in the power of people working together before *teams* was a buzzword. Twenty years old and fresh from a bad

152

experience with college, I started out in manufacturing in 1962 as an assembler in a Trane Corporation plant start-up in Lexington, Kentucky. I soon found that the work ethics I had learned from childhood in the hills of southern West Virginia—doing afterschool jobs for bosses such as Roy Chambers, Bernard Zappin, Harry Hatfield, George Spalding, and Dick Roddy—were a far cry from those I would encounter in this first factory experience.

But I found encouragement; on the third shift we had to be smarter than management to get anything accomplished. Trane was where I heard of J.F.K.'s death and where I helped tackle an employee who needed his thumb sewn back on. I experienced the meanness of union campaigns. And I learned to become a welder from experienced employees like Thad Jarras.

I left this position for 10¢ more per hour at GTE Sylvania as a forktruck driver. Because of the long lead times on delivery of fork trucks, I often had no truck to drive and spent much of my time sweeping dirt out of seams in the floor. At age 22, this was so boring that I started learning the production jobs and found a new source of money—overtime on a second shift at time-and-a-half pay. By the time Sylvania started a third shift, I landed a supervisor's job, the natural position since I knew all the jobs on the line and came to work every day. It did not matter that I knew nothing about managing people.

I soon discovered that if you treated people with decency and respect, they would work hard for you and do a good job. We outperformed the other shifts, by hook or crook. I took my first supervision training class, Effective Supervision, and learned firsthand the impact job training had on personal improvement. My eyes were open to the possibilities ahead, the start of my 30-year journey filled with new experiences that have led to the development of the reach, teach, empower, and equip approach—an evolutionary process necessary for an organization and its employees to reach a mature level of team development.

THE NASHVILLE REPAIR AND DISTRIBUTION CENTER

The Nashville Repair and Distribution Center (NRDC) had experienced a difficult and colorful past, including profitability problems, inconsistent management practices, unionization, and decertification of the union. In October 1989, we struggled for survival after a major downsizing of more than 600 employees (down to 211) and the movement of all new product manufacturing to other locations in Northern Telecom. NRDC was left with a small-scale repair business for a group of products that had been manufacturer discontinued and a horrible customer-service operation.

We survived and went forward with a small core of remaining employees and a management team that had shrunk from seven levels to three. We were going to use the teaming concept to help as NRDC moved into a new business and style of management. Not only would we survive, we would thrive. But our first step was to reach both the employees and the management group; we had to convince them to change the way we had done business and that a team environment was the best approach.

Reaching

In the reaching process, we were trying to accomplish Webster's definition of *reach:* "To communicate with; to make an impression on; to influence or affect." We also wanted to initiate change rather than inherit it from an outside source. We were in a fragile position within Northern Telecom: It would be a great challenge just to stay open. We had to understand the nature of change and implement it with as little disruption as possible. So we became a repair center for Nortel's desktop products, made up of both multimedia and business communications products; later we entered the remanufacturing equipment sales arena as well.

Once I reached the managers and the employees, the next task was to look within, to begin a process I call the *me* of getting started. It's a process of stepping back, looking inside, and evaluating whether the leader has both the position *and* the core values necessary to take the leadership role in starting the teaming process. What is required of the champion of teaming?[2]

To effectively initiate teams within an organization, the leadership and direction must come from the senior level of management within the business unit. Championing teams from this position allows for the development of strategic objectives to guide the team journey. In their book, *High Performance Enterprises,* Donna Neusch and Alan Siebenaler explain how the alignment of strategic objectives is key to the process.[3] Core values and traits such as patience, innovation, customer orientation, quality focus, as well as being a listener, learner, and change agent, are key attributes one must have to effectively move an organization to successful team implementation.

Evaluating one's ability to be the leader of change is certainly not easy. Arthur Miller Jr. calls these values and traits *gifts.*[4] He believes that a company should search out the important *me* characteristics required to accomplish certain tasks such as implementing teams. Many organizations attempt to do this in reverse order by first hiring or assigning an individual to the position of team champion without regard to the person's position or core values and traits.

Once an organization decides to move forward in team development, and the leader or champion is identified, it needs to set a course by clear strategic objectives: What is to be accomplished, and how? A few basic strategic goals allow the organization to function as a macro team unit; these objectives became directional indicators on our journey.

The newly formed Nashville Repair and Distribution Center started with five basic strategic objectives:

1. Excel in managing the business.
2. Excel in all aspects of quality.
3. Develop our people.
4. Exceed customer expectations in service.
5. Reduce overall cost.

We soon added two more goals: develop working teams and improve our environmental impact. We supported these with a vision for NRDC to become the lowest-cost/fastest North American center for repair or close it down. Out of this groundwork grew our first mission statement: Exceed customer expectations in the remanufacture, distribution, and services of Northern Telecom products.

As we prepared for teaming, we realized that many successful businesses were involved in team development. Some truths emerged: Treat people with respect and dignity. None of us is as smart as all of us together. Our team members—those employees engaged in the immediate work—know more about that work, so they should have more input in how it gets done. And, with fewer managers spending more time away from the business units in activities to grow the business, *self-managing teams* were a logical result. Finally, we recognized that managers can't solve all the problems—we had too many.

Teaching

Even though these elements were in place, we quickly found that we had to do more than talk about being a team. Following up with the right actions and skills to accomplish the objectives was the real challenge. There were few team-development tools available at a price we could afford, so we researched what team development meant and, through the efforts of Tim Smith, a member of the management team, we created NRDC team-development tools. These helped us to structure and guide our day-to-day work from a teaming perspective: team role definitions and guidelines; boundary definitions to clarify responsibilities and decision-making authority; and a transfer of responsibility matrix, which would spell out the process of what business management functions the teams would take over and when.

We learned to check the health and progress of the organization on its course of team development. In 1991, the journal of the Association of

Manufacturing Excellence, *Target* magazine, published a survey and fol-lowup article, which told us a lot about ourselves as a business unit—espe-cially in the areas of communication and training—and gave us a chance to address problems.[5] The managers held a series of meetings to decide and agree on the components of a team. In this way, we could explain to our em-ployees what we thought comprised a team and begin the teaching process.

Figure 9–1 depicts the NRDC self-managed work team components. To better prepare for what lay ahead, and continuing the self-education process, we also listed the best, worst, and most probable things that might happen to us on this journey and spent several hours sharing them with our employees (see Figure 9–2).

The exercise proved that understanding what to expect helped us to better manage the change to teams and created a readiness to learn more. Because the input from many members of the organization generated a col-lection of consistent ideas for what a team environment would look and feel like, as a group we embarked on developing the skills that would allow us to become a team-based organization at the plant level, or what I have some-times called the macro level. We were coming together, and the growing sense that we were becoming aligned and self-directed propelled us further.

Training soon became an issue: It was time to begin in earnest. Who would be the champions of this team development as we continued the teaching effort? In the past, I had not seen good long-term results from the use of a few key people as champions or specialists for developing a team

FIGURE 9-1 Components of a team

• Willing to share	• Honest
• Responsibility	• Open
• Communication	• Accountable for results
• Confidence	• Participation
• Commitment	• Incentives and rewards
• Knowledge, skills, and abilities	• Team pride
• Ownership	• Supportive
• Enthusiasm	• Maximizing skills
• Innovative	• Organized effort
• Feeling good about everything	• Making decisions
• Common task	• Success
• Evolving process	• Trusting
• Empowerment	• Loyalty
• Cross training	• Flexibility

FIGURE 9-2   Best, worst, and most probable outcomes of NRDC self-managed work teams

Best	Worst	Most probable
• Growth	• Confusion	• Prepare for degrees of best and worst
• Successful division	• Failure	
• Efficient	• No more fun	• Will take a long time
• Good for employees	• Conflict	• Confusion
• Sense of ownership	• Backstabbing	• Gradual acceptance
• High level of involvement	• Lose people	• Be prepared for setbacks
• Satisfied customers	• Competition	
• Fun place to work	• Not sharing	• Improved coordination
• Job security	• No trust	• Will cost a lot of money
• Improved attendance	• Lose common objectives	• Will need training
• Profit	• No teamwork	• Not everyone invested
• Cost-effective operation	• Individualism	• Establish proactive strategy
• Recognition	• Out of business	• Lack of management participation
		• Constant feedback
		• Benchmarking
		• Won't be for everyone
		• Some casualties
		• Peer pressure
		• Goals become common

environment. I had been part of a group of champions in a business unit that failed after several of the members moved out of the organization, an all-too-common occurrence. Each individual at NRDC needed the skill sets that a champion possessed, which would guarantee participation in team development and avoidance of the vacuum effect created by the inevitable departure of key individuals.

I researched the skills of champions I had known from my old group and checked the findings against other champions outside Northern Telecom. I found that champions were change masters; they had no fear of change, and the stress created was actually positive stress. Champions had good customer skills and received extensive training in it, averaging more than 100 training hours in the subject; they had excellent communication skills and received an average of 175 hours training in that area. These individuals were also masters of diversity; they not only understood skin-color diversity but appreciated the differences brought by age, gender, education, and job level. All of them had more than 100 hours of training in diversity awareness. Champions had extensive training in problem-solving (total quality management) tools. One champion interviewed had more than 600 hours of training in problem-solving techniques—and the average in this group was 350 hours. Overall, they averaged more than 700 hours of training in a broad range of subjects. It is easy to see that in many cases the champion possesses extensive training in the core values and skills.

We decided to provide 64 hours of training in the areas of change, customer awareness (including the internal customer), communication skills, diversity awareness, and problem-solving skills before we started to create business-unit-level teams. After the basic skills training was complete, we began the journey to self-managed teams. The designation could just as easily have been high-performance teams or self-directed, but we felt self-managed fit us best—a group of NRDC people working together to accomplish common business objectives.

Empowering

Trusting employees to form teams was the key to getting started at the micro level following initial training for champion skills. And, for the first time since the 1930s and Taylorism, we asked production employees and office-support personnel to start contributing to the growth of the business. NRDC defined empowerment as providing all our people with the resources and skills necessary to make recommendations/decisions regarding daily and long-term business decisions. It boiled down to trust.

Equipping

Will Rogers said, "Even if you are on the right road, you'll get run over if you don't move." There were many false starts and failed attempts at various team tasks. We soon found we had to restart the reach–teach–empower process because teams did not function well on the initial training only. We had to *equip* the teams with additional skills to be more effective communicators, coordinators, and managers of time.

Early Team Meetings

The weekly, one-hour team business meetings that NRDC had empowered its employees to conduct embodied this challenge. It was not enough to form teams, train them, and entrust them with responsibility, so we equipped employees with meeting-management and organization skills. There is a relevant line in Disney's *Toy Story:* "If you don't know how to fly, know how to fall with style." While the newly established climate of trust made it okay to fall once or twice, we wanted to help teams *avoid* falling if they could. We had to help teams learn effective business management skills to prevent setbacks and the additional training to equip them to deal with early failure experiences. Not only did the equipping process remedy the immediate problem, it vaulted us to a new level of sophistication, which in turn inspired a new cycle of reaching, teaching, and empowering the employees to take still greater responsibility. Awareness, skills, knowledge, and willingness to learn grew accordingly.

It took two years for the teams to reach a functioning stage. Several other things had also been developing during this time. Another significant lesson learned during this time involved our steering committee, a group originally made up of NRDC senior staff; this committee failed. We realized that staff would operate in a business-as-usual manner on the committee unless we brought representatives from the production floor and office-support teams onboard. The committee reorganized with an annually rotated makeup of three production-associate members, three support-staff members, and three senior-management staff members elected by their peer groups.

We also failed in selecting and training team facilitators. First, we tried to use the unit supervisor as the team facilitator—a bad move, because the former supervisors brought old baggage to the role and could not function as neutral facilitators. Instead, we assigned individuals from outside the immediate work area and began a facilitator training program. These corrective actions also provided development opportunities for the facilitators to learn about group dynamics and team processes, to understand new areas, and to move outside their comfort zones.

CONTINUOUS IMPROVEMENT AND SUPPORT SYSTEMS

During the growth period of getting teams to function, we found it necessary to continually improve and develop the systems that support the teaming process. These fell into several areas: the boundaries of teams, transfer of responsibilities, team versus management, measurements, the employee review process, additional training, and communications from team to management and back to team.

Boundaries were probably one of the most discussed issues in the early development of teams. Management staff members spent more than 100 hours discussing what boundaries meant, attending seminars, and reviewing various processes that different companies had used to accomplish clear

FIGURE 9–3   Decision-making boundaries

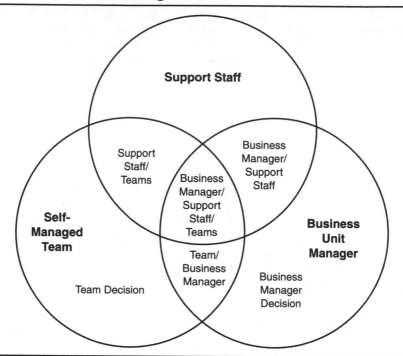

boundaries. What we ended up with was a fairly simple plan (see Figure 9–3) that stated the following: Each time a team, support staff, or management makes a decision, it should ask itself whether the decision affects any of the other groups. An example: A team is empowered to schedule overtime if it feels it is necessary, but it needs to check with engineering or facilities, to ensure that nothing is going to be shut down over the weekend, and with management, so the food services can be made available.

THE SIMPLE TRUTH ABOUT BOUNDARIES

A production associate stopped me recently and said she finally understood boundaries: "You know, it's all about respecting the other groups and communicating in the same manner you would want to be communicated with." This, of course, is the simple truth about boundaries.

The transfer of responsibilities from the NRDC management group to teams has been difficult. But a development tool created (Figure 9–4) by

FIGURE 9–4 NRDC self-directed work teams' transfer of responsibility matrix

PROCESS				
Jobs/responsibilities	Now	% Partly	Later	Review Date
1. Vacation tracking				
2. Vacation approval				
3. Scheduled cross training				
4. Track cross training				
5. Attendance tracking				
6. Scheduled overtime				

Training

_____

Expectations

_____

former training coordinator Tim Smith has helped manage the process. It accomplished several things: First, it allowed teams to establish training schedules and priorities. Second, it let our business-unit managers (the new designation for supervisor, since that term no longer fit) know the status of any team's progress in becoming self-managed. Third, it let the training coordinator look at key areas of training that would meet the needs of all teams, for example, interviewing, selecting and hiring skills to allow the teams to hire their own team members.[6]

7-Ups

Measurement of how a team is operating in relation to the overall business objectives is accomplished via a process we call 7-ups (Figure 9–5) that allows us to look at key business metrics at the team level using a continuous-improvement process specific to that team. As we moved through the team-

FIGURE 9–5 Repair customer quality index
NRDC—June 1996

Overall Results—7.50

Outgoing manufacturing quality (DPKU)	Complete correct shipments %	On-time delivery (CRD) %	Installation returns (DOA) DPKU	Service returns (warranty) %	Repair turn-around days	Customer complaints Ratio		
25.6	99.8	94.9	0.26	0.04	8	0.15	Performance Score	
2.0	100%	100%	0.1	0.05%	8	0	10	Leading
4.0	99.5%	95.0%	0.2	0.07%	9	1.0	9	Leading
6.0	99%	90.0%	0.3	0.09%	10	1.3	8	Leading
8.0	98.5%	85.0%	0.4	0.10%	11	1.6	7	Competitive
10.0	98%	80.0%	0.5	0.12%	13	1.9	6	Competitive
12.0	97.5%	75.0%	0.6	0.15%	15	2.2	5	Competitive
15.0	97%	70.0%	0.7	0.18%	16	2.5	4	Lagging
18.0	96.5%	65.0%	0.9	0.20%	17	2.8	3	Lagging
20.0	96%	60.0%	1.0	0.24%	18	3.1	2	Lagging
24.0	95.5%	55.0%	1.2	0.25%	20	3.4	1	Lagging
>24.0	<95.5%	<55.0%	>1.2	>0.25%	>20	>3.4	0	Lagging

0	9	8	8	10	10	9	Score
0.15	0.10	0.25	0.15	0.10	0.15	0.10	× Weight
0	0.090	2.00	0.90	1.00	1.50	0.90	= Index

FIGURE 9-5 Continued

Overall Results—9.2

Outgoing manufacturing quality (defects)	Efficiency %	CRD %	Materials variance $K	In-service warranty returns (%)	Labor variance $K	Safety audit (DPKU)	Performance Score	
2	143	99.3	-17	1.13	87	0		
0	104	97.6	25	0.054	0	0	10	Leading
	102	97.3	20	0.056	-5	7	9	
1	100	97	15	0.058	-10	14	8	
	98	96.7	10	0.060	-15	21	7	
2	96	96.5	5	0.062	-20	28	6	Competitive
	94	95.5	0	0.067	-25	35	5	
3	92	94.5	-5	0.071	-30	42	4	
	90	93.5	-10	0.075	-35	49	3	
4	88	92.5	-15	0.079	-40	56	2	
	86	91.5	-20	0.083	-45	63	1	Lagging
>4	<86	<91.5	-25	>0.083	-50	>63	0	

6	10	10	1	10	10	10	Score
0.2	0.2	0.1	0.2	0.1	0.1	0.1	× Weight
1.2	2	1	2	1	1	1	= Index

development process, we realized that the 7-ups had been a management document and that we had to train the teams in what each section meant by definition, the effect on the business, and how to calculate them to encourage the teams to take ownership of their businesses.

Again, the continuous-improvement process of reach, teach, empower, and equip came into play. Other measurements have since been developed from the production floor up, as teams have recognized the need. These innovations are welcome—with the stipulation that today no new measurement is taken from a team if its members are not the experts in what it means and how it contributes to the business.

Predating the current trend sweeping corporate America by several years, the traditional employee-review process evolved at NRDC from the usual one-way management review of the individual employee to a fairly simple, anonymous, written rating of one's team members in key areas (see Figure 9–6), establishing peer evaluation as part of the total review.[7] The teams were the force behind this change: Employees recognized that managers were less aware of individuals' work performances as the transfer of responsibility to teams continued, and a peer-review process was requested. Today the peer review has evolved (see Figure 9–7) into a comprehensive, formalized process and form. It counts for 50 percent of an employee's annual performance review, with direct impact on merit raises, promotions, and other personnel actions. This change was designed to promote a more complete and accurate evaluation and feedback process, but it has become a team-development tool as employees take on greater responsibility in guiding each other's performances and individual growth. The process continues to evolve as some of our more advanced teams have begun, on their own initiative, to use face-to-face, verbal feedback.[8]

FIGURE 9–6   Rating form

Employee	Productivity	Quality	Teamwork	Customer Orientation	Safety & Housekeeping
Fred	⁞	⁞	⁞	⁞	⁞
Mary					
Jim	⁞		⁞	⁞	
Shelley		⁞		⁞	⁞
Jackie	⁞	⁞	⁞	⁞	⁞
Ginnie		⁞	⁞		⁞
Bill	⁞				

FIGURE 9–7 Employee peer evaluation

MCS Multimedia Communication Systems   MAY 1995

EMPLOYEE NAME: _____

☐ Check here if SELF-EVALUATION

TEAM NAME: _____

CUSTOMER ORIENTATION:	Communicates frequently with internal/external customers Displays a sense of urgency for internal/external customers Strives to understand and meet all customer concerns	(Circle One) EX* HA MA LA NI* UN*

Comments: _____
_____
_____

TEAM PLAYER ORIENTATION & FLEXIBILITY:	Moves to other work areas as needs dictate Takes initiative to suggest and implement necessary team changes Keeps commitment to team (i.e., overtime, breaks, punctuality) Is sensitive toward diversity (i.e., race, color, gender, age, religion, sexual orientation, marital status, disability, national origin) Works on improving team-related skills (i.e., interpersonal, communication, participation) Takes initiative to suggest and implement necessary team changes	(Circle One) EX* HA MA LA NI* UN*

Comments: _____
_____
_____

QUALITY:	Initiates process changes to improve quality Makes use of continuous improvement tools where appropriate to improve quality Performs high-quality work; takes responsibility for quality	(Circle One) EX* HA MA LA NI* UN*

Comments: _____
_____
_____

PRODUCTIVITY:	Takes initiative in daily work assignments Identifies problems and offers solutions Works efficiently and effectively Utilizes time effectively	(Circle One) EX* HA MA LA NI* UN*

Comments: _____
_____
_____

SAFETY/ HOUSEKEEPING:	Maintains and ensures the work area is clean and neat Understands and follows work rules regarding safety Wears safety equipment when required Uses proper tools/techniques to prevent accidents and injuries Uses cleanup time effectively	(Circle One) EX* HA MA LA NI* UN*

Comments: _____
_____
_____

* Must have comment to make valid and possible suggestions for improvement.

PEOPLE DEVELOPMENT—THE TRAINING SEQUENCE

Sometimes we put the cart in front of the horse. An early mistake made was in trying to start this process without a full-time training coordinator. I tried to recover by putting a part-time training coordinator in place, but, ideally, a training coordinator has to be part of every step in the team-development process since people development is of primary importance.

Another discovery we made was that some of our early training was not effective because we assumed that if we trained, there would be better employees. This was not the case: Early training was not transferred back to the workstation. We were lucky to stumble upon a nonprofit organization called NashvilleREAD, a local literacy agency, which helped us test employees to determine reading skill level. It determined that we were in good shape, with better reading skills than we had expected, except for our non-native-English-speaking production associates, mainly Laotian immigrants.

The big question then was: Why aren't our people getting or retaining the training? The director of NashvilleREAD informed us we had a *learning problem* and, more specifically, we had an *adult learning problem.* Over the past 15 to 20 years, our typical employees had only read the Bible and newspapers and had not been in a learning environment. Their learning skills and strategies, along with their self-confidence as learners, had declined over time.

Another bit of luck was our encounter with Nancy Perkins, who had just moved to Nashville from South Carolina and had been involved in learning programs for the state of South Carolina. Working with Dr. Perkins, we provided all NRDC employees with 24 hours of training on how one learns, the various techniques of how to learn, and positive feedback that all can learn if they have the tools.

Seventeen employees set up a GED program. Our on-site college program attendance doubled, and our international employees were encouraged to continue their language learning in the on-site English-as-a-second-language program. The typical organization wanting to equip for teaming should first invest in some type of adult learning-to-learn program before setting out on team training. A good tracking system (what training each person has) is a must, and it is required by the ISO 9000 Certification (which NRDC obtained in the third year of our teaming development).

THE CONTINUING CHALLENGE: COMMUNICATIONS

From the beginning, with the early discussions and clarification of boundaries, a hot topic has been communication types, styles, and frequency. Effective communications have been an ongoing issue and concern at NRDC.

Although we thought we communicated fairly well with employees, we soon found that we didn't. For example, a question on our 1994 employee-satisfaction survey asked individuals whether they were satisfied with the advancement opportunities and the rate at which employees got promoted in the organization; the score was low.

I felt this was a misunderstanding—after all, many employees had been promoted. We found that 51 of 265 employees had been promoted in the past year (1994). Unfortunately we had not done a good job in making others aware and celebrating this rather high promotion rate with the entire employee population. Our pursuit of better communications continues through the use of Malcolm Baldrige Award–type assessments.[9] A team-based organization should review and improve communications continuously; its effectiveness has a powerful influence on the operation's ultimate success.

What *has* been successful is the bimonthly all-employee information meetings, in which we look both backward and forward at the business climate; recognize outstanding employees, teams, or events; discuss business subjects that are key to our growth; and just have fun. These are opportunities to come together as a large team and take time to share successes, evaluate our shortcomings, alert employees to the challenges ahead in our industry, connect our daily work to the larger Nortel mission, and teach.

Another effective program in our communication process is "Just Ask," which encourages employees to ask in writing about rumors, hearsay, or misunderstandings at the time they occur, so that the NRDC management team can respond, within 48 hours when possible, to either confirm or squelch rumors, answer any questions a team or employee might have, or review in-depth their more serious concerns.[10] Just ask has been in wide use for several years now and has proven an effective vehicle for communications.

RESULTS

Results from our new team-based management were necessary to ensure we could provide shareholder value to Nortel—solid results came during the third year of team building, in the growing teams phase. Results included 20 percent year-over-year growth, or return on assets of 121 percent for 1995. Customer-service levels reached 91 percent in 1994 and 1995. We have also been able to hold our product prices level for 1994 and 1995. And the crown jewel: NRDC received the highest employee-satisfaction rating throughout the entire corporation in a 1995 Nortel survey, attaining 84.2 percent. Internally, as measured in this same survey, some NRDC business units received 86 percent on their individual department ratings for employee satisfaction.

FIGURE 9–8   What is empowerment?

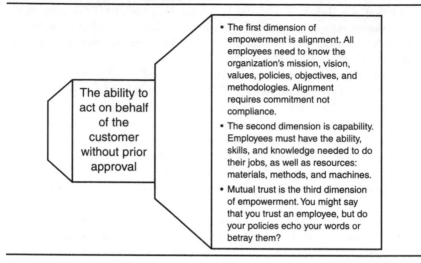

FIGURE 9–8   What is empowerment?

CONTINUOUS IMPROVEMENT—AGAIN

The continuous-improvement process helped us make more key improvements during the growing teams phase of our teaming development. We redefined empowerment (see Figure 9–8), further expanded facilitator training, provided more effective meeting training, and began monthly operations reviews by each team. We addressed the changing role of steering committees, put rewards and recognition systems in place, and began looking at future Nortel products to start retraining our entire workforce for the wireless products to come.

As our teams grew in their skills and scope of responsibility, so did our need for understanding true empowerment. In an Association of Manufacturing Excellence workshop on team development, Tom Howse of Texas Instruments used Figure 9–8 to show us how we could improve our efforts to empower teams at NRDC. For teams, as well as management, we needed a refined understanding of empowerment.

Growing team facilitators has been a constant challenge. They have been challenged to change their approach from a passive role with the team to one of a partner and coach, giving feedback and challenging the teams to grow and expand their skills and take on still greater responsibility for the business results. Beginning in 1996, the facilitators have received monthly training on their roles and skills; in addition, feedback sessions are held on what's working and what's not within the teams they facilitate. Finally, evaluation systems have been put into place to look at the teams' and facilitators' performances in the meetings.

Effective team meetings and other day-to-day processes have been a constant challenge and a focal point of training. We continue to look for a better way to meet the teams' training needs in this area. For example, in 1996, functional roles within the teams were redesigned and further expanded.[11] An in-depth, customized 12-hour training course, developed internally, has accompanied the improvement.

Between 1992 and 1995, NRDC teams did not make formal monthly reports of their operations to the management team because employees did not have confidence in their presentation skills, and each time a team tried to present what it was working on, it had a negative result. So we stopped monthly reporting and had voluntary team presentations at our bimonthly employee-information meetings, which we continue today. These employee presentations, held in a large hotel ballroom and addressing an audience of 300, are always effective and often masterful and humorous.[12]

Another improvement is that our steering committee has been challenged by the teams to review team successes and implement the recommendations of teams to enhance team processes, oversee the rewards and recognitions process, and look to the future.[13] Results include key programs in the rewards and recognition area; NRDC has two types of programs as a result. One is geared toward the individual, "Saying Thanks and Recognition" (STAR), and "Team Outstanding Performance and Service" (TOPS) addresses total team recognition. We have also asked many of our production employees to take on roles traditionally held by management personnel, such as facilitator and trainer. We now have a 2 to 4 percent merit increase attached to the roles.

It is a constant battle to stay ahead of Nortel's ever-changing product offerings. As many as 30 to 50 new products are introduced every year by our Nortel factories, for which we do warranty repairs; with the changing needs of our distributors for whom we do repair services and remanufacture sales, we are constantly challenged to change.[14]

To match these product changes and customer needs, NRDC's mission statements have evolved as follows:

1991–1993. Exceed customer expectations in the remanufacture, distribution, and services of Nortel products.

1991–1995. Team with internal and external customers to exceed expectations by continually improving communication products and services.

1996–1997. Become *the* organization that provides innovative material logistic solutions and Nortel-proven business practices to Enterprise Networks customers, which will enable them to compete more effectively in the competitive telecommunications marketplace.

FIGURE 9-9 **Seven steps to starting teams: Me—we—actions—systems— results—restarts—trusting others**

Section 1 The go decision
- Evaluation of one's ability to be the leader of change
- Objectives (thin but effective)
- Talking the talk
- Walking the talk
- Checking for success
Help! I want to go but I'm lost.

Section 2 Reaching the organization for change
- Setting the framework for a team-development process
- Looking for signs of who's going with you

Section 3 Teaching/sharing the basics
- Making everyone a champion for teaming
- Seven skill sets of the champions I have known
- What are the components of a team?
- Ops: regrouping to bring everyone along

We are in an environment of constant change. The trust factor is crucial here: I trust NRDC employees to accept this constant change. To me trust is the number-one people asset for the organization's growth and success. Developing a team-based environment is more than just saying that you're going to have teams. Figure 9–9 reflects the many simultaneous and evolutionary steps that must occur. And there are many needs to be met: physiological, psychological, and personal. Teaming development is about processes and evolution—not programs. It is people centered and requires listening and understanding, caring about and respecting individuals, feeling the emotions and empathizing, acknowledging the successes and failures, and keeping it simple and *fun*.

NOTES

1. Northern Telecom Inc., or Nortel, is a telecommunications company employing more than 63,000 people in its operations worldwide; NRDC, the only Nortel facility of its kind in the United States, is located in Nashville, Tennessee, and employs 300 people who repair Nortel's products used in the office and home environments.

2. The term *champion* as we defined it means "advocate, defender," as well as "one who shows marked superiority."

3. Oliver Wright Publications Inc., 1993.

4. "Rediscovering the Power of the Individual," PMISHARES Inc., 1991.

5. David J. Mattingly, "A View from the Factory Floor," *Target* 7(5) (1991): 23–27.

6. In the transfer of responsibility to self-managed work teams, over time this training class has grown from a two-hour session to eight hours. That is, as teams have become more sophisticated, they have taken increasing responsibility in interviewing and selecting, and the training has been updated to address their changing needs. As of January 1995, all interviewing has been done as a team task.

7. Hal Lancaster, "Performance Reviews Are More Valuable When More Join In," *The Wall Street Journal* (July 9, 1996).

8. In a process dubbed "Plus Delta," representing the next level of sophistication in self-managed teams, the members meet on a regular basis throughout the review period to provide opportunities for performance feedback and recommendations for continuous improvement.

9. More recent Baldrige-type business management assessments, at both the Nortel and state levels, have told us we are somewhat weak in the end-to-end communication of the business. At press time, we are reviewing two PC-based systems to help us tie the end-to-end programs together.

10. Adapted from the AT&T/NCR factory program, as presented in an Association of Manufacturing Excellence (AME) workshop.

11. The change has led to the establishment of 13 team roles, some specific to team meeting functions; others encompass such tasks as coordination of team training or monitoring safety.

12. In addition to the voluntary, all-employee meeting presentations, NRDC now has reinstituted formal monthly operations reviews with the senior managers, which have already demonstrated a positive result in the area of cost reduction. We read these as clear signs of the growth of confidence of our teams and their individual members.

13. The present steering committee mission statement: To be the driving force providing leadership, guidance, and strategies in the evolution to self-managed work teams.

14. The changing requirements will result in need for a 100 percent change in the skill sets of our NRDC employees. Production associates will have to become experts in wireless technology, software-driven products, and third-party–developed products. Our engineers will be involved with high-volume products with different testing requirements, and business planning will be driven by logistic services in which repair products to support distributors will create a just-in-time environment.

10 HUMAN RESOURCE MANAGEMENT STRATEGY

Robert E. McInturff

Editor's note

The 1990s and beyond will be called the people era. Although the mechanical issues (e.g., JIT, TQC) have been well developed, the formulation and execution of an appropriate human resource strategy is often not seen as a necessary component. This chapter addresses what makes good human resource management (HRM) strategy and takes us through three success stories.

Manufacturing strategy ultimately is measured by its successful implementation. Much has been written over the years about the importance of human resources to the success of an organization, but not all organizations are as successful as others in implementing new programs or concepts and maintaining a competitive edge in today's world. Why do some succeed where others fail? And why is it that a successful management team from one company or division will move to another and not achieve the same level of success?

WHAT IS STRATEGIC HUMAN RESOURCE MANAGEMENT?

By the simplest of definitions, strategic human resource planning is having in place the right number of people at the right time with the right skills to

172

meet company goals. Human resources can play an effective role in the planning and execution of corporate strategy through development of a human resource plan. The process requires a simple conversion of production requirements to labor hours, followed by specification of further staffing requirements for training, development, and review.

HOW TO DEVELOP A STRATEGIC PLAN FOR HUMAN RESOURCE MANAGEMENT

Step 1. A Product Plan Converted to Personnel Requirements

It is a fairly simple task to convert a production plan or forecast to a personnel plan. The product requirements are converted to labor hours using standards typically available in the cost accounting or materials-requirements planning (MRP) systems. The hours are factored with efficiency data and converted to head counts or labor hours.

Step 2. Short-Term Issues

Once the head count numbers have been calculated, the employee and supervisory mix needs to be determined. The following questions should help complete the list of requirements, which are then compared to actual staff levels:

1. What is the right number of employees to meet business goals?
2. What job skills will be required to meet the goals?
3. Where are the people to come from?
4. What level of education will be required of the employees?
5. What level of ongoing training will be required to maintain the proficiency of the workforce?

Complicating development of the strategic plan is companies' constant change. Sales go up and down, new products are introduced or phased out, and employees come and go. At times the rate of change varies from high to low to barely perceptible, but change is perpetual. Although we can measure the *rate* of change by quantitative methods (i.e., sales dollars, number of employees, capital expenditures) the dynamic of change as it relates to human resources cannot be quantified as easily. But they are as real and measurable as any tangible asset, computer document, or numbers blessed by the accounting department.

THREE CASES OF EFFECTIVE IMPLEMENTATION

People versus Techniques

A manager of a $30-million company states: "By cutting lead times, creating work cells, and improving vendor delivery programs we have reduced our manufacturing cycle times from months to days." This statement, as usual, focuses on the *techniques* that were successful but leaves out the *people issues* and the implementation details.

Our purpose is to identify characteristics that ensure effective implementation. We will look at three companies as examples of very different business environments operating successfully. Each of the three companies fits one of the following descriptions of internal change:

1. *Rapid or new growth.* This condition is most often associated with start-up. These companies experience rapid growth in both sales and number of employees. Their products are generally technologically advanced and require a high degree of sophistication in the manufacturing process.

2. *Loss of market share or profitability because of competition.* Companies experience problems maintaining growth and profitability as their market share erodes. Their future growth is dependent on implementation of new techniques, introduction of new products, and changing the management and performance measurements currently in place.

3. *Restructuring caused by a merger or acquisition.* Perhaps one of the most common occurrences in American industry today is the creation of a new business entity by a merger or acquisition. Companies are sold and merged, product lines are split off, and joint ventures are attempted in unprecedented numbers. The end effect is that while the plant and equipment, product, employees, and customers may all stay the same, the *corporate identity* changes overnight. The results include employee layoffs, partial plant closings, introduction of new products from other divisions or merged companies, and, most important, loss of the employees' visions of the company identity.

Following are the stories of three companies experiencing the stress of change, each coping in a different way. Their success stories are not unique, but as you will see, each followed the same road map to effective implementation.

CASE 1. RAPID OR NEW GROWTH—THE START-UP: HI-FLYER ELECTRONICS

From its founding eight years ago Hi-Flyer Electronics has experienced a rapid increase in growth, achieving sales of $300 million with 1,500 employees worldwide. The founder and president is a respected engineer well liked by everyone. Although he is articulate, he is not an impassioned speaker and does not have a charismatic personality. People are comfortable in his presence. They feel they are listened to and their opinions matter. Profitability is excellent; sales are projected to continue growing at more than 25 percent per year. The manufacturing organization is well run and has avoided the confusion and sloppiness associated with most start-ups. The vice president and all key senior- and mid-level managers are still in place from the earliest days and plan to remain onboard. Execution of the manufacturing plan is accomplished in a well-organized and timely manner.

Hi-Flyer's three major manufacturing problems are as follows:

1. The organization needs to decide how to hire enough people to meet the continual staffing needs required to support rapid growth.
2. The company wants to ensure that old and new employees have the requisite skills to keep pace with the increased production schedules and the complexity of new technology introduction.
3. With no historical precedent controlling policy and procedures, how can it maintain a common goal throughout the organization? The number of new employees added yearly exceeds the total employee population hired to date, a factor that increases the difficulty of building an internally consistent set of goals.

CASE 2. LOSS OF MARKET SHARE—THE GOOD PERFORMER UNDER ATTACK: METAL BANGERS ARE US MANUFACTURING

Erosion of market share caused by the inability to meet demand for shorter lead times was creating a major problem for this manufacturer of custom machinery. At one time, Metal Bangers Are Us Manufacturing owned the lion's share of the marketplace. In recent years new technological advances and foreign competition jeopardized its number-one position.

Design engineering responded by introducing a new generation of equipment. This restored Metal Bangers Are Us Manufacturing's lead in design, but manufacturing still could not keep pace. Located in a remote suburban area, its 10-year-old facility did not have an abundance of skilled hourly and technical workers.

The challenge facing the president of Metal Bangers was to maintain market share. He knew that it needed to improve its manufacturing capability. Options were limited, however. The current plant location could not be abandoned, and the number of employees could not be increased because of a lack of qualified workers. The president realized that any change would have to be accomplished using the current management team and factory workforce. Although he could not see a way out, he took a time-honored approach: He reorganized and got lucky.

He created a new plant manager position responsible for both design and manufacturing engineering, materials, purchasing management, and shop operations. The slot was filled by the current manufacturing manager, an assertive and well-respected employee.

Results

The newly appointed plant manager brought all functional department heads, as well as significant individual contributors, together to create a task force for the purpose of improving manufacturing response time. The result of the task force work was a reduction in internal lead times from months to days. Products are no longer built and assembled piecemeal; they are produced on an assembly line. Sales have increased by 50 percent, partly because of lead-time reductions, while employee head count has remained unchanged.

How were these improvements accomplished? Through a number of simple and direct programs. Although no one knew what the final cycle time should be for internally produced goods, it was agreed that it should be better.

- The project team became interested in the just-in-time (JIT) approach and began to implement many of its techniques.
- Design and manufacturing engineering were combined so that all new products were introduced more smoothly.
- An aggressive training program was implemented, and quality programs were put in place.

As the project progressed and many successes were achieved, the employees began to take more risks. The biggest risk was that, although it produced a custom product, typically a job-shop orientation, the organization wanted to build it on an assembly line. The result of changing to an assembly line is that average time from start to completion for a final assembly has been reduced by more than 50 percent.

CASE 3. THE LEVERAGED BUYOUT—A NEW IDENTITY: WHO ARE THESE GUYS MANUFACTURING

A division of a Fortune 500 company for years, Who Are These Guys Manufacturing was purchased through a leveraged buyout. Because its main product came to the end of its life cycle, the new owners faced a number of serious problems:

- Tight cash.
- The potential loss of 50 percent of its sales.
- An unmotivated workforce.
- A plant location unattractive to employees.

In addition, the company had chosen to revamp its traditional approach to the customer by adopting an aggressive new-product introduction campaign. This required a shift from low-tech/low-volume production to high-tech/high-volume production. It began an aggressive manufacturing program to increase efficiency, improve quality, and improve workforce morale.

Results

Despite the loss of its major product line, sales are up over 20 percent from when the company went private. Employee efficiencies are up by more than 15 percent. As measured by the human resource department, job satisfaction and employee morale is at an all-time high. Soon after the buyout, a new president was named and a new vice president of manufacturing was appointed from within.

Who Are These Guys Manufacturing integrated the three necessary components of strategic human resource management:

1. Commitment.
2. Training.
3. Measurement.

THE COMMON DENOMINATORS

Although the problems each of these companies faced were different and unique, there are some common stylistic and management approaches used by each.

The Leader or Organizational Communicator

In each of the three cases, one individual was clearly identified as the focal point, the acknowledged leader. He or she was viewed as the individual whose abilities were critical to the success of the organization and the people within it.

Although clear-cut authority was vested in one individual (generally the president), a dynamic functional manager could achieve the same level of success on a less-than-company-wide scale. Authority, charisma, and visibility do not necessarily imply comparable communication skills. Some charismatic leaders are respected by employees but not followed by them. There are authoritative leaders whom people follow but do not agree with, and there are visible leaders who are recognized but not successful. We generally equate charisma, authority, and visibility with success, but the hidden fact is that truly successful leaders are *organizational communicators*. An organizational communicator can be charismatic or authoritative or visible, but all share the following traits and business practices:

- The communicator has a written business plan that is given to every top- and middle-management individual. Everyone knows where the company is headed.
- The business plan is updated on a regular basis, and the changes are communicated to the entire organization.
- Although the communicator is usually the president, another individual could assume the role if he or she had enough visibility.
- Turf wars are lessened because all decisions are based on the need for everyone to achieve the business plan.
- Top- and mid-level managers have more autonomy in their decision making because the need to run ideas and problems up through the organization is reduced. People at lower levels are able to make better-informed decisions because they have a clearer understanding of their effects on the business plan.
- There are few hidden agendas within an organizational communicator company. If the company needs to develop three new products a year to be successful, it is common knowledge. If those three new products must fill a specific market niche, everyone knows that also. Detailed engineering specifications and marketing plans may have been on a more traditional need-to-know basis, but an overall lack of secrecy permeates the entire company.

DEVELOPING A STRATEGIC HUMAN RESOURCE PLAN

Earlier we described strategic human resource management as having the right number of people at the right time with the right skills to meet company goals. How did the three companies institute such a plan? There appear to be two critical steps in the actual implementation of a workable plan. The first is detailed planning at various functional levels, and the second is an intensive training plan supported by a budget.

Companies with organizational communicators are able to create a management plan throughout the entire organization. The plan starts from the top and works its way down throughout the organization, creating more detail at each level. For example, the vice president of manufacturing is aware that new product sales are predicted to grow by 50 percent. This involves the introduction of a new technology, so obviously it will have a major impact on the organization. The impact is reviewed in detail with the manufacturing manager, looking at its effect on employee productivity, capitalization, and potential organizational changes. The manufacturing manager then fleshes out the plan in further detail (perhaps with manufacturing engineering, purchasing, and production) and provides even greater detail as to what will happen. Finally, the operating personnel break the plan down further and develop a detailed plan at their level.

The process itself is nothing remarkable; it is probably the same process undertaken by almost every company. What makes this planning process different and unique is that *at every level,* everyone knows the company strategy—the whys and hows of what is being done. Each step of the decision-making process contributes to the health and vigor of the whole organization.

Prerequisites for Developing a Workable Plan

There are two overall conditions that impact the decision-making processes within these three companies: the ability to make autonomous decisions and the organization's support structure. The manager's ability to make his or her own decisions is dependent on the corporate plan, the source of credibility for this level of decision making. Within the organization there is a commitment to support people to prevent failure. This commitment to the success of the organization and the people within it provides checks and balances; no single plan or manager ends up off the mark. There is constant communication and consensus on direction.

The importance of the philosophy of commitment and consensus must not be understated. The people within the organization work hard on their plans and goals because they feel a sense of ownership. The effective organizational communicator creates an environment in which management's actions are recognized and its plans are implemented. It fosters a feeling that what management does counts. It is a cycle: Management feels empowered and strives to reach corporate objectives; corporate objectives are reached, and that further reinforces or validates management. This reciprocity was extremely important in all three cases.

Checks and balances are critical. Each department is allowed and encouraged to be in control of its decisions. But because all groups filter their decisions back through the entire organization, no one can get too far off track. The organization's members help each other succeed.

At Hi-Flyer Electronics, a department manager who is levels removed from the vice president of manufacturing could not conceive of being excluded from the planning process or of not making his or her own decisions on how to run the department. The corporate culture of autonomous decision making was so ingrained that the department manager could not even "imagine why I would work there or why the company would want me, unless I had a decision-making role."

DECISION MAKING

The attitudes that pervade such an autonomous decision-making environment are as follows:

1. Managing by example. As a result of the organizational communicator's constant flow of information, employees feel it's only natural to respond with information of their own.
2. Managers are proactive. They identify problems, seek input, recommend solutions, and build consensus instead of waiting to be told what to do and how to do it.
3. Each employee is chosen because of his or her quality as a person. In other words, it is not a simple choice of skill sets. Each team member must be able to contribute tangibly (e.g., technically, financially) and intangibly (e.g., creatively, proactively, communicatively). Managers are hired in part because they expect to be autonomous decision makers.

Training

The biggest surprise among the factors contributing to the success of each of these organizations is the tremendous emphasis on training and the budgeting process associated with it. In talking about the organizational communicator and the planning process, an observer might wonder how these real people in real companies are making this work and how he or she can do it, too.

The answer is that these companies used the training-budget process as the mechanism to drive human resource planning. Each company had to make sure its workforce could keep up with new demands:

• Hi-Flyer Electronics needed enough skilled workers.

- Because Metal Bangers could not bring in new people, it had to make sure its current employee base was ready.
- At Who Are These Guys Manufacturing a massive retraining program was implemented as it phased out one product and introduced many others.

The Training Budget

The training budget was key to how these companies were able to implement the strategic human resource plan. It is linked directly to the organizational communicator's strategic plan.

With an organizational communicator, short- and long-term goals and objectives for the entire organization are known and understood. Planning is done at each level. Each department manager has a crystal-clear idea of where the company and its departments are going and what this means for his or her department. The department manager has stated objectives that must be supported with an action plan.

The Training Plan

There are six questions that must be answered.

1. What is needed to implement the plan?

First, the manager identifies what skill sets are required to make the plan happen. This forces him or her to review current employees. Can the people in place be retrained? Could the required people be hired from the outside?

At Who Are These Guys Manufacturing, a decision to implement statistical process control (SPC) was made. This required specific job skills. Although the company had managers who were certified to teach SPC, now they needed employees to practice SPC.

2. How many employees are needed?
3. Who will train the employees?
4. What do the employees need to learn?
5. When should the program be given?
6. Where should the program be given?

Who Are These Guys decided the training should take place on-site during work hours for the following reasons:

- Running the program on-site ensures that it gets done.
- The company is in control, not the teacher.

- This learning program becomes mandatory, not voluntary.
- The program becomes a visible statement of the corporation's commitment to SPC.
- Employees are more committed to the learning process.

Although providing this training during work hours causes inconvenience, the company believed that to ensure success of the SPC program, it had to be done during the workday. This training program was to be ongoing since the SPC program would remain in place.

Succession Planning

Succession planning is a well-known tactic in Corporate America, and most corporations make provisions for it to some degree. The larger the company, the more sophisticated the planning. However, what makes the organizational communicator's company unique is that succession planning is a taken-for-granted, one-more-thing-to-do part of everyday responsibility. Just as one must meet schedules or prepare budgets or give a performance review, so one must constantly prepare a succession strategy. The acceptance of responsibility for and the ongoing attention to succession planning at all levels of management was evident in Metal Bangers Are Us, Hi-Flyer Electronics, and Who Are Those Guys Manufacturing. Continuous succession planning results in the right people being available at just the right time to satisfy corporate objectives.

At Metal Bangers the line supervisor planned to hire two skilled machinists in two and a half years. Although a supervisor at this level would not generally participate in long-range planning, in a company with an organizational communicator, each professional manager could translate long-range objectives into influence on his or her department. To meet the need, this supervisor chose to look internally for the talent. After planning and identifying two candidates for promotion, he also created two potential vacancies requiring replacements.

Succession planning is an integral part of this line supervisor's responsibility. Imagine walking up to the typical line supervisor and saying: "Create a succession plan." The response might be a baffled look. However, if you say, "In two years we will need two more machinists whom we can't hire from the outside. Go figure out who you want to train," then you have asked for a workable succession plan.

MEASUREMENT

Finally, each organization set up performance measurements to ensure completion of the plan. The standards were not arbitrary, and they were followed carefully. They included the following:

- Hard data rating actual performance against the plan on corporate, departmental, and individual levels. Actual performance against objectives specified in the plan measures projected benefits of using funds set aside for training and development of new managers or releasing full kits from the stockroom to production, for example.
- Soft data concerning employees' feelings on corporate, departmental, and individual levels.

Many people become suspicious and fearful when their work is measured. But the employees of the three success-story companies welcomed the opportunity because they had participated in setting the standards by which they were measured.

People became excited about setting objectives, achieving goals, and being recognized for their accomplishments. The process was contagious. At the next planning session, expectations were raised as goals were set at higher levels and the company's success continued.

At Who Are These Guys Manufacturing, the measurement process is seen as an instrument for positive recognition. Because of the lack of historical data, new-product introductions were used as an opportunity to introduce performance measurements. Working with a clean slate, management set a goal; once it had been achieved, they set a higher goal. Finally, when one of the hourly workers asked, "Why only count new products, why not count all products?" performance measures were incorporated. Good ideas came from all levels.

SUMMARY

Although most organizations will not achieve the results of the three companies profiled, partial implementation is possible. What can we do? The fundamentals discussed in this chapter—commitment, training, and measurement—can be broken down to a much smaller scale, for either individuals or departments. Although there may not be an organizational communicator within your company, that does not mean a manager cannot be one within his or her own area of control.

A strategic human resource plan for yourself or your department covering staffing levels, training and development, succession, budgets, and measurement is needed. Let people know what it is. Create the opportunity for feedback through the plan to the organization. Determine organizational needs through training and measure the results.

11 QUALITY CIRCLES AND TEAM PROBLEM-SOLVING SYSTEMS

TWELVE STEPS TO ORGANIZATION AND FACILITATION

Jackie Hammonds

Editor's note

Honda bases its success on innovation and on its associates, and Jackie Hammonds was a pioneer in the building of Honda's North American manufacturing base. She visited and worked with hundreds of supplier companies, and her patience and dedication to quality circles established a solid base for Honda's aggressive zero-defects goals.

QUALITY CIRCLES—THE REALITY

Any company can achieve successful results if it is committed to excellence, exerts much effort, and endures the frustrations of building a new system for internal culture change. A well-planned, systematic approach will assure the natural evolution of the quality circle and team problem solving. At Honda this successful concept has become a daily part of the way we work. Everyone at Honda is involved in the quality, cost, and productivity of our facilities.

Step 1: Read and Benchmark

Research, read, read, read! Learn as much as you can about the types of circle and team activities so that you can make intelligent comparisons and discuss the issues with the powers that be in your organization. Contact local and state manufacturers and other business organizations to discuss what they are doing to involve employees in problem-solving activities.

Almost all successful companies have tailored a system to fit the needs of their own organizations. Consider creating a plan that gives your company its own twist on quality circle involvement. Most companies are very willing to benchmark; talk to the executives in your company and ask for contacts—the personnel manager, human resource manager, or purchasing manager is the best source of names.

Do an analysis of the systems most likely to fit your company. Don't begin anything until the research phase is complete. And speaking about team activities intelligently will go a long way toward gaining the organizational support you will need to succeed. The creator or revitalizer of an employee-involvement system must develop a plan that management and all other levels in your company will accept.

Step 2: Analyzing Options

Next, form the committee that will help make decisions about your company's quality circles or team activities. Begin to brainstorm ideas, listing them all for discussion. Always remember who your customer is and what the customer wants. It's not enough to believe change is good and that it should occur. Management should understand what it is asking from the workforce. Someone must have responsibility to explain the group's implementation plans. You are trying to change the way people think: How will you do so? Select a champion who will act as spokesperson and motivator for the changes.

Step 3: Investigating—Is Your Company Serious?

Find out whether your company management is serious about change. Discuss the committee's ideas about team activities and the changes that must take place. The process begins with a simple question: Why does this company's management team want to implement involvement activities such as quality circles? You can tell it's serious when the answer clearly states goals and objectives, such as the following:

- Providing ongoing educational opportunities for all employees.

- Encouraging self-development and involvement company wide (all levels).
- Teaching all employees problem-solving skills (in a specified period of time).
- Getting everyone, including senior management, involved in the change.
- Making the company the best place to work through team activities.

You know management is serious when it talks about the benefits to its employees, as well as the obvious potential impact on quality, efficiency, cost savings, and so forth. If it's serious, the people side of the company, not just the technical or business aspects, will be a priority.

Committee members need to know whether management plans to recognize and reward all employees that participate in team activities. The committee should be prepared to offer recognition and reward ideas, because management may ask what would be appropriate. One idea is to look at mostly social or peer recognition rather than monetary rewards: The choice is up to you. What matters is that hard work and improvement efforts are recognized by management as well as peers. Your employees need to know the company acknowledges their value as creative, capable, responsible people.

This series of questions will prepare management for the changes:

- Who will be accountable for the success of the involvement activities?
- Who will deal with management that fails to support the initiative?
- Who will train management to understand the change in the way business is done?
- Will management be evaluated on its commitment to team activities?
- Who will be the top-management person receiving reports and feedback?

Your responsibility is to analyze your organization and to review both its strong and weak points. The involvement system should address some of the issues and concerns of the employees at all levels in your company. Consider how your plan could improve the work-life situation for everyone.

Step 4: Organizing the Team

After the preliminary preplanning work with the company management is complete and there is consensus on the purpose, conduct a series of meetings with committee members, starting with the situation appraisal:

- What is happening in the workplace, and what do employees think of the company?
- What is causing the concerns, and what countermeasures could help change them?
- What will encourage employees to become involved?
- How will you create an environment for team activities?
- Who will be responsible and accountable for the success of the teams?
- When and where will all this occur?
- What results are expected, and how will you communicate them to employees?

Use this information to create the action plan for quality circles and involvement systems.

The team must have a purpose statement, goals, and expected results of the involvement system. Plan short- and long-term goals on a milestone chart to track progress (see Figure 11–1). At Honda, we review the reasons for the involvement system:

- To train everyone to have the skills to implement ideas and solve problems in the workplace.
- To encourage employees to take responsibility for their job satisfaction.

FIGURE 11–1 Milestone Chart

| Plan   ▬▬▬▬ |
| Actual ▪▪▪▪▪▪▪▪ |

	1	2	3	4	5	6	7	8	9	10	11	12
Develop team	▬											
Brainstorm theme ideas	▬											
Select theme	▪											
Analyze problem	▬▬▬											
Set goal		▬										
Search for cause			▬▬									
Verify root cause				▬▬								
Brainstorm for countermeasure					▪							
Plan countermeasure					▬							
Do countermeasure						▬▬						
Check countermeasure							▬▬					
Standardize countermeasure								▬				
Evaluate plan versus actual								▪				
Evaluate impact analysis									▬▬			

- To allow employees to become involved and learn that work can be enjoyable when they participate in the decision making.
- To encourage employees to consider problems as opportunities.
- To create a situation in which management, supervisors, and employees at all levels communicate with each other.
- To build better relationships with peers and management.
- To learn to respect the ideas of others and become flexible and open-minded.

Always focus on the reasons you are planning to implement an employee-involvement system. The reasons should include your genuine concern for employees and the competitiveness of the company. Employee involvement should be a win–win situation.

The components of a successful new quality circle or other involvement system are training, true empowerment, commitment from everyone, time to work on projects, patience, honesty and integrity, a fearless work environment, and dedicated facilitators and advisers. Do a quick overview of quality circles to confirm an understanding of the reality.

The Reality of Circles and Problem-Solving Teams

Quality circles are typically small groups of employees voluntarily working together to help solve problems within their companies. Most of the work is done after normal work hours for some form of compensation. Companies with labor unions typically negotiate the details of employee-involvement activities when contracts are prepared. Some companies choose to use the regular workday for the teams to meet and plan their activities, which eliminates overtime. Quality circles and other team-involvement systems usually have specific guidelines to build consistency in the process.

Most circles or work teams select projects with measurable goals that help them understand the results and the real impact of team problem-solving efforts. The reality is, however, that the emphasis should be on the educational aspects and self-development of employees. Care about your people and they will learn to care about the success of the company.

Team members need to understand the purpose of quality circle involvement and the value of the concept. This is a change in company culture, and it will take time to obtain commitment from everyone. You will be asking the employees to take responsibility for changing their own workplace's communication, quality, and efficiency. The time for complaining has been replaced by a time for action—concerns become opportunities.

Why You *Must* Organize Teams

The quality circle system uses the creativity and good ideas of all the employees to build a better environment. Think about the power of all the ideas that will be generated. Employees should begin to feel pride in their companies. Anytime people have input and their voices are heard, they become more loyal to the source of this respect—the company and its success. Employees are the most valuable resource. Empower them and encourage them to participate.

Circle teams form so that they can work with management to help improve the work situation and competitiveness of the company. They should be empowered to impact almost any area or situation except labor relations issues, wages, benefits, and work hours. Self-directed work teams sometimes do work on these issues, as well as hiring and firing. However, typical circle teams usually do not venture into policy matters. Exceptions can be made if circle members are willing to work with administration on a case-by-case basis. Explain this in the guidelines. All types of team-involvement activities must be governed by standards that do not violate union contracts if your company has a union. Quality circles help break down communication barriers between hourly employees and management. Circle members learn to work cooperatively with supervisors and managers because they share information and solutions to problems.

Team members need training before they can begin to solve problems. The most common approach is to teach basic quality circle tools: checksheets, cause-and-effect diagrams (fishbone), Pareto diagrams, charts and graphs, histograms, and brainstorming techniques. There are many problem-solving courses available, and they should be taught to management along with circle members. Everyone must speak the same language when working on countermeasure problems. The facilitators of these systems will find their jobs easier when a common method is used by everyone in the company.

The level of data or course content may vary by group and by concept, and tools should be consistent throughout the organization. Your training curriculum must address what skills are needed based on specific job requirements. Be sure you have resources and the budget to deliver training.

Employees are the experts in their work areas and can help solve most of their problems given the right tools, opportunity, trust, and training. Their combined brainpower will make a big difference in the quality, productivity, and communication in your company. Quality circles encourage employees to take positive action to improve all aspects of their work lives. Most employees want to do a good job and be proud of their efforts. Everyone wants to belong to a group that does something extraordinary. Put the emphasis on people and their values. We recommend these two books to help: *What Is Total Quality Control* by Kaoru Ishikawa (Englewood Cliffs, N.J.: Prentice Hall, 1985) and *The American Spirit* by Lawrence Miller (New York: Warner Books, 1984).

Here is a summary of the steps to employee-involvement excellence:

1. Create the vision and the plan.
2. Give the employees direction.
3. Empower and trust employees.
4. Encourage involvement.
5. Educate and train.
6. Walk the talk.
7. Support employees.
8. Recognize and reward successes.

Key Success Factors

Training for Quality Circles

Train all the quality circle team members and explain the reasons for, or the value of, becoming involved; then teach them how to get involved. Your company's philosophy for the new system will probably need to be defined. Consider the reasons why the employees should commit to becoming willing problem solvers. They may want these questions answered in the introduction orientation for the system:

- What are quality circles (or teams)?
- How do they work?
- What do we have to do to start the activities?
- Why is it important and what's the benefit?
- What's in it for me?
- What's the real reason the company wants me to participate?
- Who will help us if we agree to do it?

The system must satisfy the needs of everyone in your company. Employees need a clear understanding of what they must do. You may find that there is a general lack of knowledge about basic problem solving, even among managers and supervisors. Complete the analysis of the real situation before planning the training for the quality circle or team problem-solving activities. Required skills include the following:

- The technique of brainstorming.
- Appropriate methods of collecting and analyzing data.
- Root-cause analysis.
- Pareto analysis.
- Preparing and understanding various charts and graphs.
- Countermeasures to problems.

Decision-making tools used by management will be helpful to the new involvement teams. After classes have been completed, the circle members will need guidance through their first activity. Expect to also teach them how to do research on the chosen project. Teach them that all actions should be based on facts, not assumptions. Training material sources include the Association for Quality and Participation (AQP), the American Society for Quality Control (ASQC), college libraries, local companies with involvement programs, books, and management consultants. Use these materials to create training unique to your company.

Consider the education level of the employees; for example, training should not be too technical for quick comprehension. Employees should enjoy—not fear—the learning experience; if the environment and the materials are user-friendly, people will learn. Training can be scheduled for Saturday or one-hour modules during the work week, but plan the sessions so that attendees can practice what they have learned. Remember that people quickly tire of lectures with minimal active participation. At Honda, we usually must do the thing we are studying or we lose the understanding.

The practice section of the class also allows the instructor to walk through the classroom, checking for comprehension. There is no cookbook for the perfect training program. Start with a simple process for problem solving. There will be no need for a level-up training program until all employees really understand and implement the basic concept. Keep it simple, make the learning fun, check for comprehension, and plan the training at a convenient time. (There are many good computer software packages that offer basic team activity tools. At Honda, we have circle training tools on CBT units, as well as some language classes and legal-compliance courses.)

Empowerment

No Fear. True empowerment is learning to trust and giving responsibility for communication and quality to employees. It means surrendering controlling management style. The employees become responsible for day-to-day success and quality of their job processes. Empowered employees take charge because trained, trusted, responsible people usually have the initiative and courage to make improvements when necessary.

In companies whose managers use fear to control employees, there is a sense of power when employees have no voice in day-to-day business decisions. Yet these same managers probably wonder why productivity is low, quality is poor, and the environment is not clean or organized. They just don't get it. The change to an empowered workforce requires the creation of a no-fear workplace. And the fear factor only grows with a lack of communication between upper management and other employees.

The keys to empowerment are trust, authority, respect, responsibility, training, education, fearless environment, and recognition. Employees should continue to learn and grow after they sign on. Empowerment is only a word unless managers take positive action to work with, rather than over, employees. The best managers learn new people skills and ask employees to work as team players with management rather than for management.

Most employees have creative minds, and training focuses us on the issues, but we cannot ask people to become responsible for their success unless we give them the tools and skills they need. Empowerment means trusting, training, communicating, cooperating, and then letting employees do what we ask. When managers learn to trust, life should be full of surprises, most of which will be interesting and pleasant.

RESURRECTING FALTERING QUALITY CIRCLE ACTIVITIES

What happens when successful quality circle activities begin to falter? There are many causes of loss of interest in involvement systems. You must assess the current situation and compare it to historical statistics. Consider all aspects of the quality circle activities: Who or what could be causing the loss of interest? What changes have occurred? What can you do about it? Who should be involved? How much will it cost to improve and promote increased activities? Gather statistics on these issues:

What is the current participation rate now? One year ago?

How many completed projects this year? How many last year?

How many employees are involved? Percentage increase/decrease?

What types of projects are being chosen by the teams?

What is the impact of the activities on the company?

Is there any measurable difference in employee morale?

Is there any change in absenteeism?

Display the data in chart form—column and line graphs work well. Check how many employees have been trained for quality circle activities. What specific training have they received? How much training is currently being done? Is the training adequate for today? Is the training easy to understand and implement?

Turn your attention to management and ask what it is doing to support the circle and team members. If nothing, did management support the teams when activities were first implemented? Why did it stop? Have managers and leaders been trained to understand how to visibly support quality circles? Do managers understand the benefits to them and their company? Are managers and supervisors held accountable for the success of the system, or could the system be changed to reflect more accountability?

Facilitation

There are a number of checkpoints to evaluate facilitators, including the following:

Have facilitators been trained properly?

Do they have the knowledge and ability to teach QC tools and so forth?

Are they capable of advising circle teams?

Do they have at least one quality circle project experience?

Are they committed to helping the circle activity grow?

Are they positive and do they set a good example?

Do they assist circle teams and give good direction?

Do they help focus the teams?

Do they promote the circle activities and managers and supervisors?

Do they keep accurate records and historical data?

Do facilitators attend seminars and read new books to learn creative ways to motivate team members and elevate the level of activities?

Do the facilitators understand the development of business planning: setting goals, creating objectives, and establishing realistic expectations for the quality circle system?

Are they team players?

Do the department (area) facilitators give recognition to team members separate from the company-wide recognition?

Are facilitators accessible to team members?

Do facilitators understand their roles and responsibilities? Are they serving the team members and do they know who their customers are?

Do facilitators encourage education and promote a learning environment?

Are facilitators willing to deal with difficult issues?

Are they good communicators?

Do they have credibility with other employees, especially circle members?

Do facilitators document departmental activities?

The answers to these questions indicate the level of support teams are receiving; react accordingly. What is corporate commitment? Is the quality circle system a priority at the corporate level? How do corporate managers support the circle activities? Are managers serious about empowerment and employee involvement? Were they ever really participative? If not, why? Gather facts, not opinions, for an objective assessment of upper management. Do not make assumptions: To countermeasure concerns, you must go to their root cause.

If employees are losing interest in quality circle activities, ask yourself and them why. Consider what is done today in comparison to the beginning. The time might be right for restructuring or reorganizing the administrative process. You might think about rotating new people into the positions. New ideas and fresh perspectives are refreshing, and they can bring life into dying systems. A checklist for successful quality circles includes the following:

Have the employees received appropriate training?

Do employees understand the quality circle concept?

Do they respect the concept?

Do employees understand the value and purpose of team activities?

Do they comprehend their role and responsibility for the success of the company, beyond their jobs?

Who communicates with employees about circle activities?

Do employees realize the true meaning of empowerment and the decision-making authority that quality circle teams have?

Do employees understand the self-development aspects of the membership?

Do employees have visible support from management?

Do they have a qualified facilitator?

Summary of Quality Circles, The Reality

Typically, quality circles help employees focus on issues. These team activities have been successful in empowering employees and using their creativity and energy to help solve many of the problems within the company, including, but not restricted to, quality. There are several principles for quality circles:

> Problem solving should be a cooperative effort between employees and management.
>
> The effort requires training and education for all employees.
>
> Management must learn to trust employees to become problem solvers.
>
> Employees must be recognized for their efforts.

BEGINNING THE TEAM ACTIVITIES

Quality circles can help improve quality and productivity by making employees aware of problems and their impact on their jobs and the business and by allowing them to be actively involved in solutions. Team activities give employees an opportunity to build self-confidence and leadership skills through training and involvement; they also give the employees a chance to be heard and an opportunity to participate in positive changes in the way daily work is done. You are ready to begin if these questions have been answered:

> Do we have goals, objectives, and targets?
>
> What training is needed, is it ready, who will teach, when?
>
> What are the guidelines for the activities?
>
> Who will administer the system change and who will monitor progress?
>
> Who is ultimately responsible for success or failure?
>
> When will the team activities occur?
>
> Is there a budget?
>
> Are training facilities available for training and is there time?
>
> Will teams be truly empowered?
>
> What form will recognition take?
>
> What reports or documents does the system require?
>
> Is a computer database required for the system?
>
> Does management support this?

Step 1: First Meeting

Register the team for tracking purposes. Keeping historic data is important to maintaining the system, so you must document everything the team does (for later presentation) and choose a team name, leader, subleader, and secretary.

Step 2: Identify Problems

List the possible projects on a chart and score and rank them using a high, medium, and low scoring system. Select the most serious problem by asking some questions: How important is this problem to our processes or manufacturing output? Determine whether the impact of the problem to your area is high, medium, or low and enter that on the chart. Evaluate the potential for the problem getting worse if not corrected soon and add that factor to the chart. Follow this format for all problems listed; the priority issues will score high in all or most of the categories.

Step 3: Select a Project

If you have selected a project, skip to Step 4. Most teams meet to make a decision about what project to work on. Typically, each team member has an idea that he or she believes would be a good item for team problem solving. One way to make projection easier is to have preset criteria for selecting the most important or most realistic project. Section criteria might include the following:

- Projects must be solvable in 1 to 6 months.
- Projects must be realistic and not too technical for the team's experience level.
- Projects must be measurable, attainable, within the control of the team, and worthwhile to the employees and the company and have impact on safety, quality, cost, competitiveness, production, service, employee morale, or any other company-approved initiative.

Honda Quality Circle Case: The Waste Watchers

Quality circles and problem-solving teams can and do make a difference. An example from the Honda quality circle teams is the waste watchers from the Marysville material service department. The group formed in 1988 to study recycling of corrugated cardboard. At the time, Honda wasn't saving cardboard. All of it was trucked to landfills, because it was not considered worthwhile to spend time recycling. The team began to research the cost of hauling to the landfill and dumping, and it monitored the amounts of cardboard used and discarded weekly in just one of the plants.

The team analyzed the data and set its targets. It calculated the savings from reduced trips to landfills and dumping fees. The figures amazed the team. Next the team looked for a customer to buy the cardboard, estimated at 18 to 20 tons per day. It discovered that it would need a dedicated compactor, the team's first stumbling block. It made a presentation to management and found the compactor price to be a step $100,000. At this point the team went back to the customer and made a tentative deal for the customer to finance the compactor with the promise of payback within one year.

With a customer and a compactor, the problem shifted to how to get all 5,000 associates in the auto plant to help recycle. The team spent six weekends painting special dumpsters blue so that all recyclable cardboard could be deposited in the blue containers (the trash would go into yellow dumpsters). After all the blue dumpsters were put in place, the team approached the team leaders and coordinators asking their support for recycling. Only half the supervisors monitored the separation of cardboard from the trash, which was not enough to mean success.

Team members tried again to garner support, but with insufficient cooperation, they decided to approach an executive vice president for help. He did a plant walkthrough the next day, visiting every supervisor. Those who were not monitoring the recycling were told to climb into the dumpsters and spend the day separating trash from the recyclable cardboard.

In less than six months the team paid back the compactor cost, saved several hundred thousand dollars, and sold enough recycled cardboard to claim a total impact of more than $1 million in the first year. Total savings exceeded $3 million during the time the team monitored recycling.

This activity continues today, but it is no longer a circle activity. It is now included in material service and is handled by a waste-management company. The waste watchers went to Japan to present their success to the Honda NH-C World Convention. They also won the Governor's Award from Richard Celeste of Ohio for their efforts to clean up the environment and reduce landfill waste.

Step 4: Make a Plan for the Activity

Create a milestone graph to list the items or concerns that must be done or addressed and plan a time frame for completion of each task or item. An example of a milestone shown in Figure 11–1 lists the project countermeasure plans. A team activity chart/graph should account for the entire project, including the first meeting and the documentation of the countermeasure.

Step 5: Collect Data

The team will want to decide what information is needed to begin working on the project. As a team, determine what data are relevant and how or where to begin data collection. Each circle member must be responsible for gathering data for the team's problem-solving efforts. Keep accurate records and date all information. Checksheets, control charts, and variable data charts help.

Step 6: Analyze/Interpret Data

All the information gathered must be carefully organized. Illustrate the data on charts and graphs when possible. The typical charts and graphs include Pareto diagrams, histograms, line graphs, area graphs, column and bar graphs, and scatter diagrams.

Step 7: Root-Cause Analysis

The most common means of analysis is the cause-and-effect diagram known also as the fishbone or Ishikawa diagram. We also use the affinity diagram and the tree diagram.

Step 8: Develop Countermeasures

Consider all the potential causes for the problem and brainstorm for the most likely countermeasures (corrections).

Step 9: Try the Countermeasures

Plan the corrections and notify everyone who needs to know about them. Decide what will be done, who will do it, when, where, and how the countermeasures will be implemented.

Step 10: Test the Results and Analyze the Impact

Collect data and compare with the situation before you implemented changes. If the results were good, test again in a week. If results remain good, go to Step 11. If results were not as good as expected, go back to Steps 7 and 8.

Step 11: Document the Countermeasures

Write the change into the process standards if possible and train employees on any countermeasures that require a change in the way work or a process is done.

Step 12: Follow-Up

Follow up on the countermeasures after one month and again after six months. Show the data on charts and graphs for comparison with the pre-corrective action situation.

Quality circle and the team problem-solving activities are thriving in many companies throughout the world. Most companies have their own unique approach to the implementation and administration of the systems. They have discovered that employee involvement can be a key component to continued success and customer satisfaction. Team activities encourage education, training, communication, and improvements in production and efficiency. Everyone wins in an environment that provides opportunities for all employees to take ownership for the way their company operates every day. We began associate involvement at Honda of America in 1985 and know the value of the ideas that come from the 11,500 people working in our Ohio manufacturing plants.

12 TIME-BASED COMPETITION

Joseph D. Blackburn

Editor's note

Time-based competition is a logical approach to the next frontier in competitiveness. Time compression, looking for improved customer service through quick response, results in manufacturer cost savings. This chapter explores the whole exciting topic of time-based competition, lists the successful innovators, and will help your company take non–value-added time out of your delivery cycle.

In their struggle to regain a competitive advantage, U.S. manufacturers have too often neglected to use their most potent weapon: time. Physically located within the world's most lucrative market, U.S. manufacturers should have an overwhelming advantage in terms of responsiveness to customers. Unfortunately, rather than exploit this advantage, many U.S. firms are in the uncomfortable but familiar position of observing Japanese firms demonstrate the significance of time as a dimension of competition. In the process, these Japanese firms are successfully negating the geographical advantage held by U.S. firms.

TIME AS A COMMODITY AND COMPETITIVE WEAPON

According to Fred Smith, the founder and CEO of FedEx,

Time—as both a commodity and a competitive weapon—is an emerging issue that business people can't ignore if they expect to survive in this increasingly competitive world. We will see the demise of marginal firms who do not adopt time-based strategies. And the longer they wait, the faster they will fall. In short, where everything else is equal, time-based strategies become a key factor in widening the gap between those who adopt them and those who do not.[1]

Time is indeed displacing cost as a critical dimension of competition (see Figure 12–1), and firms that ignore the importance of time in their own processes are clearly at risk. The potential vulnerability of traditional manufacturers is clearly illustrated by the following statistic: In the average firm, *less than 5 percent* of the total time required to manufacture and deliver a product to a customer is spent on actual work. The remaining 95 percent is non–value-added time, which represents a gaping window of opportunity for the time-based competitor.

The just-in-time (JIT) revolution of the past few years was perhaps the first manifestation of a new type of time-based competition. Yet JIT is not an end in itself for a firm but an evolutionary step toward the long-term goal of total time compression. Zero inventory and proximity to suppliers, while important, have only a limited impact on the bottom line. The real benefits—the ones that provide a sustainable competitive advantage—are created by a shrinkage of the whole manufacturing cycle. This type of time compression translates into faster asset turnover, increased output and flexibility, and satisfied customers. Viewed in this way, the diminished inventory often associated with JIT is seen as more of a side benefit than a driving force.

What Is Time-Based Competition?

The phrase *time-based competition* originated with George Stalk and his colleagues at the Boston Consulting Group. In the research for their book, *Kaisha: The Japanese Corporation,* Stalk and Abegglen observed the evolution of JIT at companies such as Toyota. In their view, time-based competi-

FIGURE 12–1 Progression of competitive advantage in manufacturing

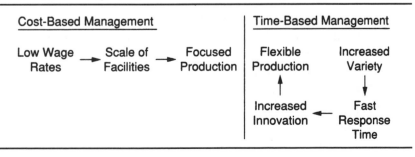

tion is the extension of JIT principles into every facet of the product delivery cycle, from research and development through marketing and distribution. When one firm achieves such a significant advantage in product or service delivery, the nature of competition in its entire industry is changed: Cost becomes secondary to response time. Companies in the textile and apparel business have dubbed this new capability "quick response."

IDLE TIME EQUALS WASTE

Both JIT and time-based competition have identical objectives: Eliminate all waste in the production of a product or delivery of a service. With JIT, small production runs, quick changeovers, and low inventories enhance production speed. The percentage of time when value is being added to the product is maximized. This is also the essence of time-based competition. Eliminate idle or dead time wherever it exists, make sure that work can be processed in small batches, and maximize the value-added time. Time-based competition, however, goes one step further, encompassing not just manufacturing but the complete product cycle.

Order Processing

Consider the order-processing function. In many cases it takes longer for the firm to process the order and place it on its master schedule than it does to manufacture the product. Most of the processing time is wasted time. No value is added while batches of paper pile up. The reasons for delay are frequently the same as in manufacturing: Information is processed in large batches; orders are moved in batches from one location to another; large inventories of orders await some form of approval; processing of orders is sequential rather than parallel.

Compressing order-processing time requires actions almost identical to the changes needed for JIT implementation in manufacturing:

- Simplification of the process itself, cutting out all unnecessary steps.
- Better tracking to reduce dead spots.
- Cross training of workers to eliminate single-minded focus on a small part of the total process.
- Higher in-process quality to eliminate checking and rechecking (inspections).
- Group training.
- Running some efforts in parallel rather than in sequence (e.g., simultaneous engineering).

The implication, then, is that firms that are or have been successful with JIT will have a leg up on their competitors in time compressing other phases of the business. This notion, however, may be wishful thinking. Many companies have not started to look at the front end of their processes. Of those that have, the area is still relatively new and filled with opportunity to try out JIT manufacturing ideas or to develop new ones to speed the process.

Northern Telecom, a leading manufacturer of telecommunications equipment, found that although it had dramatically compressed time in one manufacturing process for large digital switches, months were needed to convert a customer order into an approved (engineered) order ready for manufacture. To understand the bottlenecks in the process and alleviate them, the company sent individuals out to track specific orders through the processing function to the factory floor. What Northern Telecom found was that paperwork processing, not machines, caused their long lead times. Northern Telecom started to correct the problem areas to make order processing as efficient as manufacturing and to achieve sizable financial and competitive gains in the process. Time and processing steps cut out of the order-administration cycle represent dollar savings as a result of the following:

- Fewer clerical hours required.
- Improved cash flows.
- Fewer communications dollars (e.g., phone charges, faxes, computer time) spent in trucking and expediting orders.

Northern Telecom's efforts paid off when fire destroyed a district telephone switching office in Brooklyn, New York, affecting service for thousands of phone users. The phone company went to the largest producers of digital switches to find a replacement unit. Because of emergency conditions, price was not a major consideration. Northern Telecom's bid quoted a delivery time of two weeks—four weeks less than the competitor's. It had even loaded the replacement switching system on a truck before getting approval for the order. Guess which firm received the order.

Acme Boot Company, a division of Farley Industries, is the world's largest manufacturer of Western boots. Until recently it took up to 35 working days from the time a decision was made to manufacture a certain style and size of shoe until the completed batch was delivered to the distribution center. Of those 35 days, actual work was performed for no more than about 14 hours. For 95 percent of the time, then, no value was added to the product (see Figure 12–2).

Acme recently found that about 10 days could be excised by improving the order-processing function and coordinating the ordering of raw materials. This increased the amount of time that value is being added by about 20

FIGURE 12–2 Acme Boot: Idle time in the production process

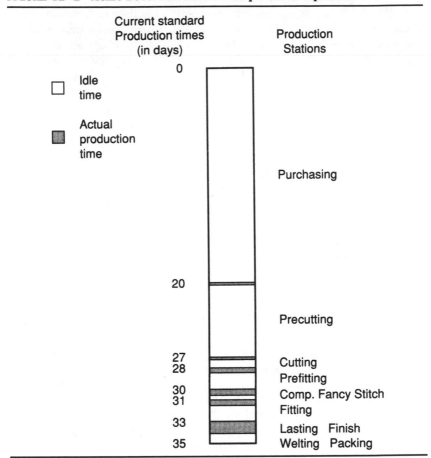

percent. More important, it shortened Acme's response time to customers, giving the company the opportunity to sharpen its forecasts and thus reduce finished-goods inventory.

LONG-TERM, TIME-BASED COMPETITION RESULTS

What are the ultimate long-term results of a transition to time-based competition? George Stalk claims that "growth rates of three times the industry average, with two times the industry profit margins are exciting—and achievable—targets." Thus, once a company falls behind competitors capable of achieving such results, it may never be able to achieve any sort of industry preeminence.

Stalk describes as typical the example of a firm making equipment for the paper industry. The firm had the largest share of the U.S. market but could not get any more of the business. The reason was delivery times that averaged 22 weeks and were highly variable (plus or minus 10 weeks). Through time-compression efforts, it reduced the lead time to 8 weeks plus or minus 1 day. Volume went up 16 percent and is growing at a projected annual rate of 40 percent. Not only are costs down by more than 5 percent but, with quicker and more consistent lead times, prices can also be increased. As a result, profit margins are up by 10 to 15 percent, placing them well above the industry average.

Keys to Becoming a Time-Based Competitor

Becoming a time-based competitor demands major transformations in the way the traditional manufacturing firm is managed. Not surprisingly, these changes are precisely the ones required to convert the manufacturing process itself to a JIT system.

Traditional Manufacturing

Consider the traditional manufacturer. The typical Western manufacturer produces components and products in large batches. Why? To achieve scale economies because the cost of setup, or changeover from one component to another, is so high. In addition, long batch-production runs also contribute to high machine-utilization rates, and this is viewed as superior performance according to conventional accounting standards. However, these large batches lead to high work-in-process (WIP) inventories and, worse, long factory response times.

The traditional manufacturing process is often characterized by a process layout. Processing equipment is grouped according to function, again with the objective of control over machine utilization and efficiency. Product typically follows a slow, disjointed path through such facilities. WIP inventories tend to build up at machine centers, increasing throughput time and making the scheduling task more complex.

To cope with the challenge of a complex scheduling problem, a central scheduling system is typically employed, usually involving an expensive computer system. Elaborate materials-requirements planning (MRP) systems are necessary in this environment to avoid losing track of the large component inventories in the intricate flow process.

JIT Manufacturing

Contrast the traditional manufacturing process with the JIT process. Process batches are small because changeover costs have been minimized. Smaller batches of components yield reduced WIP inventories and dramatically diminished factory response times. By achieving increased product speed through the factory, the transition to a JIT process develops the rapid manufacturing response necessary to be a time-based competitor.

The layout in a JIT factory typically follows product, rather than process, lines. Instead of grouping machines by function, they are grouped into flow lines supporting similar components or products. A simple layout of this type is helpful, of course, when components are being transferred in small batches. As a side benefit, space requirements (space usually taken up by inventory) are also reduced by sizable amounts.

The simpler process flow and more responsive factory minimizes the need for centralized control. Local scheduling rules can be effective in this elemental environment. To schedule production, simple pull systems—"Use one, make one"—can be used. There is less need for a central requirements plan with a complex computer program controlling the flow of components through the plant. As a consequence, the number of dispatchers and expediters should be reduced sharply under local control. With shorter throughput times, forecasting requirements far out into the future is no longer necessary.

None of this surprises managers who have survived a JIT implementation. What is surprising, however, and key to becoming a time-based competitor are the even greater benefits possible by applying JIT principles beyond manufacturing. To see this clearly, examine how these concepts are applied in an entirely different area.

Time Compressing the New-Product Introduction Process

The most positive impact on profits from time-compression activities comes from new-product development (Figure 12–3). A recent McKinsey & Company study of the effects of new-product introduction, using these market assumptions—an industry with 20 percent market growth, a five-year product life cycle, and 12 percent annual price erosion—found that a six-month delay in entering a market can result in a 33 percent reduction in after-tax profit. To put this in perspective, a six-month delay is five times more costly than a 50 percent development-cost overrun and about 30 percent more costly than having production costs run 10 percent too high.

Getting the jump on competitors by being first to market offers a powerful competitive advantage (see Figure 12–4). The time required to design and engineer a product and then produce it in volume is becoming, in many industries, the key measure of competitiveness.

Japan: Some of the best Japanese firms (Honda and Sony, for example) can introduce products twice as fast as their Western counterparts—and have staffs half as large (see Box 12–1). Coupled with a flexible JIT manufacturing system, these firms clobber the competition with an array of new

FIGURE 12–3   Factors affecting profit

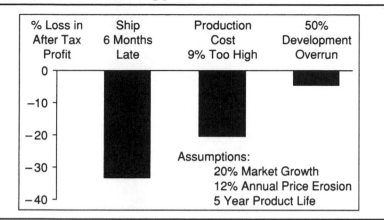

products at substantially lower costs. This is probably the reason why it is virtually impossible to find a radio, VCR, or CD player designed and manufactured in the United States.

A more detailed review of comparative new-product development data is shown in Figure 12–5. In seven of the eight development steps, the Japanese company took less than half the time the Western company

FIGURE 12–4   Who casts the biggest shadow?

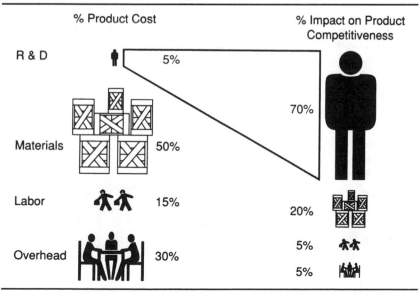

BOX 12–1   Increased response time in nonmanufacturing functions

Client observations

Projection T.V.

- Japanese can develop systems in one-third the time required by U.S. organizations

Plastic injection molds

- Japanese can develop molds in one-third the time required by U.S. competitors at 30 percent lower cost

Automotive engineering

- Japanese are developing new cars in half the time with half as many people as required by U.S. manufacturers

---

needed. The total difference added up to approximately 18 months; the Japanese got to market 1½ years before the competition.

The United States: Many U.S. firms are hindered in their efforts to engineer and introduce new products quickly by supply chains accustomed to traditionally slow responses. The following case history illustrates the problem.

FIGURE 12–5   Improving response time in new-product development

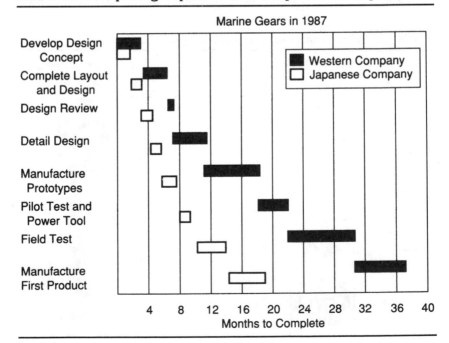

A producer of small air compressors in Ohio was introducing a new consumer product. The product concept and price were excellent, but it was crucial to get to market before its major competitor had staked out a claim to that segment of the market. In developing this new product, the firm had two options: (1) produce a prototype for testing at the plant in Ohio or (2) produce the prototype in Hong Kong and then farm out production elsewhere. The costs of the two options were equal. The decision turned on one fact: The prototype could be produced in half the time in Hong Kong. Lead time to obtain the injection molding dies was more than three months from U.S. manufacturers; the response in Hong Kong was: "When do you need it?" The pressures of time-based competition in new-product introductions forced the firm to move development and, ultimately, full-scale production offshore.

Leading U.S. high-technology firms have learned the benefits of rapid new-product introductions and made great strides in improving this part of the process (see Table 12–1). Notably, Hewlett-Packard observed that more than half of its sales orders are for products that have been introduced in the last three years. Firms such as Honeywell and Xerox, which have also undertaken major campaigns to increase the pace of new-product introductions, have had similar market experiences.

Team Engineering

These firms have time compressed the new-product introduction process by applying the same concepts that enabled their manufacturing arms to adopt JIT. To improve the flow of new ideas, team engineering practices have been introduced. Instead of following a *process* orientation, the objective here is to bring together a team focused on the *product*.

In a team environment, centralized scheduling or monitoring of activities is less necessary. With an automated information process, parallel activities, rather than sequential ones, become the norm—dramatically reducing the time required to develop the new product. Parallel activities, or simulta-

TABLE 12–1   Improvement of new-product development times

Company	New Product	Development Time	
		Before	**Now**
Honda	Automobiles	5 years	3 years
AT&T	Telephones	2 years	1 year
Navistar	Trucks	5 years	2.5 years
Hewlett-Packard	Printers	4.5 years	22 months

Source: Fortune, February 13, 1989

neous engineering as it is known in some circles, also tend to diminish the need for time-consuming product changes and looping back through the development process.

Design Automation

Design automation is employed so that information can be disseminated quickly to all members of the team. This is analogous to the small-batch production so necessary to a JIT process. Design automation means more than buying workstations equipped with CAD (computer-aided design) systems for the engineers. It requires linking all members of the product-development team together in a network so that new information can be transferred immediately. Shared databases with information on components and their manufacturability not only speed up the design process, they also yield a product that can be produced more easily, thus compressing the time required for process engineering.

Organizations That Foster Time-Based Competition

What type of organizations are positioned to become time-based competitors? Firms most likely to succeed in a time-based environment are those that are flexible and adaptable and that have top-management leadership willing to cut through bureaucratic red tape. Rapid change is required, which dictates a nimble organization. The leaders of such organizations will typically have created an atmosphere of constant improvement and change.

Notably, the strategic plans for two leading U.S. time-based competitors, Hewlett-Packard and Northern Telecom, both employ the term *stretch objectives* to describe plans to reduce time in their processes. Top management typically sets company objectives (e.g., time, cost, profitability) for the year 2000. Using the long-term objectives as targets, they then lay out intermediate goals to be reached over the next six months, year, two years, and so forth. The overall effects of the program are to stretch the capabilities of the entire organization continually over a long time and to keep the firm ahead of its competition.

Flexible Organization Structures

Firms with rigid organizational boundaries will be hindered in their efforts to become time-based competitors. Reducing the cycle time to get products from concept to customer requires teamwork among all the functional areas of the organization. A lack of cooperation among departments easily can frustrate these efforts. Another obstacle is organizational inertia that leads to rigid bureaucratic procedures. People who believe that what they are doing is correct because it's always been done that way (another version of the "if it ain't broke" syndrome) are major roadblocks to change.

Teamwork

Organizational structures that support and encourage teamwork seem to be successful, particularly in time compressing the new-product development process. Structures based on function tend to create barriers to team performance. A more flexible organizational structure based on product rather than function will be better suited for time-based competition. To speed the process of bringing a new product from concept through engineering to the factory floor, the team must be devoted to the objective of completing the process successfully in the shortest possible time.

To be effective, the members of the team must be recruited from different functional areas within the organization. This team cannot perform effectively when the team members must maintain allegiance to their functional leaders. Leading U.S. firms (e.g., Honeywell's building controls division, Xerox, and Hewlett-Packard) have embraced the team concept to spearhead rapid new-product introductions. Honeywell has reduced the time required to introduce new thermostats and other control products from 38 to 14 months with further reductions forthcoming.

Systems Support

Traditional performance measures must be discarded to move into the arena of time competition. Managers are evaluated in terms of time performance rather than traditional cost-based accounting measures. Machine loadings and overhead allocations are not only outmoded, they are dysfunctional for the time-based competitor: They reward managers for bad decisions. In fact, the same revisions in accounting practices and performance measures required for JIT are needed for time compression throughout the organization.

In designing new systems to support time-based competition, the goal is simple: Focus on time (and quality, of course), measure improvements in the firm's performance along these dimensions, and reward managers on that basis. As with JIT, production speed is of vital importance; things must move and not wait to be counted or batched. Consequently, the importance of individual work centers, around which many accounting systems are based, is diminished. Asset turnover should increase dramatically as the firm becomes more agile and productive, and this should become a key measure.

Information systems play a critical role in time compression by supporting teamwork and coordination across the organization. Rapid exchange of design information among work groups is necessary for the process of simultaneous engineering that is responsible for rapid reductions in new-product introduction cycles. Most of the reductions in customer-service cycle times have come in the order-processing functions; these changes usually require faster information processing so that orders are processed immediately in batches of one (again applying a basic JIT principle). In fact, much of FedEx's reputation for reliable, time-specific customer service is attributable to its state-of-the-art information systems. For example, FedEx now employs a terminal in a truck that provides constant contact with the field for tracking packages, expediting deliveries, and planning last-minute pickups.

TIME-BASED COMPETITORS

Toyota

How long does it take to become a time-based competitor? For Toyota, the process appears to be evolutionary and never ending. Toyota has been refining its production system for more than 20 years and, after making great strides in manufacturing, has now moved successfully to slice the idle time out of the distribution chain.

Photo Processing

At the other extreme are situations in which technological changes make dramatic time compression possible virtually overnight. For example, new automated equipment for photo processing has reduced the time required for this service from several days to less than an hour. With most manufacturing firms, however, experience indicates that the time-compression process takes years. Implementation must often be achieved incrementally, one department at a time.

Cost is not really a major factor. Most case studies on time-based competition have shown that the competitive benefits far outweigh the costs. Unless costly computer technology is used to speed information flows, most applications involve simple, inexpensive solutions. The time spent planning for necessary changes in a process is often a wiser investment than computerization of every task. Evaluating the costs and benefits of a time-compression program is remarkably similar to observing total quality control (TQC) implementations. With TQC, firms repeatedly report that while the cost of a quality improvement program may appear large at the outset, the process changes that result tend to drive costs down. Time compression, like quality, actually is free.

Service Industries

The strategic opportunities of time-based competition are not restricted to manufacturing; time has been the critical dimension of competition in many service industries for years. The fast-food business, of which McDonald's is a leading example, represents the essence of time-based competition. Instead of making customers wait 15 minutes before the lunch arrives, fast-food establishments have food ready and waiting.

The financial services industry also offers significant opportunities. Here the key to gaining a competitive advantage in the marketplace is quick response. The ability to be the first to develop and introduce a new product in response to a change in the tax law is a powerful weapon. Note that the process is remarkably similar to introducing a new product in a manufacturing environment: The financial instrument must be designed, engineered (in the accounting and legal departments), manufactured, marketed, and distributed to the customer. The first firm with a quality product usually gains the lion's share of the market. In the banking industry, for example, we are seeing the emergence of time-based competitors seizing larger shares of the business. By streamlining the process, some banks can now offer 24- or 36-hour mortgages—a process that in the past typically took over a month. Similar changes are sweeping through the commercial loan business.

In the overnight parcel business, FedEx has used time-based competition to stake out a dominant position while charging premium prices. To maintain that market position, FedEx has sought to enhance its reputation as a leading time-based competitor. In two years alone, it has spent $1.5 billion on capital improvements to make its process more efficient. With this system, FedEx can handle more than a million packages daily and track down any one of them anywhere in the world within 30 minutes of a request. The time-based strategy has rewarded FedEx for the past year with revenues of nearly $4 billion and pretax profits exceeding $300 million.

In a dramatic recent development, UPS has decided to compete head-to-head on the same dimension—the overnight market. The consumer will be the obvious winner in this confrontation. Marginal competitors in the overnight business will probably be the first casualties.

Identifying the Time-Based Competitor

Firms that have achieved a distinct time advantage should be readily identifiable. Customers are the first to know, so one of the best ways to identify an emerging star is either to ask customers or to assume a customer's vantage point. For the customer, a key barometer is the rate of introduction of new products or technological innovations in current products. Product introductions are a litmus test for time-based competition because this process is the most difficult to speed up. It requires coordination among all functional areas—from R&D and engineering through manufacturing and marketing.

Benetton is a time-based competitor in the fashion apparel business. Through an innovation in the dying process, it dyes only finished garments, so production can proceed without a decision on colors until the last minute. If American customers want red sweaters, Benetton can dye more versions red and reduce shipments of other colors. This, of course, helps the company respond more quickly to fashion whims, and it overcomes the disadvantage of the distance between production facilities in Italy and the U.S. market. By being ultraresponsive to the market, the company can keep its investment in finished goods low and increase its profitability.

In the automobile industry, it is easy to spot the time-based competitors. Honda, for example, has one of the highest rates of new-product introductions. On the other hand, General Motors has been criticized for a lack of innovation and variety in its product line. With respect to product innovations such as four-wheel steering, for example, U.S. auto manufacturers have not exhibited the rapid product-development capabilities of a time-based competitor.

The computer software market is another area where new-product delivery and product upgrades are critical to market success. Spotting the time-based competitor is again relatively easy. Key indicators are the abilities to meet promised delivery dates and to deliver updates quickly whenever new personal computer hardware is introduced. Success flows quickly and surely to the bottom line.

With consumer products, observing how quickly a competitor responds to a product innovation is a useful exercise. When Heinz introduced ketchup in translucent, squeezable plastic bottles, it immediately gained a sizable advantage over its rivals. Caught unprepared, Heinz's competitors have taken a long time to catch up.

At an operational level a key identifier of an emerging time-based competitor is customer-response time. The manufacturer with a time advantage can promise and deliver orders on short notice. Inventory levels will be lower. In addition, the marketing campaigns of such companies typically will stress their exemplary customer-service records.

Equally important is the ability to discern companies that are not time-based competitors. Just ask: Whose products look the same year after year? Whose lead times keep increasing? Whose working capital is tied up in inventories? Whose orders are always late and show few signs of improving? Once these questions are answered, the time-bloated firms become obvious.

Early identification of true time-based competitors is also vital to investors. These are the firms that achieve dominant market positions, lead their industries in profitability, and ultimately outperform stock market indicators. Again, the most successful time-based competitors should already have made great strides in implementing JIT systems (Hewlett-Packard, for example). Many of the firms emerging today as formidable competitors in the arena of time-based competition have already achieved world-class quality and low cost; they have simply added the additional weapon of speed to their arsenal. JIT is an important first step but not the ultimate act of gaining long-term competitive advantage.

NOTES

1. Fredrick W. Smith, "Time: Tomorrow's Weapon for Global Competition," Speech to Time-Based Competition Conference, Vanderbilt University, December 16, 1988.

13 KAIZEN—A TOOL FOR CHANGE

AN AMERICAN PERSPECTIVE

Anthony C. Laraia

Editor's note

The term *kaizen* means make better, but in English the word has become a verb meaning to take a process or a product or a design and using the power of the internal experts, the people on the shop floor and in the design room, to make something measurably better. To kaizen a process requires much planning, concentration, and focus until the job is over, which it never truly is.

Monday 7 A.M. The team—machine operators, assemblers, an engineer, a tool designer, a sales representative, a local supplier, an executive from corporate headquarters—assembled in the cramped conference room for the kickoff meeting. Their team leader, the department supervisor, presented their objective: Solve a chronic problem—build a manufacturing cell that cuts in half the process time for machined components—by Friday! The plant manager and the team's facilitator, an experienced kaizen veteran, added their exhortations and the work began.

Much of the morning was spent cleaning the workplace, scrubbing machines and floor, cleaning out cabinets, discarding unneeded items, and so forth. Cleaning and organizing would be part of each day's routine for the rest of the week.

216

By early afternoon, the team had decided on an initial configuration for the new cell and along with several maintenance tradespeople had begun the process of disconnecting and relocating equipment. No precise engineering drawings were needed, just some chalk marks on the floor following a familiar U-shaped pattern. No hard wiring or plumbing was necessary either—after a few trials they'd probably be moving things around again, anyway. (It had taken a few kaizen projects for the plant engineer to get used to the idea, but now quick-connect devices were becoming the standard for machine hookups.)

At the late-afternoon review meeting with the plant manager and facilitator, the team leader presented progress reports and plans for the evening and next day. The plant manager asked anxiously how long it would be before production was restored—the month's schedule was heavy and the production quota still had to be met.

After a quick dinner in the cafeteria, the team broke up into subteams, one continuing with the move, another sorting out needed tooling and coming up with a point-of-use storage system; a third was designing a kanban system to regulate the flow of work to and from the new cell. By late evening, when it was apparent that the move was a larger undertaking than expected, the first-shift maintenance crew stayed on to work with the second shift. But it looked like the move still couldn't be completed before Tuesday afternoon. The team called it quits at 10 P.M. and agreed to assemble at 6:30 the next morning.

The next day was similar but more intense. Under pressure from the plant manager and the facilitator to step up the pace, the team was able to begin running some test parts in time for the 4 P.M. status meeting. By early evening it was clear that the cell configuration needed to change, and the three machines had to be relocated to better balance work among the cell operators. The team again worked until 10 P.M. to get the job done and planned an early-morning trial.

On Wednesday morning, the team began running the new cell in earnest, changing from one product to another to develop and refine the new process and ensure that it would work on all required parts. Equipment operators and machine setters were the keys to this part of the process, bringing real skill and experience to the team.

The new pull system began to come together; taped squares on the floor would be painted once the team was satisfied. The tooling subteam's work had begun to come together. Tooling was being moved from a central crib to new point-of-use locations in the cell and individual shadow boards with outlines of individual hand tools were being made for each machine. Another 4 P.M. status meeting and another late night and the team was on the home stretch.

Thursday would be a short day. By 5 P.M. the team had run and refined procedures for all of the part configurations the cell would handle. The team had demonstrated a process time reduction of more than 60 percent, exceeding its goal. Standard work documentation was being prepared to institutionalize the changes the team had made, and the finishing touches were going into the tool racks and kanban squares. After three days of fast food at the plant, the team enjoyed a celebratory dinner at a local restaurant.

On Friday, the team did a final cleanup and prepared and presented its final report, including some recommendations for follow-up improvements to be accomplished over the following month. By noon it was over. Another kaizen team had met its targets, leaving behind a dramatically improved process.

Kaizen is a term known throughout the world yet widely misunderstood. Kaizen first came to prominence as a part of the Toyota Production System (TPS)—the manufacturing system credited by many with Japan's leap to the top in manufacturing efficiency and global competitiveness. Often confused with TPS itself, kaizen is rather the primary implementation tool used to establish the lean manufacturing environment; kaizen is the method that drives improvement in all manufacturing and related practices throughout the enterprise.

First, let's talk about lean manufacturing. Lean manufacturing stresses the elimination of waste, cutting out all non–value-added activities while severely focusing on the remaining value-added parts of the process. Originally, the concept of lean manufacturing was applied to the internal manufacturing of the business. The supply chain, from raw material suppliers through the product-distribution system, was added quickly.

Today, the concept of the lean enterprise has taken center stage with the same focus on waste elimination being applied to *all* of the business, from product development to finance to sales. But, whether they are applied more narrowly or broadly, common themes emerge. While there are as many variations on the theme of lean manufacturing as the number of companies trying to adopt its tenets, three underlying principles stand out:

Takt Time (from the German for meter or tempo). Pacing or regulating operations to customer demand; literally being driven by the customers' consumption of product.

One Piece Flow. Establishing or changing processes to produce goods one at a time or in the smallest increments possible, always with the aim of finishing a product in the form in which it can be sold, for each unit started.

Pull systems. Demand-based flow (as opposed to scheduled flow) of materials through a process, most often through simple visible means, linked to the customer.

In application, kaizen is the preferred tool for moving the organization, the business process, into alignment with these key principles. Kaizen can be translated simply as continuous improvement, but in what sense? American businesses have pursued continuous improvement for years under various total quality or world-class manufacturing movement banners. Progress is most often incremental, delivering small improvements over prolonged periods. Focus is broad, frequently across the whole organization; breakthroughs are rare. Risks can most often be characterized as sins of omission—too little change too late.

How is kaizen different? Kaizen is a highly focused improvement process aimed at producing step function performance improvements—20, 50, 90 percent—in a short time in narrowly targeted areas.

- Wiremold, a Connecticut-based manufacturer of wiring devices, realized a fourfold improvement in inventory turns in four years and reduced press setup times from several hours to less than two minutes.
- Pratt & Whitney has reduced process times for commercial jet engines from over 16 months to 5 months.
- Johnson & Johnson has employed kaizen to speed production flows.

Kaizen places great demands on team participants, as well as on management that charters the team. While improvements can be dramatic, they tend to be in specific areas with broad-based improvement coming from the cumulative effects of a number of wisely chosen projects. Misapplication, doing the right things in the wrong places and for the wrong reasons, is a common danger.

WHAT EXACTLY IS KAIZEN, HOW DOES IT WORK, AND WHY?

There are several types of kaizens, ranging from those that focus on developing solutions, to problems on the factory floor, to implementing a predetermined plan for change, to streamlining the flow of paperwork. The most familiar and common type, the factory kaizen, provides a good example of the technique.

Kaizen is a Top-Down Process

The kaizen process must begin with the process owner, the individual with real ownership and responsibility who has the authority to change the process and is answerable for the consequences. He or she may be the general manager, president, or in some cases plant manager; it is *always* the person in charge. Kaizen cannot be successful without strong support and direction from the top.

Kaizen begins with the selection of a project. The choice might be a bottleneck machine limiting product capacity or responsiveness. The needed improvement, let's say in changeover time, is established and a specific goal set for the team by the plant manager.

Kaizen is a Team Process

A team of individuals is selected from a range of functional disciplines, usually with a core of members from the area attacked. The team's work involves the intense application of a few simple tools in a straightforward, commonsense approach to bringing about real and profound change.

In a typical scenario, the team is brought together before or at the beginning of the project period (2 to 10 days) and given basic education in the principles of lean manufacturing and training in the kaizen tools required to do the work. These tools include the following:

Waste elimination—Value-added versus non–value-added

Standard work analysis

Cell design

Pull system and kanban design

Setup-reduction techniques

The team then spends 2 to 10 days (average 3 to 5 days) defining and carrying out the actions necessary to change the process and bring about the needed improvement. Several 12- to 16-hour days are spent developing, testing, and implementing their ideas. In a well-planned and well-executed kaizen project, team training is provided by trained kaizen experts who also facilitate during the project itself, working with teams and management to ensure success. (Some of the facilitation techniques employed in Japan and by a number of Japanese consultants in the United States have become noted for their severity. Most North American practitioners have found that a toned-down yet firm approach gets the most satisfactory results in the long run.) A daily feedback session with the process owner and his or her management team serves to maintain direction and momentum and to provide opportunities for course corrections.

Kaizen Principles

The kaizen process is based on several rules that may vary in detail from company to company. However, the underlying concepts are the same:

- Reject the status quo, be open-minded.
- Maintain a positive attitude.
- Reject excuses, seek solutions.
- Ask why. Why? Why? Why? There are *no* stupid questions.
- Take action—implement ideas immediately, don't seek perfection; that is, do what can be done *now,* with the resources at hand.
- Use all of the team's knowledge. The experts are frequently found on the factory floor.
- Disregard rank. All team members are equal and everyone has something to contribute.
- *Just do it!*

Kaizen Is Doing, Not Proposing

Kaizen fundamentally differs from traditional continuous improvement processes because it is almost entirely action based. Teams are charged with both developing and implementing their solutions; they create new processes or change existing processes, leaving a *new* process in place. Success meeting team goals is achieved by first demonstrating the changed process and then by putting in place the new standard practices that ensure continuation of the process in the future.

Kaizen is very much a hands-on process. Team participants not only plan, they clean equipment, sort tools, move machinery (within the bounds of safety), assemble, build, and run the process. They get tired, they get frustrated, and they get dirty together. Rank is not recognized. Factory managers and company officers work side by side with machine operators to find and implement the best of their ideas. The team's job is to make change happen and to create and leave in place a new way of doing things.

Kaizen Is a Low-Budget Process

As a tool for bringing about improvement in a rapid and targeted manner, Kaizen is a low-cost process. When a team is charged with demonstrating and implementing changes to a live process in three to five days, there is no time to spend money on new equipment, complex and expensive tooling, and elaborate systems solutions. Most teams will be allowed only modest budgets to support their projects—the kind of challenge that often leads to the most creative solutions.

The kaizen technique itself teaches that eliminating waste and developing creative solutions using the equipment and tools at hand are the preferred methods for achieving improvement goals. Many companies that have adopted kaizen improvement techniques as part of an overall lean manufacturing or lean enterprise initiative report that their more effective application of the means already at hand has resulted in significant reductions in their new equipment costs.

While kaizen projects themselves are inexpensive, learning the effective application kaizen technique can be costly. Even moderately sized companies report substantial expenditures for consulting services to provide effective education, training, and development of internal-resources expenditures before their programs begin to pay off. Certainly, many opportunities exist for companies to sample the process, but in reality, the biggest payoff comes to those willing to commit the resources required to do it right—to choose, to train, to follow up. Kaizen is not a process easily mastered. Guidance by experienced practitioners, usually on a prolonged basis, is cited time after time as an underlying fundamental of success. And, as with most business improvement processes, the rewards are commensurate with the investment.

Although the range of projects that a kaizen team might be asked to carry out is large, the scope and focus must be narrowly defined and clearly bounded. Results must be unambiguously measured. In a factory environment, a team might be assigned to build a manufacturing cell from individual functionally applied machines, another might attack changeover times on a key bottleneck machine, and yet another might create a pull system to regulate a part or all of a process.

What Works and What Doesn't

Because kaizen is an effective tool for bringing about quick change, it should be applied where a need for specific improvement can be identified and where necessary resources can be assembled. Beginning with its roots in Toyota's auto plants, kaizen has proved to be an effective tool for improvement in a broad array of manufacturing and business processes. From Pratt & Whitney (jet engines) to Wiremold (wiring devices) to Johnson & Johnson (medical products), from metal stamping, to turning, to cost accounting systems, to product distribution, kaizen has proved its value in cutting to the core of what we do and how we do it.

Focus and Commitment

One of the keys to kaizen's success is the close focus that this method brings to a process. Often, management is unwilling or unable to give full authority to those charged with bringing about a change. Problems range from the possible impact on other parts of the operation to the real risks, the unforeseen impact, of dramatically changing too large a part of the business. The larger the area affected, the larger the potential risks. Intended actions become recommendations as the fruits of change are watered down in endless studies. Risk avoidance outweighs the opportunity for gain.

In kaizen, a more narrowly defined focus is established along with clear, measurable improvement goals. The team's target might be a machine, a cell, or a department, but the scope is generally such that the risks of unforeseen consequences are minimized. An authorization to do what needs to be done becomes feasible. Further, since kaizen is a short-term change process, typically spanning no more than several days, whatever is changed can be changed back.

Commitment Is Key

Management *must* be ready to make a real commitment to change—not only to agree to the need for change, but to lead the process. A kaizen team should be directed to do what needs to be done. If you're not ready to see a new process in place by next Monday, not just proposed but in place and functioning as the new way of doing business, then don't start. Kaizen just isn't for you.

With leadership commitment comes resource commitment:

Time away from normal duties for the team to do its job.

Disruption of a part of the business for several days.

Education, training, and competent oversight (perhaps outside resources) for the team and probably much of the management staff.

A *real* commitment to the people affected by the change. The surest way to kill a kaizen initiative is to let the improvements in productivity and efficiency and elimination of non–value-added activities be translated into lost jobs. If you must make cuts—an unfortunate fact of life for many—do it first. Move past it before you begin the kaizen journey. Kaizen is a process that depends for its success on the commitment, hard work, and creativity of its team members. They cannot rationally be expected to effectively participate in a process that eliminates their jobs or diminishes their opportunities for reward and advancement.

IMPLEMENTATION STRATEGIES AND TACTICS

There are many reasons for wanting to begin or at least explore the kaizen process. Some will be interested in the technique as part of a commitment to adopting lean manufacturing. Others see kaizen as a tool for addressing a few specific problems or opportunities. Yet others will see it as a mechanism for demonstrating that radical change can happen and that it's safe to try, to do it fast, and to do it now. All are equally valid objectives.

Purists argue that a company-wide commitment to adopting a variant of the Toyota production system or going lean are necessary for a serious kaizen effort, but the process offers benefits at many levels. What's important is a clear understanding of real objectives and a realistic commitment to the process commensurate with those objectives.

Getting Started

Begin kaizen as an exploration. Most firms employ the services of professional consultants, at least in the initial stages of implementation. Senior management should take a lead role in the resource selection, education, and training processes, meeting with the management of other firms using kaizen. Senior management should participate on an actual team in another company to gain first-hand experience with the process. Professional organizations such as the Association for Manufacturing Excellence with its Kaizen Blitz^{SM} program offer such opportunities. A typical implementation, at any level, begins with an effective education and training program for the management staff and the selection of a lead resource within the organization to promote the kaizen concept and to become a key internal expert resource.

Selection of First Project

Select a series of demonstration projects to validate the process within the organization. Choose projects carefully based on several criteria. Projects must

- Be clearly and unambiguously measurable (e.g., reduce setup time, work-in-process).
- Be highly visible operations (i.e., make it clear that something is changing).
- Meet a need easily recognized by the organization (e.g., relieve a bottleneck operation, reduce cost).
- Highlight the contributions of all levels of the organization, especially the lower-level workers.

Selecting the Team

Choose team participants for the role they need to play in the team's efforts, for what they know, but also for what they don't know. An outsider's seemingly silly question may be the key to a real breakthrough. Make sure that the core of the kaizen team includes several associates who will operate and own the process once the team's work is done. The most effective teams create solutions that are strongly supported by the people who have ongoing responsibilities for or within the process.

Ensuring Success

Advocacy versus Sponsorship. Change agents aren't enough. Kaizen cannot become an effective tool for change within an organization unless it is sponsored strongly from the top. Don't confuse sponsorship with advocacy. To sponsor means to give support in a real sense, not merely as a cheerleader. The sponsor of the kaizen initiative, the senior manager who owns the business, must demonstrate in tangible ways his or her commitment to the process. The sponsor must not only suggest change but be prepared to describe it as an imperative so that the whole organization can clearly see its direction and need.

For a kaizen team to be successful it must carry out the actions needed, or better yet demanded, by management for the success of the business. Since the changes are radical, the need for clear top-management support is all the more acute.

Following Up—Securing the Gain

A key measure of the value of kaizen to an organization is the effectiveness with which the dramatic gains achieved during the project period are sustained in the weeks and months that follow. As a process of step-function improvement, expect some slippage from the initial results, but limit this backslide so that a substantial gain remains as the stepping off point for the next improvement initiative. Management follow-up and a serious and disciplined approach to measuring the performance of the process are the keys to securing the gain.

You Get What You Measure

Part of a team's work is to establish the standard work practices to be followed in the future. Management must ensure that these work practices are followed and that the old practices are not readopted through a formal and consistent follow-up process. As part of this process, key measures must be established and monitored regularly.

Make the measures simple and direct. If you want parts per shift, then measure parts per shift, not standard hours earned or some indirectly derived analogue of operator or machine efficiency. If you want quick and frequent setups, then track minutes per setup and setups per day, not setup hours earned versus some standard.

Any supervisor or manager worth his or her salt or intent on earning a bonus soon learns how to maximize results by almost any measure that one can apply. Therefore the right measure must be the one that shows the performance desired in the simplest and most direct fashion.

For kaizen to provide real and lasting benefits, management needs to follow through by establishing and monitoring clear and simple measures, providing emphasis and taking actions to ensure that the new practices that kaizen delivers are maintained. Remember that in the long run only the simple processes work.

Kaizen is a simple process. The results it brings come from the application of simple, commonsense principles in an organized and disciplined fashion. Kaizen stresses linkages of simple steps that build on each other to reach a goal rather than development of complicated, broadly focused systems. Complex solutions are hard to maintain and harder to monitor. Most organizations lack the energy and attention span required to make them work. The simple, easy-to-follow solutions, the kind that kaizen delivers, are those that last.

14 PULL SYSTEMS

A SIMPLE VISUAL APPROACH TO COMPLEX PROCESSES

Wayne K. Smith

Editor's note

Pull systems more directly link production and material pipelines to customer demand. They are simply designed to respond with minimal cost and waste and to quickly flex the process to meet volume and mix changes. Author Smith, whose industry experience is heavily influenced by process industries, recommends a few simple tools to implement a pull system, including powerful visual methods.

INTRODUCTION

Over the past 10 years, many progressive companies have found that pull-system scheduling concepts have helped them simplify the problems of scheduling, inventory management, and customer service. Pull systems are simple, visual, and owned/operated by people on the shop floor. As such, pull has also been an effective aid in employee-involvement efforts. Pull

This chapter is extracted from the "Time Out" implementation series handbook, copyright P/TM 1996.

concepts originated in discrete-parts operations, most notably the auto industry. Even today, examples in the process industry are rare, and many managers assume that pull does not apply in that environment.

Pull is closely aligned with and supports a cycle-time strategy. Cycle time (Ct) is the time it takes material to flow through the process from raw material to delivery to the customer and is defined as Ct = inventory/demand, or inventory in terms of days' supply. Cycle-time strategy is based on the belief that there is a direct link between the time trapped in a process and the quality of that process. Cycle-time strategy results in an endless quality/time improvement cycle: The only way time can be extracted is to eliminate waste activities from the process. Also, as time is extracted stations become more closely connected, making cause/effect relationships more obvious, which results in the ability to further improve quality. Pull scheduling is an integral part of minimizing cycle time.

This discussion will show that pull principles are universal; the basic principles simply need to be adapted to the specific environment. This chapter describes a simplified structure and logic base for pull, introduces some new adaptations, and lays out a detailed pull design methodology. All will be applicable in any manufacturing environment, but the examples will be process-industry based.

THE PULL CONCEPT

One way to define pull is to describe its alternative: push scheduling. Push is the traditional way a BAU organization (business as usual, the old school of thinking) does its scheduling. A sales forecast is developed and converted into production schedules for each area; then each area runs as hard as it can against that schedule, pushing material downstream. Under push, the definition of success can be to have your downstream customer buried in product.

Given all that has been written about just-in-time (JIT) and cycle-time strategy, you should understand the fallacy: Excess production equates to waste activities (*waste* is defined as any activity that does not have customer value, for example, waiting, sorting, reworking, transporting) and disconnection of workstations one from the other because of the inventory/time delay between them. Pull strategy is intended to link stations together and to cause upstream stations to produce only in direct response to downstream demand, to minimize time between the two, and to maximize connection.

The Origination of Pull

The creator of the pull concept was Mr. Ohno of Toyota, author of *The Toyota Production System.* Have you heard people speak of an "aha" moment. . . . the moment that a breakthrough idea registers? Mr. Ohno's aha moment came when viewing an American supermarket. Japan does not have supermarkets, relying on mom-and-pop specialty stores on every corner. Because Ohno was a scheduling/inventory/distribution person for Toyota, he was drawn to how supermarkets handle that problem.

Supermarkets manage by dividing up the shelf space by product: so much space for toothpaste, so much for carrots, so much for detergent, and so on. And, when they have extra time, the warehouse people do not bring in pallet loads of toilet paper and stack it in the aisles; that would be wasteful. Instead they wait for shelf space to empty, which becomes *visible permission* to bring in more.

The classic supermarket example is the Frito delivery person. The market does not issue specific purchase orders but a blanket order to Frito-Lay. It then allocates shelf space to Fritos, based on demand and the attractiveness of the profit margin enjoyed. The driver shows up every day and refills the shelves. If demand goes up, the store expands the shelf allocation and the delivery person reacts. Periodically, Frito-Lay sends an invoice. Given that simple, powerful system, would you want to go back to forecasts and specific purchase orders? Once you understand the concept of pull, it's fun to look for everyday examples. Box 14–1 is a favorite.

BOX 14–1   The Corner Liquor Store

Until recently, I lived in center-city Wilmington, Delaware. Like most large East Coast cities, Wilmington is a mix of nice restored areas and war zones. Sometimes the dividing line can be no more than a single street.

I won't tell you which area I lived in, but at the border of my neighborhood there was a liquor store. To give you an idea of the quality of that store, you couldn't buy a bottle of wine with a cork in it—only wine in screw-cap bottles was available. Further, if you bought a bottle, the assumption was that you were going to drink that bottle *immediately*. . . . maybe even before you left that store.

So, the owner only sold chilled wine; he didn't offer an option. The way he did that was, after you chose your bottle from the shelves, he took it to his cooler and performed a switch for a cold one. And when he had extra time he was not loading bottles into the cooler. That would be wasteful. He waited for me to make that purchase decision, made the switch, and then restocked his shelves each evening.

If he ever goes to that cooler to perform the switch and finds that he doesn't have a cold one ready, he adds a bottle to the cooler. Conversely, if he finds that he always has extra in the cooler, he takes one out. He doesn't know it, but he is running that cooler on a simple but very clever pull system.

Pull Systems in Industry

The objective of pull is to simplify the scheduling problem, to minimize time (inventory) in the operation, and to link stations more closely together (to make cause/effect relationships visible). The classical pull tool is kanban, typically a kanban square. In Japan, the term *kanban* has a dual meaning, referring both to inventory itself and to visible permission to produce. This chapter will keep it simple: Inventory will be called inventory and kanban will refer only to permission to produce. (Actually, the Japanese root of *kanban* goes back to its word for sign board.)

The kanban square is just that: a square painted on the floor or on the table between me (the producer) and you (the downstream user or next production station). The rules are simple. If there is space in the square there is permission to produce; if there is not, there is some problem and production must wait. Or, better yet, since there is some problem, the producer might as well go and see whether he or she can help because nothing can be produced until space is cleared. (The purpose of pull is *not* to shut operations down. As we'll see, the purpose is to keep them running smoothly.)

Once you understand the concept represented by the square, you can be as creative as you wish in your own kanban examples:

- Cards attached to the product as it is made and then removed and sent back as the product is consumed.
- Storage containers: When an empty container is returned, it is a sign of permission to refill.
- Tanks: An upper maximum and lower minimum tank level can clearly signal permission to put more into the tank.
- Shipping labels: When a container of product is pulled into use, a copy of the shipping label can be faxed back to the producer as a signal of need.
- Kanban signals can also be electronic (as long as the floor understands and has ownership for that signal).

Kanban Pull in the Process Industry

The concept of pull or JIT or the Toyota system swept first the automobile industry, then the parts suppliers to the auto industry, and then the entire discrete manufacturing world. The reasons for its acceptance were its simplicity, its power, and the impact it had on cost, quality, inventory, and customer service *simultaneously*. (Previously, BAU management had been a trade-off style of management. "You want better quality? Fine, I'll tighten the standards, reject more, and build that into the cost. Want lower cost? I can do that if we make fewer product variations.")

Why, then, have we not seen it sweep through the process industry as well? There are two reasons: the "we're-different syndrome" and the practical problem of applying the concepts in our environment. The we're-different syndrome stems from the contrast between some of the classical features of a JIT approach in a discrete manufacturing operation and the realities of a process plant (see Box 14–2). The practical problems of applying pull in a process environment go back to the inherent structure of a process operation. Discrete operations *converge* from many parts to one assembled final product. In contrast, process operations *diverge* from few common raw materials into many (hundreds or thousands of) final product variations.[1]

Consider the classic pull tool of the kanban square. In discrete parts, a station may have many upstream supply kanbans but only one downstream output kanban. When assembling carburetors, there may be several upstream kanbans for component parts but downstream only the kanban for finished carburetors. In that environment, control is simple: The one output kanban controls production.

In contrast, in a process environment, there may be many downstream kanban controls. How do we figure that out? Which square dictates? It is this problem of divergence that has lead to the we're-different conclusion. Companies assume they are free from worrying about these ideas because they don't apply to them. We now know that this is wrong. A little creativity about how to adapt the basic principles to one's special circumstances is all that's required. And more importantly, the first in each market environment to break the common paradigm will be a decisive winner for a long time while others scramble to recover.

Pull Concepts for a Process Environment

This article will introduce five special adaptation concepts, and, although these concepts help adapt pull to a process environment, all will work in a discrete environment as well:

BOX 14–2 We're Different: JIT Features versus Process Reality

- Cell manufacturing. "Our process plants have large, fixed general-purpose equipment. Rearrangement into cells doesn't apply."

- Operator line stop. "Starting/stopping process operations are difficult and time-consuming (certainly hours and sometimes *days*), so the concept of stopping operations to fix problems doesn't make sense."

- Lots of one unit. "Our transitions are difficult and start-up quality is unpredictable, so small or single-unit production lots are not possible."

- "We're continuous already, so what's the big deal?"

- *Takt* rate.
- Bottleneck control.
- Produce-to-order (PTO) point.
- Functional kanbans.
- Product wheels.

Takt Rate

Takt, a German word that translates to "beat of the music," is the *pace* at which we expect the operation to run. In the spirit of balanced production, it is the pace at which we expect *all* stations to run. Notice that this does not suggest balanced or equal capacity. That is neither possible nor desirable. The concept *does* call for all stations to produce in harmony to the whole. That means that a *takt* rate will be set for the end-of-the-line output, and then all stations will be linked to that *takt* rate. Somewhere in the supply chain, the bottleneck (see the next section) will be straining to meet *takt,* and all other stations will be holding back to balance with the bottleneck.

Exit *takt* rate is usually set by the business team. In the presence of an MRP system (covered later), the MRP procedures will provide the *takt* rate. Overall or exit *takt* rate is not going to be reset constantly; frequency will relate to the planning period. If plans are revised once a month, that will be when *takt* is revisited. It is unlikely that *takt* will be reset more frequently than once a week or less frequently than once a month.

A much shorter planning period (a day, a shift, a four-hour interval) is then set for each station. Stations communicate their expectations over that period, and internal *takt* rates are adjusted accordingly. If the overall *takt* rate is 10,000 pounds per hour but the immediate downstream station is going to be down for the next eight hours and there is only 40,000 pounds of space in the intervening kanban, the immediate *takt* rate would be adjusted to 5,000 pounds per hour in order to compensate. (Note that this may be an unnecessary sophistication in your system. In a well-designed system, as a kanban starts to approach saturation, alarms should force a decision to slow down anyway.)

Bottleneck Control

Bottleneck is very much a special-case pull adaptation. As Eli Goldratt has shown, every operation has a definitive singular bottleneck. That step is the one operating at the highest percentage capacity use, the one step that is closest to the peg. In the case where the plant is sold out completely, the bottleneck step is operating at 100 percent capacity use, which is all it can do. In that sold-out case, by definition, the bottleneck determines and limits the output of the entire system. Hence, control of the bottleneck controls the full system (see Figure 14–1).

FIGURE 14–1   A simple press flow

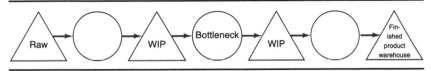

Consider an operation that consists of three steps with intervening work-in-process (WIP) inventory, drawing from a raw material stock and feeding to a finished-product warehouse. The middle step is the bottleneck, and the system is sold out. (The diagram in Figure 14–1 uses a simple symbology convention: Circles represent operations and triangles represent storage or inventory piles.)

In this situation, sales amounts are determined by the output of the bottleneck. Steps downstream of the bottleneck have excess capacity and can work only on material that gets through the bottleneck. Before the bottleneck, steps have excess capacity and need produce no more than the bottleneck needs. To be sure that the bottleneck runs, the WIP pile before the bottleneck needs to be large enough to ensure that all surprises and variability are taken care of so that there is always material for the bottleneck to work on. Below the bottleneck, no safety inventory is needed.

This control system—a special case of pull—can be very simple. Adequate just-in-case inventory is needed behind the bottleneck. Then, the bottleneck is linked to the injection of new raw material into the system. If raw material input is always equal to bottleneck output, the protective pile stays constant, the bottleneck always runs, and output of the total system is as high as possible. The key to this approach is the demand signal linking bottleneck output to raw input; that link controls the entire system—easily, simply, visually, shop floor, operator owned (see Figure 14–2).

Produce-to-Order (PTO) Point

PTO point is a good example of how thinking about cycle time and attempting to apply to concepts of pull can cause one to rethink some basic para-

FIGURE 14–2   A bottleneck-based pull system

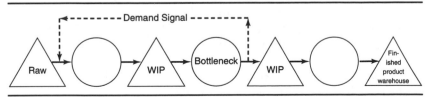

FIGURE 14–3 Conventional order entry

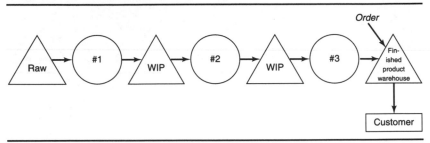

digms and effect major gains through simple changes in approach. The conventional BAU thinking is that customers are supplied from finished-product inventory and that the manufacturing process runs to refill the warehouse (see Figure 14–3).

Cycle-time thinking recognizes that the preceding is not necessarily correct and looks at how early in the process the order can be entered. This means comparing customer order lead time (the quoted interval between receipt of an order and the promise to ship that order) and cycle time, working back from the warehouse through the process. Assume that the order lead time is seven days, that Step 1 is the bottleneck step, and that cycle time for each step in the supply chain is as follows:

Raw material:	5 days
Step 1 (and downstream WIP):	3 days
Step 2 (and downstream WIP):	5 days
Step 3 (not including warehouse):	1 day
Warehouse:	5 days

(The last step is obviously an arbitrary policy.) Note that in this example orders can be entered at Step 1 WIP inventory (literally attach the order to stock in that inventory) and that material can move through Steps 2 and 3 successfully before the order is due to ship. Hence, the PTO point is just before Step 2, Steps 2 and 3 will run in response to customer order, Step 1 will run in response to its downstream WIP (its kanban), inventory downstream of Step 2 will be only material attached to a customer order on its direct way toward shipping, and the only other inventory needed is just-in-case (JIC) inventory in the collapsed warehouse to protect key customers against unexpected outages of Steps 2 and 3 (see Figure 14–4).

Note that all the objectives of cycle time and pull have been accomplished: Each station is running in response to demand, inventory and cycle

FIGURE 14–4 Order entry at the PTO point

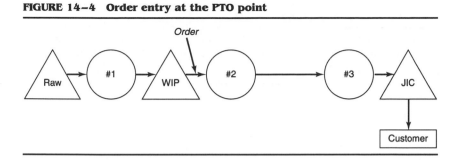

time are minimized, and all was accomplished simply by a different way of looking at the scheduling problem and the supply chain. This is a clear illustration of what is often a point of confusion: push/pull versus make-to-stock (MTS) and make-to-order (MTO). The two sets of terms are often confused as being interchangeable, with MTO equating pull and MTS relating to push, which is not true. MTS resides *before* the PTO point, while MTO resides *after* the PTO point. In this example, Step 1 is MTS, whereas Steps 2 and 3 are MTO, and *all* run under the concept of pull, running in response to customer demand.

FUNCTIONAL KANBANS

A functional kanban is nothing more than a single kanban that accepts multiple products (see Figure 14–5). The kanban is a specific size; space left in the kanban gives permission to produce and no space requires that production must stop. In a simple system with few products, this system will work well, given a little thought and inspection. "Well, there is space, but there are a lot of As and a lot of Bs. I guess I should make some Cs." In more complex systems, you can't rely on people interpreting functional kanbans. The additional tool that often works is the product wheel.

FIGURE 14–5 A functional kanban

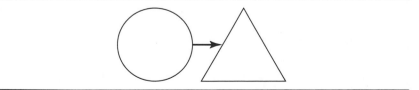

BOX 14–3 The BAU Product Wheel

"Give me long runs (as long as possible) so that I minimize the impact of transitions, maximize capacity, minimize cost per unit, and isolate myself from the turmoil of the marketplace."

Product Wheels

The product wheel has been around for a long time but it can appear dramatically different from the cycle-time viewpoint. The basic idea of a product wheel is that specific products are made in planned quantities and in a fixed order; when the sequence is completed, production will loop back through the sequence again and again.

Product wheels always show up where there is a functional need to run products in a specific order: lightest color to darkest color, heaviest unit weight or thicknesses to lightest, thin viscosity toward thick, and so forth. However, the concept of wheels can simplify the scheduling problem even when there is not a functional need to run in a given order. Traditional and/or conventional (BAU) managers have a classical approach to product wheel construction and management (see Box 14–3). At the same time, BAU managers demand better forecasts, not recognizing that they are contributing to a paradox (see Box 14–4). Once we recognize the nature of the paradox, the question becomes how short should our runs be?

Evolution of the Cycle-Time Product Wheel

Evolution of the cycle-time product wheel is the key concept here and may well be the key concept in the entire series. When product wheels are examined in light of cycle time and pull, the critical principle is the relation-

---

BOX 14–4 The Manufacturing versus Forecast Paradox

- "I desire long runs for maximum efficiency."

    but

- Long runs mean long cycle time.

    and

- Long cycle time means we must forecast further out.

    so

- Long runs mean less-accurate forecasts.

    Conclusion:

- The prime way to improve forecasts is to reduce cycle time. A key way to do that is to make *shorter* runs.

---

ship among excess production, cycle time, and waste (nonvalue) activity. It follows that production must be matched to demand and that campaign lengths of individual products and/or the time to move through the full wheel schedule must be timed exactly. This is referred to as wheel time (Wt) and can be calculated precisely. Here is how that formula evolved. The basic fundamental is that, over the Wt interval,

Production = sales (no excess production or waste)

Production = (time in production) × (CAP) = (Wt(1 − OUT) − ΣT) CAP

Sales = DEM (Wt),

where OUT = percentage equipment unavailability

DEM = sales demand per unit of time

CAP = net production capacity per unit of time

ΣT = sum of transition times throughout one turn of the wheel.

This simplifies to

$$Wt = \Sigma T/(1 - OUT - DEM/CAP).$$

The formula can be expanded by equating capacity to the throughput rate and net downstream yield:

$$CAP = THRU \times YLD,$$

where THRU = the rate at which material moves through the unit when it is up and running

YLD = yield through the process to the point where DEM is measured (DEM may be either final sales rate or demand for material at the next station; be sure to set DEM and YLD on the same basis).

The final formula then becomes

$$Wt = \Sigma T/\{1 - OUT - [DEM/(THRU \times YLD)]\}.$$

For example, assume an extruder used to blend fillers into a polymeric resin. The basic data are as follows:

Number of products: 10

Transition times: one hour per product plus one day at the end of the wheel to clean out.

OUT:	20 percent due to both mechanical downtime and to operator unavailability
DEM:	15,000 pounds per day (average over the 10 products)
THRU:	1,000 pounds per hour when up and running
YLD:	80 percent

From the formula,

$$Wt = 33 \text{ hours}/\{1 - 0.2 - [15/(24 \times 0.8)]\}$$
$$= 33 \text{ hours}/(1 - 0.2 - 0.78)$$
$$= 33 \text{ hours}/(0.02)$$
$$= 1,650 \text{ hours or } 68.5 \text{ days.}$$

Let's play a little what-if game. Suppose your technical force does a great statistical process control (SPC) job and cuts yield loss in half? What happens? Check it with the Wt formula:

$$Wt = 33 \text{ hours}/\{1 - 0.2 - [15/(24 \times 0.9)]\}$$
$$= 33 \text{ hours}/(1 - 0.2 - 0.694)$$
$$= 12.97 \text{ days.}$$

What's happened here? Obviously, capacity has been gained by cutting yield loss. But an 80 percent reduction in Wt for 10 percent in yield? Apparently, the relationship between Wt and capacity may be more important than might be immediately obvious.

Wt and Capacity

When the Wt formula was developed, it led to the recognition of a critical relationship between wheel time and the amount of capacity being utilized.

Wheel Time

The superficial message of this curve is that Wt goes up as sales increase; however, the relationship is not linear, it is asymptotic to 100 percent utilization. At high utilization, the curve gets *very steep* (see Figure 14–6). The underlying Aha is that, when operation is on the steep portion of the curve, a slight change in either sales or effective current capacity produces a *huge* change in needed Wt (see Box 14–5). In contrast, if operation is back on the relatively flat portion, large changes in capacity/demand have little influence on the machine schedule. On the flat of the curve, the operation is

FIGURE 14–6 Wheel time versus capacity use

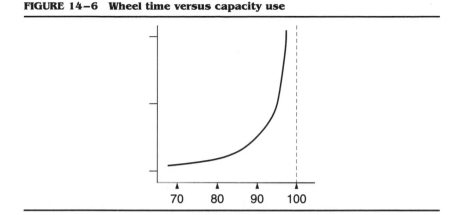

bulletproof to surprises, while on the steep portion it is unstable and vulnerable to any deviation. When that deviation occurs, recovery is not possible
until a lucky break in the other direction occurs. This is why, in the sample
Wt calculation earlier, such a huge Wt reduction resulted when yield was increased. We were resident at the end of the Wt curve (98 percent utilization), and so a slight change had tremendous leverage on Wt. Traditional
managers are *choosing* to be in that same vulnerable position. Now here is
where it gets *really* interesting.

Wt and Inventory

The Wt formula literally defines the amount of inventory downstream of
this extruder to assure meeting demand of the customer or the next station.
For the moment, ignore the problems of variation and the safety stock that
would require. Assume a perfect world:

- As each product is made, a 68.5-day supply will be required.
- Therefore, on average, at any point in time, inventory of each product
  will be 68.5/2 = 34.25 days' supply.
- Therefore, the downstream functional kanban fed by this wheel will
  have a total capacity of 34.25 × 15,000 = 517,500 pounds. (This is to
  give same-day service with no lead time to the customer. Every day of
  lead-time cushion will shrink the kanban by 15,000 pounds.)

BOX 14–5 Wt and Capacity Management

- Management desires high/maximum capacity utilization.
- High capacity utilization ensures that the system will be *unstable*.

FIGURE 14–7 Wheel control by a kanban

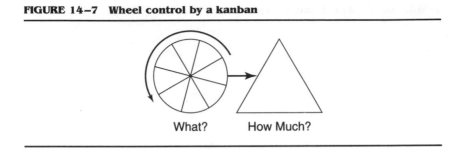

What?   How Much?

The concepts of a functional kanban have been linked with a product wheel to produce an effective pull-system tool (see Figure 14–7). The wheel turns to describe the normal production schedule, but deviations in the kanban state *force* management decisions:

- Low sales cause the functional kanban to fill up. As the kanban approaches a maximum, it can be used as a signal to *speed up* the wheel to respond to the inventory/capacity condition by making shorter runs and moving material more quickly through the system.
- High sales (or poor production) causes the kanban to drift toward a low level. That would be a signal to increase capacity by *slowing* the wheel, or extending runs.

Wheel time has been linked automatically to the real-time sales/production dynamic.

A more complex and sophisticated system would involve a product wheel feeding multiple kanbans, one for each product within that wheel. In that case, an instance of low sales would result in an individual product kanban reaching a maximum early, which in turn would automatically kick the wheel over into the next product segment, necessarily speeding the wheel by shortening runs. The converse of high sales would give permission for longer runs by virtue of available space in the depleted kanban. In either the functional or the multiple kanban example the result is a simple and almost automatic method for trimming the speed of the wheel by virtue of real-world experience.

Designing Pull Systems

Designing a pull system requires some simple yet powerful tools: using the bottleneck, shifting order entry to the PTO point, and using wheels and kanbans. Every pull system is different and individual, adapted to the particular characteristics of the manufacturing environment. But there are always some common characteristics (see Box 14–6).

Structured Inventory

Structured inventory means that each segment of inventory consciously has been placed into the manufacturing process and its size or limits have been defined precisely. The questions to ask in designing inventory follow:

1. Where is the PTO point? Downstream of the PTO point, all material is associated with a hard order. Inventory will consist only of work-in-process associated with filling current due orders, plus protective inventory at three possible points: the last point at which we service the customer, behind a station operating on a wheel, and behind the system bottleneck.

2. Where is the bottleneck? If the bottleneck limits sales (if we are sold out), then the bottleneck *must* be protected with inventory.

3. Which (if any) stations will operate on a wheel? If a station does operate on a wheel, there will of necessity be a downstream kanban to assure supply of all wheel products to the next station. That kanban will consist of two stocks:

   - Cycle stock. The amount of cycle stock for an individual product will be the sales rate per day times the number of days between product runs, or the Wt minus this product's campaign length. If you intend to use only one functional kanban, the average product in that kanban at any time will have half its cycle stock remaining, so the size of the overall functional kanban will be one-half the production made during one revolution of the wheel. If you have elected to provide multiple kanbans, one for each product in the wheel, the reasoning is the same. Each kanban must be sized to accommodate the full output of the campaign, but over time each kanban on average will be half full.

   - Safety stock. Safety stock absorbs variability as it occurs and is approximated by the following formula:

$$z\sqrt{\sigma_R^2 D^2 + \sigma_D^2 R^2},$$

where R = replenishment time

D = sales demand rate

σR = standard deviation in replenishment time

σD = standard deviation in sales rate

Z = service rate coefficient.

This formula assumes no lead time: The product must be delivered on demand. If that is not the case, lead time may be factored into the formula. Replenishment time is the *average* time to the next production campaign. Without lead time, R would be one-half of Wt minus campaign length. With lead time, R would be reduced by the lead time available. Z is a recognition of the on-time performance desired. The range of options is listed in Box 14–7. This formula applies whether you are designing safety stock for a single functional kanban or for multiple-product kanbans.

Don't be put off or intimidated by the need to develop variability information for demand and/or replenishment time. Since a well-designed system will literally retune itself, all that is needed is a good estimate at this point. One way to do that is to *assume* that you are dealing with a normal distribution and work with the fact that—in a normal distribution—more than 99 percent of the population is represented by a six-sigma range. If sales average 10T/day, you might also estimate that the range of variation in daily sales is never less than 2T/day and never more than 20T/day. Therefore, $\sigma = (20 - 2)/6 = 3T/day$. That's all you need at this point.

The safety stock formula, which includes a service objective and a lead-time consideration, introduces the general idea that designing inventory is a matter of making choices and trade-offs. In designing inventory, there are three variables but only two degrees of freedom: Any two can be set by arbitrary policy, but the third must then float to current capability (see Figure 14–8).

BOX 14–7 On-time safety factors

% On-Time Goal	'Z' Factor
84%	1.0
85%	1.04
90%	1.28
95%	1.65
97%	1.88
99%	2.33
100%	3.09

FIGURE 14–8   Trade-offs

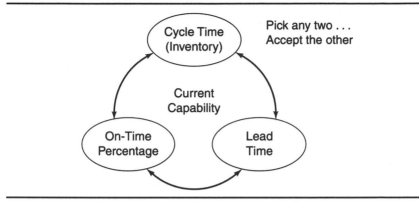

Pick any two . . .
Accept the other

For example, given a current capability, if the competitive situation dictates a certain lead time and a specific on-time performance against that lead time, one must accept the required inventory level. If economics limit inventory and there is a firm lead-time maximum, then the on-time performance that results must be accepted. After coming to grips with what the current reality must be, you can set out to improve your future-state capability and take advantage of that improvement in one of those three parameters.

A Design Example

To illustrate the principles of pull design, an implementation at a Vermont paperboard company will be used as a real-life example. A basic flowchart of its process is shown in Figure 14–9. The critical factors in this company's performance included the following:

FIGURE 14–9   Paperboard company pull installation

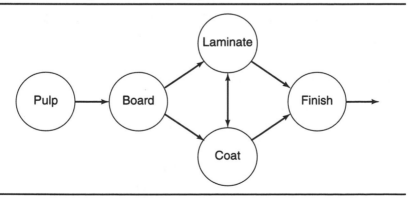

- A four-week customer-order lead time.
- 65 percent on-time delivery performance.
- 10 percent board machine mechanical downtime.
- High (~95 percent) board machine capacity utilization.
- 15 percent yield-loss downstream of the board machine.
- A cycle time (inventory in terms of days' supply) in excess of 60 days.
- A general knowledge that there was more market available, *if* it could find the capacity to service that market and *if* it could provide better service to attract that market.
- A general recognition that the board machine was the bottleneck, but a practice of focusing on the finishing steps to expedite due orders, leading to a tendency to jerk the board machine around.
- A practice of attempting to run all ~80 paper grades on the board machine in a ~6 = week production cycle.
- A recognition that it required about 5 days to move material through the operations downstream of the board machine.

Given that environment, management was concerned with finding means to gain capacity, reduce inventories, and provide better service.

An initial analysis clearly showed that priority had to be given to the board machine and to development of better discipline around the management of that bottleneck. A Wt for a simple 80-product board machine wheel showed that 83 days were required to meet demand at current service levels. That clarified why the plant ran in a chaos mode and why delivery performance was so poor; it was trying to follow a production cycle that was almost exactly half of that required. Little wonder it was scrambling continually. That Wt review also led us into the subject of using Wt analysis as an improvement planning tool.

Using Wt Analysis as an Improvement Planning Tool

When this company began its cycle-time and pull efforts, it had recognized its inventory/capacity issues and had formed three independent teams: transitions, maintenance, and yield. To gauge the impact potential, each team was asked to estimate the improvement it might expect to make in its parameter; each improvement estimate was then plugged independently into the Wt formula. The potential impact for each team on wheel time was shown to be as follows:

Maintenance	6-day reduction in Wt
Transitions	7-day impact
Yield	*67-day Wt reduction*

This is a living example of life on the steep portion of the Wt curve. This company was at 95 percent capacity utilization and was unstable but had a major opportunity to move down the curve and gain tremendous improvements.

Further, what is the chance that one team will have a negative impact on another? If we are trying to get back on production quicker after a production change, what is the chance that we will add to yield loss? If we are trying to keep equipment up and running, or get a machine back quicker after a failure, what is the probability of hurting yield? Obviously, both the transitions and maintenance teams had little chance to improve Wt and significant opportunity to hurt yield. Both teams were quickly disbanded and focus was directed toward the major opportunity—yield.

Complex Wheel Design

Going to the calculated 83-day wheel was certainly not in the final best interests of this company. The inventory required to bridge 83-day intervals between production campaigns for all 80 products was staggering. Obviously, a more creative and satisfactory solution was needed.

One of the best ways of reducing Wt is the reduction of transition times. Since ΣT is the numerator, a reduction in transitions is directly translatable to a reduction in Wt: X percent reduction in one produces an identical X percent reduction in the other. One approach to ΣT is to do the single minute exchange of dies (SMED) work of reducing transition times. The other is to (artificially) reduce the number of transitions contained in the wheel, which can be done by building more-complex wheel structures. In the case of this company, using a Pareto analysis to represent its produce line, the company created three product groupings:

- A products: high-volume strategic.
- B products: mid-volume but strategic.
- C products: low-volume maintenance.

With that distinction, the team then built three wheels (see Figure 14–10).

FIGURE 14–10   A complex three-wheel design

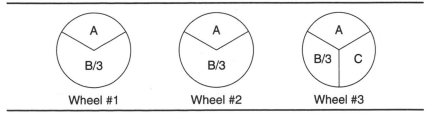

In this design, all As appear in each wheel, Bs are spread across all three wheels, and some Cs appear in Wheel #3. In the case of Cs, customers are contacted as the schedule approaches Wheel #3, customer needs are determined, and about one-third of the Cs are run in each Wheel #3, providing enough to cover the next two three-wheel sequences. Because each of these wheels has a limited number of products, ΣT for each wheel is much less than for the 80-product wheel and Wt is also proportionally less. With some supporting improvements in transition times and in yields, these three wheels calculated to wheel times of about 20 days each, which produced an interesting benefit: Since As carried a 30-day lead time and were produced every 20 days, they could be produced to customer order instead of to inventory.

Similarly, since it had solicited customer need for Cs at the start of Wheel #3, the company could produce 180-day need for those products included in that particular wheel. Hence Cs also were produced to order. Only Bs, which were to be produced every 60 days against a 30-day lead time, needed to be produced to a maintained inventory. Notice what this does: It positions different categories of products on different portions of the Wt curve (see Figure 14–11).

By putting As into a position where they are produced within customer lead time and to customer order, As have been made stable and predictable. Similarly, Bs have been improved by virtue of a building of planned inventories. Granted, Cs have been put out at the extreme end of the curve, but there is a chance every 60 days to review the bidding on individual products that you have planned to make on 180-day intervals. Lastly, since it was now known that B inventory had to bridge 60-day intervals, the company's planners were in a position to define precisely the structure of the B inventory:

FIGURE 14–11 Managing products on the Wt curve

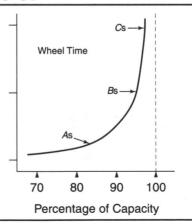

both cycle stock and just-in-case safety stock inventory. This leads to consideration of the second characteristic of pull systems, creating visible demand.

Creating Visible Demand

The general principle of creating visible demand is that each station should be able to see concrete evidence of its downstream customer's need: If that customer is about to run out, there should be panic. If the customer is not taking product for some reason, the upstream response should be to slow down. In the trivial case where stations are side by side, visible demand is easy; you can see the kanban square. In cases where visibility is not direct, design is limited only by imagination, as shown by the following examples:

- Cards can be attached to each production unit and sent back to the producing station when the material is used.
- The transportation container (e.g., box, tank, pallet) can be sent back when empty.
- A variation of the container for the film or paper industry can be the roll core, returned to be rewound with product when it is empty.
- Product labels can be faxed from thousands of miles away from customer to supplier as the containers are moved into production.

Demand signals can also be electronic, such as material inventories on a display screen. But that is a second or perhaps last choice because it does not carry the involvement, connection, or intimacy of a manual signal. People are less likely to feel ownership for a computer-generated signal. In the case of the paper-company example, cards were chosen for the demand signal. Steps in setting up and activating that system were straightforward:

1. Because the paper company calculated the Wt, the campaign length for each product, and the safety stock required, it then knew the size of the kanban for each product (the amount of material that would be in inventory immediately after each campaign was completed).
2. The design team put up an array of card racks by the board machine—a set of racks for each of the three wheels, one individual rack for each *B* product. The racks themselves were arranged from left to right in the same order that products were positioned in the three-wheel structure (picture a time-card rack).
3. Plastic-laminated roll cards were issued for each *B* product. The number of cards issued was equivalent to a completely full kanban for every product.

4. Team members then went through the inventory and tagged all existing rolls. In many cases, there were more rolls in inventory than there were cards. Necessarily, those rolls were left untagged and used first. Extra cards went in the card rack as evidence that there was demand for that product.

The result was an array of card racks, one for each product in the three wheels, arranged in left-to-right order matching the planned production sequence. Each rack resembled a bar graph; the full height indicated the size of the kanban. Within each rack, empty slots indicated that rolls were in the kanban, whereas cards indicated demand for production into the kanban. The system was completed by adding some bells and whistles for the purpose of management alarms.

Management Alarms

Whatever your demand display system, you'll want to be alerted if the system is drifting from plan. Drift includes demand above expectation and/or production shortfalls. In other words, the kanban might fill up because of either lack of sales or excess production. Kanbans might empty because of either sales booms or production losses. You want to know and react before you get into an extreme position. In the paper-company case, the team came up with some creative alarm signals:

• Kanban alarms. When a product campaign is completed and the kanban for that product is full, the card rack is empty. The expectation is for the rack to slowly refill as other products are being made, reaching full just as the wheel turns back to that product. Therefore, management needed to be alerted if the rack was refilling too fast and if there was danger of running out before the wheel completed its cycle. To do that, each wheel was color coded in red, blue, or green. Then a specific card slot could be identified for each product that should coincide with completing each wheel. If product X in the red wheel has just been completed, the last slot that should remain empty as we finish the red, blue, and green wheels can be identified. If that slot gets filled before the wheel completes, we are either refilling the racks (consuming product) faster than expected or the wheels are turning slower than expected and are falling behind schedule. Either way, there is a danger of running out of that product before production begins again.

The specific mechanism was to use colored tape stripes such that if there is a card in that slot, the tape stripe is covered and can't be seen. With no card in the slot, the color stripe is visible. In the general case, then, anyone should be able to quickly scan the card racks and see every alarm slot corresponding in color to the wheel now running. If one is in the middle of the red wheel, and for product Y over in the green wheel the red slot is covered, then product Y is in alarm state.

Kanban alarms are reported in the production meeting every morning. Are alarms okay? It depends. You don't want to *never* have alarms because the system would be too fat. But, the more alarms on, the more likely you'll actually have a stock out. Once the paper-company system settled down, two to three alarms for ~35 kanbans was normal.

• Wheel position. The three example wheels were expected to turn in 20 days each. It was important for decision making to know where actual wheel position was at given time. The team's solution to this was clever. Since the racks were arranged in production order from left to right, two race-car icons—one for plan and one for actual—were put above the rack display and moved every day to show the current state.

• System discipline. BAU attitudes are hard to kill; people will always want to extend a run that is going well, to dump a transition over onto the next shift, and so forth. The team wanted ways to make this behavior obvious. The result was two special kanbans.

  • Overrun stock. Because there is a significant time lag between batch pulp makeup and the board machine, it is difficult to time the end of the run exactly. Recognizing that, the team set up a small kanban of overrun cards. If workers ran out of kanban cards before a run completed, they could use the overrun cards. The procedure then called for retagging the overrun roll with a proper product card as soon as one was returned from downstream. If manufacturing used *all* the overrun cards, it was discussed in the morning meeting to discover *why* they had abused the system.

  • Held stock. In some cases, quality of a particular roll is in question when it is first made and put into inventory. In the old environment, there was no reason to push for final disposition, and inventory got clogged with material held up for quality disposition. Here again, a small held kanban was established and rolls tagged accordingly when a full release could not be made. If the supply of held cards ran out, the only way to get more was to release something currently held. Morning meeting discussions on this issue became *very* brief.

These alarm conditions are discussed at every shift change and in the morning production meeting. Even if stock outs ultimately do not occur, alarms enter into decisions. Questions concerning maintenance priority, schedule changes, customer special requests, and lead-time adjustments all become almost self-evident when you relate them to the kanban/wheel conditions.

Results—Paper-Company Example

The paper-company example involved more than simply installing a pull system. Yields, transition capability, product line, and order policies were questioned and revised. However, the pull system was a major contributor to

- An inventory reduction of 66 percent. Cycle time went from 60 to 20 days.
- Lead-time reduction from 4 to 2 weeks.
- On-time performance from 65 to 95 percent.
- No kanban actually emptying (this implies there is still room for cycle-time improvement).
- Significant capacity gains through yield and through bottleneck management. (Process changes were made at the same time and relative impact can't be separated, but estimates would be at least 10 percent in capacity through management/policy changes.)

Managing/Maintaining the System

Since the environment is dynamic and ever-changing, a pull system is never completed. You must have a mechanism for keeping the system in tune. In the paper example, the team set up two such mechanisms:

- The simple system. The direct way to retune the system is to use the information the system gives you—in the form of alarms and stock outs—to do the retuning. The team set up a simple retuning process used at the end of every three-wheel cycle that follows these rules:
  - If a kanban alarms, desensitize the alarm by moving the color stripe down one slot (in this design, racks are filled from top to bottom). This shift will allow the return of one more card before the alarm goes into effect.
  - If the kanban empties, add one card and one slot to the kanban.
  - If the kanban does not empty, take away one card and one slot.
- The formal system. A spreadsheet was developed to do the initial kanban calculations: Wt, run lengths, cycle and safety stocks, alarm points. This spreadsheet is rerun quarterly or whenever a major product offering change occurs. With the new spreadsheet, it is relatively easy to rebuild the system by adding/removing cards and slots. Changes are made only if the product line has been changed (a product added or discontinued) or if a kanban is off by more than 20 percent (deviations of less than 20 percent are left to the simple system).

The only other maintenance considerations are special situations, typically shutdowns or special selling opportunities. If a shutdown is upcoming, and inventory must be built to bridge the shutdown outage, it is a simple matter to temporarily expand the kanbans, issue temporary cards (which gives additional permission to produce, automatically causing the wheels to slow down), and then extract the extra cards to reduce the kanbans back to normal when the shutdown is over.

Occasionally, the sales manager may have a special (one-time) sales opportunity. He or she may not be certain of the sale or willing to build the added volume into the ongoing forecast but may want to invest in the inventory. In this case, a special kanban is built, the inventory is made to fill it, but the resultant cycle time is the responsibility of the sales office rather than the manufacturing group. Inventory is held until sold or until sales renounces the need.

Isn't This in Conflict with MRP?

Often, a critical issue occurs when companies have invested heavily in computerized scheduling systems, central scheduling organizations, or both. If management has not been clear about objectives, roles, and security there can be *major* conflict between the scheduling function and the idea of pull. After all, we're talking simple, visual, shop floor, and operator owned. How can that not be seen as incompatible and threatening to the central scheduling people?

The generic conflict here is between MRP and pull. To understand, we need to define MRP. The main ideas of traditional MRP were central, automated, and computerized. A sales forecast was converted into a production schedule and that was carried into area master schedules. The primary concern over MRP is that it seems like push. In traditional MRP, schedules were fixed and stations were measured against schedule attainment. If that resulted in mismatches in pace between stations, buildup of materials, and disconnection between stations, so be it. Competition between stations and local optimization by each station were encouraged. Happily, traditional MRP has evolved.

There are many positive aspects of MRP. MRP begins with sales and operational planning, a necessary feature for managing/planning the business and the overall supply chain. It provides long-range inventory, resource, and capacity planning, and it sets up accountability for performance against the plan. One of the products of the S&OP process is setting *takt* rate for the plant based on the dynamics of sales, capacity, shutdown plans, seasonality, product development/test time, and new-product introductions.

What happens, then, when a well-structured MRP planning process runs up against a manufacturing process that is capable of flowing materials through the process in response to a needed exit rate while maintaining planned internal inventory levels and alerting management to internal deviations as they occur? With newer MRP approaches, the S&OP process is used to set *takt* for output from the plant, and the bill of materials is one level. The MRP system thinks that end products come straight from raw materials and the intervening stations are left to manage themselves. (When raw-materials vendors are integrated into the pull system, they also may be invisible to MRP.) Progressive MRP designers see pull as positive because it makes the design and operation of MRP easier. All the control and accountability (to S&OP) is maintained, but the detail complexity is simplified. That degree of understanding and compatibility between MRP and pull is obtained only if management works hard at clarifying roles, responsibilities, and objectives for everyone.

SUMMARY

What we have described is a shop floor system for scheduling production, defining inventory, connecting workstations, achieving service objectives, minimizing cycle time, and providing a basis and direction for continuous improvement. The system may be as simple and visual as those we've described, or it may be powered by a computer-based information system. In either case, the system is understood, owned, and operated by workers on the shop floor.

Design of such a system will force management to *understand* the capabilities of its operation and to reach true clarity on *objectives* and business *strategy*, which is often one of the major benefits of undertaking pull. Operation of pull provides tools to the shop floor workers for managing their own destinies; *involvement* is achieved by *empowerment*. Further, design of the system provides management alarms as the system fluctuates in its operation. Attention to the current status of the pull system will provide a basis for the ongoing management decisions concerning operator scheduling, maintenance, special customer requests, test scheduling, and so forth. Decisions will be by fact instead of by emotion and will be made to optimize the whole rather than encourage destructive area competition. Continuous improvement will be focused by understanding the largest opportunity to extract time and to speed the pull operation.

Extension of a pull system offers opportunity to establish partnerships, internally among areas and externally with vendors and customers. This offers nothing less than integration of your supply chain—not insignificant results from such a simple concept.

NOTE

1. See *Synchronous Manufacturing* (Chapter 8) by M. L. Shrikanth and M. M. Umble (Cincinnati: South-Western Publishing Company) for a complete discussion of 'A' plants versus 'V' plants.

15 PRODUCTION PLANNING SIMPLICITY

Mark Louis Smith

Editor's note

The following success story shows how one pharmaceutical producer has become more responsive to market demand by cutting production lead times without sacrificing quality or building inventories. The keys to this major change in operations are (1) the empowerment of production workers and (2) scheduling and control systems that are simple, inexpensive, and easily understood by the organization. This chapter describes the planning process from development of the national plan to daily production schedules. The results are impressive.

- Manufacturing lead times have been cut in half not only once, but twice. And the goal for this facility in the next two years is to cut lead times in half five more times. The final lead-time objective, to make yesterday's sales today, will result in make-to-order manufacturing in a make-to-stock environment.

- Not too surprisingly, over the same five-year period, the work-in-process inventory investment (in dollars not adjusted for inflation) has been reduced by 77 percent. The final objective is to ensure perfect customer service in a volatile, market-driven business.

Does this sound like the saga of a high-technology firm under attack by Pacific Basin countries? Or perhaps a firm that has spent hundreds of millions in capital to completely retool and install supercomputer technology for a lights-out factory? It is neither. It is in fact the oldest manufacturing facility at a leading consumer pharmaceutical company. Further, the primary investment has been directed toward the *simplification* of the production-planning process and the empowerment of its stakeholders, the production workers, to do the scheduling.

HISTORY

This particular manufacturing facility evolved from a small ethical pharmaceutical producer. Over a period of 10 to 15 years, the facility expanded to become the sole production facility of market-leading consumer pharmaceuticals. Today, the facility is one of several highly focused facilities producing multiingredient products with low sales volumes and many stock-keeping units.

Ten years ago, the production-planning tools were a collection of homegrown, loosely linked, mainframe computer systems. Today, the tools focus on simplicity and are built around the core of an MRP II system. The critical parts of the MRP II system are its bill of materials (BOM), master production scheduling (MPS), and materials-requirement planning (MRP) modules. The remaining critical parts of a production-planning system (e.g., strategic planning, shop floor control) have been simplified to the point that personal computers, magnetic scheduling boards, and flip chart paper are the state-of-the-art tools.

THE STRATEGIC PLANNING PROCESS

The planning process begins at the corporate level and ends with daily machine assignments being made by the production operators. Let's look at the four steps required to get to daily scheduling:

1. The national resource plan (biannual).
2. The tactical plan (monthly).
3. The rough-cut capacity, material, and finished-goods plans, all at plant level (weekly).
4. The production schedules, tracked by shift (daily).

The first step in the planning process is the development of the five-year national resource plan, published biannually. Corporate planning uses the five-year national resource plan to develop the 12-month rolling tactical plan. The tactical plan is further broken down into 13 weekly and 9 monthly buckets before being passed on to the individual plant planning organizations. At the plant level, the production and inventory control department develops the master production schedule (MPS), the rough-cut capacity plan, and the material plan, as well as a consolidated finished-goods inventory plan for the plant. The master production schedule is passed on to the individual production centers, where the employees and the production control supervisor develop daily schedules through material lead times. Execution of the daily schedule is tracked at the end of each shift, with necessary schedule adjustments made by the employees in each production center. Concurrently, the closed-loop MRP II system tracks inventory, which feeds back to the plant and corporate planning groups.

Step 1: The National Resource Plan

The five-year national resource plan (NRP) provides aggregate rough-cut capacities for both capital and skilled labor resources by manufacturing location. It is prepared and reviewed with each manufacturing location twice annually. Local plant management uses the NRP as a template to develop its business and operating plans. The NRP has evolved from a document hand calculated annually with no simulation capability to today's computer-driven model with the ability to regenerate simulations every six to eight minutes. The model uses simple planning concepts and can be set up on a mainframe using a database language (FOCUS or QUERY UPDATE) or on a personal computer using either a database (dBASE or PFS) or spreadsheet language (LOTUS 1-2-3 or EXCEL).

From the NRP, the following strategic operational decisions are made:

- To change a plant's focus, for example, from manufacturing high-volume, single-ingredient products with few stockkeeping units (SKUs) to manufacturing low-volume, multiingredient products with many SKUs.
- To change the manufacturing location for a product line to eliminate a capacity constraint or to take advantage of a cost differential.
- To make appropriation requests for capital funds to support new products, line extensions, and sales growth and to upgrade or replace aged capital.
- To request approval or justifications for additional skilled-labor sources.

Calculation of the NRP starts with two pieces of information:

- The current annual sales forecast in SKU detail.
- The five-year forecasted growth for each product family (see Table 15–1).

TABLE 15-1 Five-year growth forecast for two product families

	SKU	Current Year	Year 2	Year 3	Year 4	Year 5
		Product Family A				
Forecasts	1	1,000				
	2	5,000				
	3	3,000				
Total		9,000				
Forecasted growth			5%	4%	4%	4%
		Product Family B				
Forecasts	1	6,000				
	2	4,000				
	3	2,000				
Total		12,000				
Forecasted growth			7%	8%	8%	9%

In Table 15-1, for example, the term *Product Family A* represents a group of common SKUs (e.g., 20-, 50-, and 100-count packages) of cough medication. The next step in the planning process is to develop five years of SKU detail. Each SKU is extended by the forecasted growth for its product family. For instance, in Table 15-1, SKU 1 in year 2 for Product Family A is calculated by extending the current year value of 1,000 by the year-2 forecasted growth of 5 percent, to yield a value of 1,050 (1,000 × 1.05 = 1,050). In year 3, the value of SKU 1 for Product Family A is calculated from the year-2 (1,050) value, extended by the forecasted growth of 4 percent, yielding a value of 1,092 (1,050 × 1.04 = 1,092). This process continues for all SKUs and all product families. Table 15-2 shows the completed forecast extensions. If, however, marketing or sales has unique plans for a given SKU, such as a promotional campaign, the extension by growth may be overridden manually.

Explosion of forecasts. Once the forecasts have been developed, they are exploded through the bills of material and extended, using standard-machine and labor-planning values in the routings, into machine and labor requirements (see Table 15-3).

Equipment planning value: The expected annual output for a specific SKU on a specific production center. Example: Product Family A, SKU 1: annual output = 2,000 units.

Equipment demand: The amount of equipment needed to support the forecast for a specific SKU (also expressed as machine shifts, machine hours, and so on). Example: Product Family A, SKU 1: forecast =

TABLE 15–2 Five-year growth forecast with SKU detail

	SKU	Current Year	Year 2	Year 3	Year 4	Year 5
		Product Family A				
Forecasts	1	1,000	1,050	1,092	1,136	1,181
	2	5,000	5,250	5,460	5,678	5,906
	3	3,000	3,150	3,276	3,407	3,543
Total		9,000	9,450	9,828	10,221	10,630
Forecasted growth			5%	4%	4%	4%
		Product Family B				
Forecasts	1	6,000	6,420	6,934	7,488	8,162
	2	4,000	4,280	4,622	4,992	5,441
	3	2,000	2,140	2,311	2,496	2,721
Total		12,000	12,840	13,867	14,976	16,324
Forecasted growth			7%	8%	8%	9%

1,000, equipment planning value = 2,000, equipment demand = 1,000/2,000 = 0.5 machines or lines.

Labor planning value: The amount of labor required to run the equipment. Example: Product Family A, SKU 1: crew size or labor-planning value = 6.

Labor demand: The average amount of labor required to support the forecast for a specific SKU. Example: Product Family A, SKU 1: equipment demand = 0.5 machines/annually, labor-planning value = 6, average annual demand = (0.5)(6) = 3.

Equipment and labor supply: Assumed values for the example representing the actual resources available.

Following the template provided by the NRP, the corporate planning department and the plant production and inventory control departments begin development of the tactical plan.

Step 2: The Tactical Plan (Master Schedule)

The tactical plan is developed at each manufacturing location by the production and inventory-control departments. First, a 12-month rolling forecast is loaded into a traditional MRP II system. Corporate planning works with sales and marketing to develop the forecast. Most of the negotiations revolve around balancing promotions for different product families with available capacities of the manufacturing locations. The goal is to ensure that manufacturing will be able to provide adequate inventory (to prevent back order) on a timely basis to support customer service.

TABLE 15-3 Five-year growth forecast's implications for production

	SKU	Current Year	Year 2	Year 3	Year 4	Year 5	Planning Values
		Product Family A					
Forecasts	1	1,000	1,050	1,092	1,136	1,181	
	2	5,000	5,250	5,460	5,678	5,906	
	3	3,000	3,150	3,276	3,407	3,543	
Equipment Demand	1	0.5	0.5	0.5	0.6	0.6	2,000
	2	0.6	0.7	0.7	0.7	0.7	8,000
	3	0.8	0.8	0.8	0.9	0.9	4,000
Total		1.9	2.0	2.0	2.2	2.2	
Labor Demand	1	3	3	3	3	4	6
	2	4	4	4	4	4	6
	3	7	7	7	8	8	9
Total		14	14	14	15	16	
		Product Family B					
Forecasts	1	6,000	6,420	6,934	7,488	8,162	
	2	4,000	4,280	4,622	4,992	5,441	
	3	2,000	2,140	2,311	2,496	2,721	
Equipment Demand	1	0.5	0.6	0.6	0.7	0.7	11,000
	2	0.8	0.9	0.9	1.0	1.1	5,000
	3	0.7	0.7	0.8	0.8	0.9	3,000
Total		2.0	2.2	2.3	2.5	2.7	
Labor Demand	1	3	4	4	4	4	6
	2	5	5	6	6	7	6
	3	6	6	7	7	8	9
Total		14	15	17	17	19	
		Equipment and Labor Totals					
Equipment demand		3.9	4.1	4.4	4.6	5.0	
Equipment supply		5	5	5	5	5	
Loading		78%	82%	87%	93%	99%	
Labor demand		28	29	31	33	35	
Labor supply		86	86	86	86	86	
Variance		58	57	55	53	51	

Step 3: Capacity, Material, and Finished-Goods Planning

Corporate planning aggregates each plant's tactical plan to determine the need for temporary transfers of production volume among manufacturing locations to relieve capacity constraints resulting from oversales or seasonality. Additionally, corporate planning provides an audit function of the individual plants, keeping an eye out for plan oversights or overextended available resources. Finally, the tactical plan is used to identify excess or dated finished goods. Once these have been identified, corporate planning negotiates with sales on methods for disposition of these inventories. The tactical planning process, which takes three to four weeks, is repeated monthly.

Step 4: Daily Production Schedules

Now let's take an overview of how the production center develops the daily schedule from the tactical plan. The first 13 weeks of the tactical plan (the MPS) are passed on to the production centers weekly. A production control supervisor (who is a member of the manufacturing staff, not the production and inventory-control department) meets with representatives from each step of the manufacturing sequence and develops the daily schedule through material lead time (typically three weeks). The daily schedule is reviewed by production and inventory control. After their sign-off, the schedule is entered into the MRP II system.

While the the the theory for developing the daily schedule is not revolutionary, the process is. In the past, the production control supervisor prepared the schedule for the manager's approval. Following approval, the schedule was passed on to the supervisor of each operation. The supervisors assigned wage employees to machines at the beginning of each shift. The employees executed the schedule in more or less the classic American fashion of doing as they were told. The process sequence is that of a typical pharmaceutical operation (see Figure 15–1).

FIGURE 15–1   Typical pharmaceutical process sequence

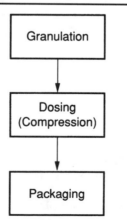

The only significant variation is that management is organized vertically; that is, each department has the required assets and bears total responsibility for all steps necessary to produce a grouping of product families. The vertical-slice structure has evolved to eliminate the over-the-fence mentality that existed when each operation was a separate department (e.g., packaging versus processing).

Additionally, by focusing each production center on a small group of product families, manufacturing and marketing have been able to form an alliance. The manufacturing organization can focus on the unique needs (e.g., seasonality, launches) of the different product families.

THE NEW SCHEDULING SYSTEM—SIMPLICITY

Today, the production-control supervisor meets with wage employees from each operation, who in turn have been empowered to develop the schedule. Once the schedule is developed, it is entered directly into the MRP II system. Although the production-center managers do not review the schedule directly they do monitor customer service (finished goods levels) and key performance indicators (costs, work-in-process levels, and cycle times).

The tools used by the employees to develop the schedule are the tactical plan, a flip chart, a marker pen, a magnetic scheduling board, a calculator, and 15 to 20 years of experience. The type of daily schedule developed by the employees could be generated with a mainframe or personal computer. In the normal course of events, however, the demands placed on production seldom work out as neatly as the computer models. Typically, there are overlapping demands, equipment out of service, production variation, and the like. Because the stakeholders (employees) are responsible for the schedule, they have the freedom to manipulate the schedule to deliver the desired result. The process used is detailed in Figure 15–2.

The process used by the employees is a combination of just-in-time (JIT) and kanban theories. It is JIT in that each operation is scheduled in the smallest possible lot sizes so that the output arrives just when the next operation is ready to begin. Kanban comes into play with the magnetic scheduling board. It is the magnetic tag on the board that signals when each successive upstream operation is to begin manufacturing. Additionally, the scheduling board allows the operators to see the capacity flow of the entire plant. The employees start the daily scheduling with the following:

- A sheet of flip chart paper.
- The tactical plan, used to indicate which SKUs are required to be produced and in what quantities.
- Planning values for each production center.

FIGURE 15–2 Simplified schedule process

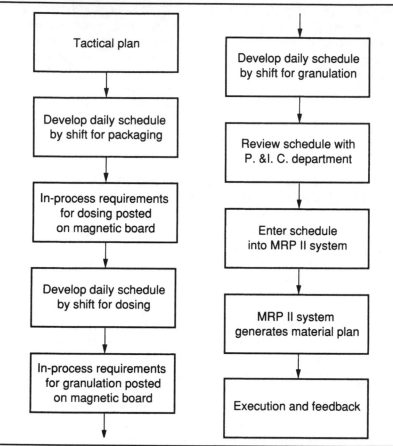

Armed with this information, the employees assign SKUs to specific production centers. During the scheduling process, the availability of skilled labor is considered and balanced. Needs for unskilled temporary labor are determined and communicated to personnel. Figure 15–3 shows a completed schedule for a three-shift operation with one skilled crew per shift supporting two packaging lines and four SKUs.

In Figure 15–3, we can see that the production crews are scheduled to alternate between the lines. The cumulative schedule is the amount of production called for in the tactical plan for each SKU (in Figure 15–3, SKU 1 = 72). Finally, each of these schedules would be prepared on separate flip chart sheets and hung at the appropriate production center at the beginning of the week.

FIGURE 15-3 Production crew flip chart schedule sheets

Packaging Line A

Day	Shift	SKU	Schedule	Production	Cumulative Schedule	Cumulative Production	Variance
Mon	3	#1	36			36	
	1		36			72	
	2		Chg. over				
Tue	3						
	1						
	2						
Wed	3						
	1	#3	36			36	
	2		36			72	
Thr	3		36			108	
	1		36			144	
	2		Chg. over				
Fri	3						
	1						
	2						
OT	3						
	1						
	2						

Packaging Line B

Day	Shift	SKU	Schedule	Production	Cumulative Schedule	Cumulative Production	Variance
Mon	3						
	1						
	2						
Tue	3	#2	45			45	
	1		45			90	
	2		45			135	
Wed	3		Chg. over				
	1						
	2						
Thr	3						
	1						
	2						
Fri	3	#4	45			45	
	1		45			90	
	2		Chg. over				
OT	3						
	1						
	2						

Once a schedule sheet is developed for each machine within an operation, the dates in-process materials are required from each primary department are posted on the magnetic scheduling board. Figure 15–4 shows how the magnetic tags would be posted for the schedules in Figure 15–3.

Figure 15–4 shows that Packaging Line A is calling for the dosing department to deliver the materials for SKU 1 at the beginning of the third shift on Monday. A tag is placed on the magnetic scheduling board to indicate the need for the remaining SKUs. Following kanban theory, these tags are the authorization for a primary process to begin manufacturing.

The packaging department requirements are used by the dosing department to develop its daily schedule sheets. After the dosing department finishes preparing its scheduling sheets, it posts when it needs in-process materials from the granulation department. The granulation department repeats the cycle of daily schedule-sheet preparation. Figure 15–5 shows the magnetic scheduling board at the end of the process.

Now that the entire schedule has been prepared, all due dates are entered into the MRP II system to generate dock dates for raw materials. Each week the entire process takes approximately 60 minutes to develop the third future week from scratch. Employees rotate the responsibility and work in teams with representatives from each shift to eliminate parochialism.

Execution and Tracking

With the production-center schedules posted and the material plan in place, all that remains is to track progress against the schedule. Tracking is simply a matter of posting the production at the end of each shift and calculating the variance. Figure 15–6 shows a typical schedule by midweek.

Packaging Line A is approximately one-third of one shift ahead of the schedule (16 units positive variance/36 units a shift = 0.44 shifts). Meanwhile Packaging Line B is behind the schedule by approximately one-third of one shift (14 units negative variance/45 units a shift = 0.31 shifts). At the beginning of Wednesday's second shift, employees would review the schedule and assign personnel to Production Line B to bring it back on schedule before continuing production on Production Line A. Previously, these decisions would have been made by management. If during the week the schedule gets one or more shifts ahead of or behind, the department behind schedule signals the variation to the upstream department by moving the appropriate kanban tag on the magnetic scheduling board. Each upstream department makes the necessary adjustments to its schedules.

CONCLUSION

How is this simple method different from the old way? Now decisions of daily production rates and mix are made by production workers and moni-

FIGURE 15–4 Production's magnetic trafficking board

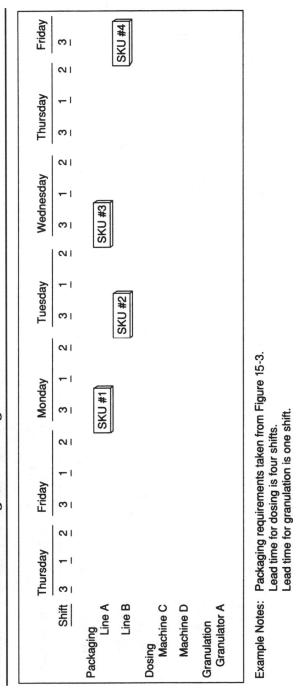

Example Notes: Packaging requirements taken from Figure 15-3.
Lead time for dosing is four shifts.
Lead time for granulation is one shift.
All lead times calculated from the start of shift.

265

FIGURE 15–5 Magnetic trafficking board at end of production process

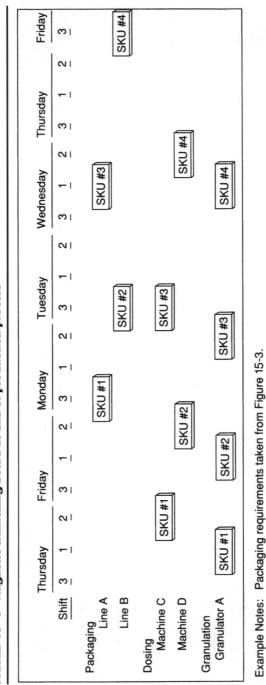

Example Notes: Packaging requirements taken from Figure 15-3.
Lead time for dosing is four shifts.
Lead time for granulation is one shift.
All lead times calculated from the start of shift.

FIGURE 15–6 Flip chart schedule at midweek

Packaging Line A

Day	Shift	SKU	Schedule	Production	Cumulative Schedule	Cumulative Production	Variance
Mon	3	#1	36	38	36	38	2
	1		36	35	72	73	1
	2		Chg. over				
Tue	3	#3	36	41	36	41	5
	1		36	42	72	83	11
	2		36	41	108	124	16
Wed	3		Chg. over		144	124	
	1						
	2						
Thr	3						
	1						
	2						
Fri	3						
	1						
	2						
OT	3						
	1						
	2						

Packaging Line B

Day	Shift	SKU	Schedule	Production	Cumulative Schedule	Cumulative Production	Variance
Mon	3						
	1						
	2						
Tue	3	#2	45	37	45	37	–8
	1		45	45	90	82	–8
	2		45	39	135	121	–14
Wed	3		Chg. over				
	1						
	2						
Thr	3						
	1						
	2						
Fri	3	#4	45	45	45		
	1		45		90		
	2		Chg. over				
OT	3						
	1						
	2						

267

tored by management. Previously, a management decision to adjust the schedule would have been less timely, if it were made at all. The reason for the delay would probably be attributed to either the untimeliness of the variance information or a preoccupation with the other important aspects of managing a dynamic business.

Although this planning and scheduling method is simple in its number-crunching aspects (flip charts, markers, and calculators), and in its visible performance-tracking feature (magnets), it requires a shift in energies. Where the hard work before might have been the mechanics—software development, user training, generation of hernia reports—now 90 percent of a production manager's job is spent working on *process*. Process in this environment is people management: setting vision and direction and removing roadblocks. Previously, a manager had one boss; now he or she works for everyone on the floor. The system requires large doses of communication, meetings, and nudges toward worker empowerment.

For years we have looked at production management hierarchically:

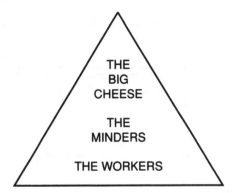

It seems that this system has turned the pyramid upside down:

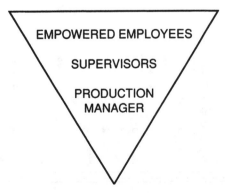

Employees call meetings. They run the business. Life goes on even if shift supervisors are away. In the words of one production manager, "I'm 50 percent cheerleader and 50 percent business manager. Some days it would be easier to sit in front of the tube for eight hours, but this is a lot more exciting, as well as profitable!"

16 PROFITABLE PURCHASING

Michael Harding

Editor's Note

This chapter examines many common practices in the purchasing discipline and offers updated and more effective alternatives. Purchasing is responsible for the price, delivery, and quality of purchased goods and services. In today's market, however, these terms take on new meaning. How does purchasing know whether the right price, delivery, and quality are achieved, *right* meaning those qualities that best serve the business and the customer? Today's right may not coincide with yesterday's definition of the purchasing function. There is a new purchasing lexicon:

Traditional purchasing	Tomorrow's purchasing
Lowest of three bids	Best installed value
Negotiate price	Cost of an effective producer
Passes inspection	Proof from suppliers that goods meet needs
Delivery when promised	Delivery as required by customer
Supplier lead times	Supplier value-added times
Design in a vacuum	Design to suppliers' capabilities and customers' needs (a syndicated process)

Purchasing is often measured on its cost-effectiveness by comparing the current or proposed purchase price with a prior purchase: The lower of the two prices is better or the lowest of three or more bids is best when deciding where to place new business. But the problem is an unspoken assumption that all other factors are identical and constant. They are not. It is the cost to use an item, its installed value, that counts, not the price to acquire the item. Before an organization can determine the value of what it has purchased, it must consider these factors:

Purchase price.

Transport—cost, time of ownership in transit, and packaging.

Foreign purchases must include brokerage fees, handling damage, currency fluctuations, added inventory requirements, duties, and communications problems.

Quality—the cost of incoming inspection, required in-process inspection, scrap, rework, and warranty repairs.

Production costs—ease of assembly, production yields, ability to automate, and minimum component variation part to part.

Suppliers—ease of doing business, predictable delivery and service, design assistance, and quick response to new demand.

Time—the amount of added inventory that must be carried to anticipate delivery problems, assembly time, and your process cycle time.

Only after all these indirect and often hidden costs are added to the purchase price will a buyer know whether he or she has obtained the best price for the business.

Sellers have difficulty establishing appropriate selling prices. They rely not only on their internal cost data but numerous external conditions:

- *The competitive market place.* What the competition is quoting, and the number of competitors. The more competitors, the greater the pressure on pricing.
- *The seller's market position.* Market leaders can usually set prices, whereas market followers must consider setting their prices below the market leader.
- *The product technology.* Product and technology maturity impact sellers' pricing. More mature products tend to compete on price while leading-edge products compete on perceived value and new functionality.

Sellers seek specific price-comparison information because the buyer is often the only consumer of a specific item, such as that made to a particular blueprint or specification. How will sellers compete in the future if they do not receive accurate feedback on current quotation efforts? A dilemma that faces many buyers is the amount and accuracy of data that should be conveyed to the seller regarding relative competitive standing. Many companies unwittingly make it expensive for suppliers to sell to them or create environments that encourage high prices by adopting these practices:

• *The lowest of three bids equals the world's third-highest price.* The bidding process is flawed. Sellers look to sell their products at the highest possible price acceptable to the buyer. Therefore, sellers will tend to offer higher-than-competitive prices and subsequently lower the price to adapt it to the competitive environment after receiving the buyer's reaction to the quote. Prices may also be lowered through negotiation. Starting off high and later lowering the price allows the seller to give up pricing position only as required to achieve the business.

• *Splitting the business for safety reasons.* Many buyers believe that they reduce their exposure to problems by awarding portions of the business to two or more suppliers, insuring against a single supplier going bankrupt, burning down, or having disruptive labor problems. Further, having several suppliers creates its own competitive environment and maintains pricing pressure on all participating suppliers. There is also an aversion to single or sole sourcing because it is perceived as poor business practice. There is a negative impact to each of these practices.

• Economies of scale may be lost by splitting the business.

• Suppliers know that the business has been split and they have a virtual license not to inform the buyer of any problem (e.g., quality, labor, financial) because they realize that the buyer has alternatives. Single sources cannot avoid the responsibility of sharing problems and concerns with the buying organization.

• Multiple sources increase the possibility that problems will arise with one or more of the suppliers. If a buyer has three sources for an item instead of one source, the likelihood of a supplier's plant burning to the ground has been increased by 200 percent.

• *Requests for quote predetermine the responses.* Buyers make several assumptions when they request a quote. One of these assumptions centers on quantity price breaks. For example, a buyer requested prices for 100, 250, and 500 pieces. The supplier had no idea how to price the product until he received the request. The buyer told him via that request that the seller should quote one price for 500, a higher price for 250, and an exorbitant price for 100. Before receiving the request the seller had only two prices; one for 1,000 and more and another for 999 and less. The buyer might do well to inquire about price breaking points or request prices on annual or greater quantities.

- *Measure the price paid by a past price or a standard cost.* If the current price is lower than a prior price paid, then the current price is a good one. Not true! Was the last price for similar quantity and quality and in a like market? Who set the standard? Is the price affordable today regardless of past prices paid? Using history as a measure of good prices is nearly always misleading and fraught with danger.

- *Short-term buys drive prices up.* Many companies will use MRP or monthly time buckets for material planning purposes, which often causes purchasing to buy or release in weekly or monthly quantities. In fact, many companies will require the same component, material, or technology for many years. Long-term contractual relationships should span the life of part, product, and/or technology. Release quantities should be totally independent of pricing and quantity break pricing. Short-term buys also give no incentive to suppliers to invest in process and product improvements, equipment, and training.

- *Suppliers not involved in product design create for cost, quality, and manufacturability.* Many buying companies fail to use the massive engineering resources of their suppliers to the fullest. The tendency is to design in a vacuum in-house and have suppliers quote on the final prints and specifications. After product release engineering change orders and value analysis efforts attest to the potential for improvement in this process. No one knows the suppliers' technologies and processes better than they do. Organizational egos aside, the buying organization can be the coordinator of the efforts of many suppliers to meet the end customers' needs and exceed their expectations.

WHAT IS THE RIGHT PRICE?

Determining price is simple and at the same time complex; it must be affordable. To determine affordability, a company must perform a reverse market cost analysis, breaking the affordable market selling price of the company's finished unit down into material, labor, overhead, and margin requirements. Purchasing will be given a bill of materials and a budget. If purchasing cannot buy the bill of materials at the affordable or budget price, there will be no product. The inverse is true; meet the budget and the company has a marketable product. If all the material can be purchased below budget, purchasing begins to contribute to the profit of the company by whatever that difference may be in dollars.

Many purchasing departments spend the major portion of their day in delivery control, although buyers have little effect on supplier lead times. The only factor that affects lead times to any significant degree is the economy. When demand is soft, prompt delivery is more readily available.

Quoted and practiced lead times tend to remain relatively fixed. A company's customers' expectations around delivery of finished product is even more demanding. Customers have not become more reasonable and understanding with time. This is particularly true the closer one gets to the end consumer.

So, as supplier lead times remain fixed and customers become more demanding, the buying organization in the middle becomes the great shock absorber between fixed supplier lead times and increasingly demanding customers. What is lead time and why is it as long as it is? Supplier lead time is the accumulation of the following:

Order entry time.

Backlog.

Priorities.

Processes.

Queue times.

Quality practices.

Internal financial measures.

Lot sizing.

Setup times.

Internal standards of performance.

Past practices.

Ninety-five percent of supplier lead time encompasses activities that are unimportant to the product and the buyer. Seldom are long lead times actively reduced because suppliers have been successful adapting their customers to their lead times. Therefore, 12-week lead times become embedded in customers' planning systems as self-fulfilling prophesies. One way to begin questioning lead times is to determine the velocity of a process. The formula compares the lead time to the actual work (labor and/or machine time content) in a product:

$$\text{Manufacturing velocity} = \frac{\text{Supplier lead time}}{\text{Work content}}$$

Work content excludes all activities and time elements that add no value to the product: queue time, material storage and handling, setup and change-over times exceeding 15 minutes, order entry processes longer than five minutes (order entry, credit and inventory checks, production scheduling, product configuration, engineering verification, and delivery and price acknowledgments), perfunctory inspection, nonfunctional testing, verification, approvals, and backlog.

A sampling of U.S. discrete manufacturers indicates that typical manufacturing velocity ratio is in the range of 200 to 300:1. Or, the average American manufacturer takes 250 hours to add 1 hour of value to a product. Here is a practical example: A transformer supplier quoted eight weeks delivery. An analysis of her process indicated that the average process cycle time is 12 minutes per transformer. This included coil winding, furnace process time, and hypotesting: 60 minutes × 8 hours × 5 days × 8 weeks = 19,200 minutes/12-minute cycle time

$$\text{Manufacturing velocity} = 1,600:1$$

There is ample opportunity to reduce lead times given the proper incentives. But for purchasing to permanently reduce supplier lead times and remove itself from the perpetual expediting mode, assign a value to lead time. No one, not suppliers and not the buyer's own accountants, values time. This is odd because process time is one of the greatest contributors to cost. The shorter the process time, the lower the cost to produce.

DELIVERY AND INVENTORY

The path to establishing a cost of lead time begins with inventory. We mentioned earlier that the buying organization is becoming the shock absorber between suppliers and customers. Often the buying organization is forced to stock increasing amounts of inventory to compensate for the expanding difference between suppliers and customers.

Management has a love–hate relationship with inventory. Inventory is an asset of the company: The more inventory, the more valuable the company. It is loan collateral and an asset on the balance sheet or annual report. On the other hand, cash flow could be better and inventory turns are linked to the flow. If a company could only turn inventory faster, regardless of the dollars in inventory, it would borrow less often and be more profitable.

Is inventory an asset, a potential asset, or a liability? Accountants say that inventory is an asset on the balance sheet, in the bank's and stockholders' minds, and in fact. But when the market or technology changes and no one wants the inventory, is it still an asset? Companies do not want to diminish their asset bases so they are slow to declare inventory obsolete and slower still to write it off. At best, inventory is a potential or conditional asset. It can be converted into sales only if the market wants it. Otherwise, it's a liability.

The Problem with Inventory

Inventory is never worth what you paid for it. It's expensive to keep track of: stock status, cycle counting, physical inventories, record accuracy. It's costly (obsolescence, space consumer, shelf life, cost to carry), difficult to work around (implementing ECOs, tracing quality problems), and requires other resources (people, systems, equipment, transactions).

Historically the annual cost has been calculated at 20 percent or twice the current prime interest rate. More recently enlightened companies have used percentages in the range of 35 to 50 of the purchase price. The real cost to carry is 75 percent, as shown in the following table:

Visible costs	Approximate percentage per year	
Interest rate of money	10%	
Taxes	5%	
Insurance	3%	
Space, occupancy, and utilities	4%	
Equipment (movement and storage)	3%	
Scrap and obsolescence	5% (to 20%)	
Subtotal		30%
Additional less-visible costs		
Personnel (planners, analysts, warehousers)	15%	
Transactions: counting, moving, retrieving, issuing, reconciling	10%	
Inspection, reinspection, return of defective material	10%	
Rework, handling damage, loss	10%	
Grand total		**75%**

Source: Michael Harding and Mary Lu Harding, *Purchasing* (New York: Barron's Educational Series, 1991), 205.

As long as inventory remained relatively inexpensive to maintain, it was the alternative to reduced lead times. Buyers acquired more to accommodate fixed or increasing supplier lead times and more demanding customers. Everybody was happy. Suppliers didn't have to change their practices and customers could be serviced from the buyers' inventories. During this time indirect (overhead) costs skyrocketed in many companies—even more than labor or material costs rose.

Suppliers are shielded from the increasing demands of their customers by standing behind their lead times, which forces their customers to stock more inventory. The longer the suppliers' lead times, the more inventory buyers must carry. The greater the difference between buyers' customer demands and the suppliers' lead times, the more inventory will be carried by buyers. Even though many buyers schedule weekly supplier deliveries, there is a tendency to carry one week's worth of inventory for each week of supplier lead time. Therefore, the cost of lead time is equal to the cost to carry inventory—75 percent per year, or 1.5 percent per week. Now we have a means of placing a value on supplier lead times and assessing that value to quoted prices and actual prices paid.

For example, a buyer sent three requests for a quote for 5,000 transformers. The buyer's standard cost is $12.30 each. The responses were as follows:

Company	Unit price	Lead time
Able Corp.	$12.25	10 weeks
Baker Ltd.	$12.65	7 weeks
Couch Inc.	$13.10	2 weeks

In this case the buyer would like to buy from Couch Inc. because delivery will become a problem sooner or later. Ideally, the buyer would like to purchase Couch's transformers at Able's prices. But the buyer must choose between the two. Finance, of course, would like the buyer to purchase the goods from Able Corp. The buyer would like to influence Able to run its business in such a manner that its lead time is two weeks or less. The new price calculation and quote comparison is as follows:

Company	Unit price × 1.5% × lead time	= New price
Able Corp.	$12.25 (1.015 × 10)	$14.09
Baker Ltd.	$12.65 (1.015 × 7)	$13.98
Couch Inc.	$13.10 (1.015 × 2)	$13.49

The prices, now weighted for lead time, must guide the buyer's source selection process. All other factors being equal, he or she must act consistently with what the weighted price prescribes. After Able starts to lose business or fails to win new business via its quotes, it will get the message that lead time is not only important but that specific costs are associated with uncompetitive lead times. Able's first reaction might be to propose to put finished goods in stock or offer consigned inventories. But these are expensive alternatives to the supplier seriously pursuing shorter process times—the buyer will ultimately pay for the new services one way or another. Able will have to become more delivery effective eventually, so why not now? Until the bite of lost business forces suppliers to work on their cycle times, they are unlikely to begin the effort.

Quality

It is axiomatic that the purchasing function of a company is responsible for supplier price, delivery, and quality, sometimes called the three-legged milking stool of purchasing. Are all the legs equal? Nearly all purchase orders have a highly contested price and a negotiated delivery date, but where is the reference to product quality? Few purchase orders specify parts quality, although they may reference a print, specification, or sample.

There are two definitions of quality: (1) the specification—what the part must look like and (2) how often the parts must look like the specification. Many companies relieve purchasing of the responsibility of communicating or specifying the second definition. This is typically the requirement for Cpk (process capability), 6+ Sigma, parts per million, and MTBF (mean time between failures). Suppliers often hear of these requirements only after their shipped goods have been found to be noncompliant.

In far too many companies purchasing gets involved in supplier quality issues after there is a problem. Purchasing's job then is to return the rejected material and expedite a replacement lot, a reactionary mode. Omitting the quality measure from the purchase order sends a strong message to suppliers that quality is less important than appearance. There may also be a contractual legal issue concerning the cause for rejection. Does a buyer have a legal right to reject for causes not called out in the contract or for variation in product that exceeds the buyer's undeclared limits or expectations? Possibly not.

Nearly all manufacturers and users of manufactured components and material have an overhead function called incoming inspection that finds errors in suppliers' products. When buying companies do not request specific quality from suppliers they institute this overhead function to catch suppliers not complying with buyers' expectations. Like all overhead expenses, this one tends to grow over time and consumes considerable resources.

Aside from the expense involved with incoming inspection there is a problem of actually finding the quality problems contained in a received lot of material. Visual inspection will find catastrophic failures (e.g., wrong part shipped, consistent flaws part to part), but companies will have great difficulty finding random failures (parts that occasionally exceed accepted limits for no apparent or consistent reason). Visual inspection will catch no more than 80 percent of lots with such failures, optimistic given the nature of sampling inspection plans such as Mil Std. 105E. These inspection plans begin with the premise that it is impractical for an organization to review or inspect every component purchased and received, so a small random sample (usually less than 0.01 percent of the total) is taken and the entire population is characterized by what is revealed in the small sample. The sampling plans also allow for a certain but small percentage of the samples to be nonconforming in the belief that perfect quality is either not achievable or would be prohibited by cost. The lot is either accepted or rejected based on the sample findings. This process is relatively simple and not very effective. More often it is manufacturing or the end customer who finds the failed components. This is expensive quality. Where a quality discrepancy is found determines the cost associated with finding the problem. The example in Figure 16–1 from a computer manufacturer makes the point.

To avoid the costs and the inevitability of some unacceptable-quality parts getting through the incoming quality system, transfer the responsibility for acceptable quality back to the source—the supplier. If suppliers are accountable for product quality they must know the product definition (specification) and the acceptable quality level (allowable defects, if any, per lot or per life of product). This requirement must be part of the purchase order or contract.

While there are many measures of quality, we will focus briefly on one—Cpk, or process capability.

$$Cp = \frac{\text{Specification width}}{\text{Process width}}$$

FIGURE 16–1 Where a problem is caught determines the cost

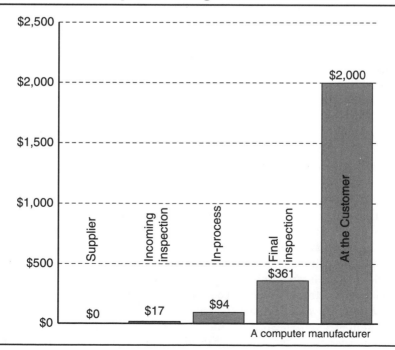

A computer manufacturer

If the process can be controlled to use only a portion of the specification tolerance, the likelihood that a part will randomly exceed the specification diminishes greatly. For example, the tolerance on a specific dimension is ±0.010″, and the process can be controlled to produce a tolerance of ±0.005:

$$0.010/0.005 = Cp\ 2 = 2\ \text{parts per billion error rate}$$

The k is the constant or mean dimension. In the preceding example, the ±0.010 is the design-allowable tolerance for a dimension of 0.200 inch. The designing engineer wants the tolerance to vary about the mean dimension or target value of 0.200. Although parts centering on 0.198 ± 0.007 (a range of 0.191 to 0.205) would comply with the specification requirement, the variation is not centered around the target value. Therefore, our definition of quality is the minimum variation part to part on a target value.

The Cpk measurement has subtle signs of perfection built into it. The statistical conversions for various Cpk are as follows:

Cpk	PPM defect	Yield
0.67	22,750	97.725%
0.83	6,210	99.379%
1.00	2,700	99.730%
1.33	63	99.9936627%
1.50	3	99.9997%
1.67	547 PPB	99.9999426%
2.00	2 PPB	99.9999998%

Remember that statistics deal with the probability of an event happening. In the case of Cpk 1.00, the data say that all parts are within specification. Statistics say that there still is a statistical probability that 2,700 random failures will occur for no specific or consistent reason.

Purchasing should consider requesting suppliers to conduct a process capability study on its process with the goal of controlling process variation to a Cpk of 2 or better. Subsequently, the purchase order should contain the specific Cpk measures of acceptable quality. The one remaining step is for the buyer to eliminate the overhead of incoming inspection. This is accomplished by moving the burden of proof of goodness from the buyer's incoming inspection to the supplier. The buyer must answer the question of what proof will be acceptable that the shipped goods are conforming to quality requirements. Proof can take the form of control charts, certificates of analysis (chemical goods), and the like. It must be impartial, empirical proof. Incoming inspection's only function will be to correlate quality data. These significant changes in the suppliers' quality practices come about more readily when they are conditions of the purchase and not left to a separate document or, worse, to an unspoken understanding.

Since the early 1980s many companies have used an evaluation process to improve supplier quality or to distinguish quality- from nonquality-producing suppliers. Often this process involved personnel from the buyer's organization who would meet suppliers armed with preprinted questions and check sheets, some more than 100 pages of forms. The goal is to evaluate a supplier, based on its past performance and an assessment of current practices, to determine whether that supplier is capable of meeting the buyer's future quality needs. There are many variations on this effort but the core procedure is flawed:

- Some suppliers will establish quality criteria for their suppliers that they themselves do not employ. Credibility is lost quickly when an evaluating organization cannot pass its own tests of quality.

- There is an assumption that the buying organization's specification and prints reflect its actual needs.

- Another assumption is the correlation between the suppliers' and the buyer's quality systems. An evaluation team must ask whether it is sufficiently knowledgeable about its suppliers' many technologies and processes to be able to fairly evaluate their capabilities. There are significant hazards in setting oneself up as a judge of others.

- A buying organization may not be a significant enough customer to a supplier to warrant the supplier's serious attention.

- Some suppliers may have as their sole objective obtaining the customer's bronze and oak certification plaque to display in their lobbies to impress other customers.

All the data collected by an evaluation team is history as soon as it is recorded, but it may not indicate the future quality performance of a supplier. What buyers really want to know is how the supplier will perform in the future. Here is an eight-step process that focuses on influencing future supplier quality performance:

1. Set quality standards for each purchased commodity—PPM, Cpk, MTBF, Sigma, inspection, and so forth. No single quality measure or standard is appropriate for the wide variety of goods purchased by most buying organizations. Chemicals, electronic components, castings, stamped parts, equipment purchases, packaging materials, and office supplies each have their own measure and requirement for quality. A matrix of purchased commodities and appropriate measures of quality can be constructed:

	Chemicals	Electronics	Castings	Stampings	Equipment	Packaging	Supplies
PPM				2000			
Cpk 1			X				
Cpk 2		X					
MTBF					20,000 hrs		
Inspect						X	
Certification/ Analysis	Reagent						
No Inspection							X

The buying organization must do its homework to establish the proper measure of quality for each commodity and establish quality goals for the future based on customer and market needs. These will be moving targets as customers' needs and expectations change.

2. What proof will the buying organization accept from suppliers of product quality? This proof may be control charts supplied before or with the shipment of goods, the supplier's own quality audits including field failures or third-party endorsements such as the Malcolm Baldrige National Quality Award application, but not other customers' certification of IOS 9000 efforts. Although the International Standards Organization has greatly improved its standards and quality criteria since being introduced to the non-European world and extensive process documentation may be of value to a limited number of world manufacturers, it does little to assist manufacturers to meet the world demands for ever-increasing levels of product quality and reliability. By the year 2000, ISO will either change to meet the needs of the world or self-extinguish because of nonrelevance.

Steps 1 and 2 require that the buying organization expend the first effort and clean its own house first. The remaining six steps involve supplier effort with the buyer's assistance.

3. What is the supplier's current quality and what is its plan for improvement? Since it is unlikely that any one customer will change a supplier's quality system, a buyer must take suppliers as they are. First, the supplier must define its current quality system and its results or yields. It must analyze the effectiveness of the system and determine whether the existing system can produce the quality its customers require. If the system is capable, the supplier will be able to produce evidence to that effect. If the system falls short, the supplier will have to assess the risks of continuing with the current system versus the potential benefits of adopting a new, more effective system. If a new system will be put in place, what are the projections for and commitment to improvement and by what dates? The supplier's plan for improvement may include the following:

Implementation of process controls.

Taking quality control to the production line with adequate training.

Massive and continuous housekeeping initiative.

Goals for PPM, Cpk, Sigma, and so forth by product line and machine.

Measuring and rewarding management based on product quality and customer delight.

Participation with customers in product/quality design.

Investment in state-of-the-art technology.

As quality improves and goals are met, the supplier will be able to furnish evidence of improvement in control charts, yield improvements, lower-quality costs, and reduced product variation.

4. What is the supplier's cost of nonconformance? Exceptionally good quality costs less than poor quality, and the evidence is buried in the over-head account. The following are costs called the price of nonconformance, or PONC, and are associated with achieving current quality levels:

Inspection	Returns to suppliers	Poor yields
Sorting	Additional space	Warranty work
Rework	Longer lead times	Premature product failure
Remakes	Nonfunctional testing	Spare parts inventories
Scrap	Delayed revenue	Added handling
Lost reputation	Lost sales	Added administrative costs

These and other associated quality costs differ from the cost of quality be-cause PONC does not include costs associated with quality training. Quality training is a healthy expenditure that produces quality dividends. The other PONC items contribute nothing to the product except cost. The more pre-dictable a supplier's processes and quality, the lower the costs to achieve su-perior quality.

5. What is the supplier's budget for quality training? Is it more or less than 3 percent of payroll? What have past budgets been? What are future projections and commitments? Is the training focused and is there a plan in place? Do all participate in training, including direct labor, middle and top management, suppliers, and customers? How are new concepts introduced to the organization?

Better-quality manufacturing companies invest 3 percent or more of payroll in training each year. In service companies the number is 5 percent or more.

6. What is the manufacturing cycle time (*velocity*) and what is the plan for improvement? For a manufacturing plant to achieve a manufacturing velocity of 10 or better, processes must be predictable. There is no time for remakes, sorting, poor yields, and the like. A short process cycle time may indicate superior quality, which in turn will shorten a supplier's lead time. A short and predictable lead time is also a statement of supplier quality. As long as a buyer is evaluating a supplier, why not look at lead and process times? Supplier qualification is more than the statistics of product quality measures. The shorter the lead time, the better the quality, the lower the cost. Product quality, costs, and lead time are inextricably mixed and co-dependent. Suppliers will be able to provide the buyer with evidence that their process times are being reduced.

There is a significant added benefit to suppliers in the learning process involved in determining and measuring velocity and PONC. Suppliers find that significant indirect costs are involved in current manufacturing practices. These two new measures point the way to lower costs and greater market acceptance of products and often provide the needed catalyst for change.

7. When will the supplier make the buyer's incoming inspection unnecessary and undesirable? When will the supplier give you the confidence to stop incoming inspection and tests? When will the buyer introduce more errors by inspecting than accepting goods without inspection? When will the buyer be able to reduce unnecessary inspection overhead? When will inspection be used only to correlate data?

8. Supplier must notify the buyer before it changes the process. Supplier must notify the buyer of all of the following:

Change in manufacturing processes or equipment.

Change of ownership.

Change in raw material suppliers.

Change in technology.

The buyer will have the opportunity to evaluate any planned major change by the supplier before it is implemented to determine impact on the buyer's process, product, and customers.

This eight-step process is forward-looking. It requires that the buying organization puts its own house in order before approaching suppliers. It is low cost and accepts suppliers' quality systems as they are. It shifts the burden of proof of goodness to the supplier where it belongs, and, finally, it does not conflict with other customer requests.

SUPPLIER EVALUATIONS

Volumes have been written on how to evaluate a supplier and its potential, including financial (Dun & Bradstreet–type) and annual reports, references, and on-site interviews and evaluations. In the end, however, the decision tends to be based on intuition.

There is another approach, involving different measures based on time and quality, that may also be beneficial:

Result		Goal	Typical U.S.
1. Manufacturing velocity $= \dfrac{\text{Lead time}}{\text{Work content (Value - added)}}$		$= <10$	250
Inventory turns (will result from manufacturing velocity)		$= >20$	3–7
2. PONC		$= <2\%$ COS	7–11%
COS		(COS $=$ cost of sales)	
3. Profit after tax		$= >10\%$	4–6%

With these three and a half measures a buyer can determine the effectiveness of a supplier while establishing goals for future performance. These metrics can be a centerpiece for in-depth discussions with suppliers. Suppliers also have an interest in performing to the goal levels. These measures take the subjectivity out of evaluations and help make the buyer–seller relationship mutually beneficial.

SOURCING STRATEGIES

Every company has at least two types of customers: core customers and opportunity customers. Core customers are those the company relies on month after month and year after year for revenue. They pay the mortgage and wages. They get the best service and careful pricing. When things get tough in the marketplace (shortages or allocations), core customers are serviced first. Core business is relationship focused. There are unspoken but real mutual obligations. Information is shared with relative ease. Opportunity customers are those sought to temporarily fill capacity, here today–gone tomorrow customers; the business is often price focused. There is no cross obligation other than that defined by the current order (there may be no future orders).

Partnering

Buyers want to do business with relationship-focused suppliers. There is, however, an equal obligation for buyers to be relationship focused and to act in accordance with the demands of such relationships. Since the early 1970s companies have encouraged their purchasing personnel to form partnerships with key suppliers, only to be directed by management shortly thereafter to demand lower prices or similar incongruous requests. The real question is whether the buying company is partnership material. Few companies stop to ask themselves this question before searching for true partners among their suppliers. Partners display certain characteristics, including

Sharing information, technology, and resources.

Participating in marketing and strategic planning.

Working cooperatively on research and development projects.

Sharing the benefits of ideas and lower costs.

Sharing the joy, pain, rewards, and risks of being in business together.

If a potential partner does not exhibit these characteristics, do not waste your time and that of your suppliers.

Supplier Reduction

A company can only partner or form relationships with a limited number of suppliers. Buyers and purchasing managers have sought in vain for a formula to give them the right number of suppliers. There are finally three formulas for determining the proper number of suppliers. Since no two companies are the same, one of the following formulas will fit any situation:

1. Take the square root of the prior or current number of suppliers.
2. Add the sum of the current ages of your children or your age times two.
3. Take your company's 1996 sales, divide by the number of miles all employees commuted to and from work in that year, times 0.28 or your 1991 income tax bracket (whichever is lower) and divide by the number of people in your purchasing department.

Any system works as long as the result is a small fraction of the prior number of suppliers. The supplier reduction process may work this way:

1. Consolidate part numbers by commodities (families of parts).
2. Within each commodity, reduce several suppliers to one per part number (assuming capacity is not a problem).
3. Where practical, place families of parts with one supplier: reduce interfacing parts problems, deliver by sets of parts, provide greater dollar leverage, and allow suppliers to be of greater design assistance.

Many buyers panic when faced with reducing the supply base because competition is then reduced and multiple-source safety nets vanish. Many professionals also feel intuitively that single sourcing is a poor purchasing strategy. Although there is validity to the concern, it is likely that more material is sole sourced through seller design than by any business plan that purchasing may devise. Sellers want to sell their products to the user (engineer, production personnel, customers, doctors) and not buyers. It is not uncommon for a purchasing department to be directed to specific sourcing in 70 percent of its buys through blueprint, specification, qualified supplier lists, and the like. And often purchasing has little input into these limiting factors.

It would be better for purchasing to have a strategy to manage the supply base by networking with users before the sale is made. At the very least purchasing should be the gatekeeper for external access to the users. To be effective, purchasing must be a service resource to the users. Some buyers call this one-stop shopping. When a user calls purchasing for a supplier resource—design assistance, samples, and technical data—purchasing must provide a resource within the desired time frame. This may be added work for purchasing but it is crucial. Purchasing will be included at the initial product stage, select an appropriate supplier, guide the relationship, and ensure that design to quality and cost is considered during design for function.

There are five critical factors a buyer will want to consider when selecting a supplier:

1. Manufacturing technology. Is the supplier using state-of-the-art technology and improving? Will it share its technology? Does the supplier support its customers with design capabilities? Does it understand its customers' technology needs for the future and invest heavily in research and development?

2. Quality. Does the supplier set aggressive quality goals and insist on the same from its suppliers—in the range of Cpk 2? Does it understand its customers' quality needs? Does the supplier have a program of continuous improvement in place? Does it visually display quality information and measures at each workstation?

3. The impact of time. Does the supplier compare lead time to work content and work toward 10? Is it reducing setup and changeover time to 15 minutes maximum?

4. Costs. Are selling prices based on the cost of raw material plus rapid valued-added time—velocity of 10? Do costs improve over time because of improved quality costs, reduced processing time, and better use of less inventory?

5. Logistics. Does the supplier get or assist in getting goods to where the customer needs them, on time, properly packaged, and without damage or mistakes?

Global or Local Sourcing Strategies

A key sourcing strategy a buyer must consider at the planning stage is whether global sourcing will be an integral part of his or her strategy. There are risks and benefits associated with international procurement. Source globally when

- The technology is not available locally.
- The cost to use (installed value) offers the buyer a competitive advantage.
- It is a condition of the selling of products in foreign markets and the difference in pricing is justified in profits gained for the corporation.
- Purchasing commodities (e.g., copper, mercury, bauxite) are directed by a customer or foreign owner.

Do not source globally when landed prices are only marginally better (less than 25 percent) than domestic prices or a buying company believes that chasing lower labor costs will yield lower prices now or in the future. The labor economies may not be there when one considers that labor represents only 2 percent of manufacturing costs in the consumer electronics industry and 3 percent in the computer industry. Foreign lead times are significantly longer than those of domestic producers, and there are risks of economic, political, or social unrest. Finally, there is a risk that a buying company may be funding its future competitors, transferring technology, and so forth.

The financial lure of lower foreign wages has drawn companies since the 1950s. The assumption is that lower labor costs translate directly into lower procurement and usage costs, which is not true. Often the pricing differential hides an increasing indirect cost. Once the buying company's financial manager has duly compared the domestic with the foreign quoted price, he or she must add the following indirect costs to the foreign quote:

added transportation costs	premium transportation costs
time in transit	duties and brokerage fees
F.O.B terms	financial document preparation
currency fluctuations	changes in local government price supports
language barriers	cost of resolving problems
local customs and holidays	fluctuations in quality
different legal systems	transit delays, dock strikes, and so forth
time differences	impact of national agendas
pilferage	ability to implement engineering changes
return policies	availability of design assistance

These factors easily add 25 to 40 percent to quoted prices. In countries where hyperinflation exists, the price can increase 1 or 2 percent per day as has been the experience with some South and Latin American countries. Even the venerable Japanese yen has ranged between 240 and 80 to the dollar in the past decade. The impact of many of these risks is often moderated by foreign governments through subsidies of raw material, export incentives, and manipulation of favorable currency-exchange rates. These incentives can be modified or withdrawn by a sponsoring government without notice, however. Newly developing nations have added price advantages in that there is often little, if any, government regulation of the environment, social welfare, or work conditions (hours, age, safety). Labor costs are also lower as witnessed by China's $60 in U.S. dollars (USD) per month wages, Vietnam's $30 (USD) per month and Mexico's $120 (USD) per month average wage. Wages are low but so is productivity.

China's low wages, for example, may be misleading. The $60 per month is for Chinese-owned sweatshops. Western-owned businesses are directed to provide subsidies to their workers such as meals, housing or housing supplements, transportation, and clothing, which drive the actual direct labor wages to $200 per month. The government often tells businesses how many people they must employ. China's inflation during 1994 was 25 percent, and 20 percent in 1995. Perhaps inflation, failure to control copyright and patent abuses, international mischief (selling nuclear technology to Pakistan, military exercises intended to intimidate Taiwan), scandals of prison labor, death orphanages, and human-rights violations will eventually creep into the collective minds and consciences of buying companies. China may also put Hong Kong and Macao at risk when they revert to the mainland in 1997 and 1999, respectively. Serious questions arise out of China's inability to deal with diversity within its walls.

The two greatest arguments against global sourcing are time and quality. Buyers must obtain goods when needed (the right product at the wrong time is the wrong product) and at predictable and appropriate quality. Buyers cannot afford suppliers that do not respond within the same time frame in which the buyer's company must respond to changes in customer and market demand. This means that suppliers must be within a four-hour radius of customers' plants.

Once buyer and seller have selected each other, the relationship is characterized by the subsequent conduct. What sort of contracts should you write to state your new relationship with suppliers (while still protecting your interests)? The contractual relationship has several growth stages: (1) A desire to be partners but also retain the right to sue newfound partners; a lack of trust. (2) Life of product and life of technology relationships in the form of requirements contracts. (3) If it is a good deal for both parties, why is a contract necessary?

Many buying companies want to enlist partners from the ranks of their suppliers but do not have the internal culture to support a reciprocal partnership relationship. These companies should not change the way they do business with their supply base; the hypocrisy shines through. Other companies want and have the ability to form true partnerships but require a growth and trust-building process. These companies will move from the use of blanket orders to requirements contracts. Blanket orders were early attempts by buyers to consolidate one year's use of materials for better pricing. Typically buyers would negotiate a price with a supplier for an estimated or forecasted one-year contract. When the quantity forecasts proved to be overstated, the buyer had a liability for the goods not taken. The liability translated into either the buyer taking unwanted goods or paying a higher unit price for the fewer goods taken. This is hardly a partnership, since the buyer is protecting the supplier from the hazards of doing business with the buyer but no one is protecting the buyer from the hazards of the marketplace in which he or she operates.

The Uniform Commercial Code, section 2, paragraph 306 (Output, Requirements and Exclusive Dealings) and its subsequent precedent-setting cases open up an entirely new and creative world of contracts. Two organizations can have a contract that specifies quantity only in terms of the buyer's need. The contract may state that the buyer proposes to purchase all (or any percentage) of his or her requirements from a supplier and/or a fixed period of time including a vague end of contract (until the product is no longer needed). With adequate and prompt sharing of projected needs (MRP reports, sales forecasts, and the like), suppliers can manage their production intelligently to serve the buyer and share equally in the rise and fall in product demand.

Companies do not purchase goods to be stored. They buy goods so that they may be processed and sold. So why do so many companies plan and execute the plan so that material ends up in raw material inventory? If goods are purchased for use, buyers should arrange for the goods to be delivered to the point of use within the organization, via kanban or other visual signaling devices, in standardized containers and with fixed counts. This not only shortens cycle times, reduces inventory, and reduces or eliminates formal releases, it also eliminates the perceived need to constantly count the received goods.

Bar coding is a useful, if not indispensable, tool in reducing the high level of material transactions that pervade most companies. Linking bar coding to the back-flush function of MRP II software can all but eliminate material transactions from the plant. One final code reading can relieve inventory of all the components used in the fabrication of the finished product and assign that product to a customer order. Components move either from a stockroom or directly from suppliers to a billable sale. There is no work-in-process inventory and no related movement transactions.

There are many false tools in the marketplace. Electronic data interchange (EDI) has been offered since the early 1980s, when it was cumbersome and expensive. EDI required buffer mailboxes to protect mainframes from unauthorized access; there were interfacing software problems and costs ranged into the hundreds of thousands of dollars. Recently EDI has become more user-friendly and cost-effective. However, buying organizations might do well to try out the theory and its effectiveness by conveying information to suppliers, common carriers, and banks by modem or fax before making the still considerable investment required by EDI.

The world is alight with procurement cards: credit cards that track and report purchases by cost center, account number, project, and individual. The issuing banks tout this as the ultimate in cost and budget control while freeing purchasing of the mounds of paperwork associated with indirect material purchases. Sounds good but why are so many banks aggressively marketing this product? The fees are high, ranging from a fixed annual charge per card, to 18-plus percent annual interest, to $2 per transaction, to some combination of all of these. The control they promote is all after the fact. At the end of the month, the department and financial managers will know who in engineering has overspent the budget or who is building the next generation of spacecraft in his or her garage.

Another broken tool is outsourcing purchasing. The premise is that when there is a unique buy or one that exceeds purchasing's technical or commercial abilities, the buy should be subcontracted to an organization that possesses the required skills. Some companies have taken outsourcing further by subcontracting key or all plant staff functions as a means of saving money. If a purchasing department accepts these arguments and practices, that department will self-destruct in short order. If a purchasing department needs new skills or information, the company and purchasing manager must invest in the training to develop the competencies to remain competitive in the world. Initial dependency fosters greater dependencies and what starts as a trickle becomes a waterfall. Once a company becomes dependent on outside organizations for competencies and cost-effectiveness, the company's end is in sight.

Outsourcing of components formerly made internally can be ominous for a company. Since the 1960s companies have asked their purchasing departments to seek suppliers that can produce goods at lower costs or higher quality than the companies themselves could produce. Often purchasing was successful. The company was happy; it obtained the business results it wanted without having to change the way it manufactured. As a result, many American companies did not have to improve and much manufacturing and product technology was given away to future competitors.

There are four traditional measures of purchasing performance:

1. Purchase price variance against a standard cost, last price paid, or target price. The intent is to measure purchasing against some standard that assumes to represent good performance. Many companies employ a standard costs system that gathers cost elements to ensure adequate margins and properly priced products in the market. The problem is that purchasing often influences or sets these standard prices. The system encourages purchasing managers to set standard prices at levels they know to be attainable and that may not reflect the needs of the business. Offering prices that come in over or under standard open the manager for criticism: Either purchasing has set the standard artificially low or it spent too much for an item. Standards typically remain in place for one year and yet the market in which the company operates may change monthly, weekly, or even daily. Meeting standard, predictable results (good or bad) is considered good managerial performance. In fact, in many companies it is preferable to produce a predictably bad performance as opposed to an unpredictably good performance.

2. Delivery measured against (a) the supplier's promised delivery, (b) a standard lead time, which is often contained in a software package, or (c) the requisitioner's request date. The first two measures have to do with predictability again. When a supplier delivers when promised it means only that it is meeting its stated delivery lead times, which is no mark of goodness.

3. Quality measured in terms of the percentage of acceptable lots passing through incoming inspection. As mentioned earlier in the chapter, incoming inspection may be no indicator of quality. It certainly does not track the inspected items through the process to find latent defects or unacceptable variation within the specification.

4. Cost reduction measures a current purchase order's price against that of a prior order to determine whether the price is lower. The assumption is that a lower purchase price contributes to company profits, which is not always the case. This logic assumes that all other factors including quality, timely deliveries, and indirect costs are equal. Other management functions are suspicious of purchasing when it reports cost-saving and cost-avoidance figures. They ask themselves who will pay for these lower prices, meaning that a price improvement may lead to a degradation in quality or functionality. It may be a savings only to purchasing and not the company as a whole.

For purchasing to be considered a corporate player and to truly reflect the profit impact the function can have it must be measured in terms of contribution to profit. None of the preceding measures clearly associates purchasing's efforts with company profits and yet purchasing controls most of the funds in many companies. Purchasing must know what costs are affordable. Sales or marketing will be required to competitively price the product in the marketplace. Purchasing will receive a costed bill of materials from finance with instructions that it must buy the listed items for a certain total sum or the company will have no product. If it can buy the items at a price lower than what is affordable, purchasing will contribute directly to company profits.

Quality and timely deliveries must also be part of the equation. An improvement in purchase price cannot be at the expense of quality, delivery, or desired inventory levels. A new measure of purchasing's contribution may be as follows:

Contribution to profit

Part Number A38596 rev 6, transformer	Standard cost $9.00
Affordable price $8.50	Price paid $8.00
Annual use 7,000 units	

Affordable price divided by price paid = 1.06% (+6%)

Delivery was in 5 weeks versus a needed date of 4 weeks = −5%
(deduct 5% for each week the delivery is beyond the needed date)

Target

Quality at incoming°	400 PPM	440 PPM	= +10% (straight percentage)
Quality in work-in-process	200 PPM	200 PPM	= 0 (straight percentage)
Finished goods°	21 parts	20 parts	= −5% (straight percentage)

°supplier-assignable errors

Price $0.50 × 7,000	=	$ 3,500
Delivery $8.00 × 0.05 × 7,000	=	−2,800
Quality $8.00 × 0.05 × 7,000	=	$ 2,800
Contribution to profit	=	$ 3,500

When constructing a measurement system, begin with the answer or behavior you want. Think profit, not cost reduction or quoted price. Sit with finance, engineering, quality, and production so that the new system will embrace the concerns of other functions. Some of the issues that require addressing include establishing costs of lead times, defects, rework, and carrying inventory. Merely asking the questions and perusing the information is part of the learning process and the benefit. Purchasing's new role is bringing resources together, education and training, and contribution to profit.

CONCLUSION

Purchasing for the new millenium will build on solid practices, teamwork, partnering, and common sense. The function will be a substantial contributor to the structure and profit of the company. Today's globally competitive companies can afford no less.

17 VISUAL ORDER

THE FOUNDATION OF EXCELLENCE IN MANUFACTURING

Gwendolyn D. Galsworth

Editor's note

Visual systems are everywhere and have been for a long time. The world's best companies have been using them for decades—and they know why. Toyota, Citizens Watch, Sony, Honda, Nissan, Matsushita, Akebono Brakes, Sumitomo, Panasonic, Hitachi, and Komatsu—some of the world's best companies—set the standard for visual excellence for the rest of the world more than two decades ago. Pockets of this excellence are beginning to appear in organizations that have more recently adopted a visual approach. Johnson Controls, AMP, Packard Electric, Fleetguard Cummins, Dana Corporation, Union Carbide, Boeing, Weyerhaeuser, Ford Motor Company, Varian, Vintech, and United Electric Controls rank high among these, along with Calsonic, Nummi, and other Pacific Rim transplants and joint ventures.

Excerpted and adapted from the book *Visual Systems: Harnessing the Power of a Visual Workplace* (Amacom, New York, 1997). Copyright © 1996, Gwendolyn D. Galsworth, all rights reserved.

Visual order, also known as industrial housekeeping or workplace organization, is the foundation of excellence in manufacturing. When it is in place on the production floor, work gets done efficiently and effectively. When it is not in place, work still gets done—but at a level of cost that is hard to justify. If you have any doubts about the power of visual order in a work environment, look at the photograph of a workbench before visual order was implemented (Figure 17–1a) and after (Figure 17–1b). Without knowing any more than your eyes tell you, you *know* which bench is the more productive, more efficient, and less frustrating place to work.

Visual order is not an end in itself. It is the indispensable first step of a more complete process called visual information sharing or *visual systems.* The ultimate outcome of this process is a *visual workplace.* There are no ifs, ands, or buts about it: You cannot achieve a visual workplace without first putting in place the principles and practices of visual order.

INDUSTRIAL HOUSEKEEPING JAPANESE STYLE

Implementing visual order is not a difficult process, but it requires a systematic methodology. That method is called 5S+1. 5S+1 is a set of principles and practices that, until recently, have not been well-known in American business and industry. In the 1980s, 5S (a narrower version of the approach) received increased attention when American companies began to send groups of managers and associates to Japan to tour that country's so-called *parlor factories.* The name derives from the cleanliness of these plants. No chips, no grease, no grime—and, in many instances, not a speak of dust, even in factories that manufacture parts. The floors shine. Safety records are flawless. Machinery is clean enough to show a single drip of oil—but of course there is none. The American visitors were stunned and clamored to know how this could be. The secret, they were told, was 5S.

5S is the Japanese code name for cleanliness and orderliness *with a vengeance.* It is as far from the notion of spring cleaning as any activity can be. This is not putting things in order one week only to have that order disappear without a trace the next week; it is order to last, a key waste-reduction strategy, and the foundation of the visual workplace.

The term *5S* is used throughout Japan and refers to the five house-keeping practices that are part of the daily routine of every Japanese household. In the mid-1950s, these practices became a corporate imperative. Here they are in Japanese, followed by an English pronunciation, and their common translation:

Seiri (*say-ree*):   proper arrangement
Seiton (*say-ton*):   orderliness

FIGURE 17–1a **Before visual order: A workstation before visual order was implemented.**

FIGURE 17–1b **After visual order: Implementing visual order triggers a simple but powerful transformation that greatly reduced motion in this work area.**

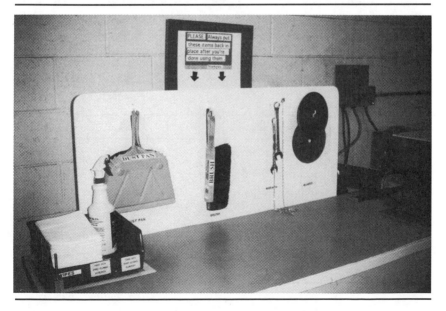

Seiso (*say-so*):	cleanliness
Seiketsu (*say-ket-soo*):	cleaned up
Shitsuke (*she-soo-kay*):	discipline

Unfortunately, something got lost in the translation and words that were meant to inspire us to action left us wondering what all the fuss was about.

5S+1: VISUAL ORDER, AMERICAN STYLE

5S+1—the principles and practices of visual order—was developed specifically for the American workplace to help companies create a work environment that is clear, clean, safe, self-explaining, and self-ordering. Box 17–1 spells this out. With each of the first five steps of the 5S+1 process, the workplace changes in a specific and unmistakable manner. Look at Figure 17–2a through 17–2g: Except for S4 (select locations), which is purely a thinking step, these photographs show you the tangible, visual shift that can result as each principle of visual order is implemented.

Why Clean Up the Workplace?

People intuitively recognize that a clean, uncluttered, safe, and well-ordered workplace is a productive one. But does it really make that much difference? Why not, the logic goes, make do with a little less than a perfect work space and just concentrate on getting product out the door? These are important questions—and unless we answer them clearly and definitively, there may be lingering doubts about whether the considerable effort required to make the shop floor self-explaining and self-ordering is worth it. Let's look at the strategic context in which visual order does make sense, a great deal of sense.

BOX 17–1   5S+1 American style

5S+1

S1:	Sort through and sort out
S2:	Scrub the workplace
S3:	Secure safety
S4:	Select locations
S5:	Set locations
+1:	Sustain the 5S habit

Text continues on page 303

S1: SORT THROUGH AND SORT OUT

FIGURE 17–2a Red-tag shelving: In this company, associates in one area regularly put any nonessential items on this metal shelving that in turn got cleared off every two weeks.

FIGURE 17–2b Roped-off area: When this first step of visual order was applied to finance and marketing departments, the team had to rope off a section of the floor to make enough room.

S2: SCRUB THE WORKPLACE

FIGURE 17–2c Before S1 and S2: A workbench before S1 and S2 were implemented. Notice the clutter and lack of uniformity in the area.

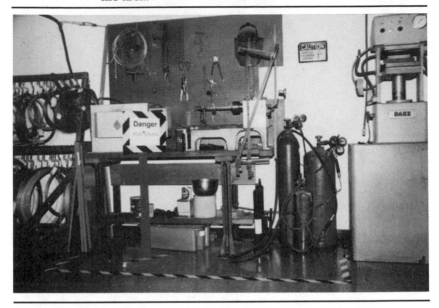

FIGURE 17–2d After S1 and S2: The same bench with the clutter gone, bright with a fresh coat of white paint.

S3: SECURE SAFETY

FIGURE 17–2e   The mystery of the pipes: There are many shop floor activities that can be made safer through visual order. One of the most important is the pipe system. Here is a network of pipes without a scrap of location information. Would you dare open any of these pipes without knowing what is inside?

S4: SELECT LOCATIONS

FIGURE 17–2f   A place for everything: Selecting proper locations means understanding the functional relationship between workplace items and locating them so that the flow between them is accelerated. In S4, this gets done through two maps similar to those you see in this photo. The first map (on the left) shows the way things are now placed. The other (on the right) shows how the same items might be placed to accelerate the flow.

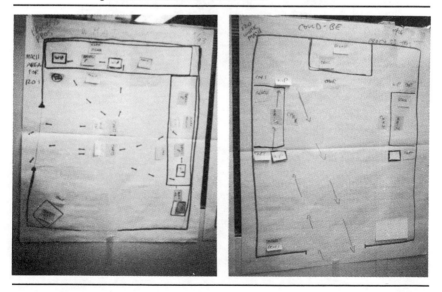

S5: SET LOCATIONS

FIGURE 17–2g **Smart placement: It is never enough just to find a good place for a workplace item. You must take the next step and ensure item recoil (that the item will find its way back to its designated location when it wanders off). That requires the three elements you see here: (1) the border around the barrel, (2) the home address above the barrel, and (3) the identification tag on the barrel itself.**

+1/SUSTAIN THE 5S HABIT

Implementing the first five principles of visual order (S1–S5) is straightforward. To ensure continued progress, you must now turn them into a *habit*—the purpose of final principle: *+1/Sustain the 5S Habit.* The +1 step is made up of nine tools that help to inspire, focus, monitor, and motivate associates and managers to get and stay involved in visual order. *Not* putting these tools in place is the fastest way for initial efforts in visual order to bite the dust.

Today's Customer Will Only Pay for Value, Not Cost

Although many businesses might prefer it otherwise, today's customers are willing to pay for value, not for cost. It wasn't always that way. Even 10 years ago, a company could get away with adding a margin of profit to the cost of making product and call that the product's price. Today, that same company must set the price at the outset—and then figure out how to include in that price both the cost of making product and the company's profit.

This is what customers expect: excellent quality, on-time delivery, superior customer service, extensive choice, *and* right pricing. And they'll wind up at your competitors' doors if you can't provide these. The paradigm for making a profit has been irreversibly altered. Many companies used to define work based on the level of activity. "We're working all the time," the boss would say, "busy getting products out the door for our customers." And everyone from hourly associate to manager would agree. Ask anyone how many hours out of a hundred he or she actually works, and every last person will say "A hundred of course!" Let's probe a little deeper. First let's find out what folks mean by *work*. When employees use the term *work*, they refer to whatever they are doing at the moment that is not mealtime or a break. We hear the same from managers and hourly employees. And we said those days are over. Today's customers will pay for the value that gets added—and nothing else. Your competitors are using a new definition of work, and it is time you do the same.

The new definition of work is moving in order to add value. That means, for example, that every time Stan, lead machinist in commercial products, walks over to the table to get a tool, he is doing something for which the customer will not pay. This activity does not add any value to the product. Stamping adds value. Casting adds value. So do grinding, coating, and assembly. But moving to get a tool, part, work order, instructions, or the like does not.

Strictly speaking, when Stan does any of those things, he is moving *without* working. There is a name for that: *motion*. By definition motion adds cost (not value) and that cost comes out of the bottom line.

> To move and add value is called *work*. To move and *not* add value is called *motion*. Motion, then, means moving without working—moving and adding cost.

The workplace is a living environment where millions of people spend the better part of their waking hours. The vast majority of these people come to work to work. Moving without working is not what a company pays its employees to do nor what employees show up for. But motion is precisely how too many people, associates and managers alike, are forced to spend their workdays. In far too many companies, motion is corporate enemy number one. Instead of working, people spend precious time searching or waiting for the tools or information they need to do their work.

What Do I Need to Know?

The magnitude of detail that workers need to know on a daily basis—but do not know—is vividly reconfirmed nearly every time a company is drawn to consider implementing visual order. In preparation for these implementations, I often call a data-gathering session and ask those who participate (usually a healthy cross section of departments and levels) to respond to a single question about their life at work: What do I need to know? (The *I* here refers to each individual in the room. If you were there, what would *you* need to know?)

> "What do I need to know?" What do I need to know that I do not know *right now* in order to do my work? What *don't* I know that I need to know to do the right work, at the right time, with the right tools, in the right quantity, of the right quality?

It is the same question for everyone. People's answers, which they commit to paper, are telling and a quick diagnostic on the state of information sharing in that organization. One of the most striking list of answers was provided one hot July morning by Hank, an assembly operator in an electronics plant in the midwest. His list is shown in Box 17–2. When he was done, Hank took me aside and said: "You should have asked what *don't* I need to know. It would have taken a lot less time and a lot less paper!"

BOX 17–2 Hank's list

What Do I Need to Know?

- Where are my pliers?
- What am I supposed to make today?
- How many am I supposed to make?
- By when?
- Who will be picking it up when I'm done?
- Who's working with me today?
- Which parts do I use?
- What's today's quality specification?
- Which are my fixtures?
- Where are the parts that were supposed to be delivered yesterday?
- Where is my supervisor?
- Who is my supervisor?

Lists like Hank's are not the exception. They are the rule. Lists from associates look much the same across industries and geographical regions, and lists from managers and supervisors everywhere also look remarkably alike. Some are identical. This is how literally millions of employees start their day: with huge information deficits that they have come to accept—along with the searching, waiting, wondering, and wandering—as a way of life.

It's about Time

Time is called the shadow of motion. That is why all wastes can be collapsed into a single massive waste called motion. Motion calls loudly to us in the language of defects, rework, scrap, and overprocessing. It speaks to us as the material handling, delays, macrosearching, microwaiting, rummaging and reaching, walking and wandering, bending and turning, and looking and glancing that occur thousands of times in any given workday. They are forms of motion. They are all about time. When we search for the sources or causes of this motion, we find that a vast number of them are linked to information deficits in the workplace. And only visual systems can solve this—beginning with visual order.

The Core Issue: Information Deficits in the Workplace

Workplace information—production schedules, customer requirements, engineering specifications, operational methods, tooling and fixtures, material procurement, work-in-process, and the thousand other details on which the daily life of the enterprise depends—changes quickly and often. Organizations need a way to ensure that this information gets shared rapidly, accurately, and completely as soon as it becomes available. Without this, the workplace is thrown into debilitating and long-lasting confusion, and the people who work there come to consider searching, waiting, wasting precious time, and making costly mistakes a way of life, a life of motion. Information deficits in the workplace come in two varieties: deficits in location information and deficits in specification information.

Deficits in Location Information

Lists like that shown in Box 17–2 speak to a distinct and compelling need for the most basic type of information in the workplace. What could be more basic than knowing where your pliers are? This is location information. As its name suggests, location information answers the *where* question. When location information is in place, work can begin. When it is missing, work stops—or it never starts.

These stops may be microevents, lasting less than a minute, but they can occur dozens of times in a single workday. Other stops are longer, consuming 5 to 10 to 45 minutes before they are resolved. Let's say such stoppages are experienced by only 10 percent of the workforce (a conservative figure; the reality is closer to 60 to 80 percent). The result is a shop floor that is limping its way to the end of a shift. The lack of location information is a serious operation barrier that impacts all phases of production.

Deficits in Specification Information

The second category of missing information is called *specification information* (spec information). Spec information refers to the details that describe products or services and the manner in which they are made. It deals with product requirements that relate to technical standards (i.e., tolerances, dimensions) and to procedural standards (i.e., operating procedures, methods). That is, once the pliers are in hand, spec information tells us how to use them to make product. Spec information is there to answer the *what, who, when, how,* and *how much/how many* questions related to work. When spec information is missing, employees do not know what is required of them.

Compensating Behaviors

Information deficits can be a serious organizational problem and can trigger a range of compensating behaviors that burden people and the production process, as well as many other sectors of the enterprise. Missing information can put the emphasis on fire fighting, not long-term solution making. Fire fighting, which happens when the symptoms rather than the true causes of a problem are attacked, is a short-term approach. Succeed at fire fighting and people call you a hero, even though you came up with a temporary half measure. Fire fighting glorifies the failures of the system instead of taking steps to put a reliable, repeatable process in place—and one of its main triggers is the scarcity of accurate, relevant, complete, and easy-to-obtain information.

Information deficits can also cause the busy syndrome—a behavior of chronic motion. When information is needed but not available, we spend time searching, asking, waiting, interrupting, looking, checking, and double-checking. These tasks consume our days. Because we are in a constant state of doing—doing this, doing that, doing this, doing that—we sometimes suppose that what we are doing must be important. This is a natural but misleading conclusion. If we persist too long in this belief we may also conclude, for example, that the company wouldn't have gotten through the day without us or that the business depends on us. Chronic busy-ness gives us a false sense of importance—false because keeping busy is not why we came to work.

When information is scarce we adopt all kinds of curious notions about what and who is important and why. The material planner, for example, carries by memory all the information on parts planning and scheduling for the company. Go to him or her and you can find out anything. And you are powerless if that person is in a meeting, out sick, or on vacation. Lack of easy access to information also forces people to interpret what something might mean instead of knowing what it does mean. Since it is often anybody's guess, everybody guesses. In the absence of facts, assumptions are everywhere.

When needed information is not available, employees begin to rely on hunches (theirs and those of others) or search out *insider* information, knowledge that has been hidden away. This is the way of the world, not because people prefer it but because a viable alternative is lacking. As a result, those in the know become power brokers and withholding information can become more important than sharing it.

The scarcer information becomes, the less employees trust each other *and* themselves. They begin to feel isolated, even immobilized; a sense of disempowerment often follows that leads people to start worrying about making mistakes. In time, *not making mistakes* becomes the driving force. When this happens, initiative, responsiveness, and flexibility disappear—and mistakes are made.

Here we have the makings of a disempowered, sluggish, and dispirited workforce for whom work becomes as demoralizing as it is empty—and the exact opposite of the clear, dynamic, and forward-moving enterprise needed in today's highly competitive marketplace. Information deficits do not just encourage mistakes, they keep us from working.

Remedies That Don't Work

Some companies attempt to address information deficits through increased supervision, hoping that a closer policing of the process will improve their performances. Other organizations use report writing and reading as tools, supported by a seemingly endless stream of memos. Meetings are often other attempts to remedy the need to know, and they usually end up triggering a lot of paper but not much news. In such work environments, the terms *disinformation* and *full disclosure* take on new and piercing significance. Looking for anything or anyone becomes everyone's worst nightmare, and changing a decision is the one decision you never want to make. These mechanisms are attempts to spread a net large enough to catch detail and meaning—and they do not work. They are themselves forms of motion.

Computers Are Not the Answer

Many companies turn to computers for a solution to their information deficits. This *seems* logical. Computers are, after all, huge information stockpiles, capable of manipulating massive quantities of data at the stroke of a key. In addition, many of the best systems are designed with lots of involvement by the users themselves. Even when quality specifications can be accessed in a nanosecond, however, and current bills of material (BOMs) are available at the touch of a button, computers are at best only a partial solution to getting the information in—and the motion out—of the production process.

The problem here is two-sided. First, the information in computers is usually not what most employees need to do their work. Second, even if computers could supply the right kind of information, they could not supply it fast enough. The information is simply in the wrong location: in a box. So the problem with computers is both the medium and the message. To serve today's workforce, information must be moment-to-moment fresh and available at a glance. It must be part of the process, as physically close to the process as possible. In short, it must be at point of use.

POINT-OF-USE INFORMATION

At its best, point-of-use information is so close to the process, it is virtually indistinguishable from the process itself. This is information that can be pulled as needed, exactly where and when it is needed. Computers can never be close enough for that. Even when they are on-line on the line, they are too far away.

Information that is at the point of its use is the long-lasting solution to information deficits in the workplace. When information is that close, we can access on demand. The information is part of the process, built into the items of the workplace—the tools, fixtures, machinery, documentation, and shelving. It is in the floor itself in the form of borders, indicators, and controls. When we need it, we pull it. We pull the exact messages we need from the workplace. This pulled information ensures quick, accurate, and complete work. Like the pull systems of JIT and lean production it supports, point-of-use information cuts the waste out of the system and enables the process to reach its highest level of function. The workplace speaks.

THE LOW-COST/HIGH-IMPACT SOLUTION

There is an excellent example of a low-cost, front-line visual solution that allows the process to speak. The company is United Electric Controls Company (UE), a small manufacturer of switches and controls in Watertown, Massachusetts. Figure 17–3 shows you a bank of ordinary bins for holding

FIGURE 17–3 Parts mix-ups. This shelf of bins holds small parts used in seven different products. Many parts seem identical, as do their part numbers, but they are not. Mix-ups were a common occurrence in this system.

small parts used in seven different subassemblies. Many of these parts look identical (but are not) and many of their part numbers differ by only one character. Up to this point, components for each subassembly were individually kitted in a central stockroom as a way to avoid parts mix-ups.

In the late 1980s, when UE eliminated the central stockroom as part of its JIT initiative, all components were moved to their point of use, right on the line of production. While this change decreased flow distance significantly, it simultaneously increased the frequency of parts mix-ups, even for the most conscientious operator. Although an operator had a computer-generated bill of material and work order with all the information needed to build a quality unit, the wrong parts still were used. Worse than that, since the subassembly was enclosed in a housing, a defective unit could move downstream to final test before the defect was spotted. No amount of training, supervision, or operator diligence solved the problem.

Figure 17-4 shows you the visual solution that eliminated the problem 100 percent. Here's how it works. Holes that correspond to the individual part bins required in a given subassembly are cut into cardboard or particle board. The template prevents the operator from picking any parts but those used in that product. This is point-of-use information at its finest: simple, low cost, easy to implement, and 100 percent effective. The process itself

FIGURE 17–4   **The end of mix-ups. Mix-ups are now impossible because of the product-specific templates that operators use to block out all the parts that a specific product does not contain. The cutouts in this cardboard visual-guarantee (*poka-yoke*) device correspond to the location of each bin of parts used in the J40–9613–9620 assembly. Notice how the numbers on the template match those on each bin, offering backup insurance on the process.**

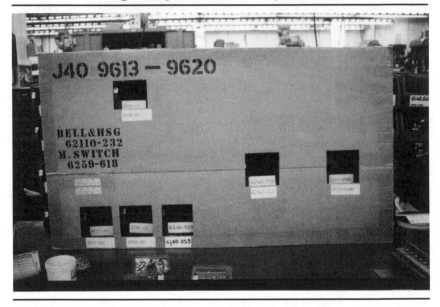

speaks to us and helps us do the right thing. We know it and have confidence in it. It supports our best intention and delivers to the customer what the customer is willing to pay for: added value.

We may be shocked to see how much location and spec information is lacking during any given workday. It is equally astonishing to realize the levels of ingenuity and resourcefulness that employees exercise to meet production objectives in the face of these glaring information deficits. One can only imagine the improved levels of output and performance that could be achieved if this burden was systematically and comprehensively lifted.

That's the point. The solution to these deficits is not more or better supervision. Nor is it more or better training. The solution is not more classes in English as a second language (ESL) or improved interpersonal communication skills. Those have already been tried. While such remedies can be effective addressing a certain group of problems, they are not designed, either singly or in combination, to solve the problems described in these pages. They cannot solve the problems caused by the absence of point of use in the workplace. They cannot let the workplace speak for itself. The journey to a visual workplace begins with implementing visual order: the principles and practices of 5S+1.

Begin by Implementing 5S+1: Visual Order

The purpose of visual order (5S+1) is (1) to prepare the physical work environment to hold location information and specification information and then (2) to install location information into the workplace—the information needed to find people, things, and places easily, quickly, and safely. Some companies think that they need to wait until they have their production system all figured out before implementing 5S+1. This is upside-down thinking, similar to the notion of cleaning up the house *before* the house cleaners arrive. While you have the option of implementing 5S+1 on the heels of another improvement process, visual order is at its best when it forms the base on which all other improvement approaches are built. Visual order is an enabler.

5S+1 is a core competency needed to maximize benefits from other improvement tools—kanban, cellular manufacturing, quick equipment changeover, statistical process control (SPC), total quality control (TQC), zero quality control (ZQC), demand flow/pull systems, 6-sigma quality, self-managed/self-directed work teams, and/or reengineering. Visual order is fundamental to them all.

Apply visual order to optimize traditional manufacturing, with its high volumes, long lead times, bottlenecks, complex material handling, and other high-cost indicators. When the time comes, let 5S+1 smooth the way for converting your production approach to a lean one with a vastly accelerated and responsive flow rate. Not only will visual order help identify what needs to change, it will also help maintain order and predictability while the change is in process.

Trackable, Bottom-Line Results

People intuitively recognize that a well-ordered, self-explaining, and self-regulating work area is a blessing. When asked for precise benefits, these same people are often left speechless, mumbling something about it being important and just plain common sense. That doesn't make for a compelling argument for the skeptics among us. In too many cases, the absence of measurable financial and operational benefits can result in a decision not to implement the process.

Following is a list of individual results compiled from American companies across a range of industries that have effectively implemented visual order as the first step in their journey to a visual workplace:

- 60% cut in floor space.
- 80% cut in flow distance.
- 68% cut in rack storage.
- 45% cut in number of forklifts.
- 62% cut in machine changeover time.
- 50% cut in annual physical inventory time.
- 55% cut in classroom training requirements.
- 96% cut in nonconformance in assembly.
- 50% increase in test yields.
- No more late deliveries.

The Uncommon Solution

Location information and the visual order that results impacts motion directly. It eliminates the cause of walking, searching, and other grosser forms of motion. By locating workplace items closer to their points of use, we automatically reduce the distance traveled. Over time, the area that we move within becomes more and more focused and requires less and less square footage. As our movements become more efficient and less scattered, we can begin to notice less-obvious forms of motion—turning, reaching, stretching, bending—and find ways to minimize even these.

Cellular manufacturing has turned motion reduction into a science and an art. One of the requirements of a work cell is that all operations be executed as efficiently as possible. If you have ever observed or worked in a cell, you know that people must maneuver in a space that is defined by the value that gets added there—the work. All the waste has been removed from the process, and motion is at an absolute minimum. In the best of cells, working looks more like dancing. Every step and each hand movement is measured and intentional, choreographed.

The same can be true of all work settings, including traditional manufacturing. Whether you work in a machine shop or stamping plant, on an assembly line or in purchasing, visual order is central to it and can create an entirely new level of work, one that blends focus and intention and results in outputs that are superior. Our focus becomes more precise and suddenly it's just us and our work. When all the unrelated movements are eliminated and all the tiny, extraneous interruptions are removed, we can simply be and do our work. We are alert and relaxed as we bring a new dimension of our attention to the task at hand. This state is possible at work, on the shop floor, in your company. You have experienced it before, but perhaps not yet at work. It is a state of intent stillness where all your resources are at your disposal and they surface to assist you when and as needed. They flow from you. Motion as you have known it no longer exists in any form. It is just you and the silent, steady rhythm of your breath as value is added. This is what you have always wanted work to feel like. This is what work is meant to be—the ease of your contribution flowing from you and into the process your company has asked you to perform. This is work that makes sense.

PART FOUR

MANAGEMENT FOCUS

Part 4, "Management Focus," pulls back from some of the detailed issues of how to execute productivity improvements and emphasizes issues of what manufacturing should and should not be doing in Roger Schmenner's "Seven Deadly Sins of Manufacturing." Frank Leonard's piece addresses how to guarantee that manufacturing and corporate strategies are linked. Chapter 20, Patricia E. Moody's description of manufacturing and the extended enterprise 15 years out, is not all Utopia, but her insights will help the transition.

18 THE SEVEN DEADLY SINS OF MANUFACTURING

Roger W. Schmenner

Editor's note

What are the practical applications of strategic manufacturing theory? The author uses analogy to explain the problems caused by the sins we hear too much about—inflexibility, waste, inconsistency, complication, meandering, impatience, permissiveness, and our favorite, sloth. His manufacturing audit suggests the starting point to identify corporate strategies and align them with production choices.

In the medieval church, there came to be known seven sins that were particularly obnoxious to God: pride, avarice, envy, anger, lust, gluttony, and sloth. These were viewed as so heinous they were termed deadly sins, punishable by hellfire.

The medieval church is now history to us but, with the resurgence of manufacturing's importance, it is intriguing to ponder what could send a manufacturing plant straight to hell. Here are my candidates for the seven deadly sins that could do just that: inconsistency, complication, waste, meandering, impatience, permissiveness, and sloth.

INCONSISTENCY

Inconsistency is the candidate for the chief deadly sin of manufacturing. Like pride, inconsistency puts a plant's, a department's, or a function's interests before the interests of the company as a whole. The economist Kenneth Boulding's phrase, "Sub-optimization is the name of the devil," expresses what is sinful about inconsistency. *Suboptimization* means consciously, happily, and often scientifically doing what seems right for the plant, department, or function but what in the end the company may not want or need.

Suboptimization in manufacturing is often caused by diverse interests tugging and pulling on production people. The needs of the company as a whole get lost in the more immediate needs of segments of the company (finance, marketing, engineering) and what manufacturing can do to further its more specialized interests. With this tugging and pulling come a host of gripes about manufacturing: Deliveries are not on time, costs are too high, quality is poorer than the competition's, and new products take forever to be launched. Manufacturing is regarded as a battleship that takes miles just to turn around. As a result, manufacturing has often felt snubbed by the rest of the corporation.

It is becoming increasingly evident, also, that to become world-class, manufacturing must do many things well. In addition to producing output of consistently high quality on time and at low cost, manufacturing must be flexible enough to accommodate diverse models, fluctuating volumes, and new-product introductions. Against world-class competitors, manufacturers no longer have the option of trading these attributes off against one another. We have learned, painfully, that quality and cost are not substitutes for one another but are, instead, complements. This has driven us to consider quality, cost, delivery, and flexibility *all* as complements. This may not be true in every instance, but it is clearly the trend.

Manufacturing Strategy

If manufacturing is to meet the challenges of world-class competition, it has to do so with clear manufacturing strategies, that is, with clear, coordinated decisions about manufacturing's role in the business and how that role ought to be carried out. Manufacturing strategy is getting more attention these days, but, regrettably, too often it lies outside corporate strategic thinking. Many thinkers about corporate strategy do not spend time discussing the intricacies of manufacturing strategy. Rather, they look to manufacturing as a source of competitive advantage solely because of two phenomena: economies of scale and the learning curve. For these strategists, manufacturing benefits a company when it can increase its scale while lowering its cost and when, through experience, manufacturing can move down the learning curve ahead of other companies. What is significant here is that both the economies-of-scale and learning-curve notions are cost related. What the strategists neglect are the many other ways in which manufacturing can be strategically important to the company.

FIGURE 18-1 **The manufacturing strategy process**

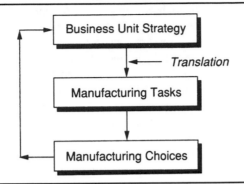

• *The manufacturing strategy process.* Manufacturing strategy is best viewed as an ongoing process rather than as a document. It is a process that feeds off the strategic planning of the company for each of its business units (see Figure 18–1). It cannot exist in a vacuum but must be derived from a business unit's strategy, and it is marketing, not manufacturing, that typically drives that process. Manufacturing's influence, while critical, plays a largely supportive role.

• *Three critical issues for business unit strategy.* Every general manager worth his or her strategic salt must address three crucial issues. In essence, these issues define business unit strategy. The first is *positioning.* The business unit must decide which products it is to produce and what the chief characteristics of those products should be. In short, it must decide which niches in the marketplace it should cover, whether they are just a few or many (a full-line producer). Mercedes Benz, for example, targets only the high end of the automobile market, while GM tries to compete across the board.

Positioning the company, however, is not enough because change is forever intruding. As long-range plans evolve, the strategy for any business unit is influenced by numerous outside factors that can shape and alter that strategy over time. Product technology is a significant influence on business unit strategy, as are the demographics of the buying population and customers' particular tastes. Competition, too, is a key influence on strategy, along with environmental concerns, including governmental influences on, and regulations of, business. Coping with these outside factors is crucial to good strategic thinking.

With such constant changes in outside influences, general managers must assess what any changes in those outside influences mean for the business unit. This is the second strategic issue general managers must confront. For example, how will the business unit be affected by demographic changes such as the aging of the baby-boom generation, or certain competitor initiatives in particular niches, or government regulation that might affect certain suppliers in the industry? General managers must sort through these influences and determine how the company can be hurt by them or how to win advantage over other competitors as a result of them.

Third, strategists must decide how the company can exploit any advantages and minimize any disadvantages that come with these likely scenarios. These are the choices of how the company is to exercise clout in its marketplace, with its customers, and with its suppliers. The examples are endless: Should a company alter the thrust of its advertising to reach older consumers? Should a company seek a distribution channel in China? Should it oppose pending legislation in Congress? Which of several new technologies seems most promising and worthy of stepped up corporate support? Answers to the questions raised by confronting these key issues are what give a company strategic direction.

The Manufacturing Task

Unfortunately, business unit strategies are not typically communicated well to manufacturing. The result of the strategy process, the five-year plan, is often reams of paper filled with marketing sales forecasts and financial pro formas. Often there is precious little that manufacturing people can sink their teeth into. The business unit strategy needs to be translated into terms that are meaningful for manufacturing managers. Such a translation is sometimes termed *the manufacturing task*.[1] A manufacturing task states what the manufacturing arm of the company must do well in order for the business unit strategy to succeed and also what it need not do well. It sets priorities for manufacturing according to the company's choice of niches it wants to compete in.

Manufacturing Tasks—Three Types

The manufacturing tasks that a company can choose to elevate or downgrade in importance can be grouped conveniently into three major categories: those that are product related, those that are delivery related, and those that are price related.

1. *Product-related tasks.* Let us consider product-related tasks first. Four come to mind: performance and features, reliability, new-product introduction, and customization. We can all think about various products and note that some companies typically compete on just one or two product-related aspects and generally not on all four. For example, some companies are known for their customization: Their products may not include all of the latest new-product features that competitors tout. They may not improve performance in many dimensions. They are, however, specific to a particu-

lar customer's needs. Likewise, firms that compete on performance and features may not be heavily into new-product introductions or customization.

The auto industry is a readily accessible example. Generally, European cars are noted for their performance and features, Japanese cars for their reliability, and the big-three American producers have historically competed with customization, allowing consumers to choose from a wide range of colors, interiors, and options. The Japanese, on the other hand, offer very few options. Their cars generally include a standard package, and while there are a number of options built into this package, individual consumers who may value one option and not another do not have the ability to request a car more customized for them.

2. *Delivery-related tasks.* Delivery-related tasks include the speed of delivery, the reliability of delivery, and what is sometimes called *volume flexibility.* Volume flexibility has to do with how quickly manufacturing can accelerate or stop production. With many consumer products companies, fads demand a quick start of production and a rapid halt when the fad dies off. Similarly important may be how quickly a product can be made or delivered to the consumer. Quickness is valued by some, but if it is without reliability, some consumers may prefer a more reliable producer, even if that producer may not be the quickest to the marketplace.

3. *Cost to produce.* This manufacturing task, of course, is the one that corporate strategists pick up on first, but low cost is a niche just like any other. In any industry there can only be one, or at most a few, low-cost producers. Others are higher cost, but with other manufacturing tasks done well, they can be every bit as profitable as the low-cost producer. Unfortunately, this truth is overlooked by many, and the result is needless pressure on manufacturing management for lower costs.

Once priorities have been set, there is still much work to do. If manufacturing is going to be successful, all of the numerous choices that manufacturers have to make about the nature of their manufacturing capabilities must be consistent with the manufacturing tasks as they have been translated from the business unit strategy.

Strategic Manufacturing Choices

There are numerous manufacturing choices possible for a company. The appendix to this chapter, "The Manufacturing Audit," lists a number of these choices, divided into three major categories:

- Technology and facilities.
- Operating policies.
- Organization.

Consistency in these choices is the hallmark of an effective manufacturer. If the choices are consistent, manufacturing will be a real asset to the company and that strength can be fed back into the business unit strategy. On the other hand, if there are inconsistencies and weaknesses in the manufacturing choices made, then this, too, must be fed back into the business unit strategy to pull the company out of businesses where ordinarily it might want to compete.

Translation: The Toughest Task

The most difficult aspect of the manufacturing strategy process is making the translation from business unit strategy to a set of manufacturing tasks. The translation must be in plain language so that manufacturing can discern its true priorities and understand how it is to be measured against those priorities. The sad fact is that the numerous manufacturing choices listed in the appendix will be made by the company by one means or another. If both manufacturing and general management do not become involved in setting tasks and in making these choices, they will be made by people lower in the organization, including workers and their direct supervisors. If companies do not engage in a dialogue about these priorities, they risk inconsistencies across the board. For general management, the question is a very real one: Who do you want to run the company? Do you want general management to run the company, or do you want supervisors' and workers' decisions on strategic matters to hold sway?

As has been argued eloquently by Wickham Skinner in his early work on focus factories, factories cannot be expected to do everything with equal vigor. There must be some choices made, some picking and choosing of exactly what kinds of technologies they are to master, with the understanding that the simpler the operation and its goals and measurements, the better its performance.

Disrupting Consistency

Manufacturing is a lot like a tennis pro who concentrates on a baseline game, where consistency is paramount to winning. Unfortunately, just as in tennis, consistency can be disrupted, and avoiding disruption demands constant vigilance. Companies frequently do not realize how important consistency can be to a factory's performance and, as a result, divergent choices are tolerated, either consciously or unconsciously. In fact, one could argue that there is not a factory on the planet that does not suffer at least one inconsistency worth addressing.

In other instances, it is professionalism, rather than inattention, that disrupts consistency. In most factories, numerous fiefdoms composed of functional work groups are controlled by experts in each function. These people often band together in professional societies, such as APICS, SME, ASQC, and others. While there is much admirable about such groups, the dark side is that they encourage overly specialized visions of manufacturing and are subject to enthusiasms out of touch with a particular company's needs. Thus, one runs the risk of having managers push for investments or systems that may be inconsistent with one another. For example, production-planning and inventory-control people may be pushing for a state-of-the-art MRP II system, while manufacturing engineers are enthralled with robots and the quality-control department is plugging Taguchi methods. Such initiatives may be totally at odds with what the operation truly needs.

Lastly, change is an enemy of consistency. If things do not change, then merely by trial and error we can devise good manufacturing choices. However, we live in a world of change, and it is change that makes manufacturing more than a trivial exercise.

Product/Process Change Dynamics

To consider the impact on change in manufacturing a bit more, consult Figure 18–2, the product/process matrix, conceived by Robert Hayes and Steven Wheelwright of the Harvard Business School. Hayes and Wheelwright consider the match of a plant's process pattern to the product mix it is responsible for. As Figure 18–2 shows, the process pattern varies from a jumbled flow, where aspects of the process are only loosely linked together, to the other extreme, where processes are continuous, are usually highly au-

FIGURE 18–2   Product/process matrix

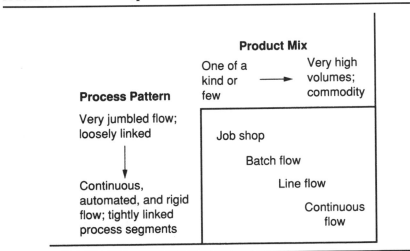

tomated, and have a rigidly defined flow to materials. Process segments are tightly linked, one to the other, so that an individual may not even have the sense of moving from one department to another within the process.

There is a continuum for the product mix as well, from one of a kind or, at most, a few units made at any one time to very high-volume commodity products. As can be seen in Figure 18–2, there is a definite correspondence between product mix descriptions and the process pattern that is most effective for making that particular product mix. The diagonal shows the kinds of processes that we have come to identify with certain mixes of product and process. These process categories cut across industry definitions and serve to unify approaches to manufacturing.

Positions off the diagonal carry penalties with them. As can be seen in Figure 18–3, if the process pattern lies more toward the continuous, rigid, and automated process but the product mix stays at high-mix and low-volume levels, the company risks incurring significant out-of-pocket costs. Yamaha attempted to take over the motorcycle market with a high-volume, narrow product line. Honda responded by roaring back with more flexibility and a broader product line. Yamaha was closed out of the high-volume motorcycle market and left with heavy overhead (plant and equipment) costs. The process must be paid for, but the volumes are simply not high enough to pay for the expense of production. This is the quick road to bankruptcy.

On the other side of the diagonal, if the product mix is low and volumes are high but the process pattern is not sufficiently continuous and linked, the plant suffers opportunity costs; that is, the plant forgoes increased contribution and profit by maintaining higher production cost than necessary. This is the slow road to bankruptcy, when the company chokes on the dust kicked by those ahead of it, the low-cost companies that are riding off into the sunset.

FIGURE 18–3   The diagonal and off diagonal

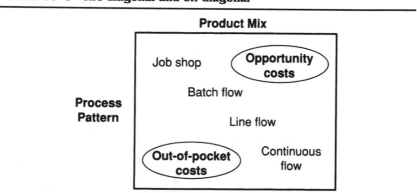

These characterizations of out-of-pocket cost and opportunity cost are important for understanding some dynamics of manufacturing change. Over time, companies frequently experience changes in the product mix that the plant is responsible for. This may often mean that the plant starts out with a low-volume product, perhaps a new product, and as the product catches on in the marketplace, volumes rise. As the product/process matrix tells us, the character of the process should also change to keep the match of product and process on the diagonal. However, it is hard to keep moving precisely along the diagonal. Investments in production tend to be lumpy, and production is seldom changed all at once. This poses a problem.

This problem is not unlike the game of golf (Figure 18–4). The golfer at the tee is faced with the task of hitting a ball onto the fairway, but even Jack Nicklaus cannot count on hitting a perfectly straight drive. Instead, Nicklaus, in his book, *Golf My Way* (New York: Simon & Schuster, 1979), encourages the judicious use of one's natural swing tendencies to hook or to slice the ball. If you naturally hook the ball, aim to the right; if you slice, aim left. There is an important difference between a hook and a slice, however. A hook can put the ball farther down the fairway because a hook has over-spin on it, and once the ball hits the ground, it can roll far. At the same time, a hook is a riskier shot to take because a ball with overspin easily can roll into the rough. Because it has backspin on it, the slice typically does not travel as far once it hits the ground and for that reason is less likely to travel into the rough. The slice is thus more conservative than the hook.

Applying the analogy to manufacturing, the hook strategy takes a company into investments in process technology before product volume is developed to the desired level. This is a risky strategy, and it puts pressure on marketing and sales to drum up the volume compatible with the investments in the process. Years ago, Texas Instruments became famous for this

FIGURE 18–4 The dynamics of product and process

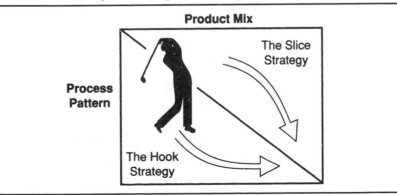

kind of preemptive strategy, and more recently the Japanese have been the masters of this approach. On the other hand, the conservative slice strategy is much more popular, but product volume must come first, with pressure on manufacturing to lower costs so that the company can compete effectively with firms that might have already hit farther down the fairway. There are advantages to both strategies, and a company may need to be able to play both hook and slice strategies effectively. Dealing with such change demands not only the courage to make timely decisions about manufacturing, but also attention to both the detail and the consistency required for manufacturing choices to mesh well with manufacturing tasks and with the business unit strategy pursued.

REMAINING CONSISTENT BY FIGHTING FOR THE FAITH

Weaning a company from the sin of inconsistency demands a good deal of faith. A number of different actions are required that involve more than merely the manufacturing function. Of course, manufacturing can do its part by developing as much internal consistency as possible along the lines emphasized earlier. This means ensuring that all aspects of operations (technology and facilities, operating policies, organization) are pulling in the same direction. More troublesome are other aspects of management (performance measurement and cost accounting systems) that can influence manufacturing heavily and cause inconsistent decisions. Manufacturing thus has to fight to bring these other aspects of management into alignment with its own consistent views.

Manufacturing Performance Measurement

Perhaps the most important battle involves changes in the way manufacturing is measured and evaluated. Current scorecards are often too preoccupied with spotting variances of actual performance from established standards or with focusing on individual cost items within what is presumed to be an accurate accounting of the structure of costs. This promotes reactive, backward-facing management.

The Problem with Cost Accounting

Cost accounting has come under increased fire recently. Even some within the profession itself have asserted that cost accounting is not providing manufacturing with the information it requires in an age filled with rapid technological advances, declining direct labor in the factory, and exploding overhead. Cost accounting is seen as preoccupied with the wrong things: direct labor, measures of labor efficiencies and machine utilizations, and managing to variances of suspect importance.

Solutions

1. *Direct costing.* There have been several suggestions for remedying the situation. Some have called for the adoption of direct-costing techniques that do not assign overhead to specific products but instead focus on contribution margins. Of course, this remedy has been espoused by a small band of followers for years. It has remained a minority position, however, largely because many people want fully allocated product costs for decision making and fear the ambiguity that lies in dealing only with contribution calculations.

2. *Activity-based accounting.* In activity-based accounting, one tries to get a much firmer grip on the real cost drivers for the various overhead accounts. With activity-based cost accounting, overhead allocations that depend only on direct labor or some other simple measure are replaced by numerous, more precise ways of allocating overhead. In this way a more precise cost for a product is developed. While activity-based accounting is conceptually appealing, many firms are likely to resist its complexity. For some, the cost of collecting and using the additional information required to allocate overhead more precisely may overwhelm the advantages of such an approach.[2]

3. *Throughput-time accounting.*[3] For those seeking a simple system, yet one without the biases inherent in allocating overhead exclusively according to direct labor, some companies (and my own sentiments) advocate substituting a different rationale as the basis of the allocation: the value of production throughput time. In this instance, the faster a product goes through the factory, the less overhead it picks up per dollar of product value. This introduces an incentive to managers to improve the flow of products in their area because reducing a product's throughput time has the added benefit of reducing its cost, as computed by the cost accounting system.

Furthermore, reducing throughput time may well stimulate a reduction in overhead. How might this occur? Many of the tasks of overhead personnel in a factory are addressed to a minority of products. The old $^{80}/_{20}$ rule may apply here, just as it does elsewhere in business; 80 percent of overhead may actually be spent working on just 20 percent of the products. Which 20 percent? My candidates are the 20 percent of products that languish in the factory. These are the products that need more materials handling, more production and inventory-control resources, more scheduling, more accounting, more quality control, and more engineering changes. If material flows are streamlined and throughput times are contracted, some of the time devoted to these overhead activities can be shed.

Finance's Role

Fighting to align management also means changing the way finance intrudes in manufacturing decisions. The capital-appropriations request process often requires justification for individual investments in new equipment and capacity. Such a mechanism forces attention on savings readily identifiable to a particular machine, such as reduced direct labor, increased output, or improved quality. This approach leads to justifications for new technology that are more conservative than required. Such an approach ignores investment initiatives that are more broadly based, anchored to a strategy for technological advance and to the potential spillover benefits that one can reap by having several investments linked together. Just because an individual project may not seem to be justifiable does not mean that all the projects, taken together, cannot be justified. Here is where suboptimization can truly be the name of the devil.

The Role of Marketing and Sales

Fighting for the faith and building consistency require a new relationship between manufacturing and the marketing and sales functions. Perhaps the most common cop-out by manufacturing is that the forecast provided is poor. The forecast is an easy target. In many industries, a disaggregated, item-by-item forecast is difficult. It makes more sense to improve manufacturing's flexibility and responsiveness than to invest more on forecasting. Of course, this means concentrating on lead time reduction and improving setups and changeovers while at the same time becoming less prey to expediting and fire fighting.

Marketing and sales can understand these trade-offs. They can understand that if manufacturing becomes more flexible, they can win new customers, and they can also learn that flagging orders as hot or entering orders slowly will only hurt their delivery performance. Perhaps the most dramatic change that has helped develop consistency in many companies has come in design engineering. Manufacturing is now involved early in the design of the product and to good advantage. We are seeing now how critical good product design is for manufacturability.

COMPLICATION

The second of manufacturing's deadly sins is complication. Simplicity is virtuous; complication is not. Complication is brought on by both love and fear. Example: a love of high technology causes companies to think that they can leapfrog the competition by incorporating new technology in their manufacturing processes. This can happen, of course, but attempts often only complicate what manufacturing should be doing.

Another example of complication derives from the love of increased size. There is scarcely a manufacturer for which bigger does not mean better. Economies of scale carry a real allure, but with increased size comes complication. Often bigger is not really better, considering the complexities that have been added to the process. There are diseconomies of scale: Large plants often suffer from poor layouts and unwieldy bureaucracies.

Finally, love of the system can complicate manufacturing. MRP and other computer-based systems have been touted for their ability to simplify manufacturing or to make it more responsive. Yet, in many instances, they lead to nothing more than complication. I am reminded of the manager who observed to me that he had never seen an MRP system that employed fewer people once it was implemented. We embrace systems, but they are often short-term fixes. We ignore the real possibility of rethinking and simplifying the process and the information flow that supports it.

Complication is also brought on by fear, such as fear of messing up a timetable. Managers do not want to be responsible for moving back the date of anything, even if it means living with complication. Taking some time upfront may be what is truly called for, but it is an option easily dismissed. Then there is fear of managing customers or of managing suppliers. Some manufacturing complications occur because managers are unwilling to take the bull by the horns to alter the way customers or suppliers operate, even when such alterations might in fact be welcomed by customers and suppliers both.

Finally, complication is often not recognized for what it is. Rationales I have heard too often are. "We may be more complicated in these operations, but our operations are different." "We serve a different market." "We have a different process." "We have particular constraints that are different from others." We have learned through the years, however, that manufacturing firms share many traits. Most companies are not different. Basically, they are really very much the same. If we recognize that, maybe we can spend some time eliminating the complication in manufacturing. It may mean not going with high technology, remaining small, developing simple systems, sacrificing the timetable, and managing customers and suppliers.

WASTE

The third deadly sin is waste. Anyone familiar with total quality control (TQC) and the just-in-time (JIT) manufacturing movement is familiar with waste as a sin. As Shigeo Shingo has pointed out, waste comes in many forms: overproduction (one more than necessary is as bad as one less than required), inventories of any size, waiting for work to be done, extraneous motion in doing the job, transportation between operations, defects that may generate rework or scrap, and processing itself (does the operation have to be done at all?). One can go far reducing cost and improving on other manufacturing tasks solely by concentrating on the reduction of waste, but diligence is required. One must move beyond the simple implementation of statistical quality control (SQC) techniques to problem solving. One must even go beyond the factory floor to push SQC and problem solving into the overhead indirect labor functions such as order entry and customer service.

Value-Adding Activities

Indeed, what needs to be done is for more of the factory's time to be devoted to value-adding activities. Still another $^{80}\!/_{20}$ rule may apply. In many companies, of all the activities actually performed, only about 20 percent typically involve value-adding steps, where a part is machined or painted or assembled. Eighty percent of the steps along the way do not add value to the product: counts, inspections, movement, handling of paper work. When we can remove the steps that do not add value, we remove waste.

Throughput-Time Reduction

The most effective strategy for pushing waste aside is concentration on throughput-time reduction.[4] We have already alluded to this in discussing cost accounting. Throughput-time reduction can promote many good things: quality improvements, lower inventory levels, rapid attention to bottlenecks, and diminished confusion in the factory caused by such things as engineering change orders or expediting. As mentioned in Solution 3 of the section "Manufacturing Performance Measurement," throughput-time reduction can also promote fewer transactions in the factory and thus less overhead.

In the pharmaceutical industry, Eli Lilly's efforts in this area have paid off. Production-process time has been reduced from between 45 and 60 days to 6 days. Harley-Davidson implemented changes that resulted in the following four improvements in its key indicators:

- Inventory turns went from 4 or 5 to between 19 and 23.
- Productivity increased 55 percent.
- Scrap and rework decreased 80 percent.
- Throughput time was cut from 72 days to 1 day.

These improvements cumulatively allowed the company to increase market share in heavy motorcycles by 10 percentage points.

Concentration on throughput-time reduction can begin to question all sorts of transactions that take time and do not add value directly to the product: counts, inspections, materials handling, monitoring of direct labor, the tracking of work-in-process inventory. Indeed, anything that generates paperwork is suspect.

Perhaps the most appealing aspect of throughput-time reduction is that it can mean something to everyone, and while that something is often different for different people, it can be useful for manufacturing performance. To the worker on the floor, for example, throughput-time reduction can be applied to work flowing through his or her workstation. It can promote improvement in the layout of the workstation itself, better materials handling, and more efficient setups and maintenance. To the department manager, concentrating on the reduction of throughput time can mean something else, such as improving the design and linking of workstations, lowering the level of inventory, and stabilizing the mix of products made. To the plant manager, reducing throughput time may mean altering the designation of what departments are responsible for and how managers are evaluated, for example, by moving to the identification of product flows that use designated equipment and are evaluated separately. To the corporate VP for manufacturing, reducing throughput time can involve multiplant strategies. What is important is that, in each case, reducing throughput time can be both understandable and helpful in the crusade to eliminate waste.

MEANDERING

Meandering, the fourth deadly sin, defined as wandering aimlessly, has dramatic consequences for manufacturing. Bad layouts, for example, have no logical flow; they wander aimlessly. It is too easy to leave a layout alone or to reorganize it only as expansion occurs or as products proliferate. Failure to move machines and people into a more organized layout has deleterious implications for a factory's competitiveness.

Meandering also means neglecting to develop the family of common parts. It is failure to see what may be common about the operation and what is truly different. Organizing for the smooth flow of a family of parts is often a more efficient way of running the business.

Chasing low-cost direct labor all over the globe is another form of meandering. In deciding where to produce a particular product or component item, current practice in many companies compares fully burdened direct labor costs in different countries. The decision disregards all the indirect and intangible costs to manufacturing competitiveness and flexibility caused by moving materials around the world. While the cost-accounting system may say that sourcing in the Far East or in Latin America is the way to reduce product costs, the aimless wandering that decision implies for the product flow is something to guard against.

Meandering can also mean that products or processes will be assigned to plants solely for the reason that space is available. Just as nature abhors a vacuum, top management abhors vacant manufacturing space. The careless assignment of products to plants causes aimless wandering of materials, technology, and management effort.

IMPATIENCE

The fifth deadly sin is impatience. Of course, there are many companies that value impatience, or urgency, in their managers. Sinful impatience refers to such evils as expediting and work around (releasing an order—without all the components on hand—with instructions to work around the components not yet there). These are misdirected rushes in the factory that interfere with manufacturing's abilities to produce quality with timely delivery. Expediting and work around ensure that the company engages in additional overhead to cope with such situations and adds to the time it takes products to go through the process.

Engineering change orders (ECOs) are another source of impatience in some companies. Many managers feel that if engineering changes are not made right away, sales will be lost because the design is not the best it could be. Yet, how many engineering changes are truly necessary, especially immediately? Many companies are willing to dribble out a never-ending stream of engineering change orders, and in some cases an ECO exists only to correct a previous ECO that was released prematurely. That it may be easy to release an engineering change order does not mean that it should be done. The process can be abused. A more patient, more deliberate approach to the matter, perhaps bunching engineering changes together, can be advantageous.

Impatience is also reflected in a company's attitude toward quality improvement. There is a difference between instant improvement and continuous improvement. Impatience can focus people on the quick fix and away from the habit of continual improvement that the company must have to be a competitor over the long term.

Lastly, there has been much written about the shortsightedness of the typical American manager, his or her preoccupation with the quarterly earnings report and willingness to forgo long-term benefits for short-term goals. It is hard to quantify this attitude. We have anecdotes but precious little hard research. However, we know the destructive effect of short-term thinking on organizations.

PERMISSIVENESS AND THE PARADOX OF FLEXIBILITY

Permissiveness is perhaps the hardest sin to comprehend, but it is firmly linked to flexibility, a key manufacturing task. Permissiveness is a sin because it breeds rigidity in the process. This seems paradoxical. How does it occur? When the process is permissive—when rescheduling is done all the time, when expediting is permitted, when engineering change orders are rampant—paralysis sets in. The process is unable to put anything out on time and loses its grip on quality. As has often been observed, when everything in the factory is tagged red for immediate action, that's as good as saying nothing is tagged red.

Conversely, discipline breeds flexibility. This is the paradox of flexibility. Consider the job shop. A job shop is tremendously flexible in the mix of products that it can produce: large quantities, small quantities, all with different characteristics. However, a job shop only operates well if it has an absolutely rigid flow to the information and record keeping within it. Tooling, setups, and the load on particular workstations can change dramatically in a job shop, but the flow of information (the paperwork, the record keeping) has to run like clockwork or the job shop becomes hopelessly snarled.

Consider another paradox, one related to quick change setups. Quick change setups are the quintessence of flexibility. But think what it takes to be able to change setups quickly: prescribed methods for making them, similar tooling designs, well-conceived workstation layouts, and strict machine maintenance schedules and procedures. Discipline breeds flexibility.

Flexibility Types

There are, of course, different kinds of flexibility that one may want to foster. There is the product mix flexibility that is best characterized by the job shop. There is also the flexibility of new-product introduction (being able to add products easily and keep up with the state of the art) and volume flexibility (being able to start production quickly or, alternatively, to cut it off quickly to capitalize on fads or to react to severe changes in marketplace conditions). These different types of flexibility demand different kinds of disciplines.

• *Product mix flexibility.* Product mix flexibility requires quick changeovers, and, as mentioned earlier, quick changeovers demand their own rigidities. Product mix flexibility requires a cross-trained workforce, able to operate several machines simultaneously and move from one bottleneck operation to another. Freezing production schedules is helpful, and expediting is not permitted. Product mix flexibility also demands discipline in the sharing of information, within the factory, with the sales staff, and with vendors.

• *New-product flexibility.* New-product introduction, on the other hand, requires a different set of disciplines. The companies that handle new-product introductions best (Digital and Hewlett-Packard, for example) make sure that a rigid set of reviews and sign-off procedures is adhered to at various stages. In addition, there may be procedures through which all the engineering drawings must pass, as well as procedures and people through which engineering changes must go. Nothing falls between the cracks. Good new-product introduction typically requires engineering follow-up. Engineers know in advance that they are responsible not only for the design but for initial production as well.

• *Volume flexibility.* Volume flexibility requires still different disciplines. The most important is maintaining a cushion of capacity resisting any management wishes to see it fill up with unnecessary product. Without a cushion of capacity, manufacturing has great difficulty increasing production quickly. Volume flexibility is enhanced by general-purpose, convertible equipment; by layouts that are easily changed; by subcontracting of jobs; by temporary hires; and by cross-trained workers willing to move from one task to another. Effectiveness in volume flexibility may also require low break-even levels derived from a more labor-intensive operation than found in plants that do not value volume flexibility.

Winnebago and Chrysler have both mastered the art of building volume flexibility. Winnebago's recreational vehicle business is subject to demand swings caused by gasoline price fluctuations. Yet the company knows how, when necessary, to cut overhead and exist on very low volumes to survive. Winnebago has also demonstrated an ability to gear up quickly. Chrysler has learned to downsize effectively. When faced with disaster, the company's restructured operations produced lower break-even points.

The Paradox of Flexibility

The paradox of flexibility is this: the extent and nature of discipline you are willing to impose on the factory will, in fact, decide the kinds of flexibilities you will be able to enjoy. Being permissive will only cause the factory to gum up and to lose the flexibility that permissiveness seeks in the first place.

SLOTH

Finally, there is sloth, the only deadly sin carried over from medieval times to current manufacturing. Sloth, of course, is a sin because in the factory as elsewhere, "cleanliness is next to godliness." Cleanliness promotes visibility of what is done in the factory. It promotes the workforce's ownership of the process. People are much more willing to go the final mile if, in fact, the factory is a pleasant and neat place to work in.

Sloth, however, is a sin for more than its housekeeping implications. Sloth is a sin because it can mean failure to get the workforce involved and participating. We have come to learn how effective workforce participation can be in improving competitiveness and productivity. Slothful management does not tap into the innovation and wisdom that exists in the workforce. A company's unwillingness to work hard at participation tempts fate. Recognizing sloth as a sin emphasizes that we want the workplace clean but that we want management's hands dirty, dirty from continual visits to the factory to pat the backs of the workforce and to gather notes and suggestions from them.

THE MATCHUP

The seven sins of manufacturing—inconsistency, complication, waste, meandering, impatience, permissiveness, and sloth—match up fairly well against the medieval admonitions. Pursuit of excellent manufacturing requires a look at the practical implications of the seven sins. A manufacturing strategy derived from cross-functional examination of the company's strengths and weaknesses can only be reinforced by attending to day-to-day operating concerns.

APPENDIX: THE MANUFACTURING AUDIT

Operations choices can be segregated into three broad categories: (1) technology and facilities, (2) operating policies, and (3) operations organization. Let us review these categories and choices in turn.

Technology and Facilities

Technology and facilities choices frequently involve large capital expenditures and long periods of time. These are the big decisions that do much to define the type of process employed.

1. *Nature of the process flow.* Is the flow of product through the plant characterized as rigid, with every product treated in the same way? At the other extreme, is the flow a jumbled one, with products routed in many different ways through the factory? Or does the flow of product through the process fall somewhere in between?

Are segments of the process tightly linked to one another, or are the connections between process segments loose? How quickly can materials flow through the process? Is the process pure or is it a hybrid?

2. *Vertical integration.* How much of a product's value is a direct result of factory operations? Could or should production involve more or less integration backward toward raw materials or more or less integration forward toward customers?

3. *Type of equipment.* Is the equipment used general purpose in design, or special purpose? Can any special-purpose, seemingly inflexible equipment be linked together in innovative ways to yield production systems that are themselves more flexible than the equipment they comprise?

Is the equipment meant for high speeds and long runs? How flexible is it for changeovers in products or models and how quickly and easily can such changes be accomplished? What possibilities exist for linking one piece of equipment with another for balanced and quicker throughput? Is the equipment operator controlled or is it automatically or computer controlled? Is its performance monitored by operators or by a computer? Can the equipment be speeded up or slowed down to match production needs? Does the equipment demand substantial nonoperation support (e.g., maintenance, repair, software, setup, tooling)? Can the company build or modify its own machines? Does it have close ties to equipment manufacturers?

4. *Degree of capital or labor intensity.* To what degree has the equipment or technology permitted labor value to be driven out of the product or service? How important could reduced labor value in the product be to costs, yields, or sustained levels of production to specifications (good quality)?

5. *Attitude toward the process technology.* To what extent does the company pioneer advances in process technology? Is the company a leader in that regard or a follower? How closely does it track other process improvements?

How committed is the company to research and development? What mix is sought between the two? How close is the alliance between manufacturing and engineering? To what extent are efforts made to design products that are easily manufactured? How are design and manufacturing teams organized for new-product introductions? Are engineering change orders numerous? To what can they be attributed? How disruptive to the process flow are they? What investments are made in manufacturing engineering and industrial engineering relative to product-design engineering?

6. *Attitude toward capacity utilization.* How close to capacity (defined as best as possible) does the company desire to operate? How willing is the company to stock out of a product because of too-tight capacity? Does capacity generally come in significant chunks? What can be done to keep capacity well balanced among segments of the process?

7. *Plant size.* How big does the company permit any one plant to grow? To what extent are either economies or diseconomies of scale present?

8. *Plant charters and locations.* Does it make sense to assign different product lines, product processes, or geographic markets to particular plants? How do the plant locations chosen mesh together into a multiplant operation?

Operating Policies

Once the process technology and facilities have been selected, management must still decide how the process technology is to be used. Three broad segments of such operating policies present themselves: loading the factory, controlling the movement of goods through it, and distributing the goods.

Loading the Factory

1. *Forecasting.* To what degree is the plant's output mix known with certainty before raw materials must be gathered or equipment or workers assigned? To what extent must forecasts be relied on to determine which raw materials ought to be ordered and which equipment or worker capacity reserved, and how much of each? How reliable have past forecasts been? Does or should manufacturing second-guess marketing's demand forecasts? What techniques best meet forecasting requirements? Is there a long product pipeline that risks pipeline momentum problems and heightens forecasting needs?

2. *Purchasing.* Given the decision on the plant's degree of vertical integration, what does the plant make for itself and what is purchased from outside suppliers? How are such suppliers chosen? What kinds of contracts (e.g., long-term versus spot) are sought? Is purchasing formally integrated with forecasting or order taking, and how much visibility is granted suppliers about the company's expected future needs? Are orders on suppliers made through an MRP system or other informal means, or are formal purchase requisitions required? How important is supplier quality against price? How and how well is supplier quality monitored?

3. *Supply logistics.* How frequently, from where, and by what mode of transportation do raw materials arrive at the plant? How sensitive are costs to changes in these factors? How readily can materials be received, inspected, and stored? Is vendor quality good enough to dispense with incoming inspection? Is vendor delivery reliable enough and frequent enough to be able to feed the plant's production needs without large raw materials inventories? How is materials handling accomplished within the plant? How much automatic, how much manual? What controls are in place?

4. *Raw materials inventory system.* How much inventory of raw materials is held? What system is used (e.g., material-requirements planning

[MRP], reorder point, periodic reorder)? How does the inventory level vary with demand, price discounts, supplier lead-time changes, supply uncertainties, or other factors? What triggers the replenishment of the raw materials inventory? How are materials controlled in the stockroom? Are records accurate enough to be relied on without ceasing production for physical inventories? All scrap reported? Are materials placed into kits, or are they fed directly to the shop or line?

5. *Production planning.* Are goods manufactured to customer order, to forecasts, or to stock finished-goods inventory? Is inventory permitted to be built in advance to cover peak-period demands and thus smooth out production, or does production try to chase demand, with little or no buildup of inventories? How are manpower needs planned for? How are model or product line changes planned for? How far in advance can changes routinely be made to the general production plan? How disruptive to the process is any expediting or rescheduling? Are routine allowances made for such situations?

Controlling Movement through the Factory

1. *Production scheduling and inventory control.* What triggers the specific production of goods: orders, forecasts, reference to a finished-goods inventory? How do factors such as the pattern of demand and product costs influence any trigger level of finished-goods inventory? How are specific departments, lines, work centers, and the like scheduled, and what factors of the process, pattern of demand, or product variations and costs affect the schedule?

What determines specific priorities in the jobs awaiting work in a department? How much expediting is permitted? How much rescheduling? What or who determines the specific priorities of work: an MRP system, direct supervisor's discretion, specific rules, simulation results?

Does instituting an MRP system make sense for the plant? How much fluctuation or stability exists for bills of materials, vendor reliability on delivery, production cycle times? What levels of accuracy and integrity exist for inventory counts and records, production or rework counts, and records for scrap? What kinds of exception reports and follow-through stand to be most helpful?

2. *Pacing of production.* Is the pace of production determined by machine setting, worker effort, management pressure or discretion, or some combination? How readily can the pace be altered?

3. *Production control.* How much information, and of what type, flows within the production process, both from management to the workforce and from the workforce to management? How easily can product variations, engineering changes, product mix changes, or production-volume changes be transmitted to the workforce? How soon can management react to ma-

chine breakdowns, parts shortages, or other disruptions of the normal flow of product and process on the plant floor? How are machines, workers, materials, and orders monitored? What early warning signals are apparent? What remedies are routinely investigated?

4. *Quality control.* Does everyone in the organization truly believe that quality (performance to specification) is his or her job and not simply the function of a quality-control department? What mechanisms and cooperative forums exist to ensure that work is done right the first time? How closely linked are design engineering, manufacturing or industrial engineering, quality control, workforce training and supervision, maintenance, and production scheduling and control? How is quality checked? How many checks are made at different steps in the process? How much authority is given to quality-control personnel?

5. *Workforce policies.* What are the skill levels required of various jobs throughout the process? How are they trained for? Is the work content of jobs broad or narrow? Is cross training of workers desirable? How do workers advance in the factory (e.g., job classification, different jobs, changes of shift, promotion to management)? How and how much are workers paid? Are any incentives, wage or otherwise, built into the process? How are workers' achievements and ideas encouraged and recognized? How does management feel about unionization, and what actions concerning unionizations does it take? What are the age and gender compositions of the workforce? What opportunities exist for job enlargement or job enrichment? Is there a place for quality-of-work-life projects? How else can the workforce be encouraged to participate in the management of the operation?

Distribution

Distribution and logistics. What are the channels of distribution and how are they filled? What are the trade-offs of service versus inventory costs? What are the benefits and costs of various geographical patterns of warehousing and distribution? What modes of transportation make sense and how should they be managed?

Operations Organization

1. *Operations control.* Are the major operating decisions retained centrally or dispersed to individual plant units? What kinds of decisions rest primarily with the plant? How is the plant evaluated and what biases might the education method introduce?

2. *Talent.* Where within the organization are the best people put? What talents are most prized for the smooth and continued successful operation of the process?

NOTES

1. This term is credited to Wickham Skinner.

2. See Robin Cooper and Robert Kaplan, "Measure Costs Right: Make the Right Decisions," *Harvard Business Review* (Sept./Oct. 1988): 96–103.

3. See Roger Schmenner, "Escaping the Black Holes of Cost Accounting," *Business Horizons* (Jan./Feb. 1988): 66–72. A worked example is included in this article.

4. See Roger Schmenner, "The Merit of Making Things Fast," *Sloan Management Review* (fall 1988): 11–17.

INTEGRATING BUSINESS AND MANUFACTURING STRATEGY

19

Frank S. Leonard

Editor's note

Why have so many companies failed to develop a successful manufacturing strategy? This chapter explores the impact on manufacturing operations of other functional activities, from sales through distribution. The author's case examples illustrate how the process can be rendered more effective by concentrating on making it interfunctional.

It has been more than two decades since the idea of a manufacturing strategy was first widely circulated. In those 20 years, despite some dramatic successes, the stark reality is that most attempts to develop a manufacturing strategy—to reconfigure manufacturing to improve performance significantly—have fallen woefully short of expectations. Although there are a multitude of reasons for the lack of success, probably the greatest single mistake made by companies in trying to develop a manufacturing strategy is to consider the process as just a manufacturing problem or a responsibility. This error and its subsequent ramifications are responsible for a majority of derailed or impotent manufacturing strategy efforts. It is also responsible for the high degree of frustration and confusion manufacturing managers have reported in this process.

THE STRATEGY-FORMATION PROCESS

In the broadest and deepest sense, the development of a competitive manufacturing strategy is a business unit problem, not a functional problem. A business unit is an organization capable in its entirety of all functions required to forecast, market, finance, design and engineer, produce, and distribute product. A functional approach segments the product design and delivery process into separate functional areas, such as finance or engineering. Each area may be moving in an opposite direction from the corporate goals or from each other.

An interfunctional approach would therefore attempt to match up, or align, parallel objectives between various interest groups. A company interested in gaining a competitive advantage as a high-tech producer dependent on fast new-product introductions might concentrate its strategy efforts on alignment of engineering and production goals. An engineering department in a company handling strategy formation intrafunctionally might, for example, pursue numerous design changes in the form of engineering change orders (ECOs) at all costs. Excessive use of ECOs throughout the product life cycle adds to production costs and delivery problems.

When viewed as an interfunctional process, the manufacturing strategy process is a valuable corporate tool to explore critical interdependencies in a business unit, to align them, and to build them into formidable competitive advantages. The alignment of major elements within manufacturing proper toward strategic requirements is a critical step in the manufacturing-strategy process. However, forces outside the manufacturing function are what often determine the effectiveness of this alignment—the ability of manufacturing to significantly increase its strategic contribution. Manufacturing's ability to change, to align itself strategically, is severely, though often subtly, hindered by these external forces. They are forces, such as marketing pressure or capital-investment policies, not easily understood by manufacturing without a great deal of insight and effort.

Manufacturing Strategy as the Integrator

When seen as an interfunctional rather than intrafunctional process, manufacturing strategy's real power is its ability to integrate the rest of the business with manufacturing. It can, for instance, ensure that the R&D strategy, marketing programs, procurement policies, technology imperatives, and management development process are aligned with manufacturing capabilities. The influence of other parts of the organization on manufacturing, from the obvious (the sales forecast) to the more subtle (the capital-appropriation procedure) to the almost invisible (accounting practices) is pervasive. World-class manufacturing firms have already discovered the necessity for understanding the nuances of this interfunctional alignment. World-class manufacturing firms are using the manufacturing strategy process as an important vehicle to obtain synergistic benefits from the coordination of various parts of the business unit, as well as to strategically position the major elements within manufacturing decision areas.

THE INDEPENDENT-FUNCTION ARGUMENT

There are, however, executives and consultants who believe in a contrary argument; let me call this the independent-function argument. This argument states that the manufacturing strategy concerns only manufacturing decisions; it can and should be formulated by the manufacturing function operating independently. This argument is based on the idea that the various functions and departments in a business unit are primarily independent of one another and that their spheres of decision making (and hence their capabilities) are relatively free from decisions in other functional areas. Pursuing this argument further, if the other functions (or the business unit as a whole) state their strategies and policies clearly, then the process of developing a manufacturing strategy can be accomplished entirely within manufacturing by using these strategies and policies as decision parameters and constraints. To the people who believe in the independent-function argument, it is the strategic planning process that should and does integrate the business unit. In other words, strategy drives manufacturing—a kind of top-down approach.

The independent-function idea is based on several tenuous if not fallacious assumptions about the reality of modern corporations. First, it assumes that the rest of the company's policies and functional strategies are correct and that manufacturing needs to fit into them. An interesting psychological corollary to this is that if manufacturing is the misfit, then somehow manufacturing is wrong.

Second, the independent-function argument assumes that manufacturing capabilities cannot be influential, much less critical, in defining and achieving market positions or in defining other functions' policies. As a counterexample to this assumption, if manufacturing is capable of delivering in two rather than four weeks, the location and stocking of distribution warehouses would be substantially different—fewer, perhaps, more spread out, and smaller.

Third, the independent-function argument assumes that the policies and strategies of other functions are compatible with one another and with manufacturing and that they have no internal contradictions that would make it impossible for manufacturing to develop a consistent strategy to fit them all. New-product introductions often display conflicting policies between R&D and marketing, leaving manufacturing without consistent time schedules. Finally, it assumes that the independencies among functions are more critical to competitive position than the interdependencies.

The preceding assumptions may have fit the corporation and organizational structure of 1950, but they do not reflect the reality and complexity of today's corporations, technologies, and global competition, in which decisions affect all functional areas. In the fullest sense, the manufacturing strategy process is a process of mutual adaptation among the various parts of a business unit. It is a process of mutually adapting manufacturing capabilities, realized or unrealized, with, for instance, engineering, marketing, sales, labor relations, management development, and strategic planning policies and procedures. It is a process of discovering intrafunctional and interfunctional contradictions and synergies that are normally left buried because of the nature of most corporate strategic planning processes. To be successful, the manufacturing strategy process must be a stimulus for examining the critical alignment of major functional strategies and business policies.

FORCES WORKING AGAINST THE PROCESS

There are many forces, however, operating to isolate the manufacturing strategy process as just a manufacturing responsibility. First, manufacturing has traditionally physically isolated itself from the rest of the organization; plants are often distant from many other corporate offices.

Second, there has been little attempt by top management to focus on cross integrating functional strategies. They assume that the strategic planning process will accomplish this integration. Most chief operating officers, unfortunately, are not from manufacturing, and they tend to want someone else to manage the details. The reality of most strategic planning is that it is a bottom-up collation of functional plans and budgets that rarely, if ever, fine-tunes interfunctional alignment below the top policy levels.

Third, a common language, what Romeyn Everdell calls a Rosetta stone, is often lacking to translate across functional lines. Each function has its own specialist jargon and perspective, which precludes a good understanding of other functional requirements and problems. Sales speaks in sales dollars, manufacturing in cost of goods sold or another unit measure, engineering may not be concerned with dollars at all, and cost accounting may concentrate on variances.

Fourth, the inevitable turf issue raises its ugly head: Functional managers like to keep control over their areas. They feel they are the experts in their areas and have little to gain from discussions with others.

Finally, the manufacturing strategy process is time-consuming, requiring a lot of patience and mutual exploration of conceptually cloudy issues without rigid methodologies. The process may take managers off-site for entire days, sometimes monthly, but at least quarterly. It is not a tidy, fill-in-the-blank process. This is hardly the type of activity busy executives find time for or are expected to do.*

Although many managers might prefer it, manufacturing can no longer operate as an independent member of a business unit. Over the last two decades, the close interdependencies necessary among all functions have been increasing dramatically. Far Eastern and European global players, such as Toyota, BMW, Sony, and Phillips, have made that quite clear. Major decisions made in engineering have a drastic impact on the ability of manufacturing to design new processes. Decisions made about sales plans have a large impact on manufacturing flexibility. Manufacturing decisions on plant location have an important effect on parts availability of service centers. The efforts over the last five years on company-wide quality programs and multi-functional team approaches to product design are important indicators of the growing awareness of these critical interdependencies. Some theorists have called the need for planning to integrate all functions a holistic approach.

Making the Connection: Interdependencies outside Manufacturing

There are many interdependencies outside of manufacturing—in engineering, marketing, sales, finance, human resource management (HRM), and accounting—that influence and can be influenced by the manufacturing strategy. Sometimes they are company specific in their impact on manufacturing. There are some critical ones, however, that time and time again across many industries inhibit manufacturing's ability to make significant strategic strides. A brief description and comment will help to illuminate the nature of these interdependencies. With any of these influences there are two key questions to keep in mind:

1. How does this interdependency shape competitive manufacturing capabilities?
2. How does this interdependency prevent manufacturing from doing something that might be turned into a competitive advantage?

Engineering

The most common processes that affect manufacturing from the engineering or R&D area are the new-product development process and the engi-

---

*Editor's Note: The information gathering and manipulation work is not easily computerized without good planning tools. See Chapter 15 for an examination of a simple planning process.

neering change order (ECO) process. The first determines the design of a new product, and the second concerns the change of an existing product. Although many companies are doing a better job of coordinating manufacturing concerns in the new-product design process, there is still a tendency to keep most decisions in the hands of technical people. Manufacturing fills a veto role, getting a change, as one manager put it, "only when I scream loud enough and long enough." The impact of these design decisions on manufacturing influences critical issues such as process design, process improvements, scheduling, plant configurations, plant layout, and manufacturing organization and staffing.

A truly creative exchange exists in the new-product design process when both engineering and manufacturing assume all design parameters are tentative and open to negotiation, including materials, shapes, technologies, and functions. Both Black & Decker and Digital Equipment Corporation use product-development teams that, from the beginning, include all functional areas and try to speed the cycle.

Manufacturing is often constrained most by existing ECO processes. Manufacturing managers frequently have no say in the number or frequency of ECOs. An indisputable (sometimes inscrutable) logic seems to prevail when it comes to ECOs. Many companies have no priority weighting for ECOs. ECOs can be generated by both internal and external sources with no decision screens to evaluate their effectiveness. Yet the ECO process is the major interruption preventing manufacturing from improving its present processes. The effect of ECOs on the stability and improvement of existing processes, and on manufacturing resources, is dramatic but frequently overlooked. One company had so many ECOs on a certain product that required tooling changes that, by the time the new tooling arrived, it was already obsolete. There was over $50,000 of tooling in inventory that had never been used.

A more subtle influence often overlooked is the relationship between the new-product design process and the ECO process. It is difficult to change one without changing the other; they are symbiotically self-perpetuating.

Marketing

Marketing, the voice of the customers, has a pervasive influence on manufacturing that is too often assumed to be positive in its present form. Frequently affecting manufacturing are warranty and service programs that marketing institutes and changes. Drastic changes in service and warranty policies are often instituted by marketing without any discussion of the impact on manufacturing. The design of product-testing equipment, the levels and types of inventories, the relationships with vendors, and the scheduling difficulties are all downstream influences that manufacturing too often has to swallow. One marketing department of a specialty chemical manufacturer instituted a marketing program based on assuring the customers a higher level of quality (fewer impurities) although the existing manufacturing process was technically unable to achieve the advertised level of product purity.

Market segmentation. Of more subtle impact are the language and concepts employed in the marketing strategy. All too often a segmentation by product or customer is effected, included in the marketing strategy, and submitted to top management. The assumption by top management is that the segmentation used for the marketing strategy is adequate, even correct, for manufacturing strategy. This can be a major source of confusion in developing a manufacturing strategy.

One basic chemical company had segmented its markets into a pulp-and-paper market and a water-treatment market. The marketing manager and the general manager then asked manufacturing to come up with a manufacturing strategy for these two markets. On deeper examination it was obvious that the two segments that would be relevant for building a competitive manufacturing strategy were markets based on manufacturing requirements. In this instance there were two segments, but not the pulp-and-paper and water-treatment segments: The two segments for manufacturing purposes were the markets where delivery was a high priority and the market where cost was a high priority. It turned out that these two segments cut across both the pulp-and-paper and water-treatment segments.

Sales

The most frequently mentioned problem affecting a manufacturing strategy from the sales area is the forecast. The predictability, variation, and time lag of the forecast affects manufacturing schedules, line changeovers, process designs, process improvements, equipment purchases, plant expansions or contractions, hiring and training of the workforce, and plant configuration. Once again, like marketing, it is too often assumed in the company (by both manufacturing and sales) that manufacturing must do whatever is required to fill customer orders, regardless of the forecast. This is frequently destructive to the consistency necessary for a manufacturing strategy to evolve.

In one company it took the general manager to intervene to prevent the sales manager from accelerating a plant start-up because of a sudden influx of orders. The result of accelerating the start-up (long-run reliability and warranty problems) would have killed the product two or three years down the road. Yet it was common practice in that company for the sales manager to determine the speed of new-product introductions according to short-run sales demand rather than through the evolution of a process/product combination.

Finance and Accounting

The two primary influences from finance and accounting are the capital-appropriation process and the cost-allocation scheme. The capital-appropriation process, including the rationale, the paperwork, the hurdle rates, the review procedures, and the inevitable politics surrounding it, has both an obvious and a subtle effect on manufacturing. At the obvious level, the quantitative payback expected (often informally communicated or implicitly understood) determines exactly what projects and what parts of what projects will be considered. This affects plant expansions, process improvements, capacity changes, and most recently, systems development and applications. It forces manufacturing to discard any long-term effect that cannot be quantified or proven.

It further forces manufacturing to submit only portions of a total project to get the required payback. I call this phenomenon chopped projects, and its result is that the infrastructural supports for an investment are not there when needed.

To hit the hurdle rate, one company decided to submit a project only with the assumption that the process would run five years without a major shutdown and overhaul rate. Not only did this give it more productive time but the company did not need to include all of the maintenance costs for the three-week shutdowns. However, when the plant had to go through a shutdown in the second year, not only did it take six weeks instead of three, it cost twice what it would have had there been proper maintenance people and spare parts. The plant start-up after the shutdown took twice as long as budgeted because the present plant management had not gone through a start-up. As a result, short-term operating results were disastrous and not planned for in the project payback estimate of two years earlier.

The accounting basis for cost allocation and subsequent product-cost determination, with its influence on management decision making, is currently under much scrutiny by the accounting community. These allocation schemes influence manufacturing decisions about staffing levels, process improvements, product-line phaseouts, benefit and compensation for the workforce, and plant configurations—without accurately reflecting true product costs. Financial and accounting procedures are often dictated by corporate-level staff groups far from the manufacturing floor who have little knowledge or concern with the inevitable impact on manufacturing decisions.

Usually connected with the accounting system is the system for measuring manufacturing performance. The aphorism, "You get what you measure," is unfortunately too true. You can be sure a plant justified, built, and measured on 90 percent utilization will get a 90 percent utilization—at the expense of quality, delivery, and flexibility.

Human Resources Management (HRM)

The influence on manufacturing strategy of HRM groups is more subtle but just as pervasive. Benefit programs, management development, training and education programs, job placement, and worker-output planning (to name a few) developed by human resource departments have an important effect on just how manufacturing strategy can use both the workforce and management people to achieve competitive advantage. The human resource policies and procedures influence how manufacturing recruits and hires people and how it promotes or rotates them. They also influence the level, type, and quality of training and educational programs available, job definitions, and, where appropriate, labor union work rules. Often locked up in inviolable policies that defy changing, manufacturing is left to use its people in highly restricted and unsatisfactory ways.

In one large multiplant complex with multiple business units, the company agreed to cover all labor relations by a single contract with standardized work rules. This was advantageous to both the union leadership and the labor relations department.

On close examination of workforce behavior as it related to competitive performance, it was apparent that the various manufacturing strategies of the businesses in the complex were drastically disparate: One needed a highly skilled, very flexible workforce with a lot of technical training; a second needed a low-skilled workforce with only minimal training at time of hiring; a third needed a workforce that combined the operators and maintenance people into discrete work groups with as little turnover as possible. Yet the labor policies of this complex did none of these well. They were, unfortunately, a compromise of political astuteness and competitive mediocrity. It is a sad fact that 50 years of insight into human relations within business has had little effect getting the traditional, hierarchical, and narrow HRM approaches to use people creatively.

Strategic Planning

Finally, the corporate-planning departments influence the effectiveness of a manufacturing strategy effort. Through their procedures and processes, they can either stifle or enhance the manufacturing strategy process. The planning process can either include the language and concepts of manufacturing strategy or exclude them. Most importantly, because most companies can't afford the time to go through the planning process twice, once officially for corporate bureaucracy and once for their own fine-tuning, it is the depth and quality of the strategic planning process, overseen by corporate analysis, that determines the quality of the entire process. Is it just a bottom-up movement of budgets and projects, or a truly interfunctional process of exploring critical interdependencies among various parts of the business? If the process is the former, chances are high that the manufacturing-strategy process, even if sanctioned at corporate level, will be an intrafunctional process with subsequent narrow results. It will be something put together from figures (i.e., profits, projections, expenses) compiled by individual departments on their own. Their first look at the big picture comes when the spreadsheet produces the bottom-up movement. If, however, the process is an interfunctional one, there is a good chance that the manufacturing strategy will make use of interfunctional synergies.

THE GOOD NEWS

A manufacturer of compressors decided to try to manage manufacturing strategically and found the road to significant change was a long and successful one. Over the course of five years, it not only restructured the entire architecture of manufacturing but also succeeded in discovering and then changing critical interdependencies outside of manufacturing. The company realized that it could not reconfigure manufacturing without also reconfiguring interfunctional influences.

In five years it changed the entire sales forecasting procedure: Any changes in schedule made by sales within 30 days of production caused a penalty payment to be made to manufacturing from the sales department's budget, a kind of forecast-change variance. The process of introducing new products was entirely revamped: All new products are developed by a joint team, headed by either a manufacturing or quality person. The team does not report to engineering or manufacturing; it reports to the general manager of the business.

The criteria on which manufacturing managers were evaluated and promoted were changed from meeting budget to increased competitive performance along five specific dimensions. The capital-appropriation review process was altered from an entirely quantitative process to an equal mix of qualitative and quantitative issues. The measurement of performance for the plants was elaborated: Each plant had specific, unique evaluation criteria depending on its strategic focus.

Finally, the strategic planning process was expanded. It now includes a thorough review of each department's goals and concerns long before the plans are rolled up to top management. As a result, manufacturing has found that it is actually helping set strategic direction.

These changes have taken almost five years to understand and implement. They required direct involvement of the general manager. They cost some managers their jobs, both in and out of manufacturing, but they resulted in catapulting the company into position as a world-class manufacturer competing with the best Asian and European companies.

THE BAD NEWS

The shift of manufacturing from more traditional stances and responses to world-class competition is not smooth, easy, or short. Experience shows that far-reaching and significant changes must be accomplished: first, in manufacturing; then, in how the corporation manages manufacturing; finally, in how manufacturing influences the corporation. The external influences on manufacturing detailed in this chapter can be considered either as ironclad constraints not open for discussion and alteration or as simply arbitrary and provisional corporate influences that can be adjusted appropriately to allow manufacturing to realize its strategic capabilities fully.

The process of understanding and managing the interfunctional aspects of strategy is not tidy; it is very real. Even if you come up with a good interfunctional manufacturing strategy—a piece of paper and a collection of ideas—you are still not home free. You have to make those ideas come alive through your organization; the ideas must be turned into forceful action. There are no simple recipes or standard paths in this process. But if you want to boost the strategic capability of manufacturing (and there are many advocates who say you probably have no choice in the matter), you will have to address concerns and issues external to manufacturing.

Pursuing a manufacturing strategy means far more than putting together a three-ring binder filled with analysis; it means challenging the very standards by which your organization evaluates and judges manufacturing performance. It means making the standard of manufacturing excellence your strategic agenda. It means relentlessly altering anything in the corporation that hinders the accomplishment of that agenda. It means change and all that change implies: effort, time, and money for corporate achievement and human satisfaction. Now, that isn't entirely bad news, is it?

NEXT-GENERATION MANUFACTURING AND THE EXTENDED ENTERPRISE

20

Patricia E. Moody

Editor's note

It's not utopia, but it's not Dante's seventh ring of hell either. Manufacturing in 15 years will be simply driven by technology and very special people.

When Francis Cabot Lowell, through a supreme act of industrial espionage, memorized the guts of the English power loom systems he had seen on an extended stay in Great Britain, he launched a 171-year run for manufacturing. His prototype mill, a complete vertical integration of the textile process on the banks of the Charles River in Waltham, Massachusetts, reached 200 percent profits within 16 months of ground breaking.

The dam's waterfall was not big enough to accommodate the incorporators' dreams of even bigger profits, and for their next initiative they acquired half a town and the Pawtucket Falls on the Merrimack River, bought under the pretense of it being a hunting preserve, and the manufacturing cities of Lowell, then Lawrence, Haverhill, Nashua, and Manchester, the biggest and one of the first to fall, followed within a few years. Economies of scale drove the concept and led to captive workers, Taylorism, piece rates, and huge profits, culminating in Malden Mills's owner Aaron Fuerstein's promise to pay his burned-out Lawrence workers three months' payroll, his commitment to maintaining the company body even after a December fire leveled the plant site.

Somewhere in the 1980s our faith in vertical integration was tested because it brought with it all varieties of costs. Its inevitable replacement, the virtual corporation, or the networked company, a galaxy of suppliers connected to each other and to one or two main customers, is the extended enterprise. Had Francis Cabot Lowell and his chief engineer/technologist Paul Moody enjoyed our gifts of nanosecond communication, teams of empowered workers, and computer-controlled machines, the extended enterprise would have been their dream as well.

PEOPLE AND SYSTEMS

Manufacturing progress has always been dependent on technology and people, but we balance and use them in different ways. In the coming decade, manufacturing professionals will be technology partners rather than servants of technology. The future isn't about size, or power, or economies of scale. It's about intelligence, values, supreme technical mastery, and constant innovation.

In the 1990s, leading edge is about people, systems, and communications. Companies that grew successful building bigger operations must now think small and light; they must reach outside their walls to find suitable teammates. And in the late 1990s and beyond, manufacturing excellence alone will not guarantee enterprise success. Simple manufacturing excellence will be, as quality has become, only the ticket to the big leagues. What does that mean for manufacturing pioneers and survivors right now?

MORE TRANSITIONS

The 1990s will continue to be a decade of the dissolution of all entities we have grown up with—our churches, schools, families, government, businesses, health care systems, music, maybe even our tax system. The bad news is that it will continue, but the good news is that it's for only another four or five years.

As for manufacturing, Deming, Juran, and Shainin reinforced the quality lessons. A few corporate leaders including Motorola, Honda, Solectron, and others have explored the dynamics of partnering and pioneered supplier-development and supplier-network integration. These leaders have had to write new rules of partnering such as how to be a world-class customer, how to retain and develop the best suppliers, how to establish and build trust, and other difficult-to-define concepts. But they all understand that partnering and advanced supply management/manufacturing practices stop where systems break down or interfere with a seamless process. And so the next (but not final) piece of the partnering challenge is finishing our systems work.

PARTNERING WITHOUT THE LIP SERVICE

When Honda of America takes on a supplier, the relationship is totally open, from financials to product plans to future strategies. As demanding as it may be with suppliers, Honda's approach is generally accepted to be data based and direct. This is what we call partnering without lip service. Other major producers, Eastman Kodak and Chrysler, for example, are working similar approaches. Purchasing and material-management professionals are a different breed, frequently technically degreed, excellent communicators, and comfortable working in teams.

KNOWLEDGE WORKERS AND EMPOWERED TEAMS

Within manufacturing's walls, where perfect process has replaced a rubber mallet and a two-by-four, and where real-time process control requires a different kind of worker, leading manufacturers including Motorola, Hewlett-Packard, and Intel understand the development and training needs of the new knowledge worker. Knowledge workers work in teams, as individuals, or both; they are a company's most valuable asset, and they will, as we slide into the next generation of manufacturing, continue to be the company's most valuable but unmeasured asset.

SYSTEMS SUPREME

MRP, JIT, kanban, and finite scheduling algorithms are not the answer to the systems challenge presented by the extended exterprise. Amazingly, the fully integrated system—launching, tracking, designing, and accounting for customer's product—from the idea to the receiving dock is a mix of very simple ideas executed with massively powerful transaction machines. And although most integrated supply-management systems are hand knit from a variety of software pieces, a few innovative software houses have begun to string together small pieces of the chain. Without on-line access to customer requirements, suppliers will be constantly whiplashed by variety conflicts and other difficult scheduling issues. Systems are the answer, and they will incorporate all the complexity and stored data that producers can tolerate: The sky is the limit and systems reign supreme.

PART FIVE

DYNAMICS OF CHANGE

Part 5, "Dynamics of Change," explores the difficult issues of disruption and culture change in organizations. Dan Ciampa looks at the responsibilities of top-level managers. The Stanadyne case outlines the history of one company's move from a traditional job shop to a just-in-time (JIT) environment, complete with pay-system changes.

21 MANAGERS AS CHANGE AGENTS

Dan Ciampa

Editor's note

What can managers do to speed effective culture change? In this chapter Dan Ciampa looks at the new role of managers in an environment of empowered employees, where responsibility is pushed down and spread out in the organization. New competitive techniques, such as simultaneous engineering, and the use of power as a motivator are also discussed. Finally, the author summarizes the seven climatic factors that build commitment and the desired competencies that should aid the selection of project managers in continuous improvement efforts.

Change as a central theme is certainly not new. Bennis, Benne, and Chin captured it quite nicely in *The Planning of Change*,[1] as did many others. The manager's role in trying to have some control over the pace of change is not new either, as anyone who has picked up one of Peter Drucker's pieces over the years knows. So, what can be said that is new and different? Well, there are quite a few things.

Let's start with the word *manager*. When Warren Bennis and colleagues penned their essays, the concept of a manager was more limited than it is today. Organizations were more hierarchical than today's are trying to become. While pushing down responsibility for decision making to lower levels was advocated by some visionaries and experiments took place, they were the exception to the rule and generally not well accepted.

EMPOWERMENT

Today, on the other hand, there is not only growing acceptance of the idea of employee empowerment, it is being enacted in every corner of the industrial landscape. The question for many leaders is not whether it makes sense to push down responsibility but how to do it fast so that employees facing problems day in and day out can solve them when they first occur or, better, can anticipate and prevent them. We want to place action at the source, not dependent on relayed direction from someone who may be more remote. This means that workers assume more responsibility and exert a certain degree of influence over their surroundings. It means that workers exercise the power for decision making—that they become their own managers. The challenge for those who are in positions we would ordinarily consider management is how to ensure that this sense of power pervades those in his or her charge.

THE CHANGING WORKPLACE

Similarly, the term *change* in the phrase managers as change agents has taken on new meaning. Change probably always has seemed unprecedented to those experiencing it. Look at the mid-1800s. In spite of the Victorian values for which that era is best known, events that truly changed the world were numerous and happened in rapid succession compared to earlier times. Within little more than a decade there were several astounding feats. John Wesley Powell led expeditions down the Colorado River to map the Grand Canyon. Othnial Marsh, not yet 40 and the country's only professor of paleontology, discovered the fossils that helped prove Darwin's theories of evolution. The Roeblings built the Brooklyn Bridge. The Union Pacific railroad was completed. The Suez Canal opened, bringing Europe and India 5,800 miles closer. These were events for which there was no precedent. They caused those who lived in the time to be astonished by their importance and the ever-more-rapid succession in which they occurred.[2]

While our grandchildren will probably see our rate of change as slow in comparison to their own, we certainly face major shifts in the manufacturing world. The most substantial ones have been brought about by the internationalization of the market and, in particular, the competition. The emphasis on quality and on gaining market share through customer satisfaction has ushered in a new way of thinking about the process of manufacturing. We are altering the nature of work itself rather than just developing faster or less-expensive ways to do the same things. The extent of these changes is even more significant than their rapidity. We are starting to change the way we do work (the technical elements of work), but at the same time we are proactively seeking to alter the work climate in our companies so that people relate with each other differently: more collaboration, more communication, and more commitment to carry through what is decided on. The most significant factor in the kind of change we face today is that it is multidisciplinary, crossing from quantitative, technical, hard sciences to the more qualitative, behavioral, soft side of the equation and back again.

TOTAL QUALITY

We are seeing developments such as the total quality (TQ) movement on a large scale and simultaneous engineering on a more functional level. TQ is typically a company-wide effort seeking to instill a climate of continuous improvement on a permanent basis toward products and services that customers will find more satisfying. First, this effort includes programs to educate employees to make them more aware of the need for, and principles of, better quality in everything they do. Second, statistically based techniques are taught so that root causes of quality problems can be identified and displayed more easily. Third, there is often more emphasis on teamwork and cooperation between departments. Training in teamwork usually takes the place of task forces asked to solve specific problems. Fourth, more emphasis is placed on customer needs through surveys and visits of managers, manufacturing workers, and engineers. Fifth, the TQ process reaches back to suppliers as well, as companies forge closer relationships with fewer suppliers—only those who can best meet their needs. While success in TQ efforts requires the leadership of the most senior person, it is equally important that all employees in the organization feel part of the effort and contribute to its success in their own ways.

SIMULTANEOUS ENGINEERING

Simultaneous engineering is a different way of designing and manufacturing products. It brings together design engineers and their counterparts from production at the time the product is being designed so that the product can be made efficiently and so that quality considerations can be taken into account as a design criterion. Problems in production are avoided by manufacturing having input upstream in the product-development process. It also paves the way for engineering help downstream while the product is in production. The essence of simultaneous engineering is the relationship that develops between people from different departments and the fact that each is focused on the task of getting the product right the first time. This sort of relationship based on common goals is unusual in the traditional product-development process where engineering–manufacturing relationships have tended to be arm's length at best.

Simultaneous engineering takes different forms. In the case of the Buick–Oldsmobile–Cadillac Group Engineering Center in Flint, Michigan, it means that design, product, and process people are one group in a single location. In another case, GE in Lexington, Kentucky, a multidisciplinary team of design engineering, manufacturing, and support people is formed when a new product idea is created. One result of all this is that the product is not designed and made by sequential and separate activities but by overlapping activities, many of which take place simultaneously. So far, this approach has been used within companies and only sparingly between companies and their suppliers; when simultaneous engineering at this level is more widespread, much more substantial gains will be made. The key is common goals, communication, common measures of success, and teamwork.

Both the total quality movement and simultaneous engineering require that technical and people-related elements of change have equal weight and work hand in hand. It may not be the Suez Canal, but for those trying to manage it, it seems as formidable.

ORIGINS AND PAWNS

This brings us to the definition of *agent* as one who acts or exerts power, a person responsible for his or her acts. In this sense of the word, there is the implication of action, of doing something, of making good use of the changes that occur. In the 1960s, when there was much change and many people trying to figure out how to manage it, there emerged the theory of origins and pawns.[3] It suggested that there are two sorts of managers in the face of rapid-fire change. *Pawns* are those who let change control them, who surrender to conditions over which they believe they have no control. *Origins* are the opposite. They are the managers who have more confidence. They will take responsibility and stand apart from others when change causes most of their peers to revert to pawnlike behavior. In basketball parlance, these are the go-to players, the ones to whom you get the ball when the game is in danger of getting out of your control or when it is on the line. They are the ones who fight to get into the right position and demand the pass. The notion that every employee, not just those with managerial titles, is a manager and the roles of various people (agents) will be explored and described next.

EVERYONE IS A MANAGER

Until fairly recently, many people believed that bosses had the sole responsibility to change how work was accomplished in their department or company. After all, he or she was at the top of the pyramid, went to corporate at the end of the year to present the unit's profit plan, and had the corner office and the reserved parking spot. Employees looked to the boss for answers. The job of the boss was to manage. That meant to take the lead and tell people what to do. One tongue-in-cheek book on managers put it this way: "For one thing, to be a real boss there were few restrictions to contend with: you hired whomever you chose, you told these people what they were to do, you paid them a nominal wage to do it, and you fired them if they didn't do it correctly."[4]

The old assumptions saw the boss as administrator. Michael Maccoby described them in this way: "The administrator is the traditional expert engineer, accountant, or lawyer. . . . he expects organizations to run by the book. . . . construct the right structure, provide proper incentives, and the industrial machine will run efficiently." He continues, "the strongman (. . . like a jungle fighter) . . . believes he can overpower distrust and gain accord by bearing down on his subordinates."[5] One of the most significant changes in the business world today has been the concept of the boss. Old assumptions are giving way to new ones that see the boss as a person with somewhat different skills than were expected in the past. What we have realized is that neither the administrator model nor the strongman model is good enough to take control of change in today's environment.

Economic incentives and the comfort of a strict order of things or structure—the main tools of the administrator—are not the powerful motivational tools they once were. The achievement-oriented worker today wants the freedom to establish goals and the sense of personal influence to attain them; he or she wants to have input and involvement. Consequently, the strongman misses the mark as well by sacrificing a sense of teamwork for personal dominance. Today's worker sees two satisfiers, equally important to personal influence and input: (1) relationships of trust with coworkers and (2) a sense of a team composed of different but interdependent parts, all moving in the same direction to achieve common goals.

POWER AS THE MOTIVATOR

We are seeing the emergence of a new set of assumptions about managing today in which the person in charge must care about developing the people under him or her by inviting input and sharing power. Management presents as an incentive the chance to influence operations rather than using the old piecework-oriented incentive method that offered more money for following the manager's rules. It is not that people today believe money is not important; the point is that they are less likely to accept money at the expense of influence over the things around them and over input into the issues that concern them. All this means that the boss must act differently. He or she must allow subordinates to be influential and find a way to ensure they take responsibility for solving problems. The boss must see that positive relationships are built, created on the basis of trust and common belief in a vision of the future. The boss must be persuasive in a way that does not diminish trust. The result should be a work environment or climate where there is continuous improvement and sharpening of the skills necessary to compete against ever better opponents.

If these are some of the elements of the boss's new mandate, what is required of the people in his or her organization? They, too, must become agents of change. They must welcome a new level of responsibility and fulfill its mandate. The simple fact is that people in the middle and lower strata of the organization chart are being called on to solve problems and make decisions. In some organizations today it is less an issue of bosses not wanting to share power than of creating the sort of climate where people can exercise the decision-making power available.

THE IMPORTANCE OF THE PILOT TEAM

The vehicle by which decisions are being made is the task team or pilot team. For example, a common building block of a TQ effort is project-by-project improvement. Teams of workers are formed to discover the root cause of a problem affecting them and are asked to find and implement solutions. Decision-making responsibility is passed from bosses through such teams, often as part of an overall company-wide improvement effort. This phenomenon is occurring with increasing frequency, and, by all indications, it will continue. For the past several years, larger companies (e.g., Hewlett-Packard, Apple Computer, Xerox, Ford, and IBM) have adopted this style. Some medium-size firms have moved in this direction as well, because their leaders found this operating style more attractive. The team-oriented, push-the-responsibility-down style has picked up more steam as large corporations have demanded that their suppliers adopt methods that require it. Zero defects and just-in-time (JIT) delivery are becoming the norm as large companies build more collaborative relationships with their suppliers. Along the way, those companies are training suppliers to operate in the way they themselves have learned to operate.

What all this means is that as much of a change of style, perhaps more, is being asked of the employees as of the boss. New ways of operating require a number of things to succeed, but the one paramount requirement is the commitment of people throughout the company to make new ways of operating work.

The techniques embodied in new ways of operating more effectively today make two requirements of employees: They must (1) go out of their way to solve problems and do the right things in the right way and (2) behave in a team-oriented way. To do so, people must want to; they cannot be mandated. People must care about how they operate and, how the work gets done, and that is where their commitment comes in.

SEVEN CLIMATE FACTORS OF COMMITMENT

How can a new level of commitment on the part of employees come about? Telling people to act differently won't make it happen and last. Simply offering to pay people more money won't work either. There is no one leverage point, no one answer. A number of things must be done simultaneously. A certain climate or environment must be created in the company for new behavior to take hold. Our experience and empirical research at Rath & Strong indicate that there are seven key elements in the climate of an organization that foster employee commitment to new ways of operating and to accepting new levels of responsibility.

1. *Influence.* The degree to which people believe they have influence over changing what is around them. Resistance to change is higher among people who have a low sense of influence because they have no sense of ownership in the process and little self-confidence about making conditions different. Many mid-level managers and supervisors believe they have less influence than they should have, given their title or spot on the organization chart. Sometimes people resist change just to exercise the little influence they believe they have.

People with a low perception of their own influence who are forced to participate in a team-oriented activity or to accept more decision-making responsibility often acquiesce, but they are usually not energetic, persistent, or committed. For people to accept more responsibility, they must develop more of a sense of influence and control, as well as confidence that they can be successful at making decisions they once depended on others to make.

2. *Responsibility.* Willingness to assume responsibility for doing the right things the right way. People who have a healthy sense of influence are comfortable accepting responsibility. Those with a low sense of influence are leery of responsibility, often believing it is a way for bosses to give them more work. Companies that have a history of compartmentalization, where engineering hardly ever talks with manufacturing and neither department relates much with sales or marketing, often have a low collective sense of responsibility across the whole organization. This sort of firm has difficulty successfully implementing change efforts requiring teamwork across department lines, including cross-functional task teams and pilot teams.

High levels of responsibility should correlate with high levels of innovativeness, a desire to change the status quo, and teamwork among workers who are willing to take responsibility for their ideas. Those who feel a sense of influence are usually also willing to push for changes they see as necessary. If one is comfortable taking responsibility, he or she is often willing to work with others to enhance the responsibility of a group.

3. *Innovativeness.* The degree to which new ideas that can improve how the company operates are encouraged, listened to, and considered seriously. Highly innovative companies get ideas from many different locations in the organizational hierarchy. This tends to happen in organizations where four conditions exist. First, where people are encouraged to experiment, they will try new and different ways of operating, knowing that mistakes for the right reasons will cause positive feedback. Second, innovation is encouraged where people are accustomed to operating in small teams or task forces. Third, those who come up with the best new ideas frequently should be held in high esteem and rewarded. Fourth, the leader should encourage people to be constantly innovative.

A climate of innovation will allow people to be different and to question the status quo. It exists in the company where employees believe that the leader wants to find new ways to solve problems and will support new ideas.

4. *Desire to change.* A healthy level of dissatisfaction with what exists, a desire to change what is and make it better. In companies where the desire to change is low, there is typically difficulty developing the sense of influence and responsibility necessary for employees to take on more of the decision-making load. At the same time, if the desire to change persists without being responded to for a significant period of time, it can turn from healthy dissatisfaction to unhealthy frustration. When employees have crossed the line from dissatisfaction to frustration, the likelihood of constructive change through employees working together and taking on more decision-making responsibility diminishes.

The desire to change often occurs when there is a crisis. Digital Equipment Company (DEC), the computer giant, is a case in point. The first quarter of 1984 was the first time DEC lost money; the stock price fell 30 points. This was the slap in the face that roused its employees and caused them to search for better ways to operate, particularly in manufacturing. DEC's continuous-improvement (TQ and JIT) effort resulted in record growth in volume and profits by 1989. While DEC's senior managers contend it would not have happened unless the company had been in a crisis, the challenge they face today is how to maintain that spirit and sense of urgency, that desire to change, during a time of success. The American attitude, "If it ain't broke, don't fix it!" is perhaps the biggest barrier to ensuring success without a crisis. Companies that foster a high desire to change tend to avoid such crises.

5. *Satisfaction*. The degree to which employees are basically satisfied. This means that for people to accept responsibility, exert influence, and become innovative they must be sure that their basic needs are met—physical, economic, and psychological. The psychological needs that must be met as a company moves to become more competitive are the individual's need to achieve and to be recognized for achievement, the need to identify with some social group (such as a work team or ad hoc task team), and the need to influence and have some control over what is affecting his or her satisfaction. When these basic needs for achievement, affiliation, and power are met, the base is established for individual motivation. Meeting these needs helps provide the motivation needed to make employees go out of their way to improve what is around them, even if they are not specifically asked to do so.

6. *Teamwork*. The working state in which people trust each other enough to work together to get a job done. In an atmosphere where there is teamwork, several elements exist:

- Issues are confronted directly, often in group meetings, and the group will stick with the issue until it reaches resolution.

- The group participates in decision making, and in so doing group members are sensitized to each other's needs.

- Feelings are expressed freely, and they are listened to and appreciated by others; motives are open and clear.

- Responsibility is distributed, and people believe they are all in it together; because of this, help is offered freely.

- Power and credit are shared. There is sufficient respect for each member's contribution that it becomes unimportant who receives credit.

- Achieving consensus is easier because people are more of one mind about what must be done. There is mutual respect for others' contributions.

7. *Common vision*. There must be a vision created by the top person and his or her closest advisers painting an image of the future that is compelling and exciting and around which employees at all levels can rally. This vision not only must be clear and compelling but consistent and consistently presented in terms that are most relevant to those at each level of the organizational ladder. It also must be based on values that are held as important by employees and to which they aspire.

It must start with agreement by top management on the values that will form the basis for the way the company will operate under TQ and JIT. TQ and JIT will not succeed if the people at the bottom or middle of the organization are operating on the basis of an idea that is dramatically different from that of the leader.

THE CHANGE-AGENT ROLE

These are the elements of the organizational climate in which a team-oriented effort can foster the sort of responsibility employees need to assume. In addition to each and every employee assuming more responsibility for change and becoming a change agent, there are specific jobs to be done in today's corporation that call for new skills. One example is the role of the leader of a company-wide continuous-improvement effort. More and more U.S. corporations are attempting to improve by way of efforts variously called total quality commitment (TQC), continuous improvement, resource management, and TQ/JIT. In many, an individual is named to be the project leader, often a former line manager. While certainly similar to roles taken in the past by people asked to implement new information systems, pay systems, and the like, this position also has some unique aspects. It is explored here because it is an example of how many companies are sharing decision-making power and spreading the responsibility for managing change.

Choosing a Project Leader

For many companies the most obvious temptation in choosing a project leader for a company-wide improvement effort is to pick someone for whom coworkers feel a sense of loyalty but who has little else to qualify him or her for this particular task. This is the wrong person, because the project leader should be a partner of the leader and the top team and because together with them he or she is responsible for pushing changes down through the organization. Although it is necessary for leaders and managers to carry the message to employees, the project leader must coordinate the effort and make certain everyone has the right information at the right time, and he or she must troubleshoot and solve problems as the process unfolds.

The project leader must be flexible and able to work in a constantly changing environment. It is imperative that the project leader be someone who is not tied to the old ways of doing business with a vested interest in seeing that one particular group within the organization gains influence disproportionately. This person must also be willing to stay in the project management position for as long as it takes to get the job done (probably 12 to 24 months), but not any longer. He or she should not use this as a stepping stone to a higher management position and should not try to make the position a permanent one requiring a staff, budget, and ever-increasing funding. His or her loyalty should be to the company head, not to other managers in the company, although the project leader must be able to get along with members of top management, and they in turn should view him or her as a valuable resource.

In one case, a client took a somewhat unusual step that worked quite well. The company had just completed a reorganization and a major cost-cutting effort. The leader did not want to pull a current manager out of a job, fearing that this would weaken an already severely trimmed-down staff. The step he took was to persuade a man who had recently retired after a successful career to return as a consultant and take responsibility for this effort. This person had no axe to grind and could not be accused of political motives. He had been well liked and respected. He constantly pushed away opportunities to collect a department under him. What he really wanted to do was finish the job and return to the farm he had bought.

Finding this person reinforced the project leader's job as temporary. The continuous-improvement effort went smoothly. After about one year he went back into retirement, and line managers assumed responsibility for the effort.

Having a project leader can make the difference between success and mediocrity in a company-wide improvement effort, but not everyone can do this job well. It takes a person who is able to balance a number of demands. (Figure 21–1) shows the characteristics that seem to make the difference between average and excellent project managers. When it is decided to have a full-time person as project leader, candidates should be measured against these 22 characteristics.

SUMMARY

We have explored the change-agent responsibility of the boss, the subordinate, and the project manager. Its central tenet is that no one person can manage strategic change successfully and that it takes the collective effort of people at every level of the organization, each doing his or her own part. It also suggests that there are certain facets of the organizational climate, the work environment, that encourage the sort of behavior needed to bring about positive strategic change.

Ultimately, it is the leader who must ensure the success of such an effort. In doing so, there are several rules (actually the five don'ts of leading a company-wide change effort) for successful, strategic organizational change that must be kept in mind.

1. Don't believe that yesterday's answers will work on today's questions. History can provide valuable lessons only after the leader has formulated a new way to proceed. Being tied to the past will often lead to replicating actions taken in a different environment for different reasons by different people—actions that may not suit today's realities.

2. Don't believe that people who have done things one way for years will change their behavior easily if at all. The wise leader will become dissat-

FIGURE 21–1 Competencies of project manager for a continuous-improvement effort

1. Able to implement without taking credit.
2. Able to organize work and bring about order from chaos.
3. Able to set priorities effectively.
4. Able to keep priorities clearly in mind.
5. Knows when to push and when to wait.
6. Gains satisfaction more from goal attainment than from teamwork.
7. Gains satisfaction from knowing things he or she is responsible for are under control.
8. Thrives on predictability and structures things he or she is responsible for so they are predictable.
9. Able to traverse organizational boundaries smoothly and is equally effective in different organizational settings.
10. Has influence skills developed to the point where he or she can be equally effective with different senior managers whose styles vary widely.
11. Able to listen actively so that the other person feels comfortable sharing information.
12. Able to figure out how to structure an effort so that people from many different camps feel involved.
13. Has loyalty to the leader and to his vision of how the TQ/JIT effort should be structured.
14. Is much more attuned to short-term goals than to a more nebulous, long-term vision.
15. Cares more about getting things started than about carrying them forward for a long time and is happy to pass off responsibilities as long as the goals set are attained.
16. Works in a deliberate way and makes steady progress, even if some see as plodding.
17. Works iteratively, in a building-block fashion.
18. Automatically breaks a long-term task into shorter-term steps that are more easily envisioned.
19. Does not care about building a staff, having a title, or creating a power group.
20. Buys into the TQ/JIT philosophy and believes deeply in its precepts but is not dogmatic.
21. Is more solid and dependable than flashy and exciting.
22. Is more practical than ideologically pure. Searches for ways to negotiate and move around obstacles. Is satisfied with having gotten 80 percent of what is needed instead of stubbornly holding out on ideological grounds and getting nothing.

isfied with the status quo *first,* before subordinates do. He or she will think about it, worry about it, ask questions about it, and formulate a way to address it. Others will be slow to grasp the significance. While the leader may not necessarily drag others along, they will feel the sense of urgency only after he or she does. Some may never feel this sense of urgency. When it is time to act (crunch time), the leader must be realistic in pulling the organization along, giving people enough time to get to the point of urgency. At the same time, he or she must not hesitate to replace people, especially high-level people, who will never achieve enough of a sense of urgency to change their behavior. Termination is not an easy decision and should be a last resort, but it is sometimes necessary.

3. Don't believe you can do it all yourself. There is a fine line between confidence and megalomania. The changes needed in most manufacturing companies are too enormous, and the problems to be solved too deeply rooted, to be resolved by any one person. Everyone has a role to play. The wise leader will find a way to have those roles defined and make sure people fulfill the requirements of each. The most effective leaders are those who understand what they do well and do it but who find others to do the things they don't do as well. The industrial graveyard is filled with epitaphs of companies that had a better mousetrap but also a leader who could not or would not bring in people to participate in the change, people who would make the firm a bigger, better competitor.

4. Don't believe you can anticipate everything or that you don't need any game plan at all. This is related somewhat to Rule 3. There are some leaders who try to anticipate everything that could possibly happen. It cannot be done, and it is the wrong way to think about it; we're talking about changing people's *attitudes* and *then* their behavior. Attitude change is something that cannot be entirely systematic; the comforting sequence of the scientific method can get in the way rather than ensure success. Changing attitudes is iterative at best; not only must one take a step back to repeat the one just taken, but one must often take a step to the side also.

At the same time, a game plan is essential. The right level of planning here is more akin to a basketball team than a football team. In a basketball team, there are only a handful of basic plays. The point guard calls a play while bringing the ball downcourt, but what actually happens depends on how the defense looks, who is overplaying, who gets double-teamed, and so forth. A football team has a play book three inches thick; the players take time to memorize the spot to go to. When a quarterback overthrows a receiver by 10 yards, it is usually because one or the other had the wrong play in mind; the quarterback throws to a spot and the receiver runs a particular pattern to a spot. Organizational change is a basketball game, not a football game.

5. Don't believe the old adage, "If it ain't broke, don't fix it!" This flies in the face of every principle of preventive maintenance, from yearly

physicals, to getting one's teeth cleaned, to a 5,000-mile checkup on your car. The wise leader is always looking for opportunities to make things better before they break. The cost of repairing a broken organization is enormous compared to the fine-tuning and constructive change required to keep it sharp.

NOTES

1. Kenneth D. Benne, Warren G. Bennis, and Robert Chin, *The Planning of Change* (New York: Holt, Rinehart & Winston, 1968).

2. This sort of passive social change has been pointed out in a much better way by David McCullough in *The Path Between the Seas* (New York: Simon & Schuster, 1977).

3. I have always attributed this theory to Dick Descharmes who wrote a paper on it in 1968 at St. Louis University.

4. E. Nevins, *Real Bosses Don't Say Thank You* (Somerville, N.J.: Nevins Publishing Co., 1983), 12.

5. Michael Maccoby, *The Leader* (New York: Ballantine Books, 1983), xiv.

22 CASE STUDY

STANADYNE, CHANGING THE MANUFACTURING STRATEGY FROM JOB SHOP TO JIT

William G. Holbrook

Editor's note

The Stanadyne case illustrates tactics required to meet the manufacturing strategy of competing on cost, quality, and customer service in the world market. Stanadyne implemented major culture changes in its two-phased restructuring from a classic job shop to JIT and work cells. All pay plans and performance-measurement systems were redesigned to match the system changes.

Added to the dynamics of implementing major culture changes, the company restructured and went private shortly after the changes described in the case. The resulting smaller, but leaner and more focused, business is more profitable.

Stanadyne Diesel Systems is part of a 100-year-old company that started supplying screw machine products in the Northeast to various companies, including Pratt & Whitney and Xerox. The company was a job shop, considered to be a quality house for screw machine products.

Forty years ago, the company began manufacturing a proprietary product based on a unique design for diesel fuel injection. The fuel injection

371

business grew and prospered while coexisting with the job-shop business. In 1976, Stanadyne was contracted to supply diesel fuel injection equipment to a large automotive company. Required volumes were so significant that the job-shop business was abandoned and manufacturing facilities were converted to production of diesel products only. During a six-year period, sales doubled three times. Facilities grew from one plant to four, one in Connecticut and three in North Carolina.

PRODUCTS

Stanadyne Diesel Systems Division supplies three major product groups to most U.S. diesel engine manufacturers. The customer base is small but well-known. The volumes and mix of business generally are predictable. Lead times from initial product design to shipment are one to two years. Sales are not off the shelf; orders are manufactured to meet customers' engine-build schedules.

The three product groups are

1. Pumps. The basic component in the fuel system is the injection pump. Containing about 150 components, the major parts are manufactured in Windsor, Connecticut; then shipped along with purchased components to Jacksonville, North Carolina, where they are assembled, tested, and sent to the customer. Volumes run in excess of 1,000 assemblies per day.
2. Nozzles. The nozzle injects fuel from the pump into the engine combustion chamber. It is made up of 15 components manufactured at Windsor and shipped to Jacksonville for assembly and test. Nozzles currently are being manufactured at a rate of 7,000 per day.
3. Filter products. The Washington, North Carolina, plant manufactures a variety of filters and fuel separators. A filter or separator consists mainly of purchased components assembled and tested at rates approximating 15,000 per day.

FACILITIES

The Windsor plant, the center of all product development and engineering, manufactures most of the components for the pump and nozzle. This site employs about 1,100 people; one-half are involved in production, the rest in engineering and administrative functions. The North Carolina plants employ about 300 to 400 people at each site, devoted almost entirely to production.

THE PROBLEM

Stanadyne faced a challenge: how to profitably survive in business with large capacity and overheads in place but with sales shrinking. Business had fallen off suddenly after a period of rapid growth. The economies of diesel-powered automobiles became less attractive; in 1981 volumes were cut in half. The company was faced with some major decisions about how to exist profitably in the face of decreasing domestic market demand.

THE RESPONSE: A NEW STRATEGY

The clear direction taken in response to decreased orders was to market fuel injection products overseas in Europe and Japan. This strategy presented more questions, however. How could the company do it and still maintain profitability? Prevailing overseas prices were at or very near direct cost to manufacture. Stanadyne was faced with either making some substantial reductions in manufacturing costs or changing the type of business it was in.

To succeed, the company had to define tactics that met these strategic objectives:

1. Improve quality to compete in the world market.
2. Deliver products when customers want them and in the quantities they need.
3. Continue the R&D effort to bring new and competitive products to market.
4. Drastically reduce overhead structures.
5. Reduce the cost of manufacturing.

Phase I: JIT

Fortunately for Stanadyne, the problem appeared at the same time some very forward-thinking people in this country began to investigate JIT (just-in-time) manufacturing techniques to achieve

- High quality levels.
- On-time delivery.
- Ever-improving cost to manufacture.
- Low overhead, low inventory.
- People involvement.

A philosophy was formed for the business incorporating these five objectives while identifying the most effective approaches for the environment existing in Stanadyne at that time. The new manufacturing strategy was based on three requirements:

1. *Culture change.* The new operating philosophy had to be part of our culture. There was no time to bring about changes through a typically lengthy project implementation with a project leader and pilot run. The change had to involve every facet of the manufacturing operation.

2. *Continual improvement.* The overriding theme had to be one of commitment to continual improvement and change. It was not adequate simply to meet a specific quality level or to meet the standard. There had to be a willingness to attempt changes without fear of making a mistake. People needed to agree that if a change did not work, they could come up with a better idea and try again.

3. *Simplicity.* We had to simplify the complexities of processes and equipment that had been put into place in the late sixties and seventies. During that period, we had purchased specialized equipment to accomplish many complex processes. We had also put complex systems into place for financial reporting and material control (i.e., material-requirements planning and standard cost-variance analysis). We needed to reevaluate our complex processes and systems to reduce the cost of doing business.

Using these three general parameters—the need for permanent culture change, continual improvement, and simplicity—we developed new tactics. We wanted to take the manufacturing facility out of the job-shop mentality and into a mindset dedicated to producing quality products on time and at a lower cost through repetitive processes (see Figure 22–1).

Process Design

The processes were redesigned to give commonality through at least 70 percent of the operations for each major family of parts. Each component started out as a common blank and traveled through a common process. Operations to make each part unique were performed in the finishing operations. After completion of the process design, the capability of each process was reviewed to ensure that the specifications called out on the blueprint could be met.

Process Control

When the process was in place and determined to be effective, the next step was a control mechanism to ensure that the process would remain in control. Statistical process control (SPC) was implemented for the key charac-

FIGURE 22–1   Stanadyne's just-in-time manufacturing strategy

Process Design
  Common blanks
  Common process—70%
  Process capability
  Process control—SPC

Manufacturing Flow
  Eliminate job shop concept of shop orders
  Phase out storeroom check-in/checkout
  Smooth the flow

Employee Involvement Plan
  Quality circle program
  Revised incentive pay plan

Material Handling
  Physically link machines—Tracking
  Standard quantity containers
  Reduce distance traveled

Machine Cells
  Dismantle general machining departments
  Develop cells by *family* of parts

Scheduling
  Daily rates of production by family
  Kanbans when logistics dictate
  Daily performance reporting
  Mix schedule through MRP
  Reduce role of production control

Lead Times/Inventories
  L/T as a planning tool to control inventory reduction
  L/T does not exist for lines and kanbans
  Inventory levels fixed by line design

teristics of each component group. As SPC was implemented, large numbers of inspectors were eliminated. Responsibility for quality was refocused on the foreperson, who became solely responsible for parts quality. Because SPC proved that the process was yielding good product, final and in-process inspections were eliminated.

We learned very early in the program that for the plan to be successful, the total workforce had to be involved. The plan would not have worked if we had tried to merely engineer the change. Because the factory employees were the ones who knew a great deal about process problems, they were brought into the problem-solving mechanism to make the improvements workable and effective.

We started massive training programs to implement a meaningful SPC program. Quality circles were instituted in all the plants to teach team problem solving.

Pay Plans

Incentive plans to change the method of paying employees were needed to foster teamwork. The individual piecework plans that had been appropriate for the job-shop environment were changed to group incentive plans. Later, the group plans were changed to straight day work. The changes in the pay plans were the most traumatic part of the total transformation. The impact was felt not only by machine operators but by supervisors who had to alter the way they ran the various manufacturing centers.

Material Flow: From Job Shop to Cells

In a classic job-shop environment, similar processes are grouped together. Parts move from one process to another based on a traveler or route sheet. Parts are batched, issued against a shop order, and expedited through the shop to meet a due date. This type of process requires large expenditures for material handling and expediting (see Figure 22–2).

To eliminate the lengthy and costly process of moving parts in and out of a queue for each operation, production equipment was reorganized into cells. Each cell performs all the operations on a specific family of similar

FIGURE 22–2 Yesterday's routing

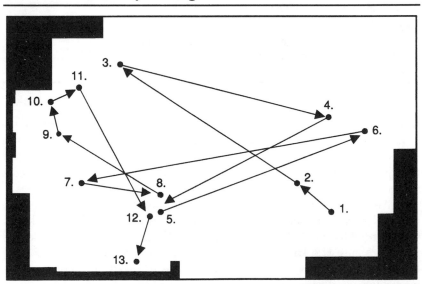

FIGURE 22–3 **Today's process routing**

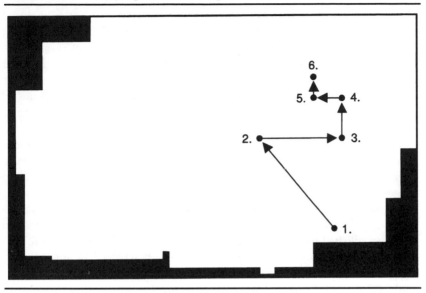

parts. The result is significant reduction in the distance a part travels through various processes. Machines are physically linked together by conveyors or tracks, using standard containers and constant container quantities (see Figure 22–3).

Shrinking Production Control's Role

Once the cells were set up and the various processes were balanced to allow a flow of material, the production control process was reduced to merely setting the cell's daily-run rate and issuing a product mix schedule. The need for expediting disappeared because the location of every part became known. Scheduling is done for the entire cell rather than for each operation within the process.

Kanban

A system of kanbans was implemented to shuttle parts between operations. A predetermined number of standard containers (unique for that component) were used as kanban to maintain flow without a complex scheduling mechanism. In the kanban system, the supplying operations run until all the containers are full; then the operation is shut off. The using operation returns empty containers to the supplying operation as the parts are consumed in the process.

Results

The results were dramatic. With the creation of cells, the entire material control system became simple. The information needed for control is merely a comparison of planned daily-run rate versus actual production. Cost control, which will be discussed in greater detail later, also became simple. Lead times typically were reduced by 75 percent, many from weeks to hours. Inventory levels were reduced. There was no need for queues or stock rooms because material continued to move through the process until it was completed.

The reorganization greatly reduced manpower in the factory. Production control slots were reduced from 32 to 4. The material expediters were no longer needed. In their place, four production planners prepare the shop schedule for components produced within the daily-run rate plan.

Quality control has been reduced from a force of more than 100 inspectors to a group of 9 people who do in-process quality checks. This reduction was accomplished by concentrating responsibility in the production cell.

Many other supporting departments were downsized by manufacturing process simplification. Areas that were *not* reduced were manufacturing engineering and industrial engineering. All the process and pay-plan changes required a great deal of engineering help. Moreover, it became clear that the only way to make so many concurrent improvements in the manufacturing process was with the help of production workers, using engineers to support them. Stanadyne's success has been the result of production workers buying into the new philosophies and management letting them work on the problems.

Other achievements have been in the area of work-in-process (WIP) inventory reduction. As the cells were formed, WIP was reduced by 50 percent. A more significant achievement is that the factory now produces on schedule. Although this is a recent accomplishment, it is important because quality improvements or cost reductions cannot be effective until operations are on schedule. When the factory is behind schedule, all efforts and focus are on getting the parts through the shop. There is little energy left to pursue better quality and correspondingly lower cost.

Phase II: Performance Measurement

After we had made many practical changes to our operations, we realized that the reporting and measurement systems were not responsive to manufacturing's new tactics. We needed a new measurement system. Further, before any measurement system could be established, we had to satisfy these prerequisites:

1. *Quality at the source.* We had to make the product right the first time before any changes would be effective in the manufacturing measure-

ment system. Without commitment to quality, it would be pointless to measure an out-of-control process. A system to measure costs and performance of product as it moves back and forth for pick out, rework, and reinspection would be far too complex.

2. *Manufacturing cells*. A manufacturing process organized into cells dedicated to the production of a similar family of components has a real opportunity to simplify the total-cost, and performance measurement system. By focusing the measurements for a family of parts onto a single set of resources (workers and machines), a simple set of measurements can be established.

3. *Business plan and critical success factors*. To measure progress effectively, we needed an effective strategic business-planning process. There was no need to measure something if it had no real impact on the success or failure of the business. The best example of this is the traditional enthusiasm that business has had for measuring the efficiency of labor. We decided to measure factors that were key to the success of the business.

The critical success factors are so important that if any one of them were out of control, the overall success of the business would be in jeopardy. Not more than five or six factors should fall into this category. The real test of their criticality was to ask whether the business will be a success if the performance objectives on each of the critical factors are met. If not, then that factor did not justify expending resources. The critical success factors change as the business changes. We review them periodically.

Measurement system design. Creating the measurement system can be overwhelming, but if addressed properly, it can be simple and easy. After we identified the critical success factors, we attacked the design of appropriate measurements. We felt performance measures for manufacturing companies competing in the world market should follow these priorities:

- Quality issues get top consideration; if the quality of the product is out of control, all other measures become meaningless.

- Second, measure delivery performance to the *customer's* demand. This requires meeting the ship schedule.

- Having met the first and second criteria, the organization should begin to concentrate on the third priority, cost.

The Universal Measure. Although measurements vary over time and from one business to another, one that is fairly consistent for all business is the actual unit cost. A universal measure for manufacturing operations makes sense because it is simple and easy to understand. The universal measure is simply the actual unit cost of production. In a cell dedicated to the production of a family of components with a uniform flow of material (all good JIT practices), it is easy to organize data collection to calculate actual cost to produce a single component. The actual cost per unit can be understood by almost everyone who has ever purchased a loaf of bread, a gallon of gasoline, or a bottle of beer.

The costs that go into the equation are the sum of direct labor and fringe, expendable tooling and supplies, maintenance supplies, and direct charges for maintenance and repair orders, divided by the pieces produced. Manufacturing supervision knows that it cannot make more than what is on the shop schedule, so it must manage spending relative to that volume.

Concentrating on actual unit costing focuses attention on actions that the foreperson can control (i.e., his or her own spending). Historically, business has concentrated on variances from standard. Discussions always bog down over the adequacy of the standard rather than on the actual spending pattern. The new system now meets all these criteria:

1. It is easy for all employees to understand.
2. It fits all levels of production and products.
3. The results are controllable by the people on the shop floor.
4. It supports the theory of continuous improvement.

Unfortunately, many organizations have been far too concerned with measuring costs and have ignored the first two criteria. This generally happens when an organization becomes a slave to traditional financial measures and does not allow creative design of a measurement system that is truly responsive to the real success factors in manufacturing.

Design Recommendations

There are a few basics that I would offer to anyone who is contemplating redesign of a measurement system:

1. *Maintain flexibility.* Start out with a personal computer to experiment with your measurement systems. Success factors change as businesses grow and mature and as business conditions change. Programming your measurement system first on a mainframe or desktop computer would result in extensive reprogramming and frustration. Also, after factors are identified the first time, it may take several attempts to successfully choose the true factors that guarantee success.
2. *Keep the measurements simple.* A complex system of measurements only understood by the designer is really no measurement system at all. JIT is based on simplicity of design and execution; its measurement system must also be simple and easy to understand. A system that is

too complex creates confusion about what must be done to improve overall performance.

3. *Pinpoint responsibility.* Merely stating that a particular factor falls short of expectations is not enough. The measurement system must be capable of tracing back to the operation or function responsible for the shortfall. For example, an indicator measuring quality failures at final-product test is fine as long as sufficient detail exists to be able to trace back to the source of the product failures. Without this capability, the system merely predicts failure without hope of preventing it.

LABOR ISSUES

Compensation Methods

There are a number of issues to be addressed when deciding how much effort should be placed on the control of labor. We decided that if labor were a small portion of the total cost of production and the policy is to not reduce manpower even if it is not 100 percent utilized, then a complex system of labor control would make little sense. If labor costs are significant, however, then some system of control is necessary. The danger here is spending more money to control labor than will ever be realized from its control. We asked ourselves the following questions:

- Is labor a small portion of direct cost?
- Is labor a scarce commodity?
- Can labor be controlled in a cost-effective manner?
- Is there an application for incentive pay?
- How does gain sharing fit into the pay system?
- Are labor standards necessary?

Advantages of Day-Rate Plan

In a JIT environment with manufacturing concentrated in cells, individual piecework incentive pay plans run contrary to the objectives of quality and schedule. An operator will not concentrate on quality if his or her pay is based on additional production. Nor will the operator produce only what is needed when he or she makes more money for each additional piece produced.

A day-rate pay plan eliminates the contradictions of an incentive system but creates some other problems. Some workers feel that the opportunity to excel has been removed when piecework is eliminated. The production supervisor's role changes dramatically because, as far as a worker's productivity is concerned, an incentive system is a self-policing mechanism. But a day-rate system requires close supervision of the productivity within the cell. The supervisor must investigate each time production falls below acceptable limits and determine the cause. The worker who is not on incentive may be less motivated to tell the supervisor that there are problems.

The real solution to this problem is not to make the supervisor into a superhuman individual. It is better to motivate each operator to be more involved in continuous improvements within the work cell. This can be done through some form of gain sharing with the employees and by making them aware of the company's objectives and the progress being made toward meeting those objectives.

To summarize our experience in changing the pay plans, we had a few problems but overall the results were appropriate to the new manufacturing strategy. In 1982, we changed from individual to group incentives for all manufacturing cells. We also changed to day rates and found that it works well in cells. It is adaptable to bar coding and allows for emphasis on quality rather than quantity.

The problems we encountered converting batch departments to day rate included losing a worker's incentive to excel or to fix problems. The work pace tends to lead off at 100 percent. Also, this method requires accurate standards and voluminous data collection. The answer to these problems is to measure differently, looking at operator productivity and overall department labor utilization.

I have briefly reviewed the points that were important at Stanadyne in setting up a responsive measurement system. It was really very simple; we knew our manufacturing goals, and we designed various checkpoints along the way to make sure we got there on time and in good condition. I think the discussion here applies to most manufacturing concerns in the United States today that count on profits as their ultimate long-term measure of success.

About the Authors

Sara L. Beckman was the manager of Hewlett-Packard's (HP) Manufacturing Strategic Planning function, where she coordinated the development of the corporation's manufacturing organization strategy. In this capacity, she was involved in decisions regarding degree of vertical integration, determination of plant focus and size, and facilities location. She is also a member of the Business School faculty of the University of California, Berkeley. She represented HP on the Advisory Board of the M.I.T. Leaders in Manufacturing Program.

Before joining corporate manufacturing at HP, she worked on the development of the Data Systems Division Manufacturing and computer-integrated manufacturing (CIM) strategies. She joined HP after four years at Booz, Allen, and Hamilton in their operations management services consulting practice.

Dr. Beckman earned her bachelor's, master's and doctoral degrees in industrial engineering from Stanford University where she also received a master's degree in statistics.

Joseph D. Blackburn is associate dean for academic affairs and professor of operations management in the Owen Graduate School of Management, Vanderbilt University. His consulting and research work covers operations strategy, material-requirements planning (MRP) systems, and new-product forecasting models. He has published numerous articles in *Management Science, Marketing Science, Journal of Operations Management,* and other journals.

He is the director of the Operations Roundtable and an associate of the market research firm Yankelovich, Clancy-Shulman. He also serves on the editorial boards of *The Journal of Operations Management* and *Corporate Strategies.*

He received his B.S. degree from Vanderbilt University, an M.S. degree from the University of Wisconsin, and a Ph.D. in operations research from Stanford University. He has also taught at Boston University, the University of Chicago, and Stanford University.

William A. Boller is the general manager of the Industrial Applications Center at Hewlett-Packard. Before holding this position he formed the Strategic Manufacturing Consulting Group. Boller was the manufacturing manager for the Data Systems Division at HP. He concurrently served on the Corporate Manufacturing Council as the Group Manufacturing Manager.

Mr. Boller has a bachelor's degree in mechanical engineering from Stanford University, a master's degree in mechanical engineering from the University of Southern California, and an M.B.A. from Stanford University.

Steven Cabana is the director of Whole System Associates, a consulting company that helps organizations plan their futures and organize themselves to get there. He received his B.S. degree in biochemistry from the University of Massachusetts and his M.A. in organizational development from American University. Mr. Cabana is also a graduate of the Gestalt Institute of Cleveland's Organization and System Development program and has sought to understand and implement the most effective methods for changing large systems for 15 years. He was the director of the Foundation for Integration of Systems and Human Resources, a five-person consulting firm specializing in large-scale projects to improve quality, productivity, and effectiveness. He began his career as a genetic researcher in the microbiology department at the University of Massachusetts.

Mr. Cabana is author, along with Fred and Merrelyn Emery, of "The Search for Effective Strategic Planning Is Over," and with Janet Fiero of "Motorola, Strategic Planning and the Search Conference" in the *Journal of Quality and Participation* (July/August 1995). He wrote the first U.S. article on Dr. Emery's innovative approach for rapid organizational redesign in the same journal, "Participative Design Works, Partially Participative Doesn't," and published a recent article in *Target,* the journal of the Association for Manufacturing Excellence, outlining some of the early North American successes of the participative design approach. He has served as a consultant to such organizations as Bank of Boston, Cabot Corp., DEC, FAA, Fidelity, Union Carbide, New England Electric, United Technologies, and the state of Maine. Mr. Cabana's primary interest is the application of the search conference and participative design methods for organizational renewal, growth, and innovation.

Dan Ciampa is the former president and chief executive officer of Rath & Strong Inc., of Lexington, Massachusetts. He frequently speaks and writes on merging total-quality, just-in-time, and computer-integrated manufacturing; on involving people in technological change; on changing the organization climate; and, in particular, on the leader's role in continuous-improvement efforts. He is the author of *Manufacturing's New Mandate* (New York: John Wiley & Sons, 1988). He has been a guest lecturer at the Harvard Business School and at Boston College.

Mr. Ciampa received his bachelor of science degree in finance and social psychology from Boston College and a master of education degree in adult education from Boston University. He is a member of the Society of Manufacturing Engineers' Computer & Automated Systems Association, of Vanderbilt University's Operations Roundtable, and of the American Arbitration Association. In addition, he is an Associate of the British Institute of Management and a member of the board of advisers for *Corporate Controller.* Listed in *Who's Who in Industry and Finance,* Mr. Ciampa is certified by the Institute of Management Consultants and the International Association of Applied Social Scientists.

Romeyn Everdell is a management consultant, educator, and writer. In 1953 he joined Rath & Strong, working in industrial engineering, quality control, and production planning, scheduling, and inventory control. He retired as executive vice president in 1985. His early industry experience included work as a quality engineer and production manager.

Mr. Everdell has been active in the American Management Association and the American Production and Inventory Control Society as a frequent speaker and writer. He has also lectured for the American Society for Quality Control, the American Institute for Industrial Engineers, the Society of American Manufacturers, the University of Wisconsin, and Simmons College.

He wrote early technical papers in the areas of master scheduling and material-requirements planning. APICS has honored his contributions to the field by establishing the Romeyn Everdell Award, given annually to the author of the best technical article in the *Production and Inventory Management Journal*. He received his B.A. with honors in chemistry from Williams College.

Janet Fiero is a management consultant for her company, IEE Consulting Inc., based in Phoenix. She received her B.S. degree in biochemistry from Pennsylvania State University and her M.B.A. from Arizona State University and is currently pursuing her Ph.D. in human and organizational development from the Fielding Institute. Ms. Fiero worked as the manager of Motorola's engineering training and education center where she developed the early progarams on statistical training for engineers and established a corporate total quality improvement strategy that was implemented worldwide. She has also worked as a wafer processing engineer, manufacturing manager, and planning manager for one of Motorola's business units. Before joining Motorola she was a manufacturing supervisor and three-shift general supervisor for Fairchild Semiconductor.

Ms. Fiero served as a Malcolm Baldrige Examiner with the Department of Commerce in 1990, 1991, 1995, and 1996. As a founding member of the Arizona Governor's Award for Quality, she has been instrumental in creating the Arizona State Quality Award. Ms. Fiero has served as a consultant on strategic planning and implementation of quality methods to a number of leading corporations. She has written numerous papers in professional journals, textbooks, and conference publications and spoken at international, national, and state professional organizations and conferences on quality and planning topics.

Gwendolyn D. Galsworth is founder/president of Quality Methods International (QMI), a training and consulting firm specializing in systematic improvement tools and strategies that support JIT/lean production. A two-term Malcolm Baldrige examiner with 15 years in the field, Dr. Galsworth has been assisting companies all over the world to accelerate their rate of improvement and become more competitive. Clients include Alpha Industries, Alcoa Aluminum/Australia, Crompton Greaves/India, Curtis Screw, Delphi Energy and Engines Systems, Fleet Engineers, Gates Rubber, General Motors, Hamilton Standard, Plymouth Rubber, Pratt & Whitney, Prince Corporation, TVS Sundaram Clayton/India, and United Electric Controls.

Previous to forming QMI, Dr. Galsworth was head of training and development at Productivity, where she worked closely with Dr. Shigeo Shingo (Toyota Production System) and Dr. Ryuji Fukuda (Sumitomo) to develop and adapt core Japanese-based methods for the American workplace.

An international speaker on methods that decomplicate, Dr. Galsworth is the author of *Smart Simple Design: Using Variety Effectiveness to Reduce Total Cost and*

Maximize Customer Selection (New York: John Wiley, 1994) and *Visual Systems: Harnessing the Power of a Visual Workplace.* She is Senior Fellow at the University of Dayton's Center for Competitive Change.

Stephen A. Hamilton is a senior consultant in HP's Strategic Manufacturing Consulting program where he focuses on the food process industry. Before joining the group, Mr. Hamilton was the project manager for the installation of major computer-integrated manufacturing (CIM) systems in Europe. He has held a variety of manufacturing management positions at HP in the United States, before which he worked for many years in public accounting in Europe and later the United States.

He earned his bachelor's degree in politics, philosophy, and economics from the University of London and is qualified as a chartered accountant in England and as a certified public accountant in the United States.

Jackie Hammonds is a senior staff administrator with Honda of America Manufacturing Inc., in Marysville, Ohio. She has been with the company for 15 years in a range of functions from paint and assembly to purchasing and supplier training. She has been manager of the voluntary involvement system; her current position is corporate associate development leader of the East Liberty, Ohio, auto-assembly plant. From 1990 to 1995 Ms. Hammonds worked with supplier companies as a member of purchasing; she has worked with 192 of Honda's 355 original equipment manufacturing (OEM) suppliers and has documented a total of 4,224 quality circles of problem-solving teams in supplier companies.

Michael Harding is a principal of Harding & Associates, a firm specializing in creating and energizing agile organizations and related consulting and education. Since 1989 Mr. Harding has been assisting manufacturing firms worldwide to restructure themselves to not merely compete in global markets but to dominate them. He is a former corporate manager of JIT education and training for Digital Equipment Corporation. Mr. Harding has more than 26 years of operations, quality, and materials experience with Texas Instruments, RCA, TRW, General Electric, and Digital.

Additionally, his firm works with a number of Fortune 500 and smaller companies to reduce manufacturing cycle times and inventory investment while substantially improving product quality and cash flow. His clients are located in North and South America, the Far East, and Europe.

Mr. Harding holds degrees in business, law, and purchasing. He authored the books *Profitable Purchasing* and *Service Velocity* and coauthored *Purchasing.* His business articles have been featured in *Electronic Buyers News, Target* magazine, *Supplier Selection & Management Report, The Distributor's & Wholesaler's Advisor, The National Productivity Association's Annual Report* (Singapore), *Insights* magazine, and the *Hospital Material Management Quarterly.* He has been a guest lecturer at the Beijing Materials College and the Alfred P. Sloan School at M.I.T. Mr. Harding conducts seminars for Clemson University, the University of Wisconsin, Duquesne University, Incolda (Colombia), and the National University of Singapore. He is certified by APICS (CPIM) and the NAPM (C.P.M.)

William G. Holbrook was the executive director of the Association for Manufacturing Excellence and the former factory manager for Stanadyne's Diesel Systems

Division, which produces fuel system components. He has been vice president of administration for the Stanadyne Automotive Products Group where he was responsible for financial reporting, data processing, purchasing, inventory, and production planning. The automotive products group has implemented a multiplant, repetitive production-planning system to support manufacturing processes and support functions for a seven-plant network. Stanadyne has used JIT techniques and systems for the past seven years.

Mr. Holbrook is a CPA with experience in public and managerial accounting. He has served as a divisional and group controller. He is a frequent APICS speaker.

Anthony C. Laraia is a senior manufacturing strategist with the Torrington Company (Ingersoll Rand). He is a vice president of the Association for Manufacturing Excellence and has more than 25 years experience in engineering and operations management. He holds a B.S. in mechanical engineering from the University of Michigan.

Frank S. Leonard is an independent management consultant specializing in the development and implementation of competitive business strategies. His consulting work includes acquisition studies, plant relocation and closings, and competitive manufacturing analysis. He has worked in production management and process engineering in several industries.

He has taught in M.B.A. and executive programs at Harvard Business School, Tulane University, and Simmons Graduate School of Management.

A frequent lecturer in the areas of strategy and operations management, his published articles have appeared in *The Harvard Business Review* and Allan Kantrow's *Survival Strategies*. Dr. Leonard's degrees include a B.S. in chemical engineering from the University of Missouri, an M.B.A. from Tulane University, and a Ph.D. in Business Administration from the Harvard Business School.

Jeanne Liedtka is a member of the faculty of the Darden School and former chair of the department of management of Simmons College where she teaches business policy and strategic management. Her industry experience includes work as a manager of strategic planning at Wang Laboratories and consulting in the Boston Consulting Group to clients on strategic planning as well as marketing, manufacturing, and distribution issues.

Her published articles appear in the *Journal of Business Ethics* and *The Proceedings of the Academy of Management*. Dr. Liedtka holds a Ph.D. in management policy from Boston University, an M.B.A. from Harvard Business School, and a B.A. from Boston University.

Robert E. McInturff is president of McInturff & Associates, of Natick, Massachusetts, an executive recruiting firm specializing in materials management, manufacturing, and distribution. Before joining the company, Mr. McInturff had more than seven years experience in plant- and corporation-level materials-management functions for Fortune 500 companies.

He writes a monthly column on career planning for *Electronic Buyer's News*, and coauthored a survey report titled "The Challenge and the Promise: Materials Management Today—An Evaluation." He was a founding member of the Middlesex Chapter of APICS and served two years as its president. He is a frequent APICS speaker for local chapters and international conferences and has lectured at Simmons College, Rhode Island College, Boston University, and the University of Massachusetts. Mr. McInturff holds a B.S. from Northeastern University and is recognized as a CPIM by APICS.

John W. Monroe is the director of the Strategic Manufacturing Consulting Group at Hewlett-Packard. This group was created to give key customers access to the management techniques used to achieve significant operating improvements within Hewlett-Packard's own factories.

He has 10 years of manufacturing experience at Hewlett-Packard. During his three years as production manager for the Data Terminals Division (now the Personal Office Computer Group), Dr. Monroe was a member of the small team of managers who introduced Dr. W. Edwards Deming to HP management. He was also a general manager at Avantek Inc., which manufactures gallium-arsenide–based microwave components and subsystems for commercial and military users. Dr. Monroe earned a bachelor's degree in electrical engineering, a masters degree in electrical engineering, and a doctorate, all from Cornell University.

Patricia E. Moody is a business thinker with more than 25 years industry experience in materials management, production planning, and business planning, including positions with Digital Equipment Corporation, Data General, and seven years with Rath & Strong; she is president of Patricia E. Moody, Inc., and she is certified by the Institute of Management Consultants. Her client list includes Motorola, Solectron, Mead Corporation, and McNeil.

She taught operations management at Simmons College in Boston. She has spoken before international, regional, and local APICS conferences, as well as the Harvard Business School AMP Program and various industry seminars. Her published articles include pieces on systems analysis, distribution requirements planning, business planning, and service management. She holds an M.B.A. from Simmons College Graduate School of Management and a B.A. from the University of Massachusetts.

Ms. Moody is editor of AME's *Target* magazine. She authored *Breakthrough Partnering*—her new book *Powered by Honda,* will be published by Wiley in 1997/1998. She is the founder, treasurer, and director of the Marblehead Community Charter Public School. Ms. Moody is a director of AME's Northeast Region Board of Directors.

Burgess Oliver is director of U.S. repair remanufacture for Northern Telecom in Nashville, Tennessee. Mr. Oliver has held a number of other operations functions in material management, industrial engineering, manufacturing, and business systems. He holds degrees from the University of Kentucky and California Coast University. He is past southeast regional president of the Association for Manufacturing Excellence and a current national board member. He is certified by APICS at the CPIM level, past president of the Brentwood Lions Club, and a director of the Nashville Junior Achievement association.

Ronald Purser is associate professor of organizational development in the Center for Organizational Development at Loyola University of Chicago. He received his B.A. degree in psychology from Sonoma State University and his Ph.D. in organizational behavior from Case Western Reserve University. He worked for several years as an internal organizational development consultant at General Electric's lighting business group. Before pursuing his college studies, he worked as an industrial electrician at the now-defunct Pullman-Standard plant in Chicago.

Dr. Purser has served as a consultant on organizational change projects for such companies as Amoco Oil, Anderson Consulting, Eastman Kodak, Exxon Chemicals, Goodyear, Polaroid, Procter & Gamble, Storage Technology, United Airlines, Whirlpool, and Xerox. He has also worked with a number of nonprofit community organizations, local school districts, and various agencies in the federal government. His research has been published in more than 25 journal articles and book chapters on such topics as the redesign of knowledge work organizations, ecologically sustainable organizations, and social creativity. He is coauthor (with Merrelyn Emery) of *The Search Conference: A Powerful Method for Planning Organizational Change and Community Action* (1996) published by Jossey-Bass. He is coeditor (with Alfonso Montuori) of *Social Creativity* (1996), a three-volume series published by Hampton Press.

Roger W. Schmenner is an associate professor at the Indiana University School of Business. He has held faculty appointments at IMEDE (Lausanne, Switzerland), Duke, Harvard, and Yale Universities.

Dr. Schmenner's major interests lie in production and operations management. He is the author of the textbook *Production/Operations Management: Concepts and Situations*, the editor of the casebook *Cases in Production/Operations Management*, and the author of *Plant Tours in Production/Operations Management*. His research interests within the field include manufacturing strategy, productivity, and industry location. He has written more than 50 published articles, book chapters, and cases that have appeared in the *Harvard Business Review*, *Sloan Management Review*, and *Journal of Operations Management*. Schmenner's book, *Making Business Location Decisions*, is a compendium of much of his stream of research on industry location. His recent research on factory productivity was sponsored by the U.S. Department of Commerce, Control Data Corporation, and IMEDE.

Dr. Schmenner has a diverse range of consulting and corporate teaching experience involving more than 40 companies, several industry groups, and more than a dozen federal, state, and local government agencies or departments. Dr. Schmenner holds an A.B. degree from Princeton and a Ph.D. from Yale in economics.

Mark Louis Smith is an industrial engineering manager and has held the positions of production manager, master scheduler, and strategic planning manager, all in the pharmaceutical industry. He has directed implementation of JIT and kanban-based programs as well as management information systems (MIS), innovations, and employee empowerment projects. He holds a B.S. in industrial engineering from Bradley University and is completing an M.S. in corporate and international planning at the University of Pennsylvania.

Wayne K. Smith is the president of the Process/Time Management Association (West Chester, Pennsylvania), a consulting firm and network association for people and organizations interested in management by time principles.

Mr. Smith spent 32 years with the DuPont company, in a wide variety of manufacturing management assignments leading to a position as manufacturing manager for a major division. His experience includes formation and operation of several Japanese joint ventures. He concluded his DuPont career by serving for three years as the corporate manager for continuous flow manufacturing. That small ex-

periment in time strategies exploded over three years into some 80 time implementations across the global company.

Mr. Smith left DuPont in 1991 to form Process/Time Management (West
Chester, Pa.) and began broader investigation of, and consulting service to, the
process industry. His work has included paper, steel, cosmetics, batch and continuous chemical, and precious metal companies. As a result of his studies, Mr.
Smith has developed unique tools for applying JIT/pull/Toyota concepts to all
work processes.

Mr. Smith is a frequent author and conference speaker. His book *Time Out:
Visible Cycle Time Implementation* will be published by Wiley in 1998. If you
meet him, he will be glad to share his granddaughter's pictures with you.

Linda G. Sprague is professor of operations management at the Whittemore
School of Business and Economics, University of New Hampshire, and was director of its executive programs from 1981 to 1986. In 1984–85 she was professor of
operations management at IMEDE, the International Management Development Institute in Lausanne, Switzerland. In 1980 she was a founding professor at
the National Center for Industrial Science and Technology Management Development at Dalian, China. She has also taught at Stanford University, the Tuck
School, and Simmons Graduate School of Management.

Professor Sprague received her doctorate from the Harvard Business School;
she also has an M.B.A. from Boston University and an S.B. in industrial management from M.I.T. Her consulting and research interests include strategic management of operations, capacity management, and operations scheduling for manufacturing enterprises and for community general hospitals, production information
systems, and productivity improvement programs. She has published articles on
material-requirements planning, international manufacturing, inventory management, and production practices in China.

Mrs. Sprague was program chair for the 1987 annual meeting of the Decision
Sciences Institute of which she is a past president. She is a vice president of the Op-
erations Management Association and was cochair of the 1987 Management Divi-
sion of the Academy of Management. She is a certified practitioner in Inventory
Management and a member of the Production Activity Control Committee of the
Certification Council of APICS. She is a fellow of the Decision Sciences Institute.

Professor Sprague is a member of the Board of Directors of Protek Inc. She is
the management advisor to SICOT, the Société Internationale de Chirugie Or-
thopaedique et de Traumatologie.

Thomas F. Wallace is an independent consultant based in Cincinnati, specializing
in sales and operations planning, manufacturing strategy, demand management,
and resource planning. Mr. Wallace has authored five books, including *The In-
stant Access Guide to World Class Manufacturing* (1994), *Customer Driven
Strategy: Winning Through Operational Excellence* (1992), and *MRP II: Making
It Happen: The Implementers' Guide to Success with Manufacturing Resource
Planning* (1985; 2d ed., 1990). He currently writes a monthly column titled "The
Customer Connection" for *APICS: The Performance Advantage* magazine. Mr.
Wallace is codirector and a distinguished fellow of the Ohio State University's
Center for Excellence in Manufacturing Management.

Index